The Wild Animal Story

In the series *Animals, Culture, and Society*,
edited by Clinton R. Sanders and Arnold Arluke

The WILD ANIMAL STORY

EDITED BY

Ralph H. Lutts

TEMPLE UNIVERSITY PRESS   PHILADELPHIA

Temple University Press, Philadelphia 19122
Collection copyright © 1998 by Ralph H. Lutts.
Published 1998
Printed in the United States of America

♾ The paper used in this book meets the requirements of the
American National Standard for Information Sciences—
Permanence of Paper for Printed Library Materials,
ANSI Z39.48-1984

Text design by Erin Kirk New

Library of Congress Cataloging-in-Publication Data
The wild animal story / edited by Ralph H. Lutts.
        p.   cm. — (Animals, culture, and society)
    Includes bibliographical references.
    ISBN 1-56639-593-3 (alk. paper)
      1. Nature stories, American—History and criticism.   2. American
fiction—20th century—History and criticism.   3. Canadian
fiction—20th century—History and criticism.   4. Nature
stories, Canadian—History and criticism.   5. Wilderness areas
in literature.   6. Nature stories—Authorship.   7. Animals in
literature.   I. Lutts, Ralph H.   II. Series.
PS374.N3W55   1998
813'.52080362—DC21   97-23906

To Merry and Jack Hudson and Dan Lutts
for their love, friendship, and support, which made
the completion of this book possible

Contents

Illustrations follow page 157

Preface

In 1986, Reading Is Fundamental surveyed a number of prominent Americans, asking them to list their favorite children's books. More than two hundred books were mentioned in the responses, but only three of them were nature books—and all of these were wild animal stories. Folk singer Pete Seeger singled out Ernest Thompson Seton's *Rolf of the Woods* as his favorite. Jack London's *Call of the Wild* was listed by John T. Walker, the Bishop of Washington, the prominent surgeon Michael DeBakey, and writer Jim Trelease. And William J. Long's *Northern Trails* helped to establish President Ronald Reagan's "lifelong love of the woods."

When they first appeared at the end of the nineteenth century, wild animal stories presented a new view of wildlife—they revealed nature as experienced by animals who lived for their own ends. The animals' worth was not measured by how they satisfied or thwarted human expectations. The stories' combination of fiction and natural history made them a powerful vehicle for promoting a love and appreciation of the natural world. Animals are ideas, as well as living creatures, and this new literary genre promoted a new way of thinking about wild animals. They lived lives independent of humans; shared many of our desires and fears, thoughts and emotions; and they had a right to live simply for their own sake. As the century progressed and environmental problems became a major social issue, wild animal stories and their vision of animals also changed—their animal heroes became ecological actors in books by such authors as Rachel Carson, Sally Carrighar, and Farley Mowat.

These are interesting times in which to be an animal. If you are a deer, you may be considered a beautiful creature worthy of protection, a vandal nibbling on suburban shrubbery, a crop managed for harvest by hunters, and an animal person worthy of rights. If you are an endangered species, you can be a precious ecological treasure that must be preserved as well as a nuisance standing in the way of progress. Conflicts abound between traditional utilitarian views of animals and the newer animal welfare, animal rights, and ecological perspectives first popularized by wild animal stories. However, the role of the wild animal story in promoting these ideas within popular culture has been largely overlooked.

The wild animal story (sometimes called the realistic wild animal story because of its apparent fidelity to natural history and life experiences of real animals) provides a marvelous window through which to view individually differing and socially changing views of nature and wildlife and the roles of wild animals in society. As such, it also provides a bridge between nature literature and environmental history, as well as case studies in the social construction of nature. Since it is a literary form that is strongly based in natural history, the wild animal story is an excellent vehicle for exploring the relationships between science and literature, reason and emotion, the head and the heart in understanding animals and our environment.

This book brings together a variety of resources to advance these efforts. The introductory essay, "The Wild Animal Story: Animals and Ideas," is an overview of the genre and how the stories and their representations of animals have changed over time. Part I, "Tales," is a diverse collection of wild animal stories, some of which are classics in the genre. It emphasizes stories first published at the beginning of the twentieth century, because many of them are long out of print, while the more recently published stories are readily available. The next part, "Controversy," reprints for the first time key documents in the famous Nature Fakers controversy in which John Burroughs and Theodore Roosevelt accused a number of prominent nature writers of literary and natural history fraud. Wild animal stories and their writers played a central role in this four-year-long debate. This book's introductory and concluding essays set that controversy within a larger context. The issues that it raised are still very much alive today. The final part, "Interpretations," is a collection of some of the most important scholarly essays examining the wild animal story.

Many people have helped to make this book possible. Thanks go to Clint Sanders, who first approached me about doing a book for Temple University Press's *Animals, Culture, and Society* series, and to the press's executive editor Janet Francendese and director David M. Bartlett (now retired) for their continuing advice, support, and flexibility. Production editors Jennifer French and Joan Vidal turned the manuscript into a book, and Mary Capouya did an outstanding job of copy editing. The staffs of the Virginia Tech, Blue Ridge Regional, and Patrick County libraries were a great help in finding materials that would otherwise have been very difficult to locate from the rural Blue Ridge region of southwestern Virginia. Bonnie Helms of the Virginia Museum of Natural History printed a number of the illustrations. I also appreciate the advice and assistance of Mark Barrus, William Cronon, John Reiger, Andrew Rowan, David Smith, and the folks participating in the Association for the Study of Literature and the Environment discussion group, including Jim Dwyer, Andrea Herrmann, Mark Hoyer, Tom Lynch, Arlene Plevin, Boria Sax, John Swift, John Tallmadge, and Charlotte Walker. The many people who helped in my study of the Nature Fakers controversy are acknowledged in my book, *The Nature Fakers: Wildlife, Science & Sentiment* (Golden, Colo.: Fulcrum Publishing, 1990).

This book includes the writing of people from the United States, Canada, and England. Out of respect for the writers and their countries, I have preserved their original spelling, punctuation, and capitalization, when reasonable. This leads to inconsistency, but it reflects the times in which they wrote and their various national and personal styles.

The Wild Animal Story

The Wild Animal Story: Animals and Ideas

RALPH H. LUTTS

The late nineteenth century witnessed the development of a new and very popular kind of animal story, the "realistic wild animal story." Called a distinctly Canadian form of literature, it also became an important part of popular culture in the United States, especially at the beginning of the twentieth century. The wild animal story combined elements of nature writing and animal fiction. Traditionally, nature essays about animals emphasized more or less detached scientific observations of animals or the author's emotional responses to them. Earlier forms of animal stories tended to be fictional accounts in which the animals were little more than humans in furry or feathery coats, whose narrative role was to instruct and morally elevate the reader. Sometimes the animal characters literally dressed in human clothing. English animal stories like Rudyard Kipling's *The Jungle Books* (1894, 1895) and Kenneth Grahame's *The Wind in the Willows* (1907), for example, presented animals as, essentially, English folks pursuing their roles in a social hierarchy. The more realistic stories of domestic animals, such as dog stories, present animals as eager to serve their masters.[1]

In the realistic wild animal story, however, the animals "live for their own ends," rather than for human ends. The stories emphasized the perspective of the animal itself. As Charles G. D. Roberts, one of the creators of the genre, put

A shorter version of this essay, "The Realistic Wild Animal Story," appears in *The Literature of Nature: An International Source Book*, ed. Patrick D. Murphy (Chicago & London: Fitzroy Dearborn Publishing, 1998).

it, "the interest centres about the personality, individuality, mentality, of an animal, as well as its purely physical characteristics." Although the accounts are presented in story form and employ fictional devices, the authors assert that their tales are factual and represent accurate natural history. This new image of wild animals can be illustrated by contrasting two forest romance novels: English naturalist W. H. Hudson's *Green Mansions* (1904) and Charles G. D. Roberts' *The Heart of the Ancient Wood* (1900).[2] Each novel involves a young woman who lives in harmony with nature, loves all wild creatures, abhors killing, and prohibits hunting in her region of the forest. The male protagonist in each realizes that he can win her love only by overcoming her independence and bringing her back into society. Despite their similarities, however, the natures of the animals in these two books differ completely. In Hudson's novel, the reader sees the animals as a part of the forest backdrop. They are generic representatives of their species with little personality and certainly no personhood. In Roberts' novel, however, they become characters with distinct personalities who are central to the plot.

Over the years, wild animal stories were neglected by scholars, perhaps because they were thought of as minor works written for children. Even Roberts' stories were rarely considered worthy of serious examination until the 1960s, despite his having been called the "father" of Canadian poetry and of Canadian literature as a result of his other writings and his having been knighted for his literary work. Ernest Thompson Seton, another Canadian founder of the genre, was also overlooked by scholars, although his wild animal stories are the only ones to have remained continually in print through the twentieth century. Since the 1960s, however, a number of scholars have studied the genre. Most of their publications focus on the work of its founders, Roberts and Seton. This is unfortunate, because so many other authors wrote wild animal stories, including William J. Long (a contemporary of Roberts and Seton), Rachel Carson, Sally Carrighar, Fred Bodworth, and Farley Mowat.

Although realistic wild animals stories are offered to readers as accurate natural history (a claim that has been disputed, as we shall see), their representations of animals differ, reflecting the differing views of the authors regarding the nature of their beasts and historical changes in societal concepts of animals and nature. For this reason, these stories provide a wonderful window through which to examine the social construction of nature and animals.

Animals are ideas as well as living, breathing creatures. Despite the fact that wild animals live lives independent from our own, throughout history people and cultures have given them special meanings and responded to them in terms of those meanings. We can only dimly interpret the complex meanings of Stone Age animal paintings found on cave walls, for example, but it seems reasonable to believe that these meanings influenced and reflected the ways that the painters thought about and interacted with the animals of their time. Deer have gone through a variety of transformations: as symbols of the erotic, femininity, innocence, holiness, the crucified Christ, nobility, nature, and wildness. They have been viewed as emblems of tragedy and innocent victims.[3] More recently, deer have been viewed as vandals (of urban shrubbery) and as a crop for harvest (by hunters). René Descartes and his followers considered animals to be machines, and the animal rights movement views them as persons.

Through all of this, the animals continue being what they are, regardless of what people think of them. But the way people think of them does have a major impact upon their lives. Despite the fact that they have an existence independent of our constructs, the ways we view wild animals are not without consequence. Our conceptions of animals help to shape our actions toward and responses to them; and they are reflected back to us by the conditions we impose upon their lives. Whether deer are viewed as a crop to be harvested or as persons with rights, for example, has an enormous impact upon them.[4]

There were a number of precursors to the wild animal story, but two books in particular paved the way and helped to create a market for the genre. The first was English writer Anna Sewell's novel about the life of a horse as told by the horse, *Black Beauty* (1877). Black Beauty thought and spoke as a four-legged human, but his message was an appeal for the humane treatment of domesticated animals. Its popularity in England and North American led to its being dubbed "The Uncle Tom's Cabin of the Horse" and marked the growing public interest in animal welfare. *Black Beauty* helped countless readers to empathize with the experiences of animals. The second book was Rudyard Kipling's *Jungle Book*.[5] Its enormous success both demonstrated the appeal of stories about wild animals, fabrications though they were, and further stimulated that market.

The realistic wild animal story burst upon the scene and achieved wide public attention with the publication of Ernest Thompson Seton's *Wild Animals I Have Known* (1898), which went through sixteen printings in its first four years alone. It was not, however, the earliest publication in this genre. United States author Charles Dudley Warner was perhaps the first North American writer to describe events from the point of view of a wild animal. His story "A-Hunting of the Deer" (1878) depicted the hunt as the deer experienced it. Seton, a Canadian, first began to experiment with the genre with "The Drummer on Snowshoes," published in 1887 in *St. Nicholas,* and brought it to fruition in his now classic tale of Lobo the Wolf, "The King of the Currumpaw: A Wolf Story," first published in 1894 and later reprinted as "Lobo: The King of Currumpaw." Charles G. D. Roberts, another Canadian, wrote poetry, novels of the Canadian wilderness, and "hook & bullet" stories that, ironically, emphasized the viciousness of animals before developing his own realistic wild animal stories. His first venture into the genre was his now classic "Do Seek Their Meat from God" (1892). This and other wild animal stories were included in his book *Earth's Enigmas* (1896).[6]

Although both Roberts and Seton have been called the creator of the realistic wild animal story, it is best to call them cocreators. The work of each paralleled and may have been influenced by that of the other. In any event, neither began cranking out wild animal stories in quantity until the publication of Kipling's *Jungle Book* and the resulting increase in public demand for animal stories.

"The literary in Canada," wrote Northrop Frye, "is often only an incidental quality of writings which, like those of many of the early explorers, are as innocent of literary intentions as a mating loon." He went on to propose that Canadian literature is best "studied as a part of Canadian life." He remarked that he found Canadian poetry reflected "a deep terror" in response to nature. This may be a result of life in isolated communities surrounded by wilderness, which also led to a "garrison mentality." Margaret Atwood further developed these ideas in her influential book *Survival,* arguing that survival is a central theme in Canadian literature, be it in the face of a hostile wilderness or threats to its culture. (By contrast, she suggested that a central theme in American literature is the frontier as a symbol of hope and new opportunities.) Associated with the survival theme is that of being a victim, which may in part be a response to the nation's colonial history. She also argued that the theme of survival is closely associated with "the will *not* to survive." "Certainly," she wrote, "Canadian authors spend a disproportionate amount of time making sure that their heroes die or fail. Much Canadian writing suggests that failure is required because it is felt—consciously or unconsciously—to be the only 'right' ending, the only thing that will support the characters' (or their authors') view of the universe." This argument stimulated a good deal of discussion, including arguments to the contrary. Nevertheless, as she wrote, "Like any theory it won't explain everything, but it may give you some points of departure."[7]

The stories by Roberts and Seton seem to support this argument. Roberts' "Do Seek Their Meat from God," for example, tells of a woodsman who finds his child being stalked by mountain lions. He kills the cats, thus saving his child. But Roberts goes on to add an ironic twist: the lions' kittens are later found dead from starvation; the life of the woodsman's son was purchased at the expense of the mountain lions' young. The woodsman and the lion pair were engaged in a common struggle to ensure the survival of their offspring. They shared the same moral ground. In another tale, one of Roberts' characters explained the nature of life in the wild by saying, "Oftentimes it's seemed to me all life was jest like a few butterflies flitterin' over a graveyard." Trappers finally managed to lure Seton's extraordinary wolf Lobo to his death by means of the scent of his beloved mate, Blanca, who had been killed earlier. When his readers complained about the deaths of so many of his animal heroes, Seton explained, "The fact that these stories are true is the reason why all are tragic. The life of a wild animal *always has a tragic end.*" He also explained, "For the wild animal there is no such thing as a gentle decline in peaceful old age. Its life is spent at the front, in line of battle, and as soon as its powers begin to wane in the least, its enemies become too strong for it; it falls."[8]

Despite their commonalities, Roberts' and Seton's animals are quite different from each other. Roberts' animals are immersed in the Darwinian struggle for survival and their deaths reflect this struggle. Yet, despite their universal deaths, life goes on—as symbolized by the "butterflies flitterin' over a grave-yard." As Joseph Gold noted of Roberts' stories, "In the long run death itself has no sting and is ironically defeated by the uses nature makes of its processes. All things conspire to sustain life and the stories create a very strong sense of rhythmic pattern and cycle of the season, of birth and death, of mating and separating, and these patterns persist no matter what the creatures, what the setting or what human interference is attempted." In addition, by including humans in this common struggle Roberts demonstrated the kinship between humans and wild animals. This insightful contribution to literature provided a theme to which Roberts returned again and again. Seton's animals, on the other hand, were virtuous creatures. As Seton wrote, he "tried to emphasize our kinship with the animals by showing that in them we can find the virtues most admired in Man. Lobo stands for Dignity and Love-constancy; Silverspot, for Sagacity; Redruff, for Obedience . . ." He even argued, "The Ten Command-ments are not *arbitrary laws given to man*, but are *fundamental laws of all highly developed animals.*"[9]

If, as Atwood and others have argued, Canadian literature reflects a struggle for survival in a fearful wilderness, why do wild animal stories not depict wil-derness animals as monsters? Atwood answers this question by arguing that the animals are all victims, they are all killed, and Canadians identify with them as victims. This becomes another bond of kinship between animals and people (in this case, Canadians).[10]

In domestic animal stories, the animals adjust to and serve the needs of their human masters. In Fred Gibson's novel *Old Yeller,* for example, the dog be-comes a hero by defending a girl from the mother of a bear cub she had found. (In a wild animal story, the mother bear would have been the hero for trying to save her cub from the human.) This emphasis of the human's interest over the animal's is characteristic of most United States literature, in which animals tend to serve as symbols or the goal of human action, as in Melville's *Moby Dick* or Faulkner's "The Bear," or in which animals accommodate themselves to humans. "Indeed," writes James Polk, "the patterns in American writing about animals seem almost inverted in Canadian counterparts, where the emphasis is not on man at all, but on the animal."[11]

Many authors in the United States, though, did produce their own body of realistic wild animal stories that emphasized the animals' perspective. However, these often presented a more romantic vision of nature and animals. The U.S. writer William J. Long,[12] for example, denied that there was a Darwinian strug-gle for survival in nature based on his belief that wild animals have no awareness of such a struggle. He believed that life in nature is a "gladsome" life and that death comes swiftly and without trauma. He also argued than wild animals can reason and teach their young in much the same way as do humans, a central premise of his book *School of the Woods* (1902). In his story, "Wayeeses the Strong One," he even claimed as factual a story of a wolf leading a pair of lost Indian children to their home.[13] This up-beat vision of nature was particularly appealing to his United States readers. Although Long has been largely forgotten, his books were quite popular and widely used in school classrooms during the first decades of the twentieth century.

Long may have been among the most romantic and anthropomorphizing of North American nature writers, but he was not the only one to idealize animals. In James Oliver Curwood's *The Grizzly King* (1916), for example, a Grizzly Bear confronted an unarmed hunter who had once shot him. The bear reared on his hind legs, ready to kill the hunter, but then decided to leave the frightened man alone and walked off. "You—you are a monster with a heart bigger than man!" the hunter exclaimed. "If I'd cornered you like that I'd have killed you! And you! You cornered me, and let me live!"[14] The animal was morally better than the man, a theme often encountered in wild animal stories.

Stories about domestic animals tended to subordinate the animals' interests to those of their human owners. However, some of these stories, especially dog stories, bridged the genres of the realistic wild animal and realistic domestic animal stories. Most notable of these is Jack London's *Call of the Wild* (1904), which begins as a traditional dog story, telling of Buck's luxurious life on a California estate, how he was kidnaped, brutalized, and sold to become a sled dog in the Yukon Gold Rush, and how he finally found kindness with a beloved master. But the novel ends as a wild animal story, as Buck becomes aware of an inner urge to independence and the fulfillment of his primitive nature as a wild creature. Throughout the book, London presents his reader with a Darwinian vision of nature and a sense that, in shedding the trappings of human society and domesticity, Buck was reverting to his true, wild identity. He even has visions of ancient times, hairy men, and his canine ancestors. With the death of his beloved master, Buck breaks free of his bond to humanity, runs off into the wilderness, and becomes the leader of a wolf pack.

Call of the Wild was a book for its time—a time of growing interest in the preservation of wilderness, disappearing species, and natural resources. The animal welfare movement was also growing, as was interest in the study of nature as a hobby and as a new pedagogical movement. Books about wilderness, such as John Muir's, were gaining popularity along with all sorts of books about nature and wildlife. In addition, the Gold Rush had stimulated great interest in the Yukon and Alaska. London's tale found an eager market.

His companion novel, *White Fang*, reversed the process: a wolf–dog born in the wilderness is found by humans and, after going through a series of owners, is tamed and goes to live on a California estate as a family pet. Although it ends as a traditional domestic animal story, *White Fang* begins as a wild animal story and the first part of the book that describes White Fang's puppyhood is an outstanding example of the genre. London made a great effort to tell these stories from White Fang's and Buck's perspectives, without making them think entirely as humans do.[15]

John Muir's extraordinary story "Stickeen," first published in *Century* magazine in 1897, clearly is not a story about a wild animal, but Muir brought to this dog story the view of animals that was characteristic of the wild animal story. "Stickeen" was written at the same time that the wild animal story was being created. Clearly, this idea about animals was "in the air" and finding expression in North America. Stickeen was a very independent and hardy mongrel but, Muir wrote, "none of us was able to make out what Stickeen was really good for. He seemed to meet danger and hardships without anything like reason, insisted on having his own way, never obeyed an order, and the hunter could never set him on anything, or make him fetch the birds he shot." Stickeen would, though, accompany Muir on his wilderness walks. On one fateful trip they became stranded on a glacier in the midst of a storm. Their only route to safety was across a seemingly impassable crevasse. Muir found and traversed a treacherous ice bridge that crossed the crevasse, but Stickeen was reluctant to venture onto it. In witnessing the dog's intelligent appraisal of the situation, his anxiety and fear of the crossing, and his ecstatic joy when he had successfully crossed the crevasse, Muir felt he had had a glimpse into the dog's soul and recognized a kindred creature with intrinsic worth. "At first the least promising and least known of my dog-friends," Muir wrote, "he suddenly became the best known of them all. Our storm-battle for life brought him to light, and through him as through a window I have ever since been looking for deeper sympathy into all my fellow mortals."[16]

Although Stickeen was hardly useful to people, he turned out to be good for himself. Like the creatures in wild animal stories, he lived for his own ends despite his enjoyment of human companionship. Muir's tale recounts both Stickeen's ordeal and achievement on a glacier and Muir's own realization of the mental, emotional, and spiritual potential of animals.[17] This is uncharacteristic of most dog stories, or other realistic stories about domestic animals.

The Darwinian Revolution was a long and difficult process of intellectual and cultural change. As a cultural phenomenon, it required the public to learn and accept a new set of ideas regarding the nature of history, organic change, and our place in the world. In a sense, this revolution is still in progress. The realistic wild animal story was a response to the Darwinism that presented readers with ways to accommodate the notion of natural selection and the amorality of nature. Robert MacDonald, for example, sees the genre as a "revolt against instinct" and Darwinian amorality. In these stories animals do have their instincts, he contends, but they are also rational and ethical; they rise above instinct. "The works of Seton and Roberts are thus celebrations of rational, ethical animals, who as they rise above instinct, reach toward the spiritual." This is certainly true of the work of the U.S. writer William J. Long, who argued that animals reason, have souls, and may even have an afterlife. Lisa Mighetto similarly argued that the efforts of many writers to demonstrate that animals live ethical lives in harmony with each other reflected an anxious rejection of the cold amorality of the Darwinian vision of nature.[18] Spiritual and moral matters aside, by the end of the nineteenth century many people recognized that instinct alone is not a sufficient explanation for much of animal behavior. However, the psychology of the day offered only options of instinct and reason to explain behavior, which encouraged some people to opt in favor of animal reasoning.

Thomas Dunlap has argued that wild animal stories helped readers not to reject Darwinism but to assimilate it. Roberts' stories, for example, often showed that humans and wild animals shared the common tasks of protecting, feeding and raising their young. If one prevailed over the other, they nevertheless shared the same moral ground and similar emotional and mental lives. At the same time, humans also stood outside nature by virtue of their ability to make and use tools and to reshape and distort nature. Seton presented a similar view of nature, although he often softened the Darwinian image of nature as a stage for carnage and placed a greater emphasis on humans as senseless killers.[19]

Although wild animal stories employed narrative devices of fiction to engage their readers and tell their stories, they were marketed as natural history, and their authors repeatedly attested to their faithfulness to nature. They frequently claimed that their stories were based on field observations and that the events of the stories actually happened. Nevertheless, in 1903 the dean of American nature writers, John Burroughs, launched a blistering attack on what he called "sham naturalists." He argued that many popular writers, including Seton, Roberts, Long, and London, were frauds who overly dramatized animal life in order to sell their books to an eager but gullible public. This began the often humorous, but no less serious, Nature Fakers controversy.[20] Most of the writers kept their heads down, did not defend themselves publicly, and escaped relatively unscathed. Long, however, aggressively defended himself in magazines and newspapers, and thus became the focus of the battle. The controversy continued for four years until Theodore Roosevelt publicly supported Burroughs' position and condemned Long. The President expressed special anger at the publishers whose classroom editions of wild animal stories introduced shoddy and even bogus natural history into the public schools.

This battle was over three closely related issues. The first was the necessity of accuracy in nature writing, including wild animal stories. The controversy helped to establish at least informal standards of accuracy in nature literature. As Clarence Hawks, a minor practitioner of the wild animal story, wrote, "I now realized that if I ever make a bad break in regards to my natural history statements I was doomed."[21] The second issue was the question of what the nature of animal mentality is; to what extent animals are governed by instincts or reason. This issue continued to be a topic of lively debate throughout the century. At its root, though, the controversy was about establishing a balance between emotion and science as means to understand and appreciate nature— the literary expression of a debate that was going on throughout the nature study movement at that time.

Although wild animal stories were an important expression of cultural responses to Darwinism, they were more overtly tied to the animal welfare movement. They presented animals as individual, sentient creatures capable of feeling mental and physical pain. They often appealed to and promoted humanitarianism by showing their readers, through the animals' own eyes, the impact of hunting and trapping. For example, T. Gilbert Pearson, who would become an early leader of the Audubon movement, wrote a school reader of bird stories to teach an understanding and appreciation of birds. It ended with a tale of boys thoughtlessly slaughtering them. One of the study questions was, "Do you suppose a bird really cares when its companions are killed?" Seton, Roberts, Long, and others presented predators in a more positive light than did most nature writing of their time. They often depicted wolves, for example, as sociable creatures who avoid humans, rather than bloodthirsty monsters eager to drag off children. Their visions of wolf behavior often turned out to be more accurate than those of Theodore Roosevelt and most professional naturalists of their time. Some writers even expressed views akin to those of the animal rights movement. Seton, for example, proposed that, since "animals are creatures with wants and feelings differing in degree only from our own, they surely have their rights. This fact, now beginning to be recognized by the Caucasian world was emphasized by the Buddhist over 2,000 years ago." Long's *Brier-Patch Philosophy* (1906) is an unrecognized "classic" in the early literature of the movement.[22]

The wild animal story seemed to die out in the early twentieth century. The Nature Fakers controversy may have contributed to this, but there were additional factors involved. Alec Lucas suggests a number of them: "Perhaps people tired of learning that animals and men are alike and learned from two world wars that they are too much alike. Perhaps urban people, now removed three or four generations from their country forebears, have lost touch with nature almost completely. Unquestionably the biological sciences have been replaced in public imagination by the physical. What might once have been a nature story is now science fiction." William Magee argued that wild animal story writers faced a problem in making animals who lived for themselves of interest to readers. They simply ran out of plots and ways to introduce variety into their stories. These writers, he argued, "expose the limits as well as the vastness of the expanded range of characters and topics for fiction. Art and life may be one, but stories of animals living only for themselves must still appeal to readers that are human."[23] Nevertheless, the wild animal story did not completely disappear.

Few women wrote wild animal stories during the first part of the twentieth century and none of their works have endured. It was two American women, however, who were responsible for the transformation and rebirth of the genre in the 1940s: Rachel Carson and Sally Carrighar. Most of the early writers of wild animal stories were interested in the lives of individual animals and their stories often promoted the humane treatment of individual animals. Carson and Carrighar wrote stories that represented animals not so much as heroes and individual personalities as representatives of their species living within an ecological community of animals.[24] Both based their stories on a careful reading of scientific literature, as well as observations in the field. Their stories, especially Carson's, arose out of an ecological worldview rather than the humanitarian and animal rights perspectives emerging at the beginning of their century.

Under the Sea-Wind (1941), Carson's first book and her only major excursion into the wild animal story, followed the activities and life cycles of marine animals and the ways their lives intertwine. Although it was not financially successful when it was first published, it became a best-seller following publication of Carson's next book, *The Sea Around Us* (1951). *Under the Sea-Wind* reflected the strong influence that Henry Williamson, English author of *Tarka the Otter* (1927) and *Salar the Salmon* (1935), had upon Carson's writing,[25] but its combination of lyrical prose, ecological vision, and careful science was uniquely Carson's.

Sally Carrighar's first book, *One Day on Beetle Rock* (1944), follows a day in the lives of a number of animals in Sequoia National Park. Each chapter tells the story of a single animal, much as in a traditional wild animal story. The animals featured in each chapter, however, also appear in the other chapters, creating an intricate tapestry depicting the animal community of Beetle Rock. Carrighar wrote that she had no model for the kind of writing she wanted to do, although Gale Lawrence has suggested that she may have been influenced by the work of Williamson and Carson.[26] Both Carson and Carrighar allowed their readers to experience animal lives through the animals' own eyes and other senses. They were, however, very careful in their language to avoid humanizing their animal characters. Theirs was a more behavioristic representation of wild animals, in contrast to earlier writers who presented animals as personalities, although Carrighar was later criticized for anthropomorphism.

Vera Norwood has argued that women nature writers present a distinctly female vision of the natural world.[27] European American women, in particular, view nature in domestic terms: they see nature as a household and often recognize their roles as protectors of this home and its residents. This was particularly true, she feels, of early writers whose roles were confined within the boundaries of their home and family. Sally Carrighar's life and work help to confirm Norwood's theory. In her autobiography, Carrighar tells of an event that occurred while she was doing field work for *One Day on Beetle Rock*. She was living in a cabin close to her animal characters. She fed them and they adapted to her presence. Outside the cabin one day, a Goshawk dropped out of the air, grabbed and flew off with a grouse. In a wave of panic, many of the other animals ran into her cabin; even a buck tried to get in. As time passed, the animals continued to spend time inside her cabin. Carrighar realized that she had found what she had sought all her life: "Here I have found it, home at last—and with all these delightful children."[28]

It is more difficult, however, to affirm that Rachel Carson's work reflects such a distinctively female vision of nature. She was trained in the biological sciences and had a very strong ecological understanding of nature. Ecology itself uses a household metaphor of nature. After all, the word "ecology" is derived from the Greek *oikos,* which means "house." Ecology is the study of our natural home. It, too, recognizes that we are all part of a larger community or household, which we must try to protect—a point of view that is now widely accepted and held by both men and women. Carson's writing may represent the convergence of female and scientific approaches to nature. Men have also adopted Carson's and Carrighar's approach to the animal story. New Zealander turned Canadian, Franklin Russell, for example, used it in his book *Watchers at the Pond* (1963).[29]

Canadian writers introduced the next innovation in the wild animal story, which reflected growing public concern about environmental destruction and the extinction of species: the themes of survival and victimization carried to an extreme.[30] These were not the first writers to pursue this theme. Seton, for example, wrote in 1901, "I do not intend primarily to denounce certain field sports, or even cruelty to animals. My chief motive, my most earnest underlying wish, has been to stop the extermination of harmless wild animals." For another example, Grey Owl (Archie Stansfield Belaney, an English emigrant to Canada who adopted the persona of an Indian) used his writing to help protect and restore the declining populations of beaver. Their stories, however, did not embody the ecological perspective and environmental angst of more recent writers. In these new stories, individual animals became representatives of their vanishing species. The curlews whose lives Fred Bodsworth followed in his *Last of the Curlews* (1955) were quite literally the last of their species. The destruction of the wolves in Farley Mowat's *Never Cry Wolf* (1963) was representative of the threat to all wolves in North America. Ecosystems, as well as species, face danger. In his *Animals of the North* (1966), William O. Pruitt, Jr., used the method of Carson and Carrighar to evoke the subarctic Canadian forest ecosystem and reveal the human threats to it. Writers in the United States also adopted this new approach. Sally Carrighar, for example, followed the life of a Blue Whale in her last book, *The Twilight Seas* (1975).[31]

Never Cry Wolf is an unusual example of the wild animal story. Mowat's humorous account of studying wolves close-up in the barren lands of northern Canada is as much a story about his evolving understanding of wolves as about the wolves he lived among. In constructing this semifictional account of his exploits in the north, Mowat came up with a solution to a central problem in the genre. As William Magee pointed out,[32] it was difficult for authors to come up with fresh plots and to maintain human interest in tales about animals who lived for themselves, rather than to meet human needs. Mowat found a way around this by letting his readers learn the ways of the wolves' lives as they unfolded to Mowat. The conflict between his initial, traditional view of wolves as savage beasts and his growing realization that they were nothing of the sort—together with the series of humorous circumstances in which he found himself—are captivating. Still, at the same time, the reader recognizes wolves as creatures who live for their own ends, as well as the human threats to those ends.

Mowat also presented a different picture of the Darwinian struggle that is so much a part of wild animal stories. The relationship between the wolves and their caribou prey was not simply one of conflict and death. Instead, the wolves seemed almost merciful, killing only the old, weak, and disabled caribou. In exchange for feeding on the herd, the wolves kept it healthy. The caribou did not even appear to be particularly fearful of their predators. This relationship of mutual exchange provided a new vision of nature that resolved many of the uncomfortable aspects of Darwinism. Nature might still be amoral, but it was not exploitative and no longer characterized by savagery and destruction.

The wild animal story genre quickly made the leap from the printed page to motion pictures and, later, television. This began with the translations from book to film; perhaps the first book to make this transition was London's *Call of the Wild*. The plot of the 1935 Fox film, starring Clark Gable and Loretta Young, was only loosely based on the novel. Young was introduced as a love interest and the film's plot was quite different from London's, placing greater emphasis on human conflict. Subsequent versions of *Call of the Wild* (including the 1972 MGM version starring Charlton Heston and a 1976 Charles Fries production based on a script by James Dickey) tended to be more faithful to the novel, but also tended to emphasize the experiences of their human characters. These problems are, in part, a product of the medium: motion pictures often must appeal to human interest to capture the attention of a large audience, including many people with little or no interest in nature; it is difficult to represent the inner life of an animal in a visual medium; the medium's time constraints place severe restrictions on what it can accomplish; and, no doubt, script writers and directors want to place their own creative stamps on their films. Although some of the filmmakers felt free to alter radically the story line regarding the human characters, most tried (with varying success) to be more faithful to the tale of Buck's answering the "call of the wild." Film versions of London's *White Fang*, beginning with the 1936 Fox version, presented similar difficulties.[33]

Disney's 1983 film version of Farley Mowat's *Never Cry Wolf* was remarkably faithful to the spirit of the novel and was, as one critic put it, "one of the most beautifully photographed wilderness films."[34] In an important departure from the novel's story, however, the bush pilot, played by Brian Dennehy, did not simply drop Mowat off in the wild wastes of the Canadian North, as in the novel; he returned as an entrepreneur who was trying to bring recreational development to the wilderness. Moreover, the human threat to wolves was emphasized with the killing of some of the wolves Mowat was studying. This introduced a plotline to what had been an episodic novel. It also reflected the enormous growth of environmental awareness and public sympathy for wolves over the twenty years since the book appeared—a sympathy that Mowat's book had helped to generate.

Given the nature of the medium, it is understandable that few efforts have been made to produce film versions of classic wild animal stories told from the animals' vantage point, but French filmmaker Jean-Jacques Annaud's *The Bear* (Columbia, 1989) represents a brilliant attempt to do just that. Based on James Oliver Curwood's novel *The Grizzly King,* the film presents the story of two bears in largely visual terms with a minimum of dialogue. If anything, the cinematic version placed less emphasis on its human characters than did the novel, or other film renditions of wild animals stories. *The Bear* demonstrates that, with the right story and cinematic approach, it is possible to render classic wild animal stories into successful films. Curwood's relatively simple story line and antihunting theme hung on the moral superiority of a bear; that, together with Annaud's cinematic technique and the visual combination of an orphaned cub, a formidable adult bear, and a spectacular landscape, made a winning combination. Even before reaching the United States, *The Bear* had earned $100 million.[35]

There are other ways, of course, to craft cinematic wild animal stories. A unifying narrative thread or story line is often employed in film and video documentaries about wild animals. The multitude of nature documentaries that have appeared in movie theaters and on television owe an enormous debt to Walt Disney's 1948 film *Seal Island,* the first of his "True-Life Adventures." Disney first became interested in filming nature when he sent cinematographers into the field to do background and motion studies in preparation for animating *Bambi* (1942). During World War II, his studio cranked out a series of informational and training films. After the war he decided to refocus on entertainment. "We'll make educational films," he said, "but they'll be sugar-coated education." Disney was interested in Alaska and hired Alaskans Alfred and Elma Milotte to spend a year photographing the region's natives and wildlife. Their footage of seals intrigued him and he had it edited into the twenty-seven minute film, *Seal Island.* RKO was reluctant to distribute a film "too short to sell." Disney set out to prove the studio wrong and arranged for a showing of *Seal Island* in a Pasadena theater in December 1948. Its reception was enthusiastic, and the film received an Academy Award, as did many of the following movies in the True-Life Adventure series.

Disney's True-Life Adventures set a new standard for nature films. Although their story lines were often minimal, their extraordinary photography (sometimes taking years to shoot) and editing grabbed the audience's attention. Anthropomorphizing animal heroes and "choreographing" the animals' movements to music provided human interest, but also drew sharp criticism from wildlife experts and film critics. Nevertheless, these films introduced millions of people to the wonders of nature and wildlife and influenced the generation that would give birth to the environmental movement of the late twentieth century. They were also good financial performers. *The Living Desert* (1953), for example, cost $300,000 to produce and earned $4 million.

Disney's True-Life Adventures represented an interesting balance between realistic wild animal stories and educational natural history films. The animals did live for their own ends, rather than those of people; indeed, human beings were absent. Disney brought still stronger and more imaginative story lines to his series of "True-Life Fantasies," beginning with *Perri* (1957), a film about the life of a squirrel based on the novel by Felix Salten, the author of *Bambi*.[36] As the name of the series implies, however, this series placed less emphasis on natural history education. Disney's groundbreaking films paved the way for the present generation of nature film and video producers, who continue to confront the same tensions among scientific documentation, good story telling, audience interest, and anthropomorphism.

The later part of the twentieth century witnessed the development of a new kind of animal story that is characterized not so much by animals that live for their own ends as by humans who live for the animals' ends. In these stories, the human heroes fight to save the life and freedom of a wild animal, often of an endangered species. The protagonists move beyond calling attention to threats to wildlife—they take action. Farley Mowat's *A Whale for the Killing* (1972), an early example of the genre, also provides an example of how an author's original, complex vision can be winnowed away in the process of turning a book into film. The book tells of Mowat's effort to save a Finback Whale, trapped in a saltwater pond on the coast of Newfoundland, Canada, from local folks who want to torment and kill it. He placed their behavior in the larger context of Canadian government policies that had reshaped and destroyed the region's economy and way of life. The townspeople were as much victims of their government as the whale was of theirs. The whale's death became symbolic, not only of the threat to all whales, but of the destruction of traditional ways of life by modern progress. The 1981 film version of the novel, produced for ABC by Playboy Productions, although it kept many elements of the novel, modified and simplified the story and stereotyped the hunters, protestors, and other characters. It was easier to label the heroes and villains. Both novel and film however, end sadly with the whale's death.[37]

The best known example of this new approach to wild animal stories on screen is *Free Willy* (Warner, 1993). A troubled boy, Jesse, is rescued from delinquency by his love for Willy, a Killer Whale he encountered in an aquarium while doing his community service there, cleaning up graffiti he had painted on its walls. The whale was thought to be untrainable, but the boy established a bond with the Orca, became his trainer, and taught him all sorts of tricks. When Willy's life was threatened, Jesse and his friends managed to release him into the ocean. The whale escaped over the final barrier to freedom by leaping on Jesse's command. Willy returned for a sequel set in Alaska, in which Jesse saved him and his family from a burning oil spill and business people who wanted to "rescue" Willy and sell him to a marine park.[38]

The Willy films rode the wave of public interest in protecting whales and made their own contribution to promoting this sentiment. The basic relationship between Willy and Jesse, however, was that of beloved pet and master, despite Jesse's role in returning the whale to the wild. The differences between Orca and human were minimized and Willy's behavior was anthropomorphized to make the film appealing to children and adults alike. The video box for *Free Willy* featured a photo of Willy leaping to freedom over Jesse at the boy's command. The box for *Free Willy II* (Warner, 1995) showed Jesse riding on the back of the whale, from the scene in which he made a big impression on his new girlfriend. This conflict between wishing to turn wild animals into cute pets and the desire to ensure their survival as autonomous beings in the wild pervades American society.

Fly Away Home (Columbia, 1996)[39] is similar to the *Free Willy* films, but draws an even closer bond between person and wild animal. A child finds more than a dozen Canada Goose eggs in a wetland destroyed by unscrupulous developers. She incubates them and raises the chicks. After a wildlife officer threatens to pinion the adult geese, she and her father train them to follow an ultralight plane. Father and daughter then show the geese how to migrate by following the aircraft south. In the process, the geese help to forge a bond between father and daughter, who had been estranged by divorce. Again, we have the story elements of a child being helped through her relationship with wild animals who need protection from the villains threatening wildlife and the environment, and of a successful effort to return animals to the freedom of the wild.

The pattern varies in *The Amazing Panda Adventure* (Warner, 1995),[40] when some boys rescue a Giant Panda from poachers in China and take it to a panda research center operated by the father of one of them. In the process, the shaky bond between father and son is strengthened. Although here the animal is temporarily taken out of the wild (and at great peril to the children), it is done only to protect the panda from danger. These films follow the pattern established by Mowat's *A Whale for the Killing,* but they provide clear and stereotyped villains, endearing and terribly cute, gentle animals, and a human interest story line in which the relationship with the animal improves the child's life. Furthermore, these films end on an upbeat and hopeful note: the animals are saved after a heroic effort by the protagonists, who devote and sometimes risk their lives to promote the best interest of their animal friends.

The "save the whales" theme also appeared in an unlikely film, one of the Star Trek series. *Star Trek IV: The Voyage Home* (Paramount, 1986)[41] was directed by Leonard Nimoy, who also helped to create the story. Here, Admiral Kirk and his crew had to go back in time to the late twentieth century to collect a pair of Humpback Whales, the only creatures who could save the Earth of the future from destruction by communicating with an all-powerful attacking alien probe. In the doing, they discover that the whales are intelligent and live for their own ends and they rescue them from the harpoon of a whaling vessel. The film was intended to promote public interest in protecting whales and may well have done so, despite some very unlikely premises. (How, for example, could the limited gene pool of a pair of whales be successful in repopulating the future Earth's oceans with Humpbacks?) This film did not fall into the trap of terminal cuteness in which the other films we have examined were caught. It did, however, portray the whales as creatures possessing a greater gentleness and, perhaps, greater wisdom and morality than do humans. In an inversion of the "save the whale" theme, the whales saved humanity and the Earth by communicating with the aliens.

This merger of science fiction and animal films opens up an interesting area for analysis. The late 1970s and 1980s witnessed a series of science fiction films in which space aliens were not out to invade and destroy Earth. Instead, they were gentle creatures of goodness—almost angels. This trend got under way with the religious imagery at the conclusion of *Close Encounters of the Third Kind* (1977) and continued with *E.T., Cocoon, Cocoon: The Return, Starman,* and others.[42] During that period, in which the world was facing the potential dooms of nuclear war and environmental collapse, filmmakers created angelic alien others to uplift their audiences. They found an eager market; Steven Spielberg's *E.T.,* for example, made more money than any previous motion picture. These aliens offered a hopeful alternative to the dark and pessimistic face of humanity that filled newspaper headlines.

Similarly, American popular culture came to view whales, wolves, pandas, and other wild creatures as representatives of the purity, gentleness, and innate wisdom that seemed missing from the late twentieth century. This appeal to an angelic other, be it a space alien or wild animal, appears to be part of a common cultural phenomenon. Lisa Mighetto argued that the view of nature in the early realistic wild animal stories provided their readers a comforting alternative to the Darwinian view of the world as one of amoral conflict and competition. Perhaps the "save the critters" films offer a similar comfort to present-day viewers.

Animals *are* ideas, as well as living, breathing creatures. And the idea that their lives are gentler and possibly wiser than ours has been a very important element in the most popular wild animal films of our time. They are also presented as animals whose lives are threatened by humans and become symbolic of the larger environmental threats that we face. These films present another idea of animals that is becoming pervasive in popular culture: that animals are persons. A December 1990 *Los Angeles Times* poll, for example, found that 47 percent of Americans believed that "animals are just like humans in all important ways."[43] This idea has been around for a century or more but has become widespread in recent decades, in part through the promotional efforts of the animal rights movement. The "save the animals" films represent a fusion of the traditional animal story, environmental concerns, and an animal rights view of animals—all wrapped up in the search for a mythic alternative to the troubles of our times.

The realistic wild animal story is likely to continue as a viable part of nature literature and other media. Over the decades, it has changed in response to the issues and concerns of the times. The early stories emphasized the personalities and lives of individual animals in response to Darwinism and public concerns regarding the humane treatment of animals. The stories of the mid-twentieth century introduced a new ecological perspective, which grew into the environmental focus of the latter part of the century. And these themes were recast from an animal rights perspective and as a mythic response to social anxiety at the end of the century. Wild animal stories will continue to evolve in response to the social challenges of the future and changing ideas about animals.

Notes

1. Keith Barker, "Animal Stories," *International Companion Encyclopedia of Children's Literature*, ed. Peter Hunt (London: Routledge, 1996), 283–294; James Polk, "Lives of the Hunted," *Canadian Literature*, no. 53 (Summer 1972): 52; William H. Magee, "The Animal Story: A Challenge in Technique," *Dalhousie Review* 44 (Summer 1964): 157. See Harriet Ritvo, "Learning from Animals: Natural History for Children in the Eighteenth and Nineteenth Centuries," *Children's Literature* 13 (1985): 72–93, for a discussion in the context of British literature.

2. Charles G. D. Roberts, "The Animal Story," *The Kindred of the Wild: A Book of Animal Life* (Boston: L. C. Page, 1902), 28. W. H. Hudson, *Green Mansions: A Romance of the Forest* (1904, repr. New York: Random House, 1944); Charles G. D. Roberts, *The Heart of the Ancient Wood* (New York: Silver, Burdett, 1900). Both novels beg for a feminist analysis. The empathetic approach to animals did not, of course, originate with these stories. See Rodney Stenning Edgecomb, "Animal Consciousness from Antiquity to the Nineteenth Century," *Dalhousie Review* 71 (Fall 1991): 269–290.

3. Matt Cartmill, *A View to a Death in the Morning: Hunting and Nature Through History* (Cambridge: Harvard University Press, 1993).

4. On the social construction of nature, see Elizabeth Ann R. Bird, "The Social Construction of Nature: Theoretical Approaches to the History of Environmental Problems," *Environmental Review* 11 (Winter 1987): 255–264; Robin Attfield, "Attitudes to

Wildlife in the History of Ideas," *Environmental History Review* 15 (Summer 1991): 71–78; Neil Evernden, *The Social Creation of Nature* (Baltimore: Johns Hopkins University Press, 1992); Gary Lease, ed., *Reinventing Nature? Responses to Postmodern Deconstruction* (Washington, D.C.: Island Press, 1995); and William Cronon, ed., *Uncommon Ground: Toward Reinventing Nature* (New York: Norton, 1995).

5. George T. Angell, "Introductory Chapter" to A. Sewell, *Black Beauty: His Grooms and Companions* (Boston: American Humane Education Society, n.d. [1890]), 6; Rudyard Kipling, *The Jungle Book* (New York: Century, 1894); see also Kipling, *The Second Jungle Book* (New York: Century, 1895). On the history of concern for animal welfare, see E. S. Turner, *All Heaven in a Rage* (New York: St. Martin's Press, 1964); Gerald Carson, *Men, Beasts, and Gods: A History of Cruelty and Kindness to Animals* (New York: Charles Scribner's Sons, 1972); and James Turner, *Reckoning with the Beast: Animals, Pain, and Humanity in the Victorian Mind* (Baltimore: Johns Hopkins University Press, 1980).

6. Michel Poirier, "The Animal Story in Canadian Literature," *Queen's Quarterly*, pt. I (January–March 1927): 298–312; and pt. II (April–June 1927): 398–419; John Henry Wadland, *Ernest Thompson Seton: Man in Nature and the Progressive Era, 1880–1915* (New York: Arno Press, 1978), 166. Charles Dudley Warner, "A-Hunting of the Deer," *Atlantic Monthly* (April 1878): 522–529; Ernest E. Thompson, "The Drummer on Snowshoes," *St. Nicholas* 14 (April 1887): 414–417; Ernest E. Thompson, "The King of Currumpaw: A Wolf Story," *Scribner's Monthly* 16 (November 1894): 618–628; Charles G. D. Roberts, "Do Seek Their Meat from God," *Harper's Magazine* 86 (December 1892): 120–123; Charles G. D. Roberts, *Earth's Enigmas* (1896; repr. Boston: L. D. Page, 1903). Seton's story of Lobo of the Currumpaw was reprinted in his *Wild Animals I Have Known* (New York: Charles Scribner's Sons, 1898). For Roberts' "hook & bullet" stories, see his *Around the Camp-fire* (Boston: Thomas Y. Crowell, 1896).

Seton published under variations of his name, including Ernest E. Thompson, Ernest Seton Thompson, Ernest Seton-Thompson, and Ernest Thompson Seton. He ultimately settled on the last version. For his explanation of this, see his autobiography, *Trail of an Artist-Naturalist* (New York: Charles Scribner's Sons, 1940), 391–393.

7. Northrop Frye, "Conclusion," in *Literary History of Canada*, ed. Carl F. Klinck (Toronto: University of Toronto Press, 1965), 821–849 (quotation on 822); Margaret Atwood, *Survival: A Thematic Guide to Canadian Literature* (1972; repr. Toronto: McClelland & Stewart, 1996), 34, 35. James Polk has similarly argued that Canadian literature reflects a survival theme and a "jittery fear of wilderness" in his "Lives of the Hunted," 52–53.

For differing views, see George Altmeyer, "Three Ideas of Nature in Canada, 1893–1914," *Journal of Canadian Studies* 11 (August 1976): 21–36; Allan Pritchard, "West of the Great Divide: A View of the Literature of British Columbia," *Canadian Literature*, no. 94 (Autumn 1982): 96–112; Pritchard, "West of the Great Divide: Man and Nature in the Literature of British Columbia," *Canadian Studies*, no. 102 (Autumn 1984): 36–53; and Mary Lu MacDonald, "The Natural World in Early Nineteenth-Century Canadian Writing," *Canadian Literature*, no. 111 (Winter 1986): 48–65.

On Canadian nature writing, see Rebecca Raglon, "Canadian Nature Writing in English," in *American Nature Writers*, ed. John Elder (New York: Charles Scribner's Sons, 1996), vol. 2:1025–1039; and Alec Lucas, "Nature Writers and the Animal Story" in *Literary History of Canada*, ed. Klinck, 364–388.

8. Roberts, *Heart of the Ancient Wood*, 243; Seton, *Wild Animals I Have Known*, 12 (emphasis in original); Ernest Seton-Thompson, *Lives of the Hunted* (Charles Scribner's Sons, 1901), 11.

9. Seton, *Lives of the Hunted*, 9; Joseph Gold, "The Precious Speck of Life," *Canadian Literature*, no. 26 (Autumn 1965): 25; Ernest Thompson Seton, *The Natural History of the Ten Commandments* (New York: Scribner's, 1907), 4 (emphasis in original).

10. Atwood, *Survival*, 75–80.

11. Lori Jo Oswald, "Heroes and Victims: The Stereotyping of Animal Characters in Children's Realistic Animal Fiction," *Children's Literature in Education* 26, no. 2 (1995): 136; Polk, "Lives of the Hunted," 52–53; Atwood, *Survival*, 74.

See Kathleen R. Johnson, "The Ambiguous Terrain of Petkeeping in Children's Realistic Animal Stories," *Society and Animals* 4 (1996): 1–17, for a content analysis of 48 children's books in the realistic animal story genre; all the books were published in the twentieth century. Johnson does not distinguish between Canadian and United States authors or between wild and domestic animal stories.

12. Little is known about Long. The most detailed biographical treatment is in Ralph H. Lutts, *The Nature Fakers: Wildlife, Science & Sentiment* (Golden, Colo.: Fulcrum Publishing, 1990).

13. William J. Long, "Wayeeses the Strong One," *Northern Trails: Some Studies of Animal Life in the Far North* (Boston: Ginn, 1905).

14. James Oliver Curwood, *The Grizzly King* (Garden City, N.Y.: Doubleday, Page, 1916), 203–207. The novel may have some basis in truth; see Judith A. Eldridge, *James Oliver Curwood: God's Country and the Man* (Bowling Green, Ohio: Bowling Green State University Popular Press, 1993), 3–8.

15. Jack London, *Call of the Wild* (New York: Macmillan, 1903); London, *White Fang* (New York: Macmillan, 1906); London, "The Other Animals," *Collier's* 41, no. 24 (September 5, 1908): 10–11, 25–26.

16. John Muir, *Stickeen* (Boston: Houghton Mifflin, 1909), 14, 72–73.

17. Ronald H. Limbaugh, "Stickeen and the Moral Education of John Muir," *Environmental History Review* 15 (Spring 1991): 25–45.

18. Ernst Mayr, "The Nature of the Darwinian Revolution," *Science* 176 (1972), 981–989; Robert H. MacDonald, "The Revolt Against Instinct: The Animal Stories of Seton and Roberts," *Canadian Literature*, no. 84 (Spring 1980), 18; William J. Long, *Brier-Patch Philosophy, by "Peter Rabbit"* (Boston: Ginn, 1906); Mighetto, "Science, Sentiment, and Anxiety: American Nature Writing at the Turn of the Century," *Pacific Historical Review* 54 (February 1985): 33–50. See also, Lisa Mighetto, "Science and Sentiment: Animals in the 'New School' of Nature Writing," in *Wild Animals and American Environmental Ethics* (Tucson: University of Arizona Press, 1991), 9–26.

19. Thomas R. Dunlap, "'The Old Kinship of Earth': Science, Man and Nature in the Animal Stories of Charles G. D. Roberts," *Journal of Canadian Studies* 22 (Spring 1987): 104–120; Dunlap, "The Realistic Animal Story: Ernest Thompson Seton, Charles Roberts, and Darwinism," *Forest & Conservation History* 36 (April 1992): 56–62.

20. Lutts, *Nature Fakers*.

21. Clarence Hawks, *The Light that Did Not Fail* (Boston: Chapman & Grimes, 1925), 118.

22. T. Gilbert Pearson, *Stories of Bird Life* (Richmond, Va.: B.F. Johnson, 1901), 223;

Seton, *Wild Animals I Have Known,* 12–13; and Long, *Brier-Patch Philosophy.* Pearson was an early, but unrecognized, contributer to the animal story genre. See also, Pearson, *Tales from Birdland* (New York: World Book, 1918). On attitudes in the United States toward wolves and other predators, see Thomas R. Dunlap, *Saving America's Wildlife* (Princeton, N.J.: Princeton University Press, 1988); and Valerie M. Fogleman, "American Attitudes Toward Wolves: A History of Misconception," *Environmental Review* 13 (Spring 1989): 63–94.

23. Lucas, "Nature Writers and the Animal Story," 388; Magee, "The Animal Story," 164.

24. Vera Norwood, *Made from This Earth: American Women and Nature* (Chapel Hill: University of North Carolina Press, 1993), 238.

25. Rachel L. Carson, *Under the Sea-Wind: A Naturalist's Picture of Ocean Life* (New York: Simon & Schuster, 1941); Carson, *The Sea Around Us* (New York: Oxford University Press, 1951); Henry Williamson, *Tarka the Otter: His Joyful Life and Death in the Country of the Two Rivers* (New York: Dutton, 1928); Williamson, *Salar the Salmon* (Boston: Little, Brown, 1936); Paul Brooks, *The House of Life: Rachel Carson at Work* (Boston: Houghton Mifflin, 1972), 5–6.

26. Sally Carrighar, *One Day on Beetle Rock* (New York: Alfred A. Knopf, 1944); Gale Lawrence, "Sally Carrighar," in *American Nature Writers,* ed. Elder, vol. 1:142.

27. Norwood, *Made from This Earth.* See reviews by Ralph H. Lutts, "Made from This Earth," *Environmental History Review* 17, no. 4 (Winter 1993): 91–93; and Linda Lear, "Made from This Earth," *ISIS* 85 (1) 130–131.

28. Sally Carrighar, *Home to the Wilderness* (Boston: Houghton Mifflin, 1973), 330.

29. Franklin Russell, *Watchers at the Pond* (New York: Alfred A. Knopf, 1961).

30. Atwood, *Survival,* 76; Dunlap, "'The Old Kinship of Earth,'" 116.

31. Seton-Thompson, *Lives of the Hunted,* 12; Fred Bodsworth, *Last of the Curlews* (New York: Dodd, Mead, 1955); Farley Mowat, *Never Cry Wolf* (Boston: Little, Brown, 1963); William O. Pruitt, Jr., *Animals of the North* (New York: Harper & Row, 1967); Sally Carrighar, *The Twilight Seas* (New York: Weybright and Talley, 1975). See Grey Owl's autobiography, *Pilgrims of the Wild* (New York: Charles Scribner's Sons, 1935).

32. Magee, "The Wild Animal Story," 156–164. Farley Mowat's books are reputed to have outsold those of any other Canadian author—14 million copies in 52 languages, according to the Houghton Mifflin Co. web site [htttp://www.hmco.com/trade/non-fiction/catalog/AboutAuthor 0-395-73528-9.html], seen March 27, 1997.

33. See "Call of the Wild" entries in Jay Robert Nash and Stanley Ralph Ross, eds., *The Motion Picture Guide: 1927–1983,* 10 vol. (Chicago: Cinebooks, 1985) vol. 2:336; Mick Martin and Marsha Porter, *Video Movie Guide 1997* (New York: Ballantine Books, 1996), 161; and *VideoHound's Golden Movie Retriever* (Detroit: Visible Ink, 1997), 131–132. The 1972 MGM Charlton Heston version is available on video, *Call of the Wild* (Van Nuys, Calif.: Bingo Video, 1989), as is the 1976 Charles Fries version, *Call of the Wild* (New York: GoodTimes Home Video, 1990). Other versions include an animated version, *Call of the Wild* (New York: GoodTimes Home Video, 1991), and a 1993 television release. See "White Fang" entries in Nash and Ross, *Motion Picture Guide, 1927–1983,* vol. 9:3823; John Miller-Mansion, ed., *The Motion Picture Guide: 1992 Annual* (New York: Baseline, 1992), 329–330; and Porter, *Video Movie Guide 1997,* 1185. Other versions of *White Fang* include a 1991 Disney release that is available on video (Burbank,

Calif.: Walt Disney Home Video, n.d.) and two sequels, *White Fang 2: Myth of the White Wolf* and *White Fang and the Hunter,* of which Jack London never even dreamed.

34. See the video version, *Never Cry Wolf* (Burbank, Calif.: Walt Disney Home Video, n.d.); and "Never Cry Wolf" in Nash and Ross, *Motion Picture Guide: 1927–1983,* vol. 6:2122. On the making of the film, see Bruce Brown, "Filming 'Never Cry Wolf,'" *New York Times Magazine,* October 16, 1983, 84–91; and Tim Cahill, "Call of the Wolf," *Rolling Stone,* no. 408 (November 10, 1983), 6868–6879.

35. The film is available on video, *The Bear* (Culver City, Calif.: Columbia TriStar Home Video, 1990). See "The Bear," *The Motion Picture Guide: 1990 Annual* (Evanston, Ill.: CineBooks, 1990), 16–17. See also Jay Carr, "Making a Bear of a Movie," *Boston Globe,* October 24, 1989, 59; and Janet Maslin, "Two Bears Who Are Just Plain Folks," *New York Times,* October 25, 1989, C15. Annaud is best known for his other films, such as *Black and White in Color* (Academy Award for Best Foreign Film, 1976), *Quest for Fire* (1981), and *The Name of the Rose* (1986). The title of *The Bear* differs from that of the novel, in large part, because it featured Kodiak Bears, rather than Grizzlies. Kodiak Bears (Big Brown Bear, *Ursa arctos middendorffi*) appear similar to, but are larger than, Grizzly Bears (*Ursa arctos horribilis*).

36. Robert DeRoos, "The Magic Worlds of Walt Disney," *Disney Discourse: Producing the Magic Kingdom,* ed. Eric Smoodin (New York: Routledge, 1994), 55–60; Bob Thomas, *Walt Disney: An American Original* (New York: Simon & Schuster, 1976), 205–240 (quotation on 206); Leonard Maltin, *The Disney Films* (New York: Bonanza Books, 1973), 18–20; Richard Schickel, *The Disney Version: The Life, Times, Art and Commerce of Walt Disney,* rev. and updated (New York: Simon & Schuster, 1985); 284–292. For descriptions of the True-Life Adventure and True-Life Fantasy films, see Maltin, *Disney Films.* Other True-Life Adventure series films included *Beaver Valley* (1950), *Nature's Half-Acre* (1951), *Water Birds* (1952), and *Bear Country* (1953), all of which received Academy Awards, as well as *Prowlers of the Everglades* (1953), *Mysteries of the Deep* (1959), and *Islands of the Sea* (1960).

37. Farley Mowat, *A Whale for the Killing* (1972; repr. Baltimore: Penguin Books, 1973); James Overton, "*A Whale for the Killing* and the Politics of Culture and Ecology," *Journal of Canadian Studies* 22, no. 1 (Spring 1987): 84–103.

38. See the videos *Free Willy* (Burbank, Calif.: Warner Home Video, 1993) and *Free Willy II: The Adventure Home* (Burbank, Calif.: Warner Home Video, 1995).

39. See the video *Fly Away Home* (Culver City, Calif.: Columbia TriStar Home Video, 1996).

40. See the video *The Amazing Panda Adventure* (Burbank, Calif.: Warner Home Video, 1996).

41. See the video *Star Trek IV: The Voyage Home* (Hollywood: Paramount, 1987).

42. See the videos *Close Encounters of the Third Kind,* special ed. (New York: GoodTimes Home Video, 1988); *E.T.: The Extra-Terrestrial* (Universal City, Calif.: MCA Home Video, 1988); *Cocoon* (Livonia, Mich.: CBS/FOX Video, 1986); *Cocoon: The Return* (New York: CBS/FOX Video, 1989); *Starman* (New York: GoodTimes Videos, 1989).

43. The more traditional animal documentaries continue to present a somewhat more objective view of animal lives. John Balzar, "Creatures Great and—Equal?" *Los Angeles Times,* December 25, 1993, A1, A30.

Tales

This selection of wild animal stories emphasizes the work of Charles G. D. Roberts, Ernest Thompson Seton, and William J. Long. Roberts and Seton are credited with creating the genre. The three of them were among the most popular and prolific animal story writers of their time. They knew that they were creating something new in literature and told their readers what they were doing, usually in prefaces to their books. These statements, some of which have been gathered here, provide a window on the early ideas and ideals of the realistic wild animal story. They also reveal the unique approaches taken by each writer. Charles G. D. Robert's "The Animal Story" is perhaps the first extended examination of the wild animal story.

Roberts' "Do Seek Their Meat from God" and Seton's "Lobo: King of the Currumpaw" are among the very first of the realistic wild animal stories and are classics in the genre. The tales by Jack London and John Muir are generally considered to be in the tradition of the dog story, rather than the wild animal story. Indeed, *Call of the Wild* (from which "The Sounding of the Call" is excerpted) and *Stickeen* are among the very best dog stories. Nevertheless, they also bridge both genres by placing an emphasis on the interests of the animals, rather than on their serving human interests. Rachel Carson's "Journey to the Sea," from her book *Under the Sea-Wind*, which revitalized the genre, reflects the strong ecological perspective that characterized the wild animal stories of the last half of the twentieth century.

Realistic wild animal stories must work both as stories and as natural history but often blur the line between fact and fiction. Roberts' tales, for example, are obviously fictional, but he argued that his natural history was accurate. Seton claimed that his stories were based on actual events, although he sometimes combined the experiences of a number of animals into a single character. London's story is a work of fiction, but he made a special effort to construct the mental life of the dog Buck in a way that was psychologically feasible. Even the tales based on the authors' own experiences are not straight factual reporting, because they have been shaped to achieve specific literary objectives. Each author must establish a balance between fact and fiction that works for him or her. And each reader needs to be cautious not to confuse fiction with fact while reading these tales.

These writers left a mark on North America; they and their colleagues promoted new visions of wild animals in the popular culture of Canada and the United States. They also cast long shadows for their individual achievements, not all of which were related to their wild animal stories. Roberts was knighted for his literary accomplishments and is now recognized as one of the founding figures in Canadian literature. Seton, became a co-founder of the Boy Scouts of America and eventually settled in New Mexico, where he was a proponent of Native American culture. Long is largely forgotten, in part because of the role he played in the Nature Fakers controversy (see Part II, "Controversy"), but schools used his popular textbooks on American and English literature for decades. London is recognized as one of the great figures in American literature. Muir is best known as a founder of the wilderness preservation movement and the Sierra Club, which carries on his work. Carson's book *Silent Spring* played a major role in establishing the environmental movement of the late twentieth century and became one of the most influential books of the century.

2

On His Animal Stories

CHARLES G. D. ROBERTS

The Animal Story

Alike in matter and in method, the animal story, as we have it to-day, may be regarded as a culmination. The animal story, of course, in one form or another, is as old as the beginnings of literature. Perhaps the most engrossing part in the life-drama of primitive man was that played by the beasts which he hunted, and by those which hunted him. They pressed incessantly upon his perceptions. They furnished both material and impulse for his first gropings toward pictorial art. When he acquired the kindred art of telling a story, they supplied his earliest themes; and they suggested the hieroglyphs by means of which, on carved bone or painted rock, he first gave his narrative a form to outlast the spoken breath. We may not unreasonably infer that the first animal story—the remote but authentic ancestor of "Mowgli" and "Lobo" and "Krag"—was a story of some successful hunt, when success meant life to the starving family; or of some desperate escape, when the truth of the narrative was attested, to the hearers squatted trembling about their fire, by the sniffings of the baffled bear or tiger at the rock-barred mouth of the cave. Such first animal stories had at least one merit of prime literary importance. They were convincing. The first critic, however supercilious, would be little likely to cavil at their verisimilitude.

Somewhat later, when men had begun to harass their souls, and their neighbours, with problems of life and conduct, then these same animals, hourly and in every aspect thrust beneath the eyes of their observation, served to point the

Prefaces from Charles G. D. Roberts, *The Kindred of the Wild: A Book of Animal Life* (Boston: L. C. Page, 1902), and *The Watchers of the Trails* (Boston: L. C. Page, 1904).

moral of their tales. The beasts, not being in a position to resent the ignoble office thrust upon them, were compelled to do duty as concrete types of those obvious virtues and vices of which alone the unsophisticated, ethical sense was ready to take cognisance. In this way, as soon as composition became a *métier*, was born the fable; and in this way the ingenuity of the first author enabled him to avoid a perilous unpopularity among those whose weaknesses and defects his art held up to the scorn of all the caves.

These earliest observers of animal life were compelled by the necessities of the case to observe truly, if not deeply. Pitting their wits against those of their four-footed rivals, they had to know their antagonists, and respect them, in order to overcome them. But it was only the most salient characteristics of each species that concerned the practical observer. It was simple to remember that the tiger was cruel, the fox cunning, the wolf rapacious. And so, as advancing civilisation drew an ever widening line between man and the animals, and men became more and more engrossed in the interests of their own kind, the personalities of the wild creatures which they had once known so well became obscured to them, and the creatures themselves came to be regarded, for the purposes of literature, as types or symbols merely, —except in those cases, equally obstructive to exact observation, where they were revered as temporary tenements of the spirits of departed kinsfolk. The characters in that great beast-epic of the middle ages, "Reynard the Fox," though far more elaborately limned than those which play their succinct roles in the fables of Aesop, are at the same time in their elaboration far more alien to the truths of wild nature. Reynard, Isegrim, Bruin, and Graybeard have little resemblance to the fox, the wolf, the bear, and the badger, as patience, sympathy, and the camera reveal them to us to-day.

The advent of Christianity, strange as it may seem at first glance, did not make for a closer understanding between man and the lower animals. While it was militant, fighting for its life against the forces of paganism, its effort was to set man at odds with the natural world, and fill his eyes with the wonders of the spiritual. Man was the only thing of consequence on earth, and of man, not his body, but his soul. Nature was the ally of the enemy. The way of nature was the way of death. In man alone was the seed of the divine. Of what concern could be the joy or pain of creatures of no soul, to-morrow returning to the dust? To strenuous spirits, their eyes fixed upon the fear of hell for themselves, and the certainty of it for their neighbours, it smacked of sin to take thought of the feelings of such evanescent products of corruption. Hence it came that, in spite of the gentle understanding of such sweet saints as Francis of Assisi, Anthony of Padua, and Colomb of the Bees, the inarticulate kindred for a long time reaped small comfort from the Dispensation of Love.

With the spread of freedom and the broadening out of all intellectual interests which characterise these modern days, the lower kindreds began to regain their old place in the concern of man. The revival of interest in the animals found literary expression (to classify roughly) in two forms, which necessarily overlap each other now and then, viz., the story of adventure and the anecdote of observation. Hunting as a recreation, pursued with zest from pole to tropics by restless seekers after the new, supplied a species of narrative singularly akin to what the first animal stories must have been, —narratives of desperate encounter, strange peril, and hairbreadth escape. Such hunters' stories and travellers' tales are rarely conspicuous for the exactitude of their observation; but that was not the quality at first demanded of them by fireside readers. The attention of the writer was focussed, not upon the peculiarities or the emotions of the beast protagonist in each fierce, brief drama, but upon the thrill of the action, the final triumph of the human actor. The inevitable tendency of these stories of adventure with beasts was to awaken interest in animals, and to excite a desire for exact knowledge of their traits and habits. The interest and the desire evoked the natural historian, the inheritor of the half-forgotten mantle of Pliny. Precise and patient scientists made the animals their care, observing with microscope and measure, comparing bones, assorting families, subdividing subdivisions, till at length all the beasts of significance to man were ticketed neatly, and laid bare, as far as the inmost fibre of their material substance was concerned, to the eye of popular information.

Altogether admirable and necessary as was this development at large, another, of richer or at least more spiritual significance, was going on at home. Folk who loved their animal comrades—their dogs, horses, cats, parrots, elephants—were observing, with the wonder and interest of discoverers, the astonishing fashion in which the mere instincts of these so-called irrational creatures were able to simulate the operations of reason. The results of this observation were written down, till "anecdotes of animals" came to form a not inconsiderable body of literature. The drift of all these data was overwhelmingly toward one conclusion. The mental processes of the animals observed were seen to be far more complex than the observers had supposed. Where instinct was called in to account for the elaborate ingenuity with which a dog would plan and accomplish the outwitting of a rival, or the nice judgment with which an elephant, with no nest-building ancestors behind him to instruct his brain, would choose and adjust the teak-logs which he was set to pile, it began to seem as if that faithful faculty was being overworked. To explain yet other cases, which no accepted theory seemed to fit, coincidence was invoked, till that rare and elusive phenomenon threatened to become as customary as buttercups. But when instinct and coincidence had done all that could be asked of them, there remained a great unaccounted-for body of facts; and men were forced at last to accept the proposition that, within their varying limitations, animals can and do reason. As far, at least, as the mental intelligence is concerned, the gulf dividing the lowest of the human species from the highest of the animals has in these latter days been reduced to a very narrow psychological fissure.

Whether avowedly or not, it is with the psychology of animal life that the representative animal stories of to-day are first of all concerned. Looking deep into the eyes of certain of the four-footed kindred, we have been startled to see therein a something, before unrecognised, that answered to our inner and intellectual, if not spiritual selves. We have suddenly attained a new and clearer vision. We have come face to face with personality, where we were blindly wont to predicate mere instinct and automatism. It is as if one should step carelessly out of one's back door, and marvel to see unrolling before his new-awakened eyes the peaks and seas and misty valleys of an unknown world. Our chief writers of animal stories at the present day may be regarded as explorers of this unknown world, absorbed in charting its topography. They work, indeed, upon a substantial foundation of known facts. They are minutely scrupulous as to their natural history, and assiduous contributors to that science. But above all are they diligent in their search for the motive beneath the action. Their care is to catch the varying, elusive personalities which dwell back of the luminous brain windows of the dog, the horse, the deer, or wrap themselves in reserve behind the inscrutable eyes of all the cats, or sit aloof in the gaze of the hawk and the eagle. The animal story at its highest point of development is a psychological romance constructed on a framework of natural science.

The real psychology of the animals, so far as we are able to grope our way toward it by deduction and induction combined, is a very different thing from the psychology of certain stories of animals which paved the way for the present vogue. Of these, such books as "Beautiful Joe" and "Black Beauty" are deservedly conspicuous examples. It is no detraction from the merit of these books, which have done great service in awakening a sympathetic understanding of the animals and sharpening our sense of kinship with all that breathe, to say that their psychology is human. Their animal characters think and feel as human beings would think and feel under like conditions. This marks the stage which these works occupy in the development of the animal story.

The next stage must be regarded as, in literature, a climax indeed, but not the climax in this genre. I refer to the "Mowgli" stories of Mr. Kipling. In these tales the animals are frankly humanised. Their individualisation is distinctly human, as are also their mental and emotional processes, and their highly elaborate powers of expression. Their notions are complex; whereas the motives of real animals, so far as we have hitherto been able to judge them, seem to be essentially simple, in the sense that the motive dominant at a given moment quite obliterates, for the time, all secondary motives. Their reasoning powers and their constructive imagination are far beyond anything which present knowledge justifies us in ascribing to the inarticulate kindreds. To say this is in no way to depreciate such work, but merely to classify it. There are stories being written now which, for interest and artistic value, are not to be mentioned in the same breath with the "Mowgli" tales, but which nevertheless occupy a more advanced stage in the evolution of this genre.

It seems to me fairly safe to say that this evolution is not likely to go beyond the point to which it has been carried to-day. In such a story, for instance, as that of "Krag, the Kootenay Ram," by Mr. Ernest Seton, the interest centres about the personality, individuality, mentality, of an animal, as well as its purely physical characteristics. The field of animal psychology so admirably opened is an inexhaustible world of wonder. Sympathetic exploration may advance its boundaries to a degree of which we hardly dare to dream; but such expansion cannot be called evolution. There would seem to be no further evolution possible, unless based upon a hypothesis that animals have souls. As souls are apt to elude exact observation, to forecast any such development would seem to be at best merely fanciful.

The animal story, as we now have it, is a potent emancipator. It frees us for a little from the world of shop-worn utilities, and from the mean tenement of self of which we do well to grow weary. It helps us to return to nature, without requiring that we at the same time return to barbarism. It leads us back to the old kinship of earth, without asking us to relinquish by way of toll any part of the wisdom of the ages, any fine essential of the "large result of time." The clear and candid life to which it reinitiates us, far behind though it lies in the long upward march of being, holds for us this quality. It has ever the more significance, it has ever the richer gift of refreshment and renewal, the more humane the heart and spiritual the understanding which we bring to the intimacy of it.

Preface to *The Watchers of the Trails*

In the preface to a former volume I have endeavoured to trace the development of the modern animal story and have indicated what appeared to me to be its tendency and scope. It seems unnecessary to add anything here but a few words of more personal application.

The stories of which this volume is made up are avowedly fiction. They are, at the same time, true, in that the material of which they are moulded consists of facts, —facts as precise as painstaking observation and anxious regard for truth can make them. Certain of the stories, of course, are true literally. Literal truth may be attained by stories which treat of a single incident, or of action so restricted as to lie within the scope of a single observation. When, on the other hand, a story follows the career of a wild creature of the wood or air or water through wide intervals of time and space, it is obvious that the truth of that story must be of a different kind. The complete picture which such a story presents is built up from observation necessarily detached and scattered; so that the utmost it can achieve as a whole is consistency with truth. If a writer has, by temperament, any sympathetic understanding of the wild kindreds; if he has any intimate knowledge of their habits, with any sensitiveness to the infinite variation of their personalities; and if he has chanced to live much among them during the impressionable periods of his life, and so become saturated in their atmosphere and their environment; —then he may hope to make his most elaborate piece of animal biography not less true to nature than his transcript of an isolated fact. The present writer, having spent most of his boyhood on the fringes of the forest, with few interests save those which the forest afforded, may claim to have had the intimacies of the wilderness as it were thrust upon him. The earliest enthusiasms which he can recollect are connected with some of the furred or feathered kindred; and the first thrills strong enough to leave a lasting mark on his memory are those with which he used to follow—furtive, apprehensive, expectant, breathlessly watchful—the lure of an unknown trail.

There is one more point which may seem to claim a word. A very distinguished author[1]—to whom all contemporary writers on nature are indebted, and from whom it is only with the utmost diffidence that I venture to dissent at all—has gently called me to account on the charge of ascribing to my animals human motives and the mental processes of man. The fact is, however, that this fault is one which I have been at particular pains to guard against. The psychological processes of the animals are so simple, so obvious, in comparison with those of man, their actions flow so directly from their springs of impulse, that it is, as a rule, an easy matter to infer the motives which are at any one moment impelling them. In my desire to avoid alike the melodramatic, the visionary, and the sentimental, I have studied to keep well within the limits of safe inference. Where I may have seemed to state too confidently the motives underlying the special action of this or that animal, it will usually be found that the action itself is very fully presented; and it will, I think, be further found that the motive which I have here assumed affords the most reasonable, if not the only reasonable, explanation of that action.

1. *Editor's note: John Burroughs; see p. 131.—RHL*

3

Do Seek Their Meat from God

CHARLES G. D. ROBERTS

One side of the ravine was in darkness. The darkness was soft and rich, suggesting thick foliage. Along the crest of the slope tree-tops came into view—great pines and hemlocks of the ancient unviolated forest—revealed against the orange disk of a full moon just rising. The low rays slanting through the moveless tops lit strangely the upper portion or the opposite steep, —the western wall of the ravine, barren, unlike its fellow, bossed with great rocky projections, and harsh with stunted junipers. Out of the sluggish dark that lay along the ravine as in a trough, rose the brawl of a swollen, obstructed stream.

Out of a shadowy hollow behind a long white rock, on the lower edge of that part of the steep which lay in the moonlight, came softly a great panther. In common daylight his coat would have shown a warm fulvous hue, but in the elvish decolorizing rays of that half hidden moon he seemed to wear a sort of spectral gray. He lifted his smooth round head to gaze on the increasing flame, which presently he greeted with a shrill cry. That terrible cry, at once plaintive and menacing, with an undertone like the fierce protestations of a saw beneath the file, was a summons to his mate, telling her that the hour had come when they should seek their prey. From the lair behind the rock, where the cubs were being suckled by their dam, came no immediate answer. Only a pair of crows, that had their nest in a giant fir-tree across the gulf, woke up and croaked harshly their indignation. These three summers past they had built in the same spot, and had been nightly awakened to vent the same rasping complaints.

The panther walked restlessly up and down, half a score of paces each way,

Charles G. D. Roberts, "Do Seek Their Meat from God," in *Earth's Enigmas* (1895; repr. Boston: L. C. Page, 1903), 12–27.

along the edge of the shadow, keeping his wide-open green eyes upon the rising light. His short, muscular tail twitched impatiently, but he made no sound. Soon the breadth of confused brightness had spread itself further down the steep disclosing the foot of the white rock and the bones and antlers of a deer which had been dragged thither and devoured.

By this time the cubs had made their meal, and their dam was ready for such enterprise as must be accomplished ere her own hunger, now grown savage, could hope to be assuaged. She glided supplely forth into the glimmer, raised her head, and screamed at the moon in a voice as terrible as her mate's. Again the crows stirred, croaking harshly; and the two beasts, noiselessly mounting the steep, stole into the shadows of the forest that clothed the high plateau.

The panthers were fierce with hunger. These two days past their hunting had been wellnigh fruitless. What scant prey they had slain had for the most part been devoured by the female; for had she not those small blind cubs at home to nourish, who soon must suffer at any lack of hers? The settlements of late had been making great inroads on the world of ancient forest, driving before them the deer and smaller game. Hence the sharp hunger of the panther parents, and hence it came that on this night they hunted together. They purposed to steal upon the settlements in their sleep, and take tribute of the enemies' flocks.

Through the dark of the thick woods, here and there pierced by the moonlight, they moved swiftly and silently. Now and again a dry twig would snap beneath the discreet and padded footfalls. Now and again, as they rustled some low tree, a pewee or a nuthatch would give a startled chirp. For an hour the noiseless journeying continued, and ever and anon the two gray, sinuous shapes would come for a moment into the view of the now well-risen moon. Suddenly there fell upon their ears, far off and faint, but clearly defined against the vast stillness of the Northern forest, a sound which made those stealthy hunters pause and lift their heads. It was the voice of a child crying, —crying long and loud, hopelessly, as if there were no one by to comfort it. The panthers turned aside from their former course and glided toward the sound. They were not yet come to the outskirts of the settlement, but they knew of a solitary cabin lying in the thick of the woods a mile and more from the nearest neighbor. Thither they bent their way, fired with fierce hope. Soon would they break their bitter fast.

Up to noon of the previous day the lonely cabin had been occupied. Then its owner, a shiftless fellow, who spent his days for the most part at the corner tavern three miles distant, had suddenly grown disgusted with a land wherein one must work to live, and had betaken himself with his seven-year-old boy to seek some more indolent clime. During the long lonely days when his father was away at the tavern the little boy had been wont to visit the house of the next neighbor, to play with a child of some five summers, who had no other playmate. The next neighbor was a prosperous pioneer, being master of a substantial frame house in the midst of a large and well-tilled clearing. At times, though rarely, because it was forbidden, the younger child would make his way by a rough wood road to visit his poor little disreputable playmate. At length it had appeared that the five-year-old was learning unsavory language from the elder boy, who rarely had an opportunity of hearing speech more desirable. To the bitter grief of both children, the companionship had at length been stopped by unalterable decree of the master of the frame house.

Hence it had come to pass that the little boy was unaware of his comrade's departure. Yielding at last to an eager longing for that comrade, he had stolen away late in the afternoon, traversed with endless misgivings the lonely stretch of wood road, and reached the cabin only to find it empty. The door, on its leathern hinges, swung idly open. The one room had been stripped of its few poor furnishings. After looking in the rickety shed, whence darted two wild and hawklike chickens, the child had seated himself on the hacked threshold, and sobbed passionately with a grief that he did not fully comprehend. Then seeing the shadows lengthen across the tiny clearing, he had grown afraid to start for home. As the dusk gathered, he had crept trembling into the cabin, whose door would not stay shut. When it grew quite dark, he crouched in the inmost corner of the room, desperate with fear and loneliness, and lifted up his voice piteously. From time to time his lamentations would be choked by sobs, or he would grow breathless, and in the terrifying silence would listen hard to hear if any one or anything were coming. Then again would the shrill childish wailings arise, startling the unexpectant night, and piercing the forest depths, even to the ears of those great beasts which had set forth to seek their meat from God.

The lonely cabin stood some distance, perhaps a quarter of a mile, back from the highway connecting the settlements. Along this main road a man was plodding wearily. All day he had been walking, and now as he neared home his steps began to quicken with anticipation of rest. Over his shoulder projected a double-barrelled fowling-piece, from which was slung a bundle of such necessities as he had purchased in town that morning. It was the prosperous settler, the master of the frame house. His mare being with foal, he had chosen to make the tedious journey on foot.

The settler passed the mouth of the wood road leading to the cabin. He had gone perhaps a furlong beyond, when his ears were startled by the sound of a child crying in the woods. He stopped, lowered his burden to the road, and stood straining ears and eyes in the direction of the sound. It was just at this time that the two panthers also stopped, and lifted their heads to listen. Their ears were keener than those of the man, and the sound had reached them at a greater distance.

Presently the settler realized whence the cries were coming. He called to mind the cabin; but he did not know the cabin's owner had departed. He cherished a hearty contempt for the drunken squatter; and on the drunken squatter's child he looked with small favor, especially as a playmate for his own boy. Nevertheless he hesitated before resuming his journey.

"Poor little devil!" he muttered, half in wrath. "I reckon his precious father's drunk down at 'the Corners,' and him crying for loneliness!" Then he re-shouldered his burden and strode on doggedly.

But louder, shriller, more hopeless and more appealing, arose the childish voice, and the settler paused again, irresolute, and with deepening indignation. In his fancy he saw the steaming supper his wife would have awaiting him. He loathed the thought of retracing his steps, and then stumbling a quarter of a mile through the stumps and bog of the wood road. He was foot-sore as well as hungry, and he cursed the vagabond squatter with serious emphasis; but in that wailing was a terror which would not let him go on. He thought of his own little one left in such a position, and straightway his heart melted. He turned, dropped his bundle behind some bushes, grasped his gun, and made speed back for the cabin.

"Who knows," he said to himself, "but that drunken idiot has left his young-ster without a bite to eat in the whole miserable shanty? Or maybe he's locked out, and the poor little beggar's half scared to death. *Sounds* as if he was scared"; and at this thought the settler quickened his pace.

As the hungry panthers drew near the cabin, and the cries of the lonely child grew clearer, they hastened their steps, and their eyes opened to a wider circle, flaming with a greener fire. It would be thoughtless superstition to say the beasts were cruel. They were simply keen with hunger, and alive with the eager passion of the chase. They were not ferocious with any anticipation of battle, for they knew the voice was the voice of a child, and something in the voice told them the child was solitary. Theirs was no hideous or unnatural rage, as it is the custom to describe it. They were but seeking with the strength, the cunning, the deadly swiftness given them to that end, the food convenient for them. On their success in accomplishing that for which nature had so exquisitely designed them depended not only their own, but the lives of their blind and helpless young, now whimpering in the cave on the slope of the moon-lit ravine. They crept through a wet alder thicket, bounded lightly over the ragged brush fence, and paused to reconnoitre on the edge of the clearing, in the full glare of the moon. At the same moment the settler emerged from the darkness of the wood road on the opposite side of the clearing. He saw the two great beasts, heads down and snouts thrust forward, gliding toward the open cabin door.

For a few moments the child had been silent. Now his voice rose again in pitiful appeal, a very ecstasy of loneliness and terror. There was a note in the cry that shook the settler's soul. He had a vision of his own boy, at home with his mother, safe-guarded from even the thought of peril. And here was this little one left to the wild beasts! "Thank God! Thank God I came!" murmured the settler, as he dropped on one knee to take a surer aim. There was a loud report (not like the sharp crack of a rifle), and the female panther, shot through the loins, fell in a heap, snarling furiously and striking with her fore-paws.

The male walked around her in fierce and anxious amazement. Presently, as the smoke lifted, he discerned the settler kneeling for a second shot. With a high screech of fury, the lithe brute sprang upon his enemy, taking a bullet full in his chest without seeming to know he was hit. Ere the man could slip in another cartridge the beast was upon him, bearing him to the ground and fixing keen fangs in his shoulder. Without a word, the man set his strong fingers desperately into the brute's throat, wrenched himself partly free, and was struggling to rise, when the panther's body collapsed upon him all at once, a dead weight which he easily flung aside. The bullet had done its work just in time.

Quivering from the swift and dreadful contest, bleeding profusely from his mangled shoulder, the settler stepped up to the cabin door and peered in. He heard sobs in the darkness.

"Don't be scared, sonny," he said, in a reassuring voice. "I 'm going to take you home along with me. Poor little lad, *I'll* look after you if folks that ought to don't."

Out of the dark corner came a shout of delight, in a voice which made the settler's heart stand still. "*Daddy*, daddy," it said, "I *knew* you'd come. I was so frightened when it got dark!" And a little figure launched itself into the settler's arms, and clung to him trembling. The man sat down on the threshold and strained the child to his breast. He remembered how near he had been to disregarding the far-off cries, and great beads of sweat broke out upon his forehead.

Not many weeks afterwards the settler was following the fresh trail of a bear which had killed his sheep. The trail led him at last along the slope of a deep ravine, from whose bottom came the brawl of a swollen and obstructed stream. In the ravine he found a shallow cave, behind a great white rock. The cave was plainly a wild beast's lair, and he entered circumspectly. There were bones scattered about, and on some dry herbage in the deepest corner of the den, he found the dead bodies, now rapidly decaying, of two small panther cubs.

4

The Rivals of Ringwaak

CHARLES G. D. ROBERTS

A white flood, still and wonderful, the moonlight lay on the naked rampikes and dense thickets of Ringwaak Hill. Beneath its magic the very rocks, harsh bulks of granite, seemed almost afloat; and every branch, spray and leaf, swam liquidly. The rampikes, towering trunks of pine, fire-blasted and time-bleached, lifted lonely spires of silver over the enchanted solitude.

Apparently, there was neither sound nor motion over all Ringwaak, or over the wide wilderness spread out below its ken. But along the secret trails, threading the thicket, and skirting the granite boulders, life went on with an intensity all the deeper and more stringent for the seal of silence laid upon it. The small, fugitive kindreds moved noiselessly about their affairs, foraging, mating, sometimes even playing, but ever watchful, a sleepless vigilance the price of each hour's breath; while even more furtive, but more intermittent in their watchfulness, the hunting and blood-loving kindreds followed the trails.

Gliding swiftly from bush to rock, from rock to thicket, now for an instant clear and terrible in a patch of moonlight, now ghost-gray and still more terrible in the sharp-cut shadows, came a round-eyed, crouching shape. It was somewhere about the size of a large spaniel, but shorter in the body, and longer in the legs; and its hind legs, in particular, though kept partly gathered beneath the body, in readiness for a lightning spring, were so disproportionately long as to give a high, humped-up, rabbity look to the powerful hind quarters. This combined suggestion of the rabbit and the tiger was peculiarly daunting in its effect. The strange beast's head was round and cat-like, but with high, tufted ears, and a curious, back-brushed muffle of whiskers under the throat. Its eyes,

From Charles G. D. Roberts, *The Watchers of the Trails* (Boston: L. C. Page, 1904).

wide and pale, shone with a cold ferocity and unconquerable wildness. Its legs, singularly large for the bulk of its body, and ending in broad, razor-clawed, furry pads of feet, would have seemed clumsy, but for the impression of tense steel springs and limitless power which they gave in every movement. In weight, this stealthy and terrifying figure would have gone perhaps forty pounds—but forty pounds of destroying energy and tireless swiftness.

As he crept through a spruce thicket, his savage eyes turning from side to side, the lynx came upon a strange trail, and stopped short, crouching. His stub of a tail twitched, his ears flattened back angrily, his long, white fangs bared themselves in a soundless snarl. A green flame seemed to flicker in his eyes, as he subjected every bush, every stone, every stump within his view to the most piercing scrutiny. Detecting no hostile presence, he bent his attention to the strange trail, sniffing at it with minute consideration.

The scent of the trail was that of a wildcat; but its size was too great for that of any wildcat this big lynx had ever known. Wildcats he viewed with utter scorn. For three years he had ruled all Ringwaak Hill; and no wildcat, in those three years, had dared to hunt upon his range. But this newcomer, with the wildcat smell, seemed about as big as three wildcats. The impression of its foot on a patch of moist mould was almost as large as that of the lynx himself—and the lynx well knew that the wildcats were a small-footed tribe. Like most of the hunting beasts, he was well-schooled in the lore of the trails, and all the signs were to him a clear speech. From the depth and definiteness of that footprint, he felt that both weight and strength had stamped it. His long claws protruded from their hidden sheaths, as he pondered the significance of this message from the unknown. Was the stranger a deliberate invader of his range, or a mere ignorant trespasser? And would he fight, or would he run? The angry lynx was determined to put these questions to the test with the least possible delay.

The trail was comparatively fresh, and the lynx began to follow it, forgetful of his hunger and of the hunt on which he had set out. He moved now more warily than ever, crouching flat, gliding smoothly as a snake, and hoping to score the first point against his rival by catching him unawares. So noiselessly did he go, indeed, that a weasel, running hard upon the trail of a rabbit, actually brushed against him, to bound away in a paroxysm of fear and rush off in another direction, wondering how he had escaped those lightning claws. In fact the lynx, intent only upon the hunting of his unknown foe, was almost as astonished as the weasel, and quite unprepared to seize the sudden opportunity for a meal. He eyed the vanishing weasel malignly for a moment, then resumed his stealthy advance. A white-footed mouse, sitting up daintily at the door of her burrow, fell over backwards, and nearly died of fright, as the ghost-gray shape of doom sped up and passed. But the lynx had just then no mind for mice, and never saw her.

The strange trail, for some hundreds of yards, kept carefully to the thickets and the shadows. In one place the marks of a scuffle, with a heap of speckled feathers and a pair of slim claws, showed that the intruder had captured and devoured an unwary partridge mothering her brood. At this evidence of poaching on his preserves, the big lynx's anger swelled hotly. He paused to sniff at the remnants, and then stole on with added caution. The blood of the victim was not yet dry, or even clotted, on the leaves.

A little further on, the trail touched the foot of a clean-stemmed young maple. Here the trespasser had paused to stretch himself, setting his claws deep into the bark. These claw-marks the lynx appeared to take as a challenge or a defiance. Rearing himself against the tree, he stretched himself to his utmost. But his highest scratch was two inches below the mark of the stranger. This still further enraged him. Possibly, it might also have daunted him a little but for the fact that his own claw-marks were both deeper and wider apart than those of his rival.

From the clawed tree, the trail now led to the very edge of the open and thence to the top of an overhanging rock, white and sharply chiseled in the moonlight. The lynx was just about to climb the rock, when there beneath it, in the revealing radiance, he saw a sight which flattened him in his tracks. The torn carcass of a young doe lay a few feet from the base of the rock; and on top of the prey, glaring savage challenge, crouched such a wildcat as the lynx had never even dreamed of.

II

A few days before this night of the white full moon, a gigantic wildcat living some fifteen miles from Ringwaak had decided to change his hunting-grounds. His range, over which he had ruled for years, was a dark, thick-wooded slope overlooking the brown pools and loud chutes of the Guimic stream. Here he had prospered hunting with continual success, and enjoying life as only the few overlords among the wild kindreds can hope to enjoy it. He had nothing to fear, as long as he avoided quarrel with a bear or a bull moose. And a narrow escape when young had taught him to shun trap and snare, and everything that savoured of the hated works of man.

Now, the lumbermen had found their way to his shadowy domain. Loud axe-strokes, the crash of falling trees, the hard clank of ox-chains, jarred the solemn stillness. But far more intolerable to the great cat's ears was the noise of laughter and shouting, the masterful insolence of the human voice unabashed in the face of the solitude. The men had built a camp near each end of his range. No retreat was safe from their incursions. And they had cut down the great pine-tree whose base shielded the entrance of his favourite lair. All through the winter the angry cat had spent the greater portion of his time slinking aside from these boisterous invaders or glaring fierce hate upon them from his densest coverts. Thus occupied, he had too little time for his hunting, and, moreover, the troubled game had become shy. His temper grew worse and worse as his ribs grew more and more obvious under his brownish, speckled fur. Nevertheless, for all his swelling indignation, he had as yet no thought of forsaking his range. He kept expecting that the men would go away.

When spring came, and the Guimic roared white between its tortuous shores, some of the loudmouthed men did go away. Nevertheless, the big cat's rage waxed hotter than ever. Far worse than the men who went were three portable steam sawmills which came in their place. At three separate points these mills were set up—and straightway the long, intolerable shriek of the circulars was ripping the air. In spite of himself, the amazed cat screeched in unison when that sound first smote his ears. He slunk away and hid for hours in his remotest lair, wondering if it would follow him. When, in the course of weeks, he grew so far accustomed to the fiendish sound that he could go about his hunting within half a mile of it, he found that the saws had worked him an unspeakable injury. They had fouled his beloved fishing-pools with sawdust.

It was the big cat's favoured custom to spend hours at a time crouched over one or another of these pools, waiting for a chance to catch a trout. Where an overhanging rock or a jutting root came out into deep water, he would lie as motionless as the rock or log itself, his round face bent close down to the glassy surface, his bright eyes intently following the movements of the big, lazy trout in their safe deeps. Once in a long while, often enough to keep his interest keen, a May-fly or a fat worm would drop close past his nose and lie kicking on top of the water. Up would sail a big trout, open-jawed to engulf the morsel. At that instant the clutching paw of the watcher would strike down and around more swiftly than eye could follow—and the next instant the fish would be flopping violently among the underbrush up the bank, with leaves and twigs clinging to its fat, silvery, dappled sides. The sport was one which gave the big wildcat never-failing delight; and, moreover, there was no other food in all the wilderness quite so exquisite to his palate as a plump trout from the ice-cool waters of the Guimic. When, therefore, he found his pools covered, all day long, with the whitey-yellow grains of sawdust, which prevented the trout feeding at the surface or drove them in disgust from their wonted haunts, he realized that his range was ruined. The men and the mills were the conquerors, and he must let himself be driven from his well-beloved Guimic slopes. But first he would have revenge. His caution somewhat undermined by his rage, he crept much nearer to the main camp than he had hitherto dared to go, and hid himself in a low tree to see what opportunity fate might fling to him.

Belonging to the camp was a brindle dog, a sturdy and noisy mongrel whose barking was particularly obnoxious to the wildcat. Of a surly yet restless temper, the mongrel was in reality by no means popular in the camp, and would not have been tolerated there but for the fact that he belonged to the Boss. In the wildcat's eyes, however, as in the eyes of all the wild kindreds, he seemed a treasured possession of the menkind, and an especially objectionable expression of all their most objectionable characteristics. Moreover, being four-footed and furred, he was plainly more kin to the wild creatures than to man—and there-fore, to the wild creature, obviously a traitor and a renegade. There was not one of them but would have taken more satisfaction in avenging its wrongs upon the loud-mouthed mongrel than upon one of the mongrel's masters; not one but would have counted that the sweetest and completest form of vengeance.

It is not surprising, therefore, that the big cat quivered with eager hate when he saw the dog come lazily out of the cook-house and wander toward the spring—which lay just beyond the thick tree! His eyes blazed green, his fur rose slightly, and he set his claws into the bark to gain firm foothold.

Confident and secure, the dog approached the tree. On the way he jumped savagely at a chipmunk, which dodged in time and whisked into its hole. For a minute or two the dog pawed and scratched at the hole, trying to dig the little fugitive out. Then he gave up the vain task, and moved on toward the spring.

The wildcat gave one quick glance on every side. There was not a man in sight. The cook was in the cook-house, rattling tins. Then the dog came be-neath the tree—and stopped to sniff at the wildcat's track.

There was a sharp scratch in the tree above—and in the next instant a brown furry shape dropped upon him noiselessly, bearing him to the ground. This thing was a mass of teeth and claws and terrific muscles. It gave one sharp screech as the dog's yelping howl arose, then made no sound but a spitting growl as it bit and ripped. From the first the brindled mongrel had no ghost of a chance; and the struggle was over in three minutes. As the cook, astonished by the sudden uproar, came rushing axe in hand from his shanty, the wildcat sprang away with a snarl and bounded into the cover of the nearest spruce bushes. He was none the worse save for a deep and bleeding gash down his fore shoulder, where his victim had gained a moment's grip. But the dog was so cruelly mauled that the woodsman could do nothing but compassionately knock him on the head with the axe which he had brought to the rescue.

Savage from the struggle, and elated from his vengeance, the wildcat with no further hesitation turned his back upon his old haunts, crossed the Guimic by great leaps from rock to rock, and set southward toward the wooded slopes and valleys overlooked by the ragged crest of Ringwaak.

The indignant exile, journeying so boldly to confront the peril of which he had no suspicion or forewarning, belonged to a species confined to the forests of New Brunswick and Nova Scotia or the neighbourhood of their boundaries. He was a giant cousin of the common wildcat, and known to the few naturalists who had succeeded in differentiating and classifying his species as *Lynx gigas*. In weight and stature he was, if anything, more than the peer of his other and more distant cousin, the savage Canada lynx. The cook of the camp, in telling his comrades about the fate of the dog, spoke of the great wildcat as a "cata-mount," to distinguish him from the common cat of the woods. These same woodsmen, had they seen the lynx who ruled on Ringwaak Hill, would have called him a "lucerfee," while any Madawaska Frenchman in their company would have dubbed him *loup cervier*. Either catamount or lucerfee was respectfully regarded by the woodsmen.

For an hour the great cat journeyed on, wary and stealthy from habit rather than intention, as he was neither hunting for prey nor avoiding enemies. But when he found himself in strange woods—a gloomy cedar swamp, dotted with dry hardwood knolls like islands—with true cat instinct he delayed his journey to look about him and investigate. Prowling from side to side, and sniffing and peering, he presently found something that he was not looking for. In a hollow beneath a granite boulder, behind the roots of two gnarled old cedars, he came upon two glossy black bear cubs, fast asleep. The mother was nowhere in sight, but the intruder shrank back with an abashed and guilty air and ran up the nearest tree. Thence he made his way from branch to branch, and did not return to the ground till he had put three or four hundred yards between him and the den. He had no mind to bring relentless doom upon his trail.

Not till he was well clear of the cedar swamp did the catamount remember that he was hungry. The idea of being suspected of an interest in young bear's meat had taken away his appetite. Now, however, coming to a series of wild meadows, he lingered to hunt meadow-mice. Among the roots of the long grass the mice had innumerable hidden runways, through which they could travel without danger from the hawks and owls. Crouching close to one of these runways, the big cat would listen till a squeak or a faint scurrying noise would reveal the passing of a mouse. Then a lightning pounce, with paws much wider apart than in his ordinary hunting, would tear away the frail covering of the runway, and usually show the victim clutched beneath one paw or the other. This was much quicker as well as craftier hunting than the more common wildcat method of lying in wait for an hour at the door of a runway. Three of these plump meadow-mice made the traveller a comfortable meal. Forgetting his wrongs, he stretched himself in the full sun under the shelter of a fallen tree, and slept soundly for an hour. Once only he awoke, when his ears caught the beat of a hawk's wings winnowing low over his retreat. He opened wide, fiercely bright eyes, completely alert on the instant, but seeing the source of the sound he was asleep again before the hawk had crossed the little meadow.

His siesta over, the exile mounted the fallen tree, dug his claws deep into the bark, stretched himself again and again, yawned prodigiously, and ended the exercise with a big, rasping miaow. At the sound there was a sudden rustling in the bushes behind the windfall. Instantly the catamount sprang, taking the risk of catching a porcupine or a skunk. But whatever it was that made the noise, it had vanished in time; and the rash hunter returned to his perch with a shame-faced air.

From this post of vantage on the edge of the meadows he could see the crest of old Ringwaak dominating the forests to the south; and the sight, for some unknown reason, drew him. Among those bleak rampikes and rocks and dark coverts he might find a range to his liking. He resumed his journey with a definiteness of purpose which kept him from squandering time on the chase. Only once he halted, and that was when the cries and flutterings of a pair of excited thrushes caught his attention. He saw their nest in a low tree—and he saw a black snake, coiled in the branches, greedily swallowing the half-fledged nestlings. This was an opportunity which he could not afford to lose. He ran expertly up the tree, pounced upon the snake, and bit through its back bone just behind the head. The strong, black coils straightened out limply. Carrying his prize between his jaws, the catamount descended to the ground, growling and jerking savagely when the wriggling length got tangled among the branches. Quick to understand the services of their most unexpected ally, the desperate birds returned to one surviving nestling, and their clamours ceased. Beneath the tree the exile hurriedly devoured a few mouthfuls of the thick meat of the back just behind the snake's head, then resumed his journey toward Ringwaak.

It was close upon sunset when he reached the first fringes of the northward slope of the mountain. Here his reception was benign. On the banks of a tiny brook, rosy-gold in the flooding afternoon light, he found a bed of wild catnip. Here for a few minutes he rolled in ecstasy, chewing and clawing at the aromatic leaves, all four paws in air, and hoarsely purring his delight. When, at last, he went on up the slope, he carried with him through the gathering shadows the pungent, sweet aroma of the herb. In a fierce gaiety of spirit he would now and then leap into the air to strike idly at some bird flitting high above his reach. Or he would jump and clutch kittenishly with both paws at a fluttering, overhanging leaf, or pounce upon an imaginary quiet mouse crouched among the leaves.

About twilight, as he was nearing the summit of the hill, he came across a footprint which somewhat startled him out of his intoxication. It was a footprint not unlike his own, but distinctly larger. Being an old sign, there was no scent left to it—but its size was puzzling and disquieting. From this on he went warily, not knowing when he might be called upon to measure forces with some redoubtable possessor of the range. When the moon rose, round and white and all-revealing, and threw sinister shadows from rampike and rock, he kept to the densest thickets and felt oppressed with strangeness. But when he succeeded in surprising a hen partridge hovering over her brood, with the blood warm in his mouth he began to feel at home. This fine range should be his, whoever might contest the sovereignty. Coming across a deer trail leading beneath an overhanging rock, he climbed the rock and crouched in ambush, waiting to see what might come by.

For an hour he crouched there, motionless as the eternal granite itself, while the moon climbed and whitened, and the shadows of the rampikes changed, and the breathless enchantment deepened over Ringwaak. At long intervals there would be a faint rustling in some near-by clump of juniper, or a squeak and a brief scuffle in the thickets; or, on wings as soundless as sleep, a great owl would pass by, to drop sharply behind a rock, or sail away like a ghost among the rampikes. But to none of these furtive happenings did the watcher on the rock pay any heed. He was waiting for what might come upon the trail.

At last, it came. Stepping daintily on her small, fine hoofs, her large eyes glancing timorously in every direction, a little yearling doe emerged from the bushes and started to cross the patch of brilliant light. The strange, upright pupils of the catamount's eyes narrowed and dilated at the sight, and his muscles quivered to sudden tension. The young doe came beneath the rock. The cat sprang, unerring, irresistible; and the next moment she lay kicking helplessly beneath him, his fangs buried in her velvet throat.

This was noble prey; and the giant cat, his misgivings all forgotten, drank till his long thirst was satiated. His jaws dripping, he lifted his round, fierce face, and gazed out and away across the moonlit slopes below him toward his ancient range beyond the Guimic. While he gazed, triumphing, something made him turn his head quickly and eye the spruce thicket behind him.

III

It was at this moment that the old lynx, master of Ringwaak, coming suddenly out into the moonlight, saw the grim apparition beneath the rock, and flattened to the ground.

Through long, momentous, pregnant seconds the two formidable and matched antagonists scrutinized each other, the lynx close crouched, ready to launch himself like a thunderbolt, the catamount half risen, his back bowed, one paw of obstinate possession clutching the head of his prey. In the eyes of each, as they measured each other's powers and sought for an advantage, flamed hate, defiance, courage, and savage question.

Seen thus near together, catamount by lucerfee, they were obviously akin, yet markedly different. The cat was heavier in the body, outweighing his rival by perhaps not far from ten pounds, but with shorter and more gracefully shaped legs, and smaller feet. His head was more arched, seeming to indicate a greater intelligence, and his flaming eyes were set wider apart; but his mouth was smaller, his fangs less long and punishing. His fur was of a browner, warmer hue than that of the lynx, whose gray had a half-invisible ghostliness in the moonlight. The tails of both were ridiculously short, not six inches in length, but that of the catamount was straight and stiff, while that of the lucerfee had a curious upward twist that somehow mocked the contortions of his huge and overlong hind legs. The eyes of the lynx, under his flatter forehead, were the more piercing, the less blazing. Altogether the great wildcat was the more beautiful of the two beasts, the more intelligent, the more adaptable and resourceful. But the lynx, with his big, uncouth, hind quarters, and great legs gathered under him, and exaggerated paws, looked to be the more formidable fighting machine.

Thus, unstirring, they eyed each other. Then with a strident screech that seemed to tear the spell of the night to tatters, the gray body of the lynx shot through the air. It landed, not upon the catamount, but squarely upon the carcass of the doe, where, a fraction of a second before, the catamount had stood. The wary intruder had not waited to endure the full shock of that charge, but lightly as a puff of down had leaped aside. The next instant he had pounced, with a yowl of defiance, straight for the lynx's neck.

Lightning quick though he was, the lynx recovered in time to meet the attack with deadly counter-stroke of bared claws, parrying like a skilled boxer. In this forearm work the catamount, lighter of paw and talon, suffered the more; and being quick to perceive his adversary's advantage, he sought to force a close grapple. This the lynx at first avoided, rending and punishing frightfully as he gave ground; while the solemn height of old Ringwaak was shocked by a clamour of spitting and raucous yowling that sent every sleepy bird fluttering in terror from its nest.

Suddenly, perceiving that the lynx was backing dangerously close to the face of the rock, the great cat sprang, took a frightful, ripping buffet across the face, broke down his foe's guard and bore him to the ground by sheer weight. Here, in this close embrace, the hinder claws of both came into play with hideous effect. The clamour died down to a tense, desperate, gasping snarl; for now the verdict of life or death was a matter of moments. But in this fearful and final test, when there was no more room for fencing, no more time for strategy, the more powerful hind legs and longer, more eviscerating claws of the lynx had the decisive advantage. Though borne down, and apparently getting the worst of the fight, the master of Ringwaak was in reality ripping his enemy to pieces from beneath. All at once the latter sprang away with a scream, stood for a second erect and rigid, then sank limp beside the torn carcass of the doe.

The lynx, badly torn and bitten, but with no fatal injury, pounced upon the unresisting body of the catamount and mauled it till well assured of the completeness of his victory. Then, heedless of his wounds, he mounted the carcass of the doe, lifted his head high, and screeched his challenge across the night. No answer coming, he tore a mouthful of the meat to emphasize possession, stepped down, and crept off to nurse his hurts in some dark retreat; for not easy had been the task of defending his lordship. When all was still once more on Ringwaak, presently descended again the enchantment of the mystic light. And under its transforming touch even the torn bodies lying before the bright face of the rock lost their hideousness, becoming remote, and unsubstantial and visionary.

5

On His Animal Stories

ERNEST THOMPSON SETON

"Note to the Reader" in *Wild Animals I Have Known*

These stories are true. Although I have left the strict line of historical truth in many places, the animals in this book were all real characters. They lived the lives I have depicted, and showed the stamp of heroism and personality more strongly by far than it has been in the power of my pen to tell.

I believe that natural history has lost much by the vague general treatment that is so common. What satisfaction would be derived from a ten-page sketch of the habits and customs of Man ? How much more profitable it would be to devote that space to the life of some one great man. This is the principle I have endeavored to apply to my animals The real personality of the individual and his view of life are my theme, rather than the ways of the race in general, as viewed by a casual and hostile human eye.

This may sound inconsistent in view of my having pieced together some of the character, but that was made necessary by the fragmentary nature of the records. There is, however, almost no deviation from the truth in Lobo, Bingo, and the Mustang.

Lobo lived his wild romantic life from 1889 to 1894 in the Currumpaw region, as the ranchmen know too well, and died, precisely as related on January 31, 1894. . . .

Silverspot, Raggylug, and Vixen are founded on real characters. Though I

From Ernest Seton-Thompson, *Wild Animals I Have Known* (New York: Charles Scribner's Sons, 1898), *Lobo, Rag & Vixen* (New York: Charles Scribner's Sons, 1899), and *Lives of the Hunted* (New York: Charles Scribner's Sons, 1901).

have ascribed to them the adventures of more than one of their kind, every incident in their biographies is from life.

The fact that these stories are true is the reason why all are tragic. The life of a wild animal *always has a tragic end.*

Such a collection of histories naturally suggests a common thought—a moral it would have been called in the last century. No doubt each different mind will find a moral to its taste, but I hope some will herein find emphasized a moral as old as Scripture—we and the beasts are kin. Man has nothing that the animals have not at least a vestige of, the animals have nothing that man does not in some degree share.

Since, then, the animals are creatures with wants and feelings differing in degree only from our own, they surely have their rights. This fact, now beginning to be recognized by the Caucasian world, was emphasized by the Buddhist over 2,000 years ago.

This book was made by my wife, Grace Gallatin Thompson. Although the handiwork throughout is my own, she chiefly is responsible for designs of cover, title page, and general make-up. Thanks are due her also for the literary revision, and for the mechanical labor of seeing the book through the press.

"Note to the Reader" in *Lobo, Rag & Vixen*

These Stories, selected from those published in "Wild Animals I Have Known," are true histories of the animals described, and are intended to show how their lives are lived.

Though the lower animals have no language in the full sense as we understand it, they have a system of sounds, signs, touches, tastes, and smells that answers the purpose of language, and I merely translate this, when necessary, into English.

"Note to the Reader" in *Lives of the Hunted*

In offering this volume of Animal Stories, I might properly repeat much of the Introduction to "Wild Animals I Have Known."

In my previous books I have tried to emphasize our kinship with the animals by showing that in them we can find the virtues most admired in Man. Lobo stands for Dignity and Love-constancy; Silverspot, for Sagacity; Redruff, for Obedience; Bingo, for Fidelity; Vixen and Molly Cottontail, for Mother-love; Wahb, for Physical Force; and the Pacing Mustang, for the Love of Liberty. In this volume, Majesty, Grace, the Power of Wisdom, the sweet Uses of Adversity, and the two–edged Sorrows of Rebellion are similarly set forth.

The material of the accounts is true. The chief liberty taken, is in ascribing to one animal the adventures of several. . . .

For the wild animal there is no such thing as a gentle decline in peaceful old age. Its life is spent at the front, in line of battle, and as soon as its powers begin to wane in the least, its enemies become too strong for it; it falls. . . .

I have been bitterly denounced, first, for killing Lobo; second, and chiefly, for telling of it, to the distress of many tender hearts.

To this I reply: In what frame of mind are my hearers left with regard to the animal? Are their sympathies quickened toward the man who killed him, or toward the noble creature who, superior to every trial, died as he had lived, dignified, fearless, and steadfast?

In answer to a question many times put, I may say that I do not champion any theory of diet. I do not intend primarily to denounce certain field sports, or even cruelty to animals. My chief motive, my most earnest underlying wish, has been to stop the extermination of harmless wild animals; not for their sakes, but for ours, firmly believing that each of our native wild creatures is in itself a precious heritage that we have no right to destroy or put beyond the reach of our children.

I have tried to stop the stupid and brutal work of destruction by an appeal— not to reason: that has failed hitherto—but to sympathy, and especially the sympathies of the coming generation.

Men spend millions of dollars each year on pictures. Why not? It is money well spent; good pictures give lasting and elevating pleasure to all who see them. At the same time men spend much labor and ingenuity in destroying harmless wild animals. No good, but great mischief, comes of this extermination. The main reason for preserving good pictures applies to the preservation of most animals. There will always be wild land not required for settlement; and how can we better use it than by making it a sanctuary for living Wild Things that afford pure pleasure to all who see them?

6

Lobo: The King of the Currumpaw

ERNEST THOMPSON SETON

I

Currumpaw is a vast cattle range in northern New Mexico. It is a land of rich pastures and teeming flocks and herds, a land of rolling mesas and precious running waters that at length unite in the Currumpaw River, from which the whole region is named. And the king whose despotic power was felt over its entire extent was an old gray wolf.

Old Lobo, or the king, as the Mexicans called him, was the gigantic leader of a remarkable pack of gray wolves, that had ravaged the Currumpaw Valley for a number of years. All the shepherds and ranchmen knew him well, and, wherever he appeared with his trusty band, terror reigned supreme among the cattle, and wrath and despair among their owners. Old Lobo was a giant among wolves, and was cunning and strong in proportion to his size. His voice at night was well-known and easily distinguished from that of any of his fellows. An ordinary wolf might howl half the night about the herdsman's bivouac without attracting more than a passing notice, but when the deep roar of the old king came booming down the cañon, the watcher bestirred himself and prepared to learn in the morning that fresh and serious inroads had been made among the herds.

Old Lobo's band was but a small one. This I never quite understood, for usually, when a wolf rises to the position and power that he had, he attracts a numerous following. It may be that he had as many as he desired, or perhaps his ferocious temper prevented the increase of his pack. Certain is it that Lobo

From Ernest Thompson Seton, *Wild Animals I Have Known* (New York: Charles Scribner's Sons, 1898).

had only five followers during the latter part of his reign. Each of these, however, was a wolf of renown, most of them were above the ordinary size, one in particular, the second in command, was a veritable giant, but even he was far below the leader in size and prowess. Several of the band, besides the two leaders, were especially noted. One of those was a beautiful white wolf, that the Mexicans called Blanca; this was supposed to be a female, possibly Lobo's mate. Another was a yellow wolf of remarkable swiftness, which, according to current stories had, on several occasions, captured an antelope for the pack.

It will be seen, then, that these wolves were thoroughly well-known to the cowboys and shepherds. They were frequently seen and oftener heard, and their lives were intimately associated with those of the cattlemen, who would so gladly have destroyed them. There was not a stockman on the Currumpaw who would not readily have given the value of many steers for the scalp of any one of Lobo's band, but they seemed to possess charmed lives, and defied all manner of devices to kill them. They scorned all hunters, derided all poisons, and continued, for at least five years, to exact their tribute from the Currumpaw ranchers to the extent, many said, of a cow each day. According to this estimate, therefore, the band had killed more than two thousand of the finest stock, for, as was only too well-known, they selected the best in every instance.

The old idea that a wolf was constantly in a starving state, and therefore ready to eat anything, was as far as possible from the truth in this case, for these freebooters were always sleek and well-conditioned, and were in fact most fastidious about what they ate. Any animal that had died from natural causes, or that was diseased or tainted, they would not touch, and they even rejected anything that had been killed by the stockmen. Their choice and daily food was the tenderer part of a freshly killed yearling heifer. An old bull or cow they disdained, and though they occasionally took a young calf or colt, it was quite clear that veal or horseflesh was not their favorite diet. It was also known that they were not fond of mutton, although they often amused themselves by killing sheep. One night in November, 1893, Blanca and the yellow wolf killed two hundred and fifty sheep, apparently for the fun of it, and did not eat an ounce of their flesh.

These are examples of many stories which I might repeat, to show the ravages of this destructive band. Many new devices for their extinction were tried each year, but still they lived and throve in spite of all the efforts of their foes. A great price was set on Lobo's head, and in consequence poison in a score of subtle forms was put out for him, but he never failed to detect and avoid it. One thing only he feared—that was firearms, and knowing full well that all men in this region carried them, he never was known to attack or face a human being. Indeed, the set policy of his band was to take refuge in flight whenever, in the daytime, a man was descried, no matter at what distance. Lobo's habit of permitting the pack to eat only that which they themselves had killed, was in numerous cases their salvation, and the keenness of his scent to detect the taint of human hands or the poison itself, completed their immunity.

On one occasion, one of the cowboys heard the too familiar rallying-cry of Old Lobo, and stealthily approaching, he found the Currumpaw pack in a hollow, where they had 'rounded up' a small herd of cattle. Lobo sat apart on a knoll, while Blanca with the rest was endeavoring to 'cut out' a young cow, which they had selected; but the cattle were standing in a compact mass with their heads outward, and presented to the foe a line of horns, unbroken save when some cow, frightened by a fresh onset of the wolves, tried to retreat into the middle of the herd. It was only by taking advantage of these breaks that the wolves had succeeded at all in wounding the selected cow, but she was far from being disabled, and it seemed that Lobo at length lost patience with his followers, for he left his position on the hill, and, uttering a deep roar, dashed toward the herd. The terrified rank broke at his charge, and he sprang in among them. Then the cattle scattered like the pieces of a bursting bomb. Away went the chosen victim, but ere she had gone twenty-five yards Lobo was upon her. Seizing her by the neck he suddenly held back with all his force and so threw her heavily to the ground. The shock must have been tremendous, for the heifer was thrown heels over head. Lobo also turned a somersault, but immediately recovered himself, and his followers falling on the poor cow, killed her in a few seconds. Lobo took no part in the killing—after having thrown the victim, he seemed to say, "Now, why could not some of you have done that at once without wasting so much time?"

The man now rode up shouting, the wolves as usual retired, and he, having a bottle of strychnine, quickly poisoned the carcass in three places, then went away, knowing they would return to feed, as they had killed the animal themselves. But next morning, on going to look for his expected victims, he found that, although the wolves had eaten the heifer, they had carefully cut out and thrown aside all those parts that had been poisoned.

The dread of this great wolf spread yearly among the ranchmen, and each year a larger price was set on his head, until at last it reached $1,000, an unparalleled wolf-bounty, surely; many a good man has been hunted down for less. Tempted by the promised reward, a Texan ranger named Tannerey came one day galloping up the cañon of the Currumpaw. He had a superb outfit for wolf-hunting—the best of guns and horses, and a pack of enormous wolf-hounds. Far out on the plains of the Pan-handle, he and his dogs had killed many a wolf, and now he never doubted that, within a few days, old Lobo's scalp would dangle at his saddle-bow.

Away they went bravely on their hunt in the gray dawn of a summer morning, and soon the great dogs gave joyous tongue to say that they were already on the track of their quarry. Within two miles, the grizzly band of Currumpaw leaped into view, and the chase grew fast and furious. The part of the wolf-hounds was merely to hold the wolves at bay till the hunter could ride up and shoot them, and this usually was easy on the open plains of Texas; but here a new feature of the country came into play, and showed how well Lobo had chosen his range; for the rocky cañons of the Currumpaw and its tributaries intersect the prairies in every direction. The old wolf at once made for the nearest of these and by crossing it got rid of the horsemen. His band then scattered and thereby scattered the dogs, and when they reunited at a distant point of course all of the dogs did not turn up, and the wolves no longer outnumbered, turned on their pursuers and killed or desperately wounded them all. That night when Tannerey mustered his dogs, only six of them returned, and of these, two were terribly lacerated. This hunter made two other attempts to capture the royal scalp, but neither of them was more successful than the first, and on the last occasion his best horse met its death by a fall; so he gave up the chase in disgust and went back to Texas, leaving Lobo more than ever the despot of the region.

Next year, two other hunters appeared, determined to win the promised bounty. Each believed he could destroy this noted wolf, the first by means of a newly devised poison, which was to be laid out in an entirely new manner; the other a French Canadian, by poison assisted with certain spells and charms, for he firmly believed that Lobo was a veritable 'loup-garou,' and could not be killed by ordinary means. But cunningly compounded poisons, charms, and incantations were all of no avail against this grizzly devastator. He made his weekly rounds and daily banquets as aforetime, and before many weeks had passed, Calone and Laloche gave up in despair and went elsewhere to hunt.

In the spring of 1893, after his unsuccessful attempt to capture Lobo, Joe Calone had a humiliating experience, which seems to show that the big wolf simply scorned his enemies, and had absolute confidence in himself. Calone's farm was on a small tributary of the Currumpaw, in a picturesque cañon, and among the rocks of this very cañon, within a thousand yards of the house, old Lobo and his mate selected their den and raised their family that season. There they lived all summer, and killed Joe's cattle, sheep, and dogs, but laughed at all his poisons and traps, and rested securely among the recesses of the cavernous cliffs, while Joe vainly racked his brain for some method of smoking them out, or of reaching them with dynamite. But they escaped entirely unscathed, and continued their ravages as before. "There's where he lived all last summer," said Joe, pointing to the face of the cliff, "and I couldn't do a thing with him. I was like a fool to him."

II

This history, gathered so far from the cowboys, I found hard to believe until in the fall of 1893, I made the acquaintance of the wily marauder, and at length came to know him more thoroughly than anyone else. Some years before, in the Bingo days, I had been a wolf-hunter, but my occupations since then had been of another sort, chaining me to stool and desk. I was much in need of a change, and when a friend, who was also a ranch-owner on the Currumpaw, asked me to come to New Mexico and try if I could do anything with this predatory pack, I accepted the invitation and, eager to make the acquaintance of its king, was as soon as possible among the mesas of that region. I spent some time riding about to learn the country, and at intervals, my guide would point to the skeleton of a cow to which the hide still adhered, and remark, "That's some of his work."

It became quite clear to me that, in this rough country, it was useless to think of pursuing Lobo with hounds and horses, so that poison or traps were the only available expedients. At present we had no traps large enough, so I set to work with poison.

I need not enter into the details of a hundred devices that I employed to circumvent this 'loup-garou'; there was no combination of strychnine, arsenic, cyanide, or prussic acid, that I did not essay; there was no manner of flesh that I did not try as bait; but morning after morning, as I rode forth to learn the result, I found that all my efforts had been useless. The old king was too cunning for me. A single instance will show his wonderful sagacity. Acting on the hint of an old trapper, I melted some cheese together with the kidney fat of a freshly killed heifer, stewing it in a china dish, and cutting it with a bone knife to avoid the taint of metal. When the mixture was cool, I cut it into lumps, and making a hole in one side of each lump, I inserted a large dose of strychnine and cyanide, contained in a capsule that was impermeable by any odor; finally I sealed the holes up with pieces of the cheese itself. During the whole process, I wore a pair of gloves steeped in the hot blood of the heifer, and even avoided breathing on the baits. When all was ready, I put them in a raw-hide bag rubbed all over with blood, and rode forth dragging the liver and kidneys of the beef at the end of a rope. With this I made a ten-mile circuit, dropping a bait at each quarter of a mile, and taking the utmost care, always, not to touch any with my hands.

Lobo, generally, came into this part of the range in the early part of each week, and passed the latter part, it was supposed, around the base of Sierra Grande. This was Monday, and that same evening, as we were about to retire, I heard the deep bass howl of his majesty. On hearing it one of the boys briefly remarked, "There he is, we'll see."

The next morning I went forth, eager to know the result. I soon came on the fresh trail of the robbers, with Lobo in the lead—his track was always easily distinguished. An ordinary wolf's forefoot is 4½ inches long, that of a large wolf 4¾ inches, but Lobo's, as measured a number of times, was 5½ inches from claw to heel; I afterward found that his other proportions were commensurate, for he stood three feet high at the shoulder, and weighed 150 pounds. His trail, therefore, though obscured by those of his followers, was never difficult to trace. The pack had soon found the track of my drag, and as usual followed it. I could see that Lobo had come to the first bait, sniffed about it, and finally had picked it up.

Then I could not conceal my delight. "I've got him at last," I exclaimed; "I shall find him stark within a mile," and I galloped on with eager eyes fixed on the great broad track in the dust. It led me to the second bait and that also was gone. How I exulted—I surely have him now and perhaps several of his band. But there was the broad paw-mark still on the drag; and though I stood in the stirrups and scanned the plain I saw nothing that looked like a dead wolf. Again I followed—to find now that the third bait was gone—and the king-wolf's track led on to the fourth, there to learn that he had not really taken a bait at all, but had merely carried them in his mouth. Then having piled the three on the fourth, he scattered filth over them to express his utter contempt for my devices. After this he left my drag and went about his business with the pack he guarded so effectively.

This is only one of many similar experiences which convinced me that poison would never avail to destroy this robber, and though I continued to use it while awaiting the arrival of the traps, it was only because it was meanwhile a sure means of killing many prairie wolves and other destructive vermin.

About this time there came under my observation an incident that will illustrate Lobo's diabolic cunning. These wolves had at least one pursuit which was merely an amusement, it was stampeding and killing sheep, though they rarely ate them. The sheep are usually kept in flocks of from one thousand to three thousand under one or more shepherds. At night they are gathered in the most sheltered place available, and a herdsman sleeps on each side of the flock to give additional protection. Sheep are such senseless creatures that they are liable to be stampeded by the veriest trifle, but they have deeply ingrained in their nature one, and perhaps only one, strong weakness, namely, to follow their leader. And this the shepherds turn to good account by putting half a dozen goats in the flock of sheep. The latter recognize the superior intelligence of their bearded cousins, and when a night alarm occurs they crowd around them, and usually are thus saved from a stampede and are easily protected. But it was not always so. One night late in last November, two Perico shepherds were aroused by an onset of wolves. Their flocks huddled around the goats, which being neither fools nor cowards, stood their ground and were bravely defiant; but alas for them, no common wolf was heading this attack. Old Lobo, the weir-wolf, knew as well as the shepherds that the goats were the moral force of the flock, so hastily running over the backs of the densely packed sheep, he fell on these leaders, slew them all in a few minutes, and soon had the luckless sheep stampeding in a thousand different directions. For weeks afterward I was almost daily accosted by some anxious shepherd, who asked, "Have you seen any stray OTO sheep lately?" and usually I was obliged to say I had; one day it was, "Yes, I came on some five or six carcasses by Diamond Springs"; or another, it was to the effect that I had seen a small 'bunch' running on the Malpai Mesa; or again, "No, but Juan Meira saw about twenty, freshly killed, on the Cedra Monte two days ago."

At length the wolf traps arrived, and with two men I worked a whole week to get them properly set out. We spared no labor or pains, I adopted every device I could think of that might help to insure success. The second day after the traps arrived, I rode around to inspect, and soon came upon Lobo's trail running from trap to trap. In the dust I could read the whole story of his doings that night. He had trotted along in the darkness, and although the traps were so carefully concealed, he had instantly detected the first one. Stopping the on-ward march of the pack, he had cautiously scratched around it until he had disclosed the trap, the chain, and the log, then left them wholly exposed to view with the trap still unsprung, and passing on he treated over a dozen traps in the same fashion. Very soon I noticed that he stopped and turned aside as soon as he detected suspicious signs on the trail and a new plan to outwit him at once suggested itself. I set the traps in the form of an H; that is, with a row of traps on each side of the trail, and one on the trail for the cross-bar of the H. Before long, I had an opportunity to count another failure. Lobo came trotting along the trail, and was fairly between the parallel lines before he detected the single trap in the trail, but he stopped in time, and why or how he knew enough I cannot tell, the Angel of the wild things must have been with him, but without turning an inch to the right or left, he slowly and cautiously backed on his own tracks, putting each paw exactly in its old track until he was off the dangerous ground. Then returning at one side he scratched clods and stones with his hind feet till he had sprung every trap. This he did on many other occasions, and although I varied my methods and redoubled my precautions, he was never deceived, his sagacity seemed never at fault, and he might have been pursuing his career of rapine to-day, but for an unfortunate alliance that proved his ruin and added his name to the long list of heroes who, unassailable when alone, have fallen through the indiscretion of a trusted ally.

III

Once or twice, I had found indications that everything was not quite right in the Currumpaw pack. There were signs of irregularity, I thought; for instance there was clearly the trail of a smaller wolf running ahead of the leader, at times, and this I could not understand until a cowboy made a remark which explained the matter.

"I saw them to-day," he said, "and the wild one that breaks away is Blanca." Then the truth dawned upon me, and I added, "Now, I know that Blanca is a she-wolf, because were a he-wolf to act thus, Lobo would kill him at once."

This suggested a new plan. I killed a heifer, and set one or two rather obvious traps about the carcass. Then cutting off the head, which is considered useless offal, and quite beneath the notice of a wolf, I set it a little apart and around it placed two powerful steel traps properly deodorized and concealed with the utmost care. During my operations I kept my hands, boots, and implements smeared with fresh blood, and afterward sprinkled the ground with the same, as though it had flowed from the head; and when the traps were buried in the dust I brushed the place over with the skin of a coyote, and with a foot of the same animal made a number of tracks over the traps. The head was so placed that there was a narrow passage between it and some tussocks, and in this passage I buried two of my best traps, fastening them to the head itself.

Wolves have a habit of approaching every carcass they get the wind of, in order to examine it, even when they have no intention of eating of it, and I hoped that this habit would bring the Currumpaw pack within reach of my latest stratagem. I did not doubt that Lobo would detect my handiwork about the meat, and prevent the pack approaching it, but I did build some hopes on the head, for it looked as though it had been thrown aside as useless.

Next morning, I sallied forth to inspect the traps, and there, oh, joy! were the tracks of the pack, and the place where the beef-head and its traps had been was empty. A hasty study of the trail showed that Lobo had kept the pack from approaching the meat, but one, a small wolf, had evidently gone on to examine the head as it lay apart and had walked right into one of the traps.

We set out on the trail, and within a mile discovered that the hapless wolf was Blanca. Away she went, however, at a gallop, and although encumbered by the beef-head, which weighed over fifty pounds, she speedily distanced my companion who was on foot. But we overtook her when she reached the rocks, for the horns of the cow's head became caught and held her fast. She was the handsomest wolf I had ever seen. Her coat was in perfect condition and nearly white.

She turned to fight, and raising her voice in the rallying cry of her race, sent a long howl rolling over the cañon. From far away upon the mesa came a deep response, the cry of Old Lobo. That was her last call, for now we had closed in on her, and all her energy and breath were devoted to combat.

Then followed the inevitable tragedy, the idea of which I shrank from afterward more than at the time. We each threw a lasso over the neck of the doomed wolf, and strained our horses in opposite directions until the blood burst from her mouth, her eyes glazed, her limbs stiffened and then fell limp. Homeward then we rode, carrying the dead wolf, and exulting over this, the first death-blow we had been able to inflict on the Currumpaw pack.

At intervals during the tragedy, and afterward as we rode homeward, we heard the roar of Lobo as he wandered about on the distant mesas, where he seemed to be searching for Blanca. He had never really deserted her, but knowing that he could not save her, his deep-rooted dread of firearms had been too much for him when he saw us approaching. All that day we heard him wailing as he roamed in his quest, and I remarked at length to one of the boys, "Now, indeed, I truly know that Blanca was his mate."

As evening fell he seemed to be coming toward the home cañon, for his voice sounded continually nearer. There was an unmistakable note of sorrow in it now. It was no longer the loud, defiant howl, but a long, plaintive wail; "Blanca! Blanca!" he seemed to call. And as night came down, I noticed that he was not far from the place where we had overtaken her. At length he seemed to find the trail, and when he came to the spot where we had killed her, his heart-broken wailing was piteous to hear. It was sadder than I could possibly have believed. Even the stolid cowboys noticed it, and said they had "never heard a wolf carry on like that before." He seemed to know exactly what had taken place, for her blood had stained the place of her death.

Then he took up the trail of the horses and followed it to the ranch-house. Whether in hopes of finding her there, or in quest of revenge, I know not, but the latter was what he found, for he surprised our unfortunate watchdog outside and tore him to little bits within fifty yards of the door. He evidently came alone this time, for I found but one trail next morning, and he had galloped about in a reckless manner that was very unusual with him. I had half expected this, and had set a number of additional traps about the pasture. Afterward I found that he had indeed fallen into one of these, but such was his strength, he had torn himself loose and cast it aside.

I believed that he would continue in the neighborhood until he found her body at least, so I concentrated all my energies on this one enterprise of catching him before he left the region, and while yet in this reckless mood. Then I realized what a mistake I had made in killing Blanca, for by using her as a decoy I might have secured him the next night.

I gathered in all the traps I could command, one hundred and thirty strong steel wolf-traps, and set them in fours in every trail that led into the cañon; each trap was separately fastened to a log, and each log was separately buried. In burying them, I carefully removed the sod and every particle of earth that was lifted we put in blankets, so that after the sod was replaced and all was finished the eye could detect no trace of human handiwork. When the traps were concealed I trailed the body of poor Blanca over each place, and made of it a drag that circled all about the ranch, and finally I took off one of her paws and made with it a line of tracks over each trap. Every precaution and device known to me I used, and retired at a late hour to await the result.

Once during the night I thought I heard Old Lobo, but was not sure of it. Next day I rode around, but darkness came on before I completed the circuit of the north cañon, and I had nothing to report. At supper one of the cowboys said, "There was a great row among the cattle in the north cañon this morning, maybe there is something in the traps there." It was afternoon of the next day before I got to the place referred to, and as I drew near a great grizzly form arose from the ground, vainly endeavoring to escape, and there revealed before me stood Lobo, King of the Currumpaw, firmly held in the traps. Poor old hero, he had never ceased to search for his darling, and when he found the trail her body had made he followed it recklessly, and so fell into the snare prepared for him. There he lay in the iron grasp of all four traps, perfectly helpless, and all around him were numerous tracks showing how the cattle had gathered about him to insult the fallen despot, without daring to approach within his reach. For two days and two nights he had lain there, and now was worn out with struggling. Yet, when I went near him, he rose up with bristling mane and raised his voice, and for the last time made the cañon reverberate with his deep bass roar, a call for help, the muster call of his band. But there was none to answer him, and, left alone in his extremity, he whirled about with all his strength and made a desperate effort to get at me. All in vain, each trap was a dead drag of over three hundred pounds, and in their relentless fourfold grasp, with great steel jaws on every foot, and the heavy logs and chains all entangled together, he was absolutely powerless. How his huge ivory tusks did grind on those cruel chains, and when I ventured to touch him with my riffle-barrel he left grooves on it which are there to this day. His eyes glared green with hate and fury, and his jaws snapped with a hollow 'chop,' as he vainly endeavored to reach me and my trembling horse. But he was worn out with hunger and struggling and loss of blood, and he soon sank exhausted to the ground.

Something like compunction came over me, as I prepared to deal out to him that which so many had suffered at his hands.

"Grand old outlaw, hero of a thousand lawless raids, in a few minutes you will be but a great load of carrion. It cannot be otherwise." Then I swung my lasso and sent it whistling over his head. But not so fast; he was yet far from being subdued, and, before the supple coils had fallen on his neck he seized the noose and, with one fierce chop, cut through its hard thick strands, and dropped it in two pieces at his feet.

Of course I had my rifle as a last resource, but I dill not wish to spoil his royal hide, so I galloped back to the camp and returned with a cowboy and a fresh lasso. We threw to our victim a stick of wood which he seized in his teeth, and before he could relinquish it our lassoes whistled through the air and tightened on his neck.

Yet before the light had died from his fierce eyes, I cried, "Stay, we will not kill him; let us take him alive to the camp." He was so completely powerless now that it was easy to put a stout stick through his mouth, behind his tusks, and then lash his jaws with a heavy cord which was also fastened to the stick. The stick kept the cord in, and the cord kept the stick in so he was harmless. As soon as he felt his jaws were tied he made no further resistance, and uttered no sound, but looked calmly at us and seemed to say, "Well, you have got me at last, do as you please with me." And from that time he took no more notice of us.

We tied his feet securely, but he never groaned, nor growled, nor turned his head. Then with our united strength were just able to put him on my horse. His breath came evenly as though sleeping, and his eyes were bright and clear again, but did not rest on us. Afar on the great rolling mesas they were fixed, his passing kingdom, where his famous band was now scattered. And he gazed till the pony descended the pathway into the cañon, and the rocks cut off the view.

By travelling slowly we reached the ranch in safety, and after securing him with a collar and a strong chain, we staked him out in the pasture and removed the cords. Then for the first time I could examine him closely, and proved how unreliable is vulgar report when a living hero or tyrant is concerned. He had *not* a collar of gold about his neck, nor was there on his shoulders an inverted cross to denote that he had leagued himself with Satan. But I did find on one haunch a great broad scar, that tradition says was the fang-mark of Juno, the leader of Tannerey's wolf-hounds—a mark which she gave him the moment before he stretched her lifeless on the sand of the cañon.

I set meat and water beside him, but he paid no heed. He lay calmly on his breast, and gazed with those steadfast yellow eyes away past me down through the gateway of the cañon over the open plains—his plains—nor moved a muscle when I touched him. When the sun went down he was still gazing fixedly across the prairie. I expected he would call up his band when night came, and prepared for them, but he had called once in his extremity, and none had come; he would never call again.

A lion shorn of his strength, an eagle robbed of his freedom, or a dove bereft of his mate, all die, it is said, of a broken heart; and who will aver that this grim bandit could bear the threefold brunt, heart-whole ? This only I know, that when the morning dawned, he was lying there still in his position of calm repose, his body unwounded, but his spirit was gone—the old King-wolf was dead.

I took the chain from his neck, a cowboy helped me to carry him to the shed where lay the remains of Blanca, and as we laid him beside her, the cattle-man exclaimed: "There, you *would* come to her, now you are together again."

7

The Springfield Fox

ERNEST THOMPSON SETON

I

The hens had been mysteriously disappearing for over a month; and when I came home to Springfield for the summer holidays it was my duty to find the cause. This was soon done. The fowls were carried away bodily one at a time, before going to roost or else after leaving, which put tramps and neighbors out of court; they were not taken from the high perches, which cleared all coons and owls; or left partly eaten, so that weasels, skunks, or minks were not the guilty ones, and the blame, therefore, was surely left at Reynard's door.

The great pine wood of Erindale was on the other bank of the river, and on looking carefully about the lower ford I saw a few fox-tracks and a barred feather from one of our Plymouth Rock chickens. On climbing the farther bank in search of more clews, I heard a great outcry of crows behind me, and turning, saw a number of these birds darting down at something in the ford. A better view showed that it was the old story, thief catch thief, for there in the middle of the ford was a fox with something in his jaws—he was returning from our barnyard with another hen. The crows, though shameless robbers themselves, are ever first to cry 'Stop thief,' and yet more than ready to take 'hush money' in the form of a share in the plunder.

And this was their game now. The fox to get back home must cross the river, where he was exposed to the full brunt of the crow mob. He made a dash for it, and would doubtless have gotten across with his booty had I not joined in the attack, whereupon he dropped the hen, scarce dead, and disappeared in the woods.

From Ernest Thompson Seton, *Wild Animals I Have Known* (New York: Charles Scribner's Sons, 1898).

This large and regular levy of provisions wholly carried off could mean but one thing, a family of little foxes at home; and to find them I now was bound.

That evening I went with Ranger, my hound, across the river into the Erindale woods. As soon as the hound began to circle, we heard the short, sharp bark of a fox from a thickly wooded ravine close by. Ranger dashed in at once, struck a hot scent and went off on a lively straight-away till his voice was lost in the distance away over the upland.

After nearly an hour he came back, panting and warm, for it was baking August weather, and lay down at my feet.

But almost immediately the same foxy *Yap yurrr* was heard close at hand and off dashed the dog on another chase.

Away he went in the darkness, baying like a foghorn, straight away to the north. And the loud '*Boo, boo,*' became a low '*oo, oo,*' and that a feeble 'o-o' and then was lost. They must have gone some miles away, for even with ear to the ground I heard nothing of them though a mile was easy distance for Ranger's brazen voice.

As I waited in the black woods I heard a sweet sound of dripping water: '*Tink tank tenk tink, Ta tink tank tenk tonk.*'

I did not know of any spring so near, and in the hot night it was a glad find. But the sound led me to the bough of an oak-tree, where I found its source. Such a soft sweet song; full of delightful suggestion on such a night:

Tonk tank tenk tink
Ta tink a tonk a tank a tink a
Ta ta tink tank ta ta tonk tink
Drink a tank a drink a drunk.

It was the 'water-dripping' song of the saw-whet owl.

But suddenly a deep raucous breathing and a rustle of leaves showed that Ranger was back. He was completely fagged out. His tongue hung almost to the ground and was dripping with foam, his flanks were heaving and spume-flecks dribbled from his breast and sides. He stopped panting a moment to give my hand a dutiful lick, then flung himself flop on the leaves to drown all other sounds with his noisy panting.

But again that tantalizing '*Yap yurrr*' was heard a few feet away, and the meaning of it all dawned on me.

We were close to the den where the little foxes were, and the old ones were taking turns in trying to lead us away.

It was late night now, so we went home feeling sure that the problem was nearly solved.

II

It was well known that there was an old fox with his family living in the neighborhood, but no one supposed them so near.

This fox had been called 'Scarface,' because of a scar reaching from his eye through and back of his ear; this was supposed to have been given him by a barbed-wire fence during a rabbit hunt, and as the hair came in white after it healed, it was always a strong mark.

The winter before I had met with him and had had a sample of his craftiness. I was out shooting, after a fall of snow, and had crossed the open fields to the edge of the brushy hollow back of the old mill. As my head rose to a view of the hollow I caught sight of a fox trotting at long range down the other side, in line to cross my course. Instantly I held motionless, and did not even lower or turn my head lest I should catch his eye by moving, until he went on out of sight in the thick cover at the bottom. As soon as he was hidden I bobbed down and ran to head him off where he should leave the cover on the other side, and was there in good time awaiting, but no fox came forth. A careful look showed the fresh track of a fox that had bounded from the cover, and following it with my eye I saw old Scarface himself far out of range behind me, sitting on his haunches and grinning as though much amused.

A study of the trail made all clear. He had seen me at the moment I saw him, but he, also like a true hunter, had concealed the fact, putting on an air of unconcern till out of sight, when he had run for his life around behind me and amused himself by watching my stillborn trick.

In the springtime I had yet another instance of Scarface's cunning. I was walking with a friend along the road over the high pasture. We passed within thirty feet of a ridge on which were several gray and brown bowlders. When at the nearest point my friend said:

"Stone number three looks to me very much like a fox curled up."

But I could not see it, and we passed. We had not gone many yards farther when the wind blew on this bowlder as on fur.

My friend said, "I am sure that is a fox, lying asleep."

"We'll soon settle that," I replied, and turned back, but as soon as I had taken one step from the road, up jumped Scarface, for it was he, and ran. A fire had swept the middle of the pasture, leaving a broad belt of black; over this he skurried till he came to the unburnt yellow grass again, where he squatted down and was lost to view. He had been watching us all the time, and would not have moved had we kept to the road. The wonderful part of this is, not that he resembled the round stones and dry grass, but that he *knew he did,* and was ready to profit by it.

We soon found that it was Scarface and his wife Vixen that had made our woods their home and our barnyard their base of supplies.

Next morning a search in the pines showed a great bank of earth that had been scratched up within a few months. It must have come from a hole, and yet there was none to be seen. It is well known that a really cute fox, on digging a new den, brings all the earth out at the first hole made, but carries on a tunnel into some distant thicket. Then closing up for good the first made and too well-marked door, uses only the entrance hidden in the thicket.

So after a little search at the other side of a knoll, I found the real entry and good proof that there was a nest of little foxes inside.

Rising above the brush on the hillside was a great hollow basswood. It leaned a good deal and had a large hole at the bottom, and a smaller one at top.

We boys had often used this tree in playing Swiss Family Robinson, and by cutting steps in its soft punky walls had made it easy to go up and down in the hollow. Now it came in handy, for next day when the sun was warm I went there to watch, and from this perch on the roof, I soon saw the interesting family that lived in the cellar near by. There were four little foxes; they looked curiously like little lambs, with their woolly coats, their long thick legs and innocent expressions, and yet a second glance at their broad, sharp-nosed, sharp-eyed visages showed that each of these innocents was the makings of a crafty old fox.

They played about, basking in the sun, or wrestling with each other till a slight sound made them skurry under ground. But their alarm was needless, for the cause of it was their mother; she stepped from the bushes bringing another hen—number seventeen as I remember. A low call from her and the little fellows came tumbling out. Then began a scene that I thought charming, but which my uncle would not have enjoyed at all.

They rushed on the hen, and tussled and fought with it, and each other, while the mother, keeping a sharp eye for enemies, looked on with fond delight. The expression on her face was remarkable. It was first a grinning of delight, but her usual look of wildness and cunning was there, nor were cruelty and nervousness lacking, but over all was the unmistakable look of the mother's pride and love.

The base of my tree was hidden in bushes and much lower than the knoll where the den was. So I could come and go at will without scaring the foxes.

For many days I went there and saw much of the training of the young ones. They early learned to turn to statuettes at any strange sound, and then on hearing it again or finding other cause for fear, to run for shelter.

Some animals have so much mother-love that it overflows and benefits outsiders. Not so old Vixen it would seem. Her pleasure in the cubs led to most refined cruelty. For she often brought home to them mice and birds alive, and with diabolic gentleness would avoid doing them serious hurt so that the cubs might have larger scope to torment them.

There was a woodchuck that lived over in the hill orchard. He was neither handsome nor interesting, but he knew how to take care of himself. He had digged a den between the roots of an old pine stump, so that the foxes could not follow him by digging. But hard work was not their way of life; wits they believed worth more than elbow-grease. This woodchuck usually sunned himself on the stump each morning. If he saw a fox near he went down in the door of his den, or if the enemy was very near he went inside and stayed long enough for the danger to pass.

One morning Vixen and her mate seemed to decide that it was time the children knew something about the broad subject of Woodchucks, and further that this orchard woodchuck would serve nicely for an object-lesson. So they went together to the orchard-fence unseen by old Chuckie on his stump. Scarface then showed himself in the orchard and quietly walked in a line so as to pass by the stump at a distance, but never once turned his head or allowed the ever-watchful woodchuck to think himself seen. When the fox entered the field the woodchuck quietly dropped down to the mouth of his den; here he waited as the fox passed, but concluding that after all wisdom is the better part, went into his hole.

This was what the foxes wanted. Vixen had kept out of sight, but now ran swiftly to the stump and hid behind it. Scarface had kept straight on, going very slowly. The woodchuck had not been frightened, so before long his head popped up between the roots and he looked around. There was that fox still going on, farther and farther away. The woodchuck grew bold as the fox went, and came out farther, and then seeing the coast clear, he scrambled onto the stump, and with one spring Vixen had him and shook him till he lay senseless. Scarface had watched out of the corner of his eye and now came running back. But Vixen took the chuck in her jaws and made for the den, so he saw he wasn't needed.

Back to the den came Vix, and carried the chuck so carefully that he was able to struggle a little when she got there. A low '*woof*' at the den brought the little fellows out like schoolboys to play. She threw the wounded animal to them and they set on him like four little furies, uttering little growls and biting little bites with all the strength of their baby jaws, but the woodchuck fought for his life and beating them off slowly hobbled to the shelter of a thicket. The little ones pursued like a pack of hounds and dragged at his tail and flanks, but could not hold him back. So Vix overtook him with a couple of bounds and dragged him again into the open for the children to worry. Again and again this rough sport went on till one of the little ones was badly bitten, and his squeal of pain roused Vix to end the woodchuck's misery and serve him up at once.

Not far from the den was a hollow overgrown with coarse grass, the playground of a colony of field-mice. The earliest lesson in woodcraft that the little ones took, away from the den, was in this hollow. Here they had their first course of mice, the easiest of all game. In teaching, the main thing was example, aided by a deep-set instinct. The old fox, also, had one or two signs meaning "lie still and watch," "come, do as I do," and so on, that were much used.

So the merry lot went to this hollow one calm evening and Mother Fox made them lie still in the grass. Presently a faint squeak showed that the game was astir. Vix rose up and went on tip-toe into the grass—not crouching but as high as she could stand, sometimes on her hind legs so as to get a better view. The runs that the mice follow are hidden under the grass tangle, and the only way to know the whereabouts of a mouse is by seeing the slight shaking of the grass, which is the reason why mice are hunted only on calm days.

And the trick is to locate the mouse and seize him first and see him afterward. Vix soon made a spring, and in the middle of the bunch of dead grass that she grabbed was a field-mouse squeaking his last squeak.

He was soon gobbled, and the four awkward little foxes tried to do the same as their mother, and when at length the eldest for the first time in his life caught game, he quivered with excitement and ground his pearly little milk-teeth into the mouse with a rush of inborn savageness that must have surprised even himself.

Another home lesson was on the red-squirrel. One of these noisy, vulgar creatures, lived close by and used to waste part of each day scolding the foxes, from some safe perch. The cubs made many vain attempts to catch him as he ran across their glade from one tree to another, or spluttered and scolded at them a foot or so out of reach. But old Vixen was up in natural history—she knew squirrel nature and took the case in hand when the proper time came. She hid the children and lay down flat in the middle of the open glade. The saucy low-minded squirrel came and scolded as usual. But she moved no hair. He came nearer and at last right overhead to chatter:

"You brute you, you brute you."

But Vix lay as dead. This was very perplexing, so the squirrel came down the trunk and peeping about made a nervous dash across the grass, to another tree, again to scold from a safe perch.

"You brute you, you useless brute, scarrr-scarrrrr."

But flat and lifeless on the grass lay Vix. This was most tantalizing to the squirrel. He was naturally curious and disposed to be venturesome, so again he came to the ground and skurried across the glade nearer than before.

Still as death lay Vix, "surely she was dead." And the little foxes began to wonder if their mother wasn't asleep.

But the squirrel was working himself into a little craze of foolhardy curiosity. He had dropped a piece of bark on Vix's head, he had used up his list of bad words and he had done it all over again, without getting a sign of life. So after a couple more dashes across the glade he ventured within a few feet of the really watchful Vix, who sprang to her feet and pinned him in a twinkling.

"And the little ones picked the bones e-oh."

Thus the rudiments of their education were laid, and afterward as they grew stronger they were taken farther afield to begin the higher branches of trailing and scenting.

For each kind of prey they were taught a way to hunt, for every animal has some great strength or it could not live, and some great weakness or the others could not live. The squirrel's weakness was foolish curiosity; the fox's that he can't climb a tree. And the training of the little foxes was all shaped to take advantage of the weakness of the other creatures and to make up for their own by defter play where they are strong.

From their parents they learned the chief axioms of the fox world. How, is not easy to say. But that they learned this in company with their parents was clear. Here are some that foxes taught me, without saying a word:—

Never sleep on your straight track.
Your nose is before your eyes, then trust it first.
A fool runs down the wind.
Running rills cure many ills.
Never take the open if you can keep the cover.
Never leave a straight trail if a crooked one will do.
If it's strange, it's hostile.
Dust and water burn the scent.
Never hunt mice in a rabbit-woods, or rabbits in a henyard.
Keep off the grass.

Inklings of the meanings of these were already entering the little ones' minds—thus, 'Never follow what you can't smell,' was wise, they could see, because if you can't smell it, then the wind is so that it must smell you.

One by one they learned the birds and beasts of their home woods, and then as they were able to go abroad with their parents they learned new animals. They were beginning to think they knew the scent of everything that moved. But one night the mother took them to a field where was a strange black flat thing on the ground. She brought them on purpose to smell it, but at the first whiff their every hair stood on end, they trembled, they knew not why—it seemed to tingle through their blood and fill them with instinctive hate and fear. And when she saw its full effect she told them—

"*that is man-scent.*"

III

Meanwhile the hens continued to disappear. I had not betrayed the den of cubs. Indeed, I thought a good deal more of the little rascals than I did of the hens; but uncle was dreadfully wrought up and made most disparaging remarks about my woodcraft. To please him I one day took the hound across to the woods and seating myself on a stump on the open hillside, I bade the dog go on. Within three minutes he sang out in the tongue all hunters know so well, "Fox! fox! fox! straight away down the valley."

After awhile I heard them coming back. There I saw the fox—Scarface— loping lightly across the river-bottom to the stream. In he went and trotted along in the shallow water near the margin for two hundred yards, then came out straight toward me. Though in full view, he saw me not but came up the hill watching over his shoulder for the hound. Within ten feet of me he turned and sat with his back to me while he craned his neck and showed an eager interest in the doings of the hound. Ranger came bawling along the trail till he came to the running water, the killer of scent, and here he was puzzled; but there was only one thing to do; that was by going up and down both banks find where the fox had left the river.

The fox before me shifted his position a little to get a better view and watched with a most human interest all the circling of the hound. He was so close that I saw the hair of his shoulder bristle a little when the dog came in sight. I could see the jumping of his heart on his ribs, and the gleam of his yellow eye. When the dog was wholly baulked by the water trick, it was comical to see: —he could not sit still, but rocked up and down in glee, and reared on his hind feet to get a better view of the slow-plodding hound. With mouth opened nearly to his ears, though not at all winded, he panted noisily for a moment, or rather he laughed gleefully, just as a dog laughs by grinning and panting.

Old Scarface wriggled in huge enjoyment as the hound puzzled over the trail so long that when he did find it, it was so stale he could barely follow it, and did not feel justified in tonguing on it at all.

As soon as the hound was working up the hill, the fox quietly went into the woods. I had been sitting in plain view only ten feet away, but I had the wind and kept still and the fox never knew that his life had for twenty minutes been in the power of the foe he most feared. Ranger also would have passed me as near as the fox, but I spoke to him, and with a little nervous start he quit the trail and looking sheepish lay down by my feet.

This little comedy was played with variations for several days, but it was all in plain view from the house across the river. My uncle, impatient at the daily loss of hens, went out himself, sat on the open knoll, and when old Scarface trotted to his lookout to watch the dull hound on the river flat below, my uncle remorselessly shot him in the back, at the very moment when he was grinning over a new triumph.

IV

But still the hens were disappearing. My uncle was wrathy. He determined to conduct the war himself, and sowed the woods with poison baits, trusting to luck that our own dogs would not get them. He indulged in contemptuous remarks on my by-gone woodcraft, and went out evenings with a gun and the two dogs, to see what he could destroy.

Vix knew right well what a poisoned bait was; she passed them by or else treated them with active contempt, but one she dropped down the hole of an old enemy, a skunk, who was never afterward seen. Formerly old Scarface was always ready to take charge of the dogs, and keep them out of mischief. But now that Vix had the whole burden of the brood, she could no longer spend time in breaking every track to the den, and was not always at hand to meet and mislead the foes that might be coming too near.

The end is easily foreseen. Ranger followed a hot trail to the den, and Spot, the fox-terrier, announced that the family was at home, and then did his best to go in after them.

The whole secret was now out, and the whole family doomed. The hired man came around with pick and shovel to dig them out, while we and the dogs stood by. Old Vix soon showed herself in the near woods, and led the dogs away off down the river, where she shook them off when she thought proper, by the simple device of springing on a sheep's back. The frightened animal ran for several hundred yards, then Vix got off, knowing that there was now a hopeless gap in the scent, and returned to the den. But the dogs, baffled by the break in the trail, soon did the same, to find Vix hanging about in despair, vainly trying to decoy us away from her treasures.

Meanwhile Paddy plied both pick and shovel with vigor and effect. The yellow, gravelly sand was heaping on both sides, and the shoulders of the sturdy digger were sinking below the level. After an hour's digging, enlivened by frantic rushes of the dogs after the old fox, who hovered near in the woods, Pat called:

"Here they are, sor!"

It was the den at the end of the burrow, and cowering as far back as they could, were the four little woolly cubs.

Before I could interfere, a murderous blow from the shovel, and a sudden rush for the fierce little terrier, ended the lives of three. The fourth and smallest was barely saved by holding him by his tail high out of reach of the excited dogs.

He gave one short squeal, and his poor mother came at the cry, and circled so near that she would have been shot but for the accidental protection of the dogs, who somehow always seemed to get between, and whom she once more led away on a fruitless chase.

The little one saved alive was dropped into a bag, where he lay quite still. His unfortunate brothers were thrown back into their nursery bed, and buried under a few shovelfuls of earth.

We guilty ones then went back into the house, and the little fox was soon chained in the yard. No one knew just why he was kept alive, but in all a change of feeling had set in, and the idea of killing him was without a supporter.

He was a pretty little fellow, like a cross between a fox and a lamb. His woolly visage and form were strangely lamb-like and innocent, but one could find in his yellow eyes a gleam of cunning and savageness as unlamb-like as it possibly could be.

As long as anyone was near he crouched sullen and cowed in his shelter-box, and it was a full hour after being left alone before he ventured to look out.

My window now took the place of the hollow basswood. A number of hens of the breed he knew so well were about the cub in the yard. Late that afternoon as they strayed near the captive there was a sudden rattle of the chain, and the youngster dashed at the nearest one and would have caught him but for the chain which brought him up with a jerk. He got on his feet and slunk back to his box, and though he afterward made several rushes he so gauged his leap as to win or fall within the length of the chain and never again was brought up by its cruel jerk.

As night came down the little fellow became very uneasy, sneaking out of his box, but going back at each slight alarm, tugging at his chain, or at times biting it in fury while he held it down with his fore paws. Suddenly he paused as though listening, then raising his little black nose he poured out a short quavering cry.

Once or twice this was repeated, the time between being occupied in worrying the chain and running about. Then an answer came. The far-away *Yap-yurrr* of the old fox. A few minutes later a shadowy form appeared on the woodpile. The little one slunk into his box, but at once returned and ran to meet his mother with all the gladness that a fox could show. Quick as a flash she seized him and turned to bear him away by the road she came. But the moment the end of the chain was reached the cub was rudely jerked from the old one's mouth, and she, scared by the opening of a window, fled over the wood-pile.

An hour afterward the cub had ceased to run about or cry. I peeped out, and by the light of the moon saw the form of the mother at full length on the ground by the little one, gnawing at something—the clank of iron told what, it was that cruel chain. And Tip, the little one, meanwhile was helping himself to a warm drink.

On my going out she fled into the dark woods, but there by the shelter-box were two little mice, bloody and still warm, food for the cub brought by the devoted mother. And in the morning I found the chain was very bright for a foot or two next the little one's collar.

On walking across the woods to the ruined den, I again found signs of Vixen. The poor heart-broken mother had come and dug out the bedraggled bodies of her little ones.

There lay the three little baby foxes all licked smooth now, and by them were two of our hens fresh killed. The newly heaved earth was printed all over with tell-tale signs—signs that told me that here by the side of her dead she had watched like Rizpah. Here she had brought their usual meal, the spoil of her nightly hunt. Here she had stretched herself beside them and vainly offered them their natural drink and yearned to feed and warm them as of old; but only stiff little bodies under their soft wool she found, and little cold noses still and unresponsive.

A deep impress of elbows, breast, and hocks showed where she had laid in silent grief and watched them for long and mourned as a wild mother can mourn for its young. But from that time she came no more to the ruined den, for now she surely knew that her little ones were dead.

V

Tip the captive, the weakling of the brood, was now the heir to all her love. The dogs were loosed to guard the hens. The hired man had orders to shoot the old fox on sight—so had I, but was resolved never to see her. Chicken-heads, that a fox loves and a dog will not touch, had been poisoned and scattered through the woods; and the only way to the yard where Tip was tied, was by climbing the wood-pile after braving all other dangers. And yet each night old Vix was there to nurse her baby and bring it fresh-killed hens and game. Again and again I saw her, although she came now without awaiting the querulous cry of the captive.

The second night of the captivity I heard the rattle of the chain, and then made out that the old fox was there, hard at work digging a hole by the little one's kennel. When it was deep enough to half bury her, she gathered into it all the slack of the chain, and filled it again with earth. Then in triumph thinking she had gotten rid of the chain, she seized little Tip by the neck and turned to dash off up the wood-pile, but alas! only to have him jerked roughly from her grasp.

Poor little fellow, he whimpered sadly as he crawled into his box. After half an hour there was a great outcry among the dogs, and by their straight-away tonguing through the far woods I knew they were chasing Vix. Away up north they went in the direction of the railway and their noise faded from hearing. Next morning the hound had not come back. We soon knew why. Foxes long ago learned what a railroad is; they soon devised several ways of turning it to account. One way is when hunted to walk the rails for a long distance just before a train comes. The scent, always poor on iron, is destroyed by the train and there is always a chance of hounds being killed by the engine. But another way more sure, but harder to play, is to lead the hounds straight to a high trestle just ahead of the train, so that the engine overtakes them on it and they are surely dashed to destruction.

This trick was skilfully played, and down below we found the mangled remains of old Ranger and learned that Vix was already wreaking her revenge.

That same night she returned to the yard before Spot's weary limbs could bring him back and killed another hen and brought it to Tip, and stretched her panting length beside him that he might quench his thirst. For she seemed to think he had no food but what she brought.

It was that hen that betrayed to my uncle the nightly visits.

My own sympathies were all turning to Vix, and I would have no hand in planning further murders. Next night my uncle himself watched, gun in hand, for an hour. Then when it became cold and the moon clouded over he remembered other important business elsewhere, and left Paddy in his place.

But Paddy was "onaisy" as the stillness and anxiety of watching worked on his nerves. And the loud bang! bang! an hour later left us sure only that powder had been burned.

In the morning we found Vix had not failed her young one. Again next night found my uncle on guard, for another hen had been taken. Soon after dark a single shot was heard, but Vix dropped the game she was bringing and escaped. Another attempt made that night called forth another gun-shot. Yet next day it was seen by the brightness of the chain that she had come again and vainly tried for hours to cut that hateful bond.

Such courage and staunch fidelity were bound to win respect, if not toleration. At any rate, there was no gunner in wait next night, when all was still. Could it be of any use? Driven off thrice with gun-shots, would she make another try to feed or free her captive young one?

Would she ? Hers was a mother's love. There was but one to watch them this time, the fourth night, when the quavering whine of the little one was followed by that shadowy form above the wood-pile.

But carrying no fowl or food that could be seen. Had the keen huntress failed at last? Had she no head of game for this her only charge, or had she learned to trust his captors for his food ?

No, far from all this. The wild-wood mother's heart and hate were true. Her only thought had been to set him free. All means she knew she tried, and every danger braved to tend him well and help him to be free. But all had failed.

Like a shadow she came and in a moment was gone, and Tip seized on something dropped, and crunched and chewed with relish what she brought. But even as he ate, a knife-like pang shot through and a scream of pain escaped him. Then there was a momentary struggle and the little fox was dead.

The mother's love was strong in Vix, but a higher thought was stronger. She knew right well the poison's power; she knew the poison bait, and would have taught him had he lived to know and shun it too. But now at last when she must choose for him a wretched prisoner's life or sudden death, she quenched the mother in her breast and freed him by the one remaining door.

It is when the snow is on the ground that we take the census of the woods, and when the winter came it told me that Vix no longer roamed the woods of Erindale. Where she went it never told, but only this, that she was gone.

Gone, perhaps, to some other far-off haunt to leave behind the sad remembrance of her murdered little ones and mate. Or gone, may be, deliberately, from the scene of a sorrowful life, as many a wild-wood mother has gone, by the means that she herself had used to free her young one, the last of all her brood.

8

On His Animal Stories

WILLIAM J. LONG

Preface to *Ways of Wood Folk*

"All crows are alike," said a wise man, speaking of politicians. That is quite true—in the dark. By daylight, however, there is as much difference, within and without, in the first two crows one meets as in the first two men or women. I asked a little child once, who was telling me all about her chicken, how she knew her chicken from twenty others just like him in the flock. "How do I know my chicken? I know him by his little face," she said. And sure enough, the face, when you looked at it closely, was different from all other faces.

This is undoubtedly true of all birds and all animals. They recognize each other instantly amid multitudes of their kind; and one who watches them patiently sees quite as many odd ways and individualities among Wood Folk as among other people. No matter, therefore, how well you know the habits of crows or the habits of caribou in general, watch the first one that crosses your path as if he were an entire stranger; open eyes to see and heart to interpret, and you will surely find some new thing, some curious unrecorded way, to give delight to your tramp and bring you home with a new interest.

This individuality of the wild creatures will account, perhaps, for many of these Ways, which can seem no more curious or startling to the reader than to the writer when he first discovered them. They are, almost entirely, the records of personal observation in the woods and fields. Occasionally, when I know my hunter or woodsman well, I have taken his testimony, but never without weigh-

From William J. Long, *Ways of Wood Folk* (Boston: Ginn, 1899) and *Northern Trails* (Boston: Ginn, 1905).

ing it carefully, and proving it whenever possible by watching the animal in question for days or weeks till I found for myself that it was all true.

The sketches are taken almost at random from old notebooks and summer journals. About them gather a host of associations, of living-over-agains, that have made it a delight to write them; associations of the winter woods, of apple blossoms and nest-building, of New England uplands and wilderness rivers, of camps and canoes, of snowshoes and trout rods, of sunrise on the hills, when one climbed for the eagle's nest, and twilight on the yellow wind-swept beaches, where the surf sobbed far away, and wings twanged like reeds in the wind swooping down to decoys, —all thronging about one, eager to be remembered if not recorded. Among them, most eager, most intense, most frequent of all associations, there is a boy with nerves all a-tingle at the vast sweet mystery that rustled in every wood, following the call of the winds and the birds, or wandering alone where the spirit moved him, who never studied nature consciously, but only loved it, and who found out many of these Ways long ago, guided solely by a boy's instinct.

If they speak to other boys, as to fellow explorers in the always new world, if they bring back to older children happy memories of a golden age when nature and man were not quite so far apart, then there will be another pleasure in having written them.

Preface to *Northern Trails*

The reader who follows these trails will find them leading into a new country, a land of space and silence where it is good to be, away up among the mountains and woods and salmon rivers and mossy barren grounds of Labrador and Newfoundland. There he will find himself face to face with new animals—white wolf, fisher, salmon, wild goose, polar bear, and a score of others big and little—that stop their silent hunting to look at the intruder curiously and without fear. In his turn he will lay aside his gun and his thoughts of killing for a moment, and watch these animals with his heart as well as his eyes wide open, trying to see without prejudice just what things they are doing, and then to understand if possible why and how they do them: why, for instance, the big Arctic wolf spares the bull caribou that attacks him wantonly; why the wild goose has no fear at home; why the baby seals are white at birth; how the salmon climb the falls which they cannot jump, and why they hasten back to the sea when they are hurt; how the whale speaks without a voice; and what makes the fisher confuse his trail, or leave beside it a tempting bait for you when you are following him, —all these and twenty more curious things are waiting to be seen and understood at the end of the trail.

The reader who has not followed such trails before will ask at once, How many of these things are true? Every smallest incident recorded here is as true as careful and accurate observation can make it. In most of the following chapters, as in all previous volumes, will be found the direct results of my own experience among animals; and in the few cases where, as stated plainly in the text, I have used the experience of other and wiser men, I have taken the facts from first-hand and accurate observers, and have then sifted them carefully so as to retain only those that are in my own mind without a question as to their truth. In the long story of Wayeeses the White Wolf, for example, —in which for the greater interest I have put the separate facts into a more or less connected biography—every incident in this wolf's life, from his grasshopper hunting to the cunning caribou chase, and from the den in the rocks to the meeting of wolf and children on the storm-swept barrens, is minutely true to fact, and is based squarely upon my own observation and that of my Indians. . . .

If the reader find himself often wondering at the courage or gentleness or intelligence of these free folk of the wilderness, that need not trouble or puzzle him for an instant. He is not giving human traits to the beasts, but is simply finding, as all do find who watch animals closely, many things which awaken a sympathetic response in his own heart, and which he understands more or less clearly, in precisely the same way that he understands himself and his own children.

It is not choice, but necessity, which leads us to this way of looking at animals and of trying to understand them. If we had a developed animal psychology based upon the assumption that life in one creature is essentially different from life in another, and that the intelligence in a wolf's head, for instance, is of a radically different kind from the same intelligence in the head of some other animal with two legs instead of four, then we might use our knowledge to understand what we see upon these trails. But there is no such psychology, and the assumption itself is a groundless one. Nature is of one piece, and consistent throughout. The drop is like the ocean, though it bears no ships on its bosom; the tear on a child's cheek breaks the light into glorious color, as does the rainbow on the spray of Niagara; and the law that holds the mountains fast sleeps in the heart of every grain of sand on the seashore. When we wish to measure the interstellar spaces we seek no new celestial unit, but apply confidently our own yardstick; and the chemistry that analyzes a baby's food serves equally well for the satellites of Jupiter. This is but an analogy, to be sure, but it serves to guide us in the realm of conscious life, which also seems of one piece and under one law. Inspired writers of every age have sought to comprehend even gods and angels by the same human intelligence that they applied to the ants and the conies, and for the same reason, —that they possessed but one measure of life. Love and hate, fear and courage, joy and grief, pain and pleasure, want and satisfaction, —these things, which make so large a part of life, are found in animals as well as in men, differing much in degree but not at all in kind from the same feelings in our own hearts; and we must measure them, if we are to understand them at all, by a common standard. To call a thing intelligence in one creature and reflex action in another, or to speak of the same thing as love or kindness in one and blind impulse in the other, is to be blinder ourselves than the impulse which is supposed to govern animals. Until, therefore, we have some new chemistry that will ignore atoms and atomic law, and some new psychology that ignores animal intelligence altogether, or regards it as under a radically different law from our own, we must apply what we know of ourselves and our own motives to the smaller and weaker lives that are in some distant way akin to our own.

To cover our own blindness and lack of observation we often make a mystery and hocus-pocus of animal life by using the word *instinct* to cover it all; as if instinct were the mysterious and exclusive possession of the animals, and not a common heritage which we share with them in large measure. It is an unmeaning word at best; for no one has told us, except in the vaguest way, what instinct is, or has set the limit where instinct ends and conscious intelligence begins, or has shown how far the primary instincts of a child differ from those of any other animal. On the other hand, one who watches animals closely and sympathetically must judge from what he sees that the motives which govern an animal's action are often very much like our own, the difference being that the animal's motive is more simple and natural than ours, and that among the higher orders the greater part of an animal's life—playing, working, seeking food, making dens, outwitting other animals, avoiding traps and enemies—is directed not by a blind instinct but by a very wide-awake intelligence. And this intelligence begins by the use of native powers and is strengthened by their daily occupation, is encouraged and developed by the mother's training and example as she leads her little ones into the world, and is perfected by the animal's own experience, which he remembers in the face of new problems— precisely as we do. A wild animal's life may indeed be far below ours, but he lives much in that pleasant border-land between thought and feeling where we so often find ourselves in our quiet moments, and there is no earthly need to make a mystery of him by talking vaguely of instinct, since so much of his life corresponds to our own and becomes intelligible to us the moment we lay aside our prejudice or hostility and watch him with a patient and friendly interest.

I make no claim whatever that animals reason or think or feel as men and women do. I have watched them too long for that; and sitting beside the beaver's village in the still twilight of the wilderness I find enough to occupy eyes and mind without making any comparison with the unquiet cities of men far away. But here before me is a life to be understood before it can be described, —a life, not an automaton, with its own joys and fears, its own problems, and its own intelligence; and the only conceivable way for me to understand it is to put myself for a moment in its place and lay upon it the measure of the only life of which I have any direct knowledge or understanding, which is my own. And this, far from being visionary or hypersensitive, as the makers of mechanical natural history would have us believe, is the only rational, indeed the only possible, way of understanding any animal action.

So, whether one looks for the facts of animal life or for the motives which govern it, the reader may follow these trails, as I first followed them, with the idea of seeing with his own eyes and understanding with his own heart. He will see many things that he does not understand, and so will listen with respect to Noel and Old Tomah, who for fifty seasons and more have lived close to the Wood Folk. And he will find at the end of every trail a real animal, as true to life as I am able to see and describe it after many years of watching in the wilderness.

9

A School for Little Fishermen

WILLIAM J. LONG

There came a day when, as I sat fishing among the rocks, the cry of the mother osprey changed as she came sweeping up to my fishing grounds, —*Chip, ch'wee! Chip, chip, ch'weeeee?* That was the fisherman's hail plainly enough; but there was another note in it, a look-here cry of triumph and satisfaction. Before I could turn my head for a fish was nibbling—there came other sounds behind it, —*Pip, pip, pip, ch'weee! pip, ch'wee! pip ch'weeee!*—a curious medley, a hail of good-luck cries; and I knew without turning that two other fishermen had come to join the brotherhood.

The mother bird—one can tell her instantly by her greater size and darker breast markings—veered in as I turned to greet the newcomers, and came directly over my head, her two little ones flapping lustily behind her. Two days before, when I went down to another lake on an excursion after bigger trout, the young fishhawks were still standing on the nest, turning a deaf ear to all the old birds' assurances that the time had come to use their big wings. The last glimpse I had of them through my glass showed me the mother bird in one tree, the father in another, each holding a fish, which they were showing the young across a tantalizing short stretch of empty air, telling the young, in fishhawk language, to come across and get it; while the young birds, on their part, stretched wings and necks hungrily and tried to whistle the fish over to them, as one would call a dog across the street. In the short interval that I was absent, mother wiles and mother patience had done their good work. The young were already flying well. Now they were out for their first lesson in fishing, evi-

From William J. Long, *School of the Woods: Some Life Studies of Animal Instincts and Animal Training* (Boston: Ginn, 1902).

dently; and I stopped fishing myself, letting my bait sink into the mud—where an eel presently tangled my hooks into an old root—to see how it was done. For fishing is not an instinct with Ismaques, but a simple matter of training. As with young otters, they know only from daily experience that fish, and not grouse and rabbits, are their legitimate food. Left to themselves, especially if one should bring them up on flesh and then turn them loose, they would go straight back to the old hawk habit of hunting the woods, which is much easier. To catch fish, therefore, they must be taught from the first day they leave the nest. And it is a fascinating experience for any man to watch the way they go about it.

The young ospreys flew heavily in short irregular circles, scanning the water with their inexperienced eyes for their first strike. Over them wheeled the mother bird on broad, even wings, whistling directions to the young neophytes, who would presently be initiated into the old sweet mysteries of going a-fishing. Fish were plenty enough; but that means nothing to a fishhawk, who must see his game reasonably near the surface before making his swoop. There was a good jump on the lake, and the sun shone brightly into it. Between the glare and the motion on the surface the young fishermen were having a hard time of it. Their eyes were not yet quick enough to tell them when to swoop. At every gleam of silver in the depths below they would stop short and cry out: *Pip!* "there he is!" *Pip, pip!* "here goes!" like a boy with his first nibble. But a short, clear whistle from the mother stopped them ere they had begun to fall; and they would flap up to her, protesting eagerly that they could catch that fellow, sure, if she would only let them try.

As they wheeled in over me on their way down the lake, one of the youngsters caught the gleam of my pile of chub among the rocks. *Pip, ch'weee!* he whistled, and down they came, both of them, like rockets. They were hungry; here were fish galore; and they had not noticed me at all, sitting very still among the rocks. *Pip, pip, pip, hurrah!* they piped as they came down.

But the mother bird, who had noted me and my pile of fish the first thing as she rounded the point, swept in swiftly with a curious, half-angry, half-anxious chiding that I had never heard from her before, —*Chip chip, chip! Chip! Chip!*—growing sharper and shriller at each repetition, till they heeded it and swerved aside. As I looked up they were just over my head, looking down at me now with eager, wondering eyes. Then they were led aside in a wide circle and talked to with wise, quiet whistlings before they were sent back to their fishing again.

And now as they sweep round and round over the edge of a shoal, one of the little fellows sees a fish and drops lower to follow it. The mother sees it too; notes that the fish is slanting up to the surface, and wisely lets the young fisherman alone. He is too near the water now; the glare and the dancing waves bother him; he loses his gleam of silver in the flash of a whitecap. Mother bird mounts higher, and whistles him up where he can see better. But there is the fish again, and the youngster, hungry and heedless, sets his wings for a swoop. *Chip, chip!* "wait, he's going down," cautions the mother; but the little fellow, too hungry to wait, shoots down like an arrow. He is a yard above the surface when a big whitecap jumps up at him and frightens him. He hesitates, swerves, flaps lustily to save himself. Then under the whitecap is a gleam of silver again. Down he goes on the instant, —*ugh! boo!* —like a boy taking his first dive. He is out of sight for a full moment, while two waves race over him, and I hold my breath waiting for him to come up. Then he bursts out, sputtering and shaking himself, and of course without his fish. As he rises heavily the mother, who has been circling over him whistling advice and comfort, stops short, with a single blow of her pinions against the air. She has seen the same fish, watched him shoot away under the plunge of her little one, and now sees him glancing up to the edge of the shoal where the minnows are playing. She knows that the young pupils are growing discouraged, and that the time has come to hearten them. *Chip, chip!* —"watch, I'll show you," she whistles—*Cheeeep!* with a sharp up-slide at the end, which I soon grow to recognize as the signal to strike. At the cry she sets her wings and shoots downward with strong, even plunge, strikes a wave squarely as it rises, passes under it, and is out on the other side, gripping a big chub. The little ones follow her, whistling their delight, and telling her that perhaps now they will go back to the nest and take a look at the fish before they go on with their fishing. Which means, of course, that they will eat it and go to sleep perfectly satisfied with the good fun of fishing; and then lessons are over for the day.

The mother, however, has other thoughts in her wise head. She knows that the little ones are not yet tired, only hungry; and that there is much to teach them before the chub stop shoaling and they must all be off to the coast. She knows also that they have thus far missed the two things she brought them out to learn: to take a fish always as he comes up; and to hit a wave always on the front side, under the crest. Gripping her fish tightly, she bends in her slow flight and paralyzes it by a single blow in the spine from her hooked beak. Then she drops it back into the whitecaps, where, jumping to the top of my rock, I can see it occasionally struggling near the surface. *Cheeeep!* "try it now," she whistles. *Pip, pip!* "here goes!" cries the little one who failed before; and down he drops, *souse!* going clear under in his impatient hunger, forgetting precept and example and past experience.

Again the waves race over him; but there is a satisfied note in the mother's whistle which tells me that she sees him, and that he is doing well. In a moment he is out again, with a great rush and sputter, gripping his fish and *pip-pipping* his exultation. Away he goes in low heavy flight to the nest. The mother circles over him a moment to be sure he is not overloaded; then she goes back with the other neophyte and ranges back and forth over the shoal's edge.

It is clear now to even my eyes that there is a vast difference in the characters of young fishhawks. The first was eager, headstrong, impatient; the second is calmer, stronger, more obedient. He watches the mother; he heeds her signals. Five minutes later he makes a clean, beautiful swoop and comes up with his fish. The mother whistles her praise as she drops beside him. My eyes follow them as, gossiping like two old cronies, they wing their slow way over the dancing whitecaps and climb the slanting tree-tops to the nest.

The day's lessons are over now, and I go back to my bait catching with a new admiration for these winged members of the brotherhood. Perhaps there is also a bit of envy or regret in my meditation as I tie on a new hook to replace the one that an uneasy eel is trying to rid himself of, down in the mud. If I had only had some one to teach me like that, I should certainly now be a better fisherman.

Next day, when the mother came up the lake to the shoal with her two little ones, there was a surprise awaiting them. For half an hour I had been watching from the point to anticipate their coming. There were some things that puzzled me, and that puzzle me still, in Ismaques' fishing. If he caught his fish in his beak, after the methods of mink and otter, I could understand it better. But to catch a fish—whose dart is like lightning—under the water with his feet, when, after his plunge, he can see neither his fish nor his feet, must require some puzzling calculation. And I had set a trap in my head to find out how it is done.

When the fishermen hove into sight, and their eager pipings came faintly up the lake ahead of them, I paddled hastily out and turned loose a half-dozen chub in the shallow water. I had kept them alive as long as possible in a big pail, and they still had life enough to fin about near the surface. When the fishermen arrived I was sitting among the rocks as usual, and turned to acknowledge the mother bird's *ch'wee?* But my deep-laid scheme to find out their method accomplished nothing; except, perhaps, to spoil the day's lesson. They saw my bait on the instant. One of the youngsters dove headlong without poising, went under, missed his fish, rose, plunged again. He got him that time and went away sputtering. The second took his time, came down on a long swift slant, and got his fish without going under. Almost before the lesson began it was over. The mother circled about for a few moments in a puzzled sort of way, watching the young fishermen flapping up the slope to their nest. Something was wrong. She had fished enough to know that success means something more than good luck; and this morning success had come too easily. She wheeled slowly over the shallows, noting the fish there, where they plainly did not belong, and dropping to examine with suspicion one big chub that was floating, belly up, on the water. Then she went under with a rush, where I could not see, came out again with a fish for herself, and followed her little ones to the nest.

Next day I set the trap again in the same way. But the mother, with her lesson well laid out before her, remembered yesterday's unearned success and came over to investigate, leaving her young ones circling along the farther shore. There were the fish again, in shallow water; and there—too easy altogether! —were two dead ones floating among the whitecaps. She wheeled away in a sharp turn, as if she had not seen anything, whistled her pupils up to her, and went on to other fishing grounds.

Presently, above the next point, I heard their pipings and the sharp, up-sliding *Cheeeep!* which was the mother's signal to swoop. Paddling up under the point in my canoe, I found them all wheeling and diving over a shoal, where I knew the fish were smaller and more nimble, and where there were lily pads for a haven of refuge, whither no hawk could follow them. Twenty times I saw them swoop only to miss, while the mother circled above or beside them, whistling advice and encouragement. And when at last they struck their fish and bore away towards the mountain, there was an exultation in their dusty wing beats, and in the whistling cry they sent back to me, which was not there the day before.

The mother followed them at a distance, veering in when near my shoal to take another look at the fish there. Three were floating now instead of two; the others—what were left of them—struggled feebly at the surface. *Chip, ch'weee!* she whistled disdainfully "plenty fish here, but mighty poor fishing." Then she swooped, passed under, came out with a big chub and was gone, leaving me only a blinding splash and a widening circle of laughing, dancing, tantalizing wavelets to tell me how she catches them.

10

Trails That Cross in the Snow

WILLIAM J. LONG

Noel was stealing along warily, his arrow ready on the string. Mooka beside him was watching a faint cloud of mist, the breath of caribou, that blurred at times the dark tree-line in the distance, when one of those mysterious warnings that befall the hunter in the far North rested upon them suddenly like a heavy hand.

I know not what it is, —what lesser pressure of air, to which we respond like a barometer; or what unknown chords there are within us that sleep for years in the midst of society and that waken and answer, like an animal's, to the subtle influence of nature, —but one can never be watched by an unseen wild animal without feeling it vaguely; and one can never be so keen on the trail that the storm, before it breaks, will not whisper a warning to turn back to shelter before it is too late. To Noel and Mooka, alone on the barrens, the sun was no dimmer than before; the heavy gray bank of clouds still held sullenly to its place on the horizon; and no eyes, however keen, would have noticed the tiny dark spots that centered and glowed upon them over the rim of the little hollow where the wolves were watching. Nevertheless, a sudden chill fell upon them both. They stopped abruptly, shivering a bit, drawing closer together and scanning the waste keenly to know what it all meant.

"*Mitcheegeesookh*, the storm!" said Noel sharply; and without another word they turned and hurried back on their own trail. In a short half-hour the world would be swallowed up in chaos. To be caught out on the barrens meant to be lost; and to be lost here without fire and shelter meant death, swift and sure. So they ran on, hoping to strike the woods before the blizzard burst upon them.

Excerpted from William J. Long, "Wayeeses the Strong One," *Northern Trails* (Boston: Ginn, 1905).

They were scarcely half-way to shelter when the white flakes began to whirl around them. With startling, terrible swiftness the familiar world vanished; the guiding trail was blotted out, and nothing but a wolf's instinct could have held a straight course in the blinding fury of the storm. Still they held on bravely, trying in vain to keep their direction by the eddying winds, till Mooka stumbled twice at the same hollow over a hidden brook, and they knew they were running blindly in a circle of death. Frightened at the discovery they turned, as the caribou do, keeping their backs steadily to the winds, and drifted slowly away down the long barren.

Hour after hour they struggled on, hand in hand, without a thought of where they were going. Twice Mooka fell and lay still, but was dragged to her feet and hurried onward again. The little hunter's own strength was almost gone, when a low moan rose steadily above the howl and hiss of the gale. It was the spruce woods, bending their tops to the blast and groaning at the strain. With a wild whoop Noel plunged forward, and the next instant they were safe within the woods. All around them the flakes sifted steadily, silently down into the thick covert, while the storm passed with a great roar over their heads.

In the lee of a low-branched spruce they stopped again, as though by a common impulse, while Noel lifted his hands. "Thanks, thanks, *Keesuolukh;* we can take care of ourselves now," the brave little heart was singing under the upstretched arms. Then they tumbled into the snow and lay for a moment utterly relaxed, like two tired animals, in that brief, delicious rest which follows a terrible struggle with the storm and cold.

First they ate a little of their bread and fish to keep up their spirits; then— for the storm that was upon them might last for days—they set about preparing a shelter. With a little search, whooping to each other lest they stray away, they found a big dry stub that some gale had snapped off a few feet above the snow. While Mooka scurried about, collecting birch bark and armfuls of dry branches, Noel took off his snow-shoes and began with one of them to shovel away the snow in a semicircle around the base of the stub. In a short half-hour he had a deep hole there, with the snow banked up around it to the height of his head. Next with his knife he cut a lot of light poles and scrub spruces and, sticking the butts in his snow bank, laid the tops, like the sticks of a wigwam, firmly against the big stub. A few armfuls of spruce boughs shingled over this roof, and a few minutes' work shoveling snow thickly upon them to hold them in place and to make a warm covering; then a doorway, or rather a narrow tunnel, just beyond the stub on the straight side semicircle, and their *commoosie* was all ready. Let the storm roar and the snow sift down The thicker it fell the warmer would be their shelter. They laughed and shouted now as they scurried out and in, bringing boughs for a bed and the fire-wood which Mooka had gathered.

Against the base of the dry stub they built their fire, —a wee, sociable little fire such as an Indian always builds, which is far better than a big one, for it draws you near and welcomes you cheerily, instead of driving you away by its smoke and great heat. Soon the big stub itself began to burn, glowing steadily with a heat that filled the snug little *commoosie*, while the smoke found its way out of the hole in the roof which Noel had left for that purpose. Later the stub burned through to its hollow center, and then they had a famous chimney, which soon grew hot and glowing inside, and added its mite to the children's comfort.

Noel and Mooka were drowsy now; but before the long night closed in upon them they had gathered more wood, and laid aside some wisps of birch bark to use when they should wake, cold and shivering, and find their little fire gone out and the big stub losing its cheery glow. Then they lay down to rest, and the night and the storm rolled on unheeded.

Towards morning they fell into a heavy sleep; for the big stub began to burn more freely as the wind changed, and they need not stir every half-hour to feed their little fire and keep from freezing. It was broad daylight, the storm had ceased, and a woodpecker was hammering loudly on a hollow shell over their heads when they started up, wondering vaguely where they were. Then while Noel broke out of the *commoosie*, which was fairly buried under the snow, to find out where he was, Mooka rebuilt the fire and plucked a ptarmigan and set it to toasting with the last of their bread over the coals.

Noel came back soon with a cheery whoop to tell the little cook that they had drifted before the storm down the whole length of the great barren, and were camped now on the opposite side, just under the highest ridge of the Top Gallants. There was not a track on the barrens, he said; not a sign of wolf or caribou, which had probably wandered deeper into the woods for shelter. So they ate their bread to the last crumb and their bird to the last bone, and, giving up all thought of hunting, started up the big barren, heading for the distant lodge, where they had long since been given up for lost.

They had crossed the barren and a mile of thick woods beyond when they ran into the fresh trail of a dozen caribou. Following it swiftly they came to the edge of a much smaller barren that they had crossed yesterday, and saw at a glance that the trail stretched straight across it. Not a caribou was in sight; but they might nevertheless be feeding, or resting in the woods just beyond; and for the little hunters to show themselves now in the open would mean that they would become instantly the target for every keen eye that was watching the back trail. So they started warily to circle the barren, keeping just within the fringe of woods out of sight.

They had gone scarcely a hundred steps when Noel whipped out a long arrow and pointed silently across the open. From the woods on the other side the caribou had broken out of a dozen tunnels under the spruces, and came trotting back in their old trails, straight down-wind to where the little hunters were hiding.

The deer were acting queerly, —now plunging away with the high, awkward jumps that caribou use when startled; now swinging off on their swift, tireless rack, and before they had settled to their stride halting suddenly to look back and wag their ears at the trail. For Megaleep is full of curiosity as a wild turkey, and always stops to get a little entertainment out of every new thing that does not threaten him with instant death. Then out of the woods behind them trotted five white wolves, —not hunting, certainly! for whenever the caribou stopped to look the wolves sat down on their tails and yawned. One lay down and rolled over and over in the soft snow; another chased and capered after his own brush, whirling round and round like a little whirlwind, and the shrill *ki-yi* of a cub wolf playing came faintly across the barren.

It was a strange scene, yet one often witnessed on the lonely plains of the far North: the caribou halting, running away, and halting again to look back and watch the queer antics of their big enemies, which seemed now so playful and harmless; the cunning wolves playing on the game's curiosity at every turn, knowing well that if once frightened the deer would break away at a pace which would make pursuit hopeless. So they followed rather than drove the foolish deer across the barren, holding them with monkey tricks and kitten's capers, and restraining with an iron grip their own fearful hunger and the blind impulse to rush in headlong and have it all quickly over.

Kneeling behind a big spruce, Noel was trying nervously the spring and temper of his long bow, divided in desire between the caribou, which they needed sadly at home, and one of the great wolves whose death would give him a place among the mighty hunters, when Mooka clutched his arm, her eyes snapping with excitement, her finger pointing silently back on their own trail. A vague shadow glided swiftly among the trees. An enormous white wolf appeared, vanished, came near them again, and crouched down under a low spruce branch waiting.

Again the two trails had crossed in the snow. The big wolf as he appeared had thrust his nose into the snow-shoe tracks, and a sniff or two told him everything, —who had passed, and how long ago, and what they were doing, and how far ahead they were now waiting. But the caribou were coming, coaxed along marvelously by the cubs and the old mother; and the great silent wolf, that had left the pack playing with the game while he circled the barren at top speed, now turned to the business in hand with no thought nor fear of harm from the two children whom he had watched but yesterday.

Not so Noel. The fire blazed out in his eyes; the long bow swung to the wolf, bending like a steel spring, and the feathered shaft of an arrow lay close against the boy's cheek. But Mooka caught his arm—

"Look, Noel, his ear! *Malsunsis,* my little wolf cub," she breathed excitedly. And Noel, with a great wonder in his eyes, slacked his bow, while his thoughts jumped far away to the den on the mountains where the trail began, and to three little cubs playing like kittens with the grasshoppers and the cloud shadows; for the great wolf that lay so still near them, his eyes fixed in a steady glow upon the coming caribou, had one ear bent sharply forward, like a leaf that has been creased between the fingers.

Again Mooka broke the tense silence in a low whisper. "How many wolf trails you see yesterday, little brother?"

"Seven," said Noel, whose eyes already had the cunning of Old Tomah's to understand everything.

"Then where tother wolf? Only six here," breathed Mooka, looking timidly all around, fearing to find the steady glare of green eyes fixed upon them from the shadow of every thicket.

Noel stirred uneasily. Somewhere close at hand another huge wolf was waiting; and a wholesome fear fell upon him, with a shiver at the thought of how near he had come in his excitement to bringing the whole savage pack snarling about his ears.

A snort of alarm cut short his thinking. There at the edge of the wood, not twenty feet away, stood a caribou, pointing his ears at the children whom he had almost stumbled over as he ran, thinking only of the wolves behind. The long bow sprang back of itself; an arrow buzzed like a wasp and buried itself deep in the white chest. Like a flash a second arrow followed as the stag turned away, and with a jump or two he sank to his knees, as if to rest awhile in the snow.

But Mooka scarcely saw these things. Her eyes were fastened on the great white wolf which she had claimed for her own when he was a toddling cub. He lay still as a stone under the tip of a bending spruce branch, his eyes following every motion of a young bull caribou which three of the wolves had singled out of the herd and were now guiding surely straight to his hiding-place.

The snort and plunge of the smitten animal startled this young stag and he turned aside from his course. Like a shadow the big wolf that Mooka was watching changed his place so as to head the game, while two of the pack on the open barrens slipped around the caribou and turned him back again to the woods. At the edge of the cover the stag stopped for a last look, pointing his ears first at Noel's caribou, which now lay very still in the snow, then at the wolves, which with quick instinct had singled him out of the herd, knowing in some subtle way he was watched from beyond, and which gathered about him in a circle, sitting on their tails and yawning. Slowly, silently Mooka's wolf crept forward, pushing his great body through the snow. A terrific rush, a quick snap under the stag's chest just behind the fore legs, where the heart lay; then the big wolf leaped aside and sat down quietly again to watch.

It was soon finished. The stag plunged away, settled into his long rack, slowed down to a swaying, weakening trot. After him at a distance glided the big wolf, lapping eagerly at the crimson trail, but holding himself with tremendous will power from rushing in headlong and driving the game, which might run for miles if too hard pressed. The stag sank to his knees; a sharp yelp rang like a pistol-shot through the still woods; then the pack rolled in like a whirlwind, and it was all over.

Creeping near on the trail the little hunters crouched under a low spruce, watching as if fascinated the wild feast of the wolves. Noel's bow was ready in his hand; but luckily the sight of these huge, powerful brutes overwhelmed him and drove all thoughts of killing out of his head. Mooka plucked him by the sleeve at last, and pointed silently homewards. It was surely time to go, for the biggest wolf had already stretched himself and was licking his paws, while the two cubs with full stomachs were rolling over and over and biting each other playfully in the snow. Silently they stole away, stopping only to tie a rag to a pointed stick, which they thrust between their own caribou's ribs to make the wolves suspicious and keep them from tearing the game and eating the tidbits while the little hunters hurried away to bring the men with their guns and dog sledges.

They had almost crossed the second barren when Mooka, looking back uneasily from the edge of the woods, saw a single big wolf emerge across the barren and follow swiftly on their trail. Startled at the sight, they turned swiftly to run; for that terrible feeling which sweeps over a hunter, when for the first time he finds himself hunted in his turn, had clutched their little hearts and crushed all their confidence. A sudden panic seized them; they rushed away for the woods, running side by side till they broke into the fringe of evergreen that surrounded the barren. There they dropped breathless under a low fir and turned to look.

"It was wrong to run, little brother," whispered Mooka.

"Why?" said Noel.

"Cause Wayeeses see it, and think we 'fraid."

"But I was 'fraid out there, little sister,"confessed Noel bravely. "Here we can climb tree; good chance shoot um with my arrows."

Like two frightened rabbits they crouched under the fir, staring back with wild round eyes over the trail, fearing every instant to see the savage pack break out of the woods and come howling after them. But only the single big wolf appeared, trotting quietly along in their footsteps. Within bowshot he stopped with head raised, looking, listening intently. Then, as if he had seen them in their hiding, he turned aside, circled widely to the left, and entered the woods far below.

Again the two little hunters hurried on through the silent, snow-filled woods, a strange disquietude settling upon them as they felt they were followed by unseen feet. Soon the feeling grew too strong to resist. Noel with his bow ready, and a strange chill trickling like cold water along his spine, was hiding behind a tree watching the back trail, when a low exclamation from Mooka made him turn. There behind them, not ten steps away, a huge white wolf was sitting quietly on his tail, watching them with absorbed, silent intentness.

Fear and wonder, and swift memories of Old Tomah and the wolf that had followed him when he was lost, swept over Noel in a flood. He rose swiftly, the long bow bent, and again a deadly arrow cuddled softly against his cheek; but there were doubts and fears in his eye till Mooka caught his arm with a glad little laugh—

"My cub, little brother. See his ear, and oh, his tail! Watch um tail, little brother." For at the first move the big wolf sprang alertly to his feet, looked deep into Mooka's eyes with that intense, penetrating light which serves a wild animal to read your very thoughts, and instantly his great bushy tail was waving its friendly greeting.

It was indeed Malsunsis, the cub. Before the great storm broke he had crouched with the pack in the hollow just in front of the little hunters; and although the wolves were hungry, it was with feelings of curiosity only that they watched the children, who seemed to the powerful brutes hardly more to be feared than a couple of snowbirds hopping across the vast barren. But they were children of men—that was enough for the white-wolf packs, which for untold years had never been known to molest a man. This morning Malsunsis had again crossed their trail. He had seen them lying in wait for the caribou that his own pack were driving; had seen Noel smite the bull, and was filled with wonder; but his own business kept him still in hiding. Now, well fed and good-natured, but more curious than ever, he had followed the trail of these little folk to learn something about them.

Mooka as she watched him was brim full of an eagerness which swept away all fear. "Tomah says, wolf and Injun hunt just alike; keep ver' still; don't trouble game 'cept when he hungry," she whispered. "Says too, *Keesuolukh* made us friends 'fore white man come, spoil um everything. Das what Malsunsis say now wid hees tail and eyes; only way he can talk um, little brother. No, no" —for Noel's bow was still strongly bent, —"you must not shoot. Malsunsis think we friends." And trusting her own brave little heart she stepped in front of the deadly arrow and walked straight to the big wolf, which moved aside timidly and sat down again at a distance, with the friendly expression of a lost collie in eyes and ears and wagging tail tip.

Cheerfully enough Noel slacked his long bow, for the wonder of the woods was strong upon him, and the hunting-spirit, which leads one forth to frighten and kill and to break the blessed peace, had vanished in the better sense of comradeship which steals over one when he watches the Wood Folk alone and friendly in the midst of the solitudes. As they went on their way again the big wolf trotted after them, keeping close to their trail but never crossing it, and occasionally ranging up alongside, as if to keep them in the right way. Where the woods were thickest Noel, with no trail to guide him, swung uncertainly to left and right, peering through the trees for some landmark on the distant hills. Twice the big wolf trotted out to one side, returned and trotted out again in the same direction; and Noel, taking the subtle hint, as an Indian always does, bore steadily to the right till the great ridge, beyond which the Lodge was hidden, loomed over the tree-tops. And to this day he believes—and it is impossible, for I have tried, to dissuade him—that the wolf knew where they were going and tried in his own way to show them.

So they climbed the long ridge to the summit, and from the deep valley beyond the smoke of the Lodge rose up to guide them. There the wolf stopped; and though Noel whistled and Mooka called cheerily, as they would to one of their own huskies that they had learned to love, Malsunsis would go no farther. He sat there on the ridge, his tail sweeping a circle in the snow behind him, his ears cocked to the friendly call and his eyes following every step of the little hunters, till they vanished in the woods below. Then he turned to follow his own way in the wilderness.

A Woodcock Genius

WILLIAM J. LONG

There is one astonishing thing about Whitooweek which can scarcely be called a habit, but which is probably the discovery of one or two rare individuals here and there more original than their fellows. Like the eider-ducks and the bear and the beaver, Whitooweek sometimes uses a rude kind of surgery for binding up his wounds. Twenty years ago, while sitting quietly by a brook at the edge of the woods in Bridgewater, a woodcock suddenly fluttered out into the open and made his way to a spot on the bank where a light streak of sticky mud and clay showed clearly from where I was watching. It was the early hunting season and gunners were abroad in the land, and my first impression was that this was a wounded bird that had made a long flight after being shot, and that had now come out to the stream to drink or to bathe his wound. Whether this were so or not is a matter of guesswork; but the bird was acting strangely in broad daylight, and I crept nearer till I could see him plainly on the other side of the little stream, though he was still too far away for me to be absolutely sure of what all his motions meant.

At first he took soft clay in his bill from the edge of the water and seemed to be smearing it on one leg near the knee. Then he fluttered away on one foot for a short distance and seemed to be pulling tiny roots and fibers of grass, which he worked into the clay that he had already smeared on his leg. Again he took more clay and plastered it over the fibers, putting on more and more till I could plainly see the enlargement, working away with strange, silent intentness for fully fifteen minutes, while I watched and wondered, scarce believing my eyes. Then he stood perfectly still for a full hour under an overhanging sod, where

From William J. Long, *A Little Brother to the Bear* (Boston: Ginn, 1903).

the eye could with difficulty find him, his only motion meanwhile being an occasional rubbing and smoothing of the clay bandage with his bill, until it hardened enough to suit him, whereupon he fluttered away from the brook and disappeared in the thick woods.

I had my own explanation of the incredible action, namely, that the woodcock had a broken leg, and had deliberately put it into a clay cast to hold the bones in place until they should knit together again; but naturally I kept my own counsel, knowing that no one would believe in the theory. For years I questioned gunners closely, and found two who said that they had killed woodcock whose legs had at one time been broken and had healed again. As far as they could remember, the leg had in each case healed perfectly straight instead of twisting out to one side, as a chicken's leg does when broken and allowed to knit of itself. I examined hundreds of woodcock in the markets in different localities, and found one whose leg had at one time been broken by a shot and then had healed perfectly. There were plain signs of dried mud at the break; but that was also true of the other leg near the foot, which only indicated that the bird had been feeding in soft places. All this proved nothing to an outsider, and I kept silence as to what I had seen until last winter, twenty years afterwards, when the confirmation came unexpectedly. I had been speaking of animals before the Contemporary Club of Bridgeport when a gentleman, a lawyer well known all over the state, came to me and told me eagerly of a curious find he had made the previous autumn. He was gunning one day with a friend, when they shot a woodcock, which on being brought in by the dog was found to have a lump of hard clay on one of its legs. Curious to know what it meant he chipped the clay off with his penknife and found a broken bone, which was then almost healed and as straight as ever. A few weeks later the bird, had he lived, would undoubtedly have taken off the cast himself and there would have been nothing to indicate anything unusual about him.

So I give the observation now, at last, since proof is at hand, not to indicate a new or old habit of Whitooweek, —for how far the strange knowledge is spread among the woodcock and the wading birds no man can say, —but simply to indicate how little we know of the inner life of the hermit, and indeed of all wild birds, and how much there is yet to be discovered when we shall lay aside the gun for the field-glass and learn to interpret the wonderful life which goes on unseen all about us.

12

The Sounding of the Call

JACK LONDON

When Buck earned sixteen hundred dollars in five minutes for John Thornton, he made it possible for his master to pay off certain debts and to journey with his partners into the East after a fabled lost mine, the history of which was as old as the history of the country. Many men had sought it; few had found it; and more than a few there were who had never returned from the quest. This lost mine was steeped in tragedy and shrouded in mystery. No one knew of the first man. The oldest tradition stopped before it got back to him. From the beginning there had been an ancient and ramshackle cabin. Dying men had sworn to it, and to the mine the site of which it marked, clinching their testimony with nuggets that were unlike any known grade of gold in the Northland.

But no living man had looted this treasure house, and the dead were dead; wherefore John Thornton and Pete and Hans, with Buck and half a dozen other dogs, faced into the East on an unknown trail to achieve where men and dogs as good as themselves had failed. They sledded seventy miles up the Yukon, swung to the left into the Stewart River, passed the Mayo and the McQuestion, and held on until the Stewart itself became a streamlet, threading the upstanding peaks which marked the backbone of the continent.

John Thornton asked little of man or nature. He was unafraid of the wild. With a handful of salt and a rifle he could plunge into the wilderness and fare wherever he pleased and as long as he pleased. Being in no haste, Indian fashion, he hunted his dinner in the course of the day's travel; and if he failed to find it, like the Indian, he kept on travelling, secure in the knowledge that sooner or later he would come to it. So, on this great journey into the East,

Excerpted from Jack London, *Call of the Wild* (1903; repr. New York: Grosset & Dunlap, 1906).

straight meat was the bill of fare, ammunition and tools principally made up the load on the sled, and the time-card was drawn upon the limitless future.

To Buck it was boundless delight, this hunting, fishing, and indefinite wandering through strange places. For weeks at a time they would hold on steadily, day after day; and for weeks upon end they would camp, here and there, the dogs loafing and the men burning holes through frozen muck and gravel and washing countless pans of dirt by the heat of the fire. Sometimes they went hungry, sometimes they feasted riotously, all according to the abundance of game and the fortune of hunting. Summer arrived, and dogs and men packed on their backs, rafted across blue mountain lakes, and descended or ascended unknown rivers in slender boats whipsawed from the standing forest.

The months came and went, and back and forth they twisted through the uncharted vastness, where no men were and yet where men had been if the Lost Cabin were true. They went across divides in summer blizzards, shivered under the midnight sun on naked mountains between the timber line and the eternal snows, dropped into summer valleys amid swarming gnats and flies, and in the shadows of glaciers picked strawberries and flowers as ripe and fair as any the Southland could boast. In the fall of the year they penetrated a weird lake country, sad and silent, where wild-fowl had been, but where then there was no life nor sign of life—only the blowing of chill winds, the forming of ice in sheltered places, and the melancholy rippling of waves on lonely beaches.

And through another winter they wandered on the obliterated trails of men who had gone before. Once, they came upon a path blazed through the forest, an ancient path, and the Lost Cabin seemed very near. But the path began nowhere and ended nowhere, and it remained mystery, as the man who made it and the reason he made it remained mystery. Another time they chanced upon the time-graven wreckage of a hunting lodge, and amid the shreds of rotted blankets John Thornton found a long-barrelled flint-lock. He knew it for a Hudson Bay Company gun of the young days in the Northwest, when such a gun was worth its height in beaver skins packed flat. And that was all—no hint as to the man who in an early day had reared the lodge and left the gun among the blankets.

Spring came on once more, and at the end of all their wandering they found, not the Lost Cabin, but a shallow placer in a broad valley where the gold showed like yellow butter across the bottom of the washing-pan. They sought no farther. Each day they worked earned them thousands of dollars in clean dust and nuggets, and they worked every day. The gold was sacked in moose-hide bags, fifty pounds to the bag, and piled like so much firewood outside the spruce-bough lodge. Like giants they toiled, days flashing on the heels of days like dreams as they heaped the treasure up.

There was nothing for the dogs to do, save the hauling in of meat now and again that Thornton killed, and Buck spent long hours musing by the fire. The vision of the short-legged hairy man came to him more frequently, now that there was little work to be done; and often, blinking by the fire, Buck wandered with him in that other world which he remembered.

The salient thing of this other world seemed fear. When he watched the hairy man sleeping by the fire, head between his knees and hands clasped above, Buck saw that he slept restlessly, with many starts and awakenings, at which times he would peer fearfully into the darkness and fling more wood upon the fire. Did they walk by the beach of a sea, where the hairy man gathered shell-fish and ate them as he gathered, it was with eyes that roved everywhere for hidden danger and with legs prepared to run like the wind at its first appearance. Through the forest they crept noiselessly, Buck at the hairy man's heels; and they were alert and vigilant, the pair of them, ears twitching and moving and nostrils quivering, for the man heard and smelled as keenly as Buck. The hairy man could spring up into the trees and travel ahead as fast as on the ground, swinging by the arms from limb to limb, sometimes a dozen feet apart, letting go and catching, never falling, never missing his grip. In fact he seemed as much at home among the trees as on the ground, and Buck had memories of nights of vigil spent beneath trees wherein the hairy man roosted, holding on tightly as he slept.

And closely akin to the visions of the hairy man was the call still sounding in the depths of the forest. It filled him with a great unrest and strange desires. It caused him to feel a vague, sweet gladness, and he was aware of wild yearnings and stirrings for he knew not what. Sometimes he pursued the call into the forest, looking for it as though it were a tangible thing, barking softly or defiantly, as the mood might dictate. He would thrust his nose into the cool wood moss, or into the black soil where long grasses grew, and snort with joy at the fat earth smells; or he would crouch for hours, as if in concealment, behind fungus-covered trunks of fallen trees, wide-eyed and wide-eared to all that moved and sounded about him. It might be, lying thus, that he hoped to surprise this call he could not understand. But he did not know why he did these various things. He was impelled to do them, and did not reason about them at all.

Irresistible impulses seized him. He would be lying in camp, dozing lazily in the heat of the day, when suddenly his head would lift and his ears cock up, intent and listening, and he would spring to his feet and dash away, and on and on, for hours, through the forest aisles and across the open spaces where the niggerheads bunched. He loved to run down dry watercourses, and to creep and spy upon the bird life in the woods. For a day at a time he would lie in the underbrush where he could watch the partridges drumming and strutting up and down. But especially he loved to run in the dim twilight of the summer midnights, listening to the subdued and sleepy murmurs of the forest, reading signs and sounds as man may read a book, and seeking for the mysterious something that called—called, waking or sleeping, at all times, for him to come.

One night he sprang from sleep with a start, eager-eyed, nostrils quivering and scenting, his mane bristling in recurrent waves. From the forest came the call (or one note of it, for the call was many noted), distinct and definite as never before, —a long-drawn howl, like, yet unlike, any noise made by husky dog. And he knew it, in the old familiar way, as a sound heard before. He sprang through the sleeping camp and in swift silence dashed through the woods. As he drew closer to the cry he went more slowly, with caution in every movement, till he came to an open place among the trees, and looking out saw, erect on haunches, with nose pointed to the sky, a long, lean, timber wolf.

He had made no noise, yet it ceased from its howling and tried to sense his presence. Buck stalked into the open, half crouching, body gathered compactly together, tail straight and stiff, feet falling with unwonted care. Every movement advertised commingled threatening and overture of friendliness. It was the menacing truce that marks the meeting of wild beasts that prey. But the wolf fled at sight of him. He followed, with wild leapings, in a frenzy to overtake. He ran him into a blind channel, in the bed of the creek, where a timber jam barred the way. The wolf whirled about, pivoting on his hind legs after the fashion of Joe and of all cornered husky dogs, snarling and bristling, clipping his teeth together in a continuous and rapid succession of snaps.

Buck did not attack, but circled him about and hedged him in with friendly advances. The wolf was suspicious and afraid; for Buck made three of him in weight, while his head barely reached Buck's shoulder. Watching his chance, he darted away, and the chase was resumed. Time and again he was cornered, and the thing repeated, though he was in poor condition, or Buck could not so easily have overtaken him. He would run till Buck's head was even with his flank, when he would whirl around at bay, only to dash away again at the first opportunity.

But in the end Buck's pertinacity was rewarded; for the wolf, finding that no harm was intended, finally sniffed noses with him. Then they became friendly, and played about in the nervous, half-coy way with which fierce beasts belie their fierceness. After some time of this the wolf started off at an easy lope in a manner that plainly showed he was going somewhere. He made it clear to Buck that he was to come, and they ran side by side through the sombre twilight, straight up the creek bed, into the gorge from which it issued, and across the bleak divide where it took its rise.

On the opposite slope of the watershed they came down into a level country where were great stretches of forest and many streams, and through these great stretches they ran steadily, hour after hour, the sun rising higher and the day growing warmer Buck was wildly glad. He knew he was at last answering the call, running by the side of his wood brother toward the place from where the call surely came. Old memories were coming upon him fast, and he was stirring to them as of old he stirred to the realities of which they were the shadows. He had done this thing before, somewhere in that other and dimly remembered world, and he was doing it again, now, running free in the open, the unpacked earth underfoot, the wide sky overhead.

They stopped by a running stream to drink, and, stopping, Buck remembered John Thornton. He sat down. The wolf started on toward the place from where the call surely came, then returned to him, sniffing noses and making actions as though to encourage him. But Buck turned about and started slowly on the back track. For the better part of an hour the wild brother ran by his side, whining softly. Then he sat down, pointed his nose upward, and howled. It was a mournful howl, and as Buck held steadily on his way he heard it grow faint and fainter until it was lost in the distance.

John Thornton was eating dinner when Buck dashed into camp and sprang upon him in a frenzy of affection, overturning him, scrambling upon him, licking his face, biting his hand—"playing the general tom-fool," as John Thornton characterized it, the while he shook Buck back and forth and cursed him lovingly.

For two days and nights Buck never left camp, never let Thornton out of his sight. He followed him about at his work, watched him while he ate, saw him into his blankets at night and out of them in the morning. But after two days the call in the forest began to sound more imperiously than ever. Buck's restlessness came back on him, and he was haunted by recollections of the wild brother, and of the smiling land beyond the divide and the run side by side through the wide forest stretches. Once again he took to wandering in the woods, but the wild brother came no more; and though he listened through long vigils, the mournful howl was never raised.

He began to sleep out at night, staying away from camp for days at a time; and once he crossed the divide at the head of the creek and went down into the land of timber and streams. There he wandered for a week, seeking vainly for fresh sign of the wild brother, killing his meat as he travelled and travelling with the long, easy lope that seems never to tire. He fished for salmon in a broad stream that emptied somewhere into the sea, and by this stream he killed a large black bear, blinded by the mosquitoes while likewise fishing, and raging through the forest helpless and terrible. Even so, it was a hard fight, and it aroused the last latent remnants of Buck's ferocity. And two days later, when he returned to his kill and found a dozen wolverenes quarrelling over the spoil, he scattered them like chaff; and those that fled left two behind who would quarrel no more.

The blood-longing became stronger than ever before. He was a killer, a thing that preyed, living on the things that lived, unaided, alone, by virtue of his own strength and prowess, surviving triumphantly in a hostile environment where only the strong survived. Because of all this he became possessed of a great pride in himself, which communicated itself like a contagion to his physical being. It advertised itself in all his movements, was apparent in the play of every muscle, spoke plainly as speech in the way he carried himself, and made his glorious furry coat if anything more glorious. But for the stray brown on his muzzle and above his eyes, and for the splash of white hair that ran midmost down his chest, he might well have been mistaken for a gigantic wolf, larger than the largest of the breed. From his St. Bernard father he had inherited size and weight, but it was his shepherd mother who had given shape to that size and weight. His muzzle was the long wolf muzzle, save that it was larger than the muzzle of any wolf; and his head, somewhat broader, was the wolf head on a massive scale.

His cunning was wolf cunning, and wild cunning; his intelligence, shepherd intelligence and St. Bernard intelligence; and all this, plus an experience gained in the fiercest of schools, made him as formidable a creature as any that roamed the wild. A carnivorous animal, living on a straight meat diet, he was in full flower, at the high tide of his life, overspilling with vigor and virility. When Thornton passed a caressing hand along his back, a snapping and crackling followed the hand, each hair discharging its pent magnetism at the contact. Every part, brain and body, nerve tissue and fibre, was keyed to the most exquisite pitch; and between all the parts there was a perfect equilibrium or adjustment. To sights and sounds and events which required action, he responded with lightning-like rapidity. Quickly as a husky dog could leap to defend from attack or to attack, he could leap twice as quickly. He saw the movement, or heard sound, and responded in less time than another dog required to compass the mere seeing or hearing. He perceived and determined and responded in the same instant. In point of fact the three actions of perceiving, determining, and responding were sequential; but so infinitesimal were the intervals of time between them that they appeared simultaneous. His muscles were surcharged with vitality, and snapped into play sharply, like steel springs. Life streamed through him in splendid flood, glad and rampant, until it seemed that it would burst him asunder in sheer ecstasy and pour forth generously over the world.

"Never was there such a dog," said John Thornton one day, as the partners watched Buck marching out of camp.

"When he was made, the mould was broke," said Pete.

"Py jingo! I t'ink so mineself," Hans affirmed.

They saw him marching out of camp, but they did not see the instant and terrible transformation which took place as soon as he was within the secrecy of the forest. He no longer marched. At once he became a thing of the wild, stealing along softly, cat-footed, a passing shadow that appeared and disappeared among the shadows. He knew how to take advantage of every cover, to crawl on his belly like a snake, and like a snake to leap and strike. He could take a ptarmigan from its nest, kill a rabbit as it slept, and snap in mid air the little chipmunks fleeing a second too late for the trees. Fish, in open pools, were not too quick for him; nor were beaver, mending their dams, too wary. He killed to eat, not from wantonness; but he preferred to eat what he killed himself. So a lurking humor ran through his deeds, and it was his delight to steal upon the squirrels, and, when he all but had them, to let them go, chattering in mortal fear to the tree-tops.

As the fall of the year came on, the moose appeared in greater abundance, moving slowly down to meet the winter in the lower and less rigorous valleys. Buck had already dragged down a stray part-grown calf; but he wished strongly for larger and more formidable quarry, and he came upon it one day on the divide at the head of the creek. A band of twenty moose had crossed over from the land of streams and timber, and chief among them was a great bull. He was in a savage temper, and, standing over six feet from the ground, was as formidable an antagonist as even Buck could desire. Back and forth the bull tossed his great palmated antlers, branching to fourteen points and embracing seven feet within the tips. His small eyes burned with a vicious and bitter light, while he roared with fury at sight of Buck.

From the bull's side, just forward of the flank, protruded a feathered arrow-end, which accounted for his savageness. Guided by that instinct which came from the old hunting days of the primordial world, Buck proceeded to cut the bull out from the herd. It was no slight task. He would bark and dance about in front of the bull, just out of reach of the great antlers and of the terrible splay hoofs which could have stamped his life out with a single blow. Unable to turn his back on the fanged danger and go on, the bull would be driven into paroxysms of rage. At such moments he charged Buck, who retreated craftily, luring him on by a simulated inability to escape. But when he was thus separated from his fellows, two or three of the younger bulls would charge back upon Buck and enable the wounded bull to rejoin the herd.

There is a patience of the wild—dogged, tireless, persistent as life itself—that holds motionless for endless hours the spider in its web, the snake in its coils, the panther in its ambuscade; this patience belongs peculiarly to life when it hunts its living food; and it belonged to Buck as he clung to the flank of the herd, retarding its march, irritating the young bulls, worrying the cows with their half-grown calves, and driving the wounded bull mad with helpless rage. For half a day this continued. Buck multiplied himself, attacking from all sides, enveloping the herd in a whirlwind of menace, cutting out his victim as fast as it could rejoin its mates, wearing out the patience of creatures preyed upon, which is a lesser patience than that of creatures preying.

As the day wore along and the sun dropped to its bed in the northwest (the darkness had come back and the fall nights were six hours long), the young bulls retraced their steps more and more reluctantly to the aid of their beset leader. The down-coming winter was harrying them on to the lower levels, and it seemed they could never shake off this tireless creature that held them back. Besides, it was not the life of the herd, or of the young bulls, that was threatened. The life of only one member was demanded, which was a remoter interest than their lives, and in the end they were content to pay the toll.

As twilight fell the old bull stood with lowered head, watching his mates—the cows he had known, the calves he had fathered, the bulls he had mastered—as they shambled on at a rapid pace through the fading light. He could not follow, for before his nose leaped the merciless fanged terror that would not let him go. Three hundredweight more than half a ton he weighed; he had lived a long, strong life, full of fight and struggle, and at the end he faced death at the teeth of a creature whose head did not reach beyond his great knuckled knees.

From then on, night and day, Buck never left his prey, never gave it a moment's rest, never permitted it to browse the leaves of trees or the shoots of young birch and willow. Nor did he give the wounded bull opportunity to slake his burning thirst in the slender trickling streams they crossed. Often, in desperation, he burst into long stretches of flight. At such times Buck did not attempt to stay him, but loped easily at his heels, satisfied with the way the game was played, lying down when the moose stood still, attacking him fiercely when he strove to eat or drink.

The great head drooped more and more under its tree of horns, and the shambling trot grew weak and weaker. He took to standing for long periods, with nose to the ground and dejected ears dropped limply; and Buck found more time in which to get water for himself and in which to rest. At such moments, panting with red lolling tongue and with eyes fixed upon the big bull, it appeared to Buck that a change was coming over the face of things. He could feel a new stir in the land. As the moose were coming into the land, other kinds of life were coming in. Forest and stream and air seemed palpitant with their presence. The news of it was borne in upon him, not by sight, or sound, or smell, but by some other and subtler sense. He heard nothing, saw nothing, yet knew that the land was somehow different; that through it strange things were afoot and ranging; and he resolved to investigate after he had finished the business in hand.

At last, at the end of the fourth day, he pulled the great moose down. For a day and a night he remained by the kill, eating and sleeping, turn and turn about. Then, rested, refreshed and strong, he turned his face toward camp and John Thornton. He broke into the long easy lope, and went on, hour after hour, never at loss for the tangled way, heading straight home through strange country with a certitude of direction that put man and his magnetic needle to shame.

As he held on he became more and more conscious of the new stir in the land. There was life abroad in it different from the life which had been there throughout the summer. No longer was this fact borne in upon him in some subtle, mysterious way. The birds talked of it, the squirrels chattered about it, the very breeze whispered of it. Several times he stopped and drew in the fresh morning air in great sniffs, reading a message which made him leap on with greater speeds. He was oppressed with a sense of calamity happening if it were not calamity already happened; and as he crossed the last watershed and dropped down into the valley toward camp, he proceeded with greater caution

Three miles away he came upon a fresh trail that sent his neck hair rippling and bristling. It led straight toward camp and John Thornton. Buck hurried on, swiftly and stealthily, every nerve straining and tense, alert to the multitudinous details which told a story—all but the end. His nose gave him a varying description of the passage of the life on the heels of which he was travelling. He remarked the pregnant silence of the forest. The bird life had flitted. The squirrels were in hiding. One only he saw, —a sleek gray fellow, flattened against a gray dead limb so that he seemed a part of it, a woody excrescence upon the wood itself.

As Buck slid along with the obscureness of a gliding shadow, his nose was jerked suddenly to the side as though a positive force had gripped and pulled it. He followed the new scent into a thicket and found Nig. He was lying on his side, dead where he had dragged himself, an arrow protruding, head and feathers, from either side of his body.

A hundred yards farther on, Buck came upon one of the sled-dogs Thornton had bought in Dawson. This dog was thrashing about in a death-struggle, directly on the trail, and Buck passed around him without stopping. From the camp came the faint sound of many voices, rising and falling in a sing-song chant. Bellying forward to the edge of the clearing, he found Hans, lying on his face, feathered with arrows like a porcupine. At the same instant Buck peered out where the spruce-bough lodge had been and saw what made his hair leap straight up on his neck and shoulders. A gust of overpowering rage swept over him. He did not know that he growled, but he growled aloud with a terrible ferocity. For the last time in his life he allowed passion to usurp cunning and reason, and it was because of his great love for John Thornton that he lost his head.

The Yeehats were dancing about the wreckage of the spruce-bough lodge when they heard a fearful roaring and saw rushing upon them an animal the like of which they had never seen before. It was Buck, a live hurricane of fury, hurling himself upon them in a frenzy to destroy. He sprang at the foremost man (it was the chief of the Yeehats), ripping the throat wide open till the rent jugular spouted a fountain of blood. He did not pause to worry the victim, but ripped in passing, with the next bound tearing wide the throat of a second man. There was no withstanding him. He plunged about in their very midst, tearing, rending, destroying, in constant and terrific motion which defied the arrows they discharged at him. In fact, so inconceivably rapid were his movements, and so closely were the Indians tangled together, that they shot one another with the arrows; and one young hunter, hurling a spear at Buck in mid air, drove it through the chest of another hunter with such force that the point broke through the skin of the back and stood out beyond. Then a panic seized the Yeehats, and they fled in terror to the woods, proclaiming as they fled the advent of the Evil Spirit.

And truly Buck was the Fiend incarnate, raging at their heels and dragging them down like deer as they raced through the trees. It was a fateful day for the Yeehats. They scattered far and wide over the country, and it was not till a week later that the last of the survivors gathered together in a lower valley and counted their losses. As for Buck, wearying of the pursuit, he returned to the desolated camp. He found Pete where he had been killed in his blankets in the first moment of surprise. Thornton's desperate struggle was fresh-written on the earth, and Buck scented every detail of it down to the edge of a deep pool. By the edge, head and fore feet in the water, lay Skeet, faithful to the last. The pool itself, muddy and discolored from the sluice boxes, effectually hid what it contained, and it contained John Thornton; for Buck followed his trace into the water, from which no trace led away.

All day Buck brooded by the pool or roamed restlessly about the camp. Death, as a cessation of movement, as a passing out and away from the lives of the living, he knew, and he knew John Thornton was dead. It left a great void in him, somewhat akin to hunger, but a void which ached and ached, and which food could not fill. At times, when he paused to contemplate the carcasses of the Yeehats, he forgot the pain of it; and at such times he was aware of a great pride in himself, —a pride greater than any he had yet experienced. He had killed man, the noblest game of all, and he had killed in the face of the law of club and fang. He sniffed the bodies curiously. They had died so easily. It was harder to kill a husky dog than them. They were no match at all, were it not for their arrows and spears and clubs. Thenceforward he would be unafraid of them except when they bore in their hands their arrows, spears, and clubs.

Night came on, and a full moon rose high over the trees into the sky, lighting the land till it lay bathed in ghostly day. And with the coming of the night, brooding and mourning by the pool, Buck became alive to a stirring of the new life in the forest other than that which the Yeehats had made. He stood up, listening and scenting. From far away drifted a faint, sharp yelp, followed by a chorus of similar sharp yelps. As the moments passed the yelps grew closer and louder. Again Buck knew them as things heard in that other world which persisted in his memory. He walked to the centre of the open space and listened. It was the call, the many-noted call, sounding more luringly and compellingly than ever before. And as never before, he was ready to obey. John Thornton was dead. The last tie was broken. Man and the claims of man no longer bound him.

Hunting their living meat, as the Yeehats were hunting it, on the flanks of the migrating moose, the wolf pack had at last crossed over from the land of streams and timber and invaded Buck's valley. Into the clearing where the moonlight streamed, they poured in a silvery flood; and in the centre of the clearing stood Buck, motionless as a statue, waiting their coming. They were awed, so still and large he stood, and a moment's pause fell, till the boldest one leaped straight for him. Like a flash Buck struck, breaking the neck. Then he stood, without movement, as before, the stricken wolf rolling in agony behind him. Three others tried it in sharp succession; and one after the other they drew back, streaming blood from slashed throats or shoulders.

This was sufficient to fling the whole pack forward, pell-mell, crowded together, blocked and confused by its eagerness to pull down the prey. Buck's marvellous quickness and agility stood him in good stead. Pivoting on his hind legs, and snapping and gashing, he was everywhere at once, presenting a front which was apparently unbroken so swiftly did he whirl and guard from side to side. But to prevent them from getting behind him, he was forced back, down past the pool and into the creek bed, till he brought up against a high gravel bank. He worked along to a right angle in the bank which the men had made in the course of mining, and in this angle he came to bay, protected on three sides end with nothing to do but face the front.

And so well did he face it, that at the end of half an hour the wolves drew back discomfited. The tongues of all were out and lolling, the white fangs showing cruelly white in the moonlight. Some were lying down with heads raised and ears pricked forward; others stood on their feet, watching him; and still others were lapping water from the pool. One wolf, long and lean and gray, advanced cautiously, in a friendly manner, and Buck recognized the wild brother with whom he had run for a night and a day. He was whining softly, and, as Buck whined, they touched noses.

Then an old wolf, gaunt and battle-scarred, came forward. Buck writhed his lips into the preliminary of a snarl, but sniffed noses with him. Whereupon the old wolf sat down, pointed nose at the moon, and broke out the long wolf howl. The others sat down and howled. And now the call came to Buck in unmistakable accents. He, too, sat down and howled. This over, he came out of his angle and the pack crowded around him, sniffing in half-friendly, half-savage manner. The leaders lifted the yelp of the pack and sprang away into the woods. The wolves swung in behind, yelping in chorus. And Buck ran with them, side by side with the wild brother, yelping as he ran.

■

And here may well end the story of Buck. The years were not many when the Yeehats noted a change in the breed of timber wolves; for some were seen with splashes of brown on head and muzzle, and with a rift of white centring down the chest. But more remarkable than this, the Yeehats tell of a Ghost Dog that runs at the head of the pack. They are afraid of this Ghost Dog, for it has cunning greater than they, stealing from their camps in fierce winters, robbing their traps, slaying their dogs, and defying their bravest hunters.

Nay, the tale grows worse. Hunters there are who fail to return to the camp, and hunters there have been whom their tribesmen found with throats slashed cruelly open and with wolf prints about them in the snow greater than the prints of any wolf. Each fall, when the Yeehats follow the movement of the moose, there is a certain valley which they never enter. And women there are who become sad when the word goes over the fire of how the Evil Spirit came to select that valley for an abiding-place.

In the summers there is one visitor, however, to that valley, of which the Yeehats do not know. It is a great, gloriously coated wolf, like, and yet unlike, all other wolves. He crosses alone from the smiling timber land and comes down into an open space among the trees. Here a yellow stream flows from rotted moose-hide sacks and sinks into the ground, with long grasses growing through it and vegetable mould overrunning it and hiding its yellow from the sun; and here he muses for a time, howling once, long and mournfully, ere he departs.

But he is not always alone. When the long winter nights come on and the wolves follow their meat into the lower valleys, he may be seen running at the head of the pack through the pale moonlight or glimmering borealis, leaping gigantic above his fellows, his great throat a-bellow as he sings a song of the younger world, which is the song of the pack.

13

Stickeen

JOHN MUIR

In the summer of 1880 I set out from Fort Wrangel in a canoe to continue the exploration of the icy region of southeastern Alaska, begun in the fall of 1879. After the necessary provisions, blankets, etc., had been collected and stowed away, and my Indian crew were in their places ready to start, while a crowd of their relatives and friends on the wharf were bidding them good-by and good-luck, my companion, the Rev. S. H. Young, for whom we were waiting, at last came aboard, followed by a little black dog, that made himself at home by curling up in a hollow among the baggage. I like dogs, but this one seemed so small and worthless that I objected to his going, and asked the missionary why he was taking him.

"Such a little helpless creature will only be in the way," I said; "you had better pass him up to the Indian boys on the wharf, to be taken home to play with the children. This trip is not likely to be good for toy-dogs. The poor silly thing will be in rain and snow for weeks or months, and will require care like a baby."

But his master assured me that he would be no trouble at all; that he was a perfect wonder of a dog, could endure cold and hunger like a bear, swim like a seal, and was wondrous wise and cunning, etc., making out a list of virtues to show he might be the most interesting member of the party.

Nobody could hope to unravel the lines of his ancestry. In all the wonderfully mixed and varied dog-tribe I never saw any creature very much like him, though in some of his sly, soft, gliding motions and gestures he brought the fox to mind. He was short-legged and bunchy-bodied, and his hair, though smooth,

John Muir, *Stickeen* (Boston: Houghton Mifflin, 1909).

was long and silky and slightly waved, so that when the wind was at his back it ruffled, making him look shaggy. At first sight his only noticeable feature was his fine tail, which was about as airy and shady as a squirrel's, and was carried curling forward almost to his nose. On closer inspection you might notice his thin sensitive ears, and sharp eyes with cunning tan-spots above them. Mr. Young told me that when the little fellow was a pup about the size of a woodrat he was presented to his wife by an Irish prospector at Sitka, and that on his arrival at Fort Wrangel he was adopted with enthusiasm by the Stickeen Indians as a sort of new good-luck totem, was named "Stickeen" for the tribe, and became a universal favorite; petted, protected, and admired wherever he went, and regarded as a mysterious fountain of wisdom.

On our trip he soon proved himself a queer character—odd, concealed, independent, keeping invincibly quiet, and doing many little puzzling things that piqued my curiosity. As we sailed week after week through the long intricate channels and inlets among the innumerable islands and mountains of the coast, he spent most of the dull days in sluggish ease, motionless, and apparently as unobserving as if in deep sleep. But I discovered that somehow he always knew what was going on. When the Indians were about to shoot at ducks or seals, or when anything along the shore was exciting our attention, he would rest his chin on the edge of the canoe and calmly look out like a dreamy-eyed tourist. And when he heard us talking about making a landing, he immediately roused himself to see what sort of a place we were coming to, and made ready to jump overboard and swim ashore as soon as the canoe neared the beach. Then, with a vigorous shake to get rid of the brine in his hair, he ran into the woods to hunt small game. But though always the first out of the canoe, he was always the last to get into it. When we were ready to start he could never be found, and refused to come to our call. We soon found out, however, that though we could not see him at such times, he saw us, and from the cover of the briers and huckleberry bushes in the fringe of the woods was watching the canoe with wary eye. For as soon as we were fairly off he came trotting down the beach, plunged into the surf, and swam after us, knowing well that we would cease rowing and take him in. When the contrary little vagabond came alongside, he was lifted by the neck, held at arm's length a moment to drip, and dropped aboard. We tried to cure him of this trick by compelling him to swim a long way, as if we had a mind to abandon him; but this did no good: the longer the swim the better he seemed to like it.

Though capable of great idleness, he never failed to be ready for all sorts of adventures and excursions. One pitch-dark rainy night we landed about ten o'clock at the mouth of a salmon stream when the water was phosphorescent. The salmon were running, and the myriad fins of the onrushing multitude were churning all the stream into a silvery glow, wonderfully beautiful and impressive in the ebon darkness. To get a good view of the show I set out with one of the Indians and sailed up through the midst of it to the foot of a rapid about half a mile from camp, where the swift current dashing over rocks made the luminous glow most glorious. Happening to look back down the stream, while the Indian was catching a few of the struggling fish, I saw a long spreading fan of light like the tail of a comet, which we thought must be made by some big strange animal that was pursuing us. On it came with its magnificent train, until we imagined we could see the monster's head and eyes; but it was only Stickeen, who, finding I had left the camp, came swimming after me to see what was up.

When we camped early, the best hunter of the crew usually went to the woods for a deer, and Stickeen was sure to be at his heels, provided I had not gone out. For, strange to say, though I never carried a gun, he always followed me, forsaking the hunter and even his master to share my wanderings. The days that were too stormy for sailing I spent in the woods, or on the adjacent mountains, wherever my studies called me; and Stickeen always insisted on going with me, however wild the weather, gliding like a fox through dripping huckleberry bushes and thorny tangles of panax and rubus, scarce stirring their rain-laden leaves; wading and wallowing through snow, swimming icy streams, skipping over logs and rocks and the crevasses of glaciers with the patience and endurance of a determined mountaineer, never tiring or getting discouraged. Once he followed me over a glacier the surface of which was so crusty and rough that it cut his feet until every step was marked with blood; but he trotted on with Indian fortitude until I noticed his red track, and, taking pity on him, made him a set of moccasins out of a handkerchief. However great his troubles he never asked help or made any complaint, as if, like a philosopher, he had learned that without hard work and suffering there could be no pleasure worth having.

Yet none of us was able to make out what Stickeen was really good for. He seemed to meet danger and hardships without anything like reason, insisted on having his own way, never obeyed an order, and the hunter could never set him on anything, or make him fetch the birds he shot. His equanimity was so steady it seemed due to want of feeling; ordinary storms were pleasures to him, and as for mere rain, he flourished in it like a vegetable. No matter what advances you might make, scarce a glance or a tail-wag would you get for your pains. But though he was apparently as cold as a glacier and about as impervious to fun, I tried hard to make his acquaintance, guessing there must be something worth while hidden beneath so much courage, endurance, and love of wild-weathery adventure. No superannuated mastiff or bulldog grown old in office surpassed this fluffy midget in stoic dignity. He sometimes reminded me of a small, squat, unshakable desert cactus. For he never displayed a single trace of the merry, tricksy, elfish fun of the terriers and collies that we all know, nor of their touching affection and devotion. Like children, most small dogs beg to be loved and allowed to love; but Stickeen seemed a very Diogenes, asking only to be let alone: a true child of the wilderness, holding the even tenor of his hidden life with the silence and serenity of nature. His strength of character lay in his eyes. They looked as old as the hills, and as young, and as wild. I never tired of looking into them: it was like looking into a landscape; but they were small and rather deep-set, and had no explaining lines around them to give out particulars. I was accustomed to look into the faces of plants and animals, and I watched the little sphinx more and more keenly as an interesting study. But there is no estimating the wit and wisdom concealed and latent in our lower fellow mortals until made manifest by profound experiences; for it is through suffering that dogs as well as saints are developed and made perfect.

After we had explored the Sundum and Tahkoo fiords and their glaciers, we sailed through Stephen's Passage into Lynn Canal and thence through Icy Strait into Cross Sound, searching for unexplored inlets leading toward the great fountain ice-fields of the Fairweather Range. Here, while the tide was in our favor, we were accompanied by a fleet of icebergs drifting out to the ocean from Glacier Bay. Slowly we paddled around Vancouver's Point, Wimbleton, our frail canoe tossed like a feather on the massive heaving swells coming in past Cape Spenser. For miles the sound is bounded by precipitous mural cliffs, which, lashed with wave-spray and their heads hidden in clouds, looked terribly threatening and stern. Had our canoe been crushed or upset we could have made no landing here, for the cliffs, as high as those of Yosemite, sink sheer into deep water. Eagerly we scanned the wall on the north side for the first sign of an opening fiord or harbor, all of us anxious except Stickeen, who dozed in peace or gazed dreamily at the tremendous precipices when he heard us talking about them. At length we made the joyful discovery of the mouth of the inlet now called "Taylor Bay," and about five o'clock reached the head of it and encamped in a spruce grove near the front of a large glacier.

While camp was being made, Joe the hunter climbed the mountain wall on the east side of the fiord in pursuit of wild goats, while Mr. Young and I went to the glacier. We found that it is separated from the waters of the inlet by a tide-washed moraine, and extends, an abrupt barrier, all the way across from wall to wall of the inlet, a distance of about three miles. But our most interesting discovery was that it had recently advanced, though again slightly receding. A portion of the terminal moraine had been plowed up and shoved forward, uprooting and overwhelming the woods on the east side. Many of the trees were down and buried, or nearly so, others were leaning away from the ice-cliffs, ready to fall, and some stood erect, with the bottom of the ice-plow still beneath their roots and its lofty crystal spires towering high above their tops. The spectacle presented by these century-old trees standing close beside a spiry wall of ice, with their branches almost touching it, was most novel and striking. And when I climbed around the front, and a little way up the west side of the glacier, I found that it had swelled and increased in height and width in accordance with its advance, and carried away the outer ranks of trees on its bank.

On our way back to camp after these first observations I planned a far-and-wide excursion for the morrow. I awoke early, called not only by the glacier, which had been on my mind all night, but by a grand flood-storm. The wind was blowing a gale from the north and the rain was flying with the clouds in a wide passionate horizontal flood, as if it were all passing over the country instead of falling on it. The main perennial streams were booming high above their banks, and hundreds of new ones, roaring like the sea, almost covered the lofty gray walls of the inlet with white cascades and falls. I had intended making a cup of coffee and getting something like a breakfast before starting, but when I heard the storm and looked out I made haste to join it; for many of Nature's finest lessons are to be found in her storms, and if careful to keep in right relations with them, we may go safely abroad with them, rejoicing in the grandeur and beauty of their works and ways, and chanting with the old Norsemen, "The blast of the tempest aids our oars, the hurricane is our servant and drives us whither we wish to go." So, omitting breakfast, I put a piece of bread in my pocket and hurried away.

Mr. Young and the Indians were asleep, and so, I hoped, was Stickeen; but I had not gone a dozen rods before he left his bed in the tent and came boring through the blast after me. That a man should welcome storms for their exhilarating music and motion, and go forth to see God making landscapes, is reasonable enough; but what fascination could there be in such tremendous weather for a dog? Surely nothing akin to human enthusiasm for scenery or geology. Anyhow, on he came, breakfastless, through the choking blast. I stopped and did my best to turn him back. "Now don't," I said, shouting to make myself heard in the storm, "now don't, Stickeen. What has got into your queer noddle now? You must be daft. This wild day has nothing for you. There is no game abroad, nothing but weather. Go back to camp and keep warm, get a good breakfast with your master, and be sensible for once. I can't carry you all day or feed you, and this storm will kill you."

But Nature, it seems, was at the bottom of the affair, and she gains her ends with dogs as well as with men, making us do as she likes, shoving and pulling us along her ways, however rough, all but killing us at times in getting her lessons driven hard home. After I had stopped again and again, shouting good warning advice, I saw that he was not to be shaken off; as well might the earth try to shake off the moon. I had once led his master into trouble, when he fell on one of the topmost jags of a mountain and dislocated his arm; now the turn of his humble companion was coming. The pitiful little wanderer just stood there in the wind, drenched and blinking, saying doggedly, "Where thou goest I will go." So at last I told him to come on if he must, and gave him a piece of the bread I had in my pocket; then we struggled on together, and thus began the most memorable of all my wild days.

The level flood, driving hard in our faces, thrashed and washed us wildly until we got into the shelter of a grove on the east side of the glacier near the front, where we stopped awhile for breath and to listen and look out. The exploration of the glacier was my main object, but the wind was too high to allow excursions over its open surface, where one might be dangerously shoved while balancing for a jump on the brink of a crevasse. In the mean time the storm was a fine study. Here the end of the glacier, descending an abrupt swell of resisting rock about five hundred feet high, leans forward and falls in ice cascades. And as the storm came down the glacier from the North, Stickeen and I were beneath the main current of the blast, while favorably located to see and hear it. What a psalm the storm was singing, and how fresh the smell of the washed earth and leaves, and how sweet the still small voices of the storm! Detached wafts and swirls were coming through the woods, with music from the leaves and branches and furrowed boles, and even from the splintered rocks and ice-crags overhead, many of the tones soft and low and flute-like, as if each leaf and tree, crag and spire were a tuned reed. A broad torrent, draining the side of the glacier, now swollen by scores of new streams from the mountains, was rolling boulders along its rocky channel, with thudding, bumping, muffled sounds, rushing towards the bay with tremendous energy, as if in haste to get out of the mountains; the waters above and beneath calling to each other, and all to the ocean, their home.

Looking southward from our shelter, we had this great torrent and the forested mountain wall above it on our left, the spiry ice-crags on our right, and smooth gray gloom ahead. I tried to draw the marvelous scene in my note-book, but the rain blurred the page in spite of all my pains to shelter it, and the sketch was almost worthless. When the wind began to abate, I traced the east side of the glacier. All the trees standing on the edge of the woods were barked and bruised, showing high-ice mark in a very telling way, while tens of thousands of those that had stood for centuries on the bank of the glacier farther out lay crushed and being crushed. In many places I could see down fifty feet or so beneath the margin of the glacier-mill, where trunks from one to two feet in diameter were being ground to pulp against outstanding rock-ribs and bosses of the bank.

About three miles above the front of the glacier I climbed to the surface of it by means of axe-steps made easy for Stickeen. As far as the eye could reach, the level, or nearly level, glacier stretched away indefinitely beneath the gray sky, a seemingly boundless prairie of ice. The rain continued, and grew colder, which I did not mind, but a dim snowy look in the drooping clouds made me hesitate about venturing far from land. No trace of the west shore was visible, and in case the clouds should settle and give snow, or the wind again become violent, I feared getting caught in a tangle of crevasses. Snow-crystals, the flowers of the mountain clouds, are frail, beautiful things, but terrible when flying on storm-winds in darkening, benumbing swarms, or, when welded together into glaciers full of deadly crevasses. Watching the weather, I sauntered about on the crystal sea. For a mile or two out I found the ice remarkably safe. The marginal crevasses were mostly narrow, while the few wider ones were easily avoided by passing around them, and the clouds began to open here and there.

Thus encouraged, I at last pushed out for the other side; for Nature can make us do anything she likes. At first we made rapid progress, and the sky was not very threatening, while I took bearings occasionally with a pocket compass to enable me to find my way back more surely in case the storm should become blinding; but the structure lines of the glacier were my main guide. Toward the west side we came to a closely crevassed section in which we had to make long, narrow tacks and doublings, tracing the edges of tremendous transverse and longitudinal crevasses, many of which were from twenty to thirty feet wide, and perhaps a thousand feet deep—beautiful and awful. In working a way through them I was severely cautious, but Stickeen came on as unhesitating as the flying clouds. The widest crevasse that I could jump he would leap without so much as halting to take a look at it. The weather was now making quick changes, scattering bits of dazzling brightness through the wintry gloom; at rare intervals, when the sun broke forth wholly free, the glacier was seen from shore to shore with a bright array of encompassing mountains partly revealed, wearing the clouds as garments, while the prairie bloomed and sparkled with irised light from myriads of washed crystals. Then suddenly all the glorious show would be darkened and blotted out.

Stickeen seemed to care for none of these things, bright or dark, nor for the crevasses, wells, moulins, or swift flashing streams into which he might fall. The little adventurer was only about two years old, yet nothing seemed novel to him, nothing daunted him. He showed neither caution nor curiosity, wonder nor fear, but bravely trotted on as if glaciers were playgrounds. His stout, muffled body seemed all one skipping muscle, and it was truly wonderful to see how swiftly and to all appearance heedlessly he flashed across nerve-trying chasms six or eight feet wide. His courage was so unwavering that it seemed to be due to dullness of perception, as if he were only blindly bold; and I kept warning him to be careful. For we had been close companions on so many wilderness trips that I had formed the habit of talking to him as if he were a boy and understood every word.

We gained the west shore in about three hours; the width of the glacier here being about seven miles. Then I pushed northward in order to see as far back as possible into the fountains of the Fairweather Mountains, in case the clouds should rise. The walking was easy along the margin of the forest, which, of course, like that on the other side, had been invaded and crushed by the swollen, overflowing glacier. In an hour or so, after passing a massive headland, we came suddenly on a branch of the glacier, which, in the form of a magnificent ice-cascade two miles wide, was pouring over the rim of the main basin in a westerly direction, its surface broken into wave-shaped blades and shattered blocks, suggesting the wildest updashing, heaving, plunging motion of a great river cataract. Tracing it down three or four miles, I found that it discharged into a lake, filling it with icebergs.

I would gladly have followed the lake outlet to tide-water, but the day was already far spent, and the threatening sky called for haste on the return trip to get off the ice before dark. I decided therefore to go no farther, and, after taking a general view of the wonderful region, turned back, hoping to see it again under more favorable auspices. We made good speed up the cañon of the great ice-torrent, and out on the main glacier until we had left the west shore about two miles behind us. Here we got into a difficult network of crevasses, the gathering clouds began to drop misty fringes, and soon the dreaded snow came flying thick and fast. I now began to feel anxious about finding a way in the blurring storm. Stickeen showed no trace of fear. He was still the same silent, able little hero. I noticed, however, that after the storm-darkness came on he kept close up behind me. The snow urged us to make still greater haste, but at the same time hid our way. I pushed on as best I could, jumping innumerable crevasses, and for every hundred rods or so of direct advance traveling a mile in doubling up and down in the turmoil of chasms and dislocated ice-blocks. After an hour or two of this work we came to a series of longitudinal crevasses of appalling width, and almost straight and regular in trend, like immense furrows. These I traced with firm nerve, excited and strengthened by the danger, making wide jumps, poising cautiously on their dizzy edges after cutting hollows for my feet before making the spring, to avoid possible slipping or any uncertainty on the farther sides, where only one trial is granted—exercise at once frightful and inspiring. Stickeen followed seemingly without effort.

Many a mile we thus traveled, mostly up and down, making but little real headway in crossing, running instead of walking most of the time as the danger of being compelled to spend the night on the glacier became threatening. Stickeen seemed able for anything. Doubtless we could have weathered the storm for one night, dancing on a flat spot to keep from freezing, and I faced the threat without feeling anything like despair; but we were hungry and wet, and the wind from the mountains was still thick with snow and bitterly cold, so of course that night would have seemed a very long one. I could not see far enough through the blurring snow to judge in which general direction the least dangerous route lay, while the few dim, momentary glimpses I caught of mountains through rifts in the flying clouds were far from encouraging either as weather signs or as guides. I had simply to grope my way from crevasse to crevasse, holding a general direction by the ice-structure, which was not to be seen everywhere, and partly by the wind. Again and again I was put to my mettle, but Stickeen followed easily, his nerve apparently growing more unflinching as the danger increased. So it always is with mountaineers when hard beset. Running hard and jumping, holding every minute of the remaining daylight, poor as it was, precious, we doggedly persevered and tried to hope that every difficult crevasse we overcame would prove to be the last of its kind. But on the contrary, as we advanced they became more deadly trying.

At length our way was barred by a very wide and straight crevasse, which I traced rapidly northward a mile or so without finding a crossing or hope of one; then down the glacier about as far, to where it united with another uncrossable crevasse. In all this distance of perhaps two miles there was only one place where I could possibly jump it, but the width of this jump was the utmost I dared attempt, while the danger of slipping on the farther side was so great that I was loath to try it. Furthermore, the side I was on was about a foot higher than the other, and even with this advantage the crevasse seemed dangerously wide. One is liable to underestimate the width of crevasses where the magnitudes in general are great. I therefore stared at this one mighty keenly, estimating its width and the shape of the edge on the farther side, until I thought that I could jump it if necessary, but that in case I should be compelled to jump back from the lower side I might fail. Now, a cautious mountaineer seldom takes a step on unknown ground which seems at all dangerous that he cannot retrace in case he should be stopped by unseen obstacles ahead. This is the rule of mountaineers who live long, and, though in haste, I compelled myself to sit down and calmly deliberate before I broke it.

Retracing my devious path in imagination as if it were drawn on a chart, I saw that I was redressing the glacier a mile or two farther up stream than the course pursued in the morning, and that I was now entangled in a section I had not before seen. Should I risk this dangerous jump, or try to regain the woods on the west shore, make a fire, and have only hunger to endure while waiting for a new day? I had already crossed so broad a stretch of dangerous ice that I saw it would be difficult to get back to the woods through the storm, before dark, and the attempt would most likely result in a dismal night-dance on the glacier; while just beyond the present barrier the surface seemed more promising, and the east shore was now perhaps about as near as the west. I was therefore eager to go on. But this wide jump was a dreadful obstacle.

At length, because of the dangers already behind me, I determined to venture against those that might be ahead, jumped and landed well, but with so little to spare that I more than ever dreaded being compelled to that jump back from the lower side. Stickeen followed, making nothing of it, and we ran eagerly forward, hoping we were leaving all our troubles behind. But within the distance of a few hundred yards we were stopped by the widest crevasse yet encountered. Of course I made haste to explore it, I hoping all might yet be remedied by finding a bridge or a way around either end. About three-fourths of a mile upstream I found that it united with the one we had just crossed, as I feared it would. Then, tracing it down, I found it joined the same crevasse at the lower end also, maintaining throughout its whole course a width of forty to fifty feet. Thus to my dismay I discovered that we were on a narrow island about two miles long, with two barely possible ways of escape: one back by the way we came, the other ahead by an almost inaccessible sliver-bridge that crossed the great crevasse from near the middle of it!

After this nerve-trying discovery I ran back to the sliver-bridge and cautiously examined it. Crevasses, caused by strains from variations in the rate of motion of different parts of the glacier and convexities in the channel, are mere cracks when they first open, so narrow as hardly to admit the blade of a pocket-knife, and gradually widen according to the extent of the strain and the depth of the glacier. Now some of these cracks are interrupted, like the cracks in wood, and in opening, the strip of ice between overlapping ends is dragged out, and may maintain a continuous connection between the sides, just as the two sides of a slivered crack in wood that is being split are connected. Some crevasses remain open for months or even years, and by the melting of their sides continue to increase in width long after the opening strain has ceased; while the sliver-bridges, level on top at first and perfectly safe, are at length melted to thin, vertical, knife-edged blades, the upper portion being most exposed to the weather; and since the exposure is greatest in the middle, they at length curve downward like the cables of suspension bridges. This one was evidently very old, for it had been weathered and wasted until it was the most dangerous and inaccessible that ever lay in my way. The width of the crevasse was here about fifty feet, and the sliver crossing diagonally was about seventy feet long; its thin knife-edge near the middle was depressed twenty-five or thirty feet below the level of the glacier, and the upcurving ends were attached to the sides eight or ten feet below the brink. Getting down the nearly vertical wall to the end of the sliver and up the other side were the main difficulties, and they seemed all but insurmountable. Of the many perils encountered in my years of wandering on mountains and glaciers none seemed so plain and stern and merciless as this. And it was presented when we were wet to the skin and hungry, the sky dark with quick driving snow, and the night near. But we were forced to face it. It was a tremendous necessity.

Beginning, not immediately above the sunken end of the bridge, but a little to one side, I cut a deep hollow on the brink for my knees to rest in. Then, leaning over, with my short-handled axe I cut a step sixteen or eighteen inches below, which on account of the sheerness of the wall was necessarily shallow. That step, however, was well made; its floor sloped slightly inward and formed a good hold for my heels. Then, slipping cautiously upon it, and crouching as low as possible, with my left side toward the wall, I steadied myself against the wind with my left hand in a slight notch, while with the right I cut other similar steps and notches in succession, guarding against losing balance by glinting of the axe, or by wind-gusts, for life and death were in every stroke and in the niceness of finish of every foothold.

After the end of the bridge was reached I chipped it down until I had made a level platform six or eight inches wide, and it was a trying thing to poise on this little slippery platform while bending over to get safely astride of the sliver. Crossing was then comparatively easy by chipping off the sharp edge with short, careful strokes, and hitching forward an inch or two at a time, keeping my balance with my knees pressed against the sides. The tremendous abyss on either hand I studiously ignored. To me the edge of that blue sliver was then all the world. But the most trying part of the adventure, after working my way across inch by inch and chipping another small platform, was to rise from the safe position astride and to cut a step-ladder in the nearly vertical face of the wall, —chipping, climbing, holding on with feet and fingers in mere notches. At such times one's whole body is eye, and common skill and fortitude are replaced by power beyond our call or knowledge. Never before had I been so long under deadly strain. How I got up that cliff I never could tell. The thing seemed to have been done by somebody else. I never have held death in contempt, though in the course of my explorations I have oftentimes felt that to meet one's fate on a noble mountain, or in the heart of a glacier, would be blessed as compared with death from disease, or from some shabby lowland accident. But the best death, quick and crystal-pure, set so glaringly open before us, is hard enough to face, even though we feel gratefully sure that we have already had happiness enough for a dozen lives.

But poor Stickeen, the wee, hairy, sleekit beastie, think of him! When I had decided to dare the bridge, and while I was on my knees chipping a hollow on the rounded brow above it, he came behind me, pushed his head past my shoulder, looked down and across, scanned the sliver and its approaches with his mysterious eyes, then looked me in the face with a startled air of surprise and concern, and began to mutter and whine; saying as plainly as if speaking with words, "Surely, you are not going into that awful place." This was the first time I had seen him gaze deliberately into a crevasse, or into my face with an eager, speaking, troubled look. That he should have recognized and appreciated the danger at the first glance showed wonderful sagacity. Never before had the daring midget seemed to know that ice was slippery or that there was any such thing as danger anywhere. His looks and tones of voice when he began to complain and speak his fears were so human that I unconsciously talked to him in sympathy as I would to a frightened boy, and in trying to calm his fears perhaps in some measure moderated my own. "Hush your fears, my boy," I said, "we will get across safe, though it is not going to be easy. No right way is easy in this rough world. We must risk our lives to save them. At the worst we can only slip, and then how grand a grave we will have, and by and by our nice bones will do good in the terminal moraine."

But my sermon was far from reassuring him: he began to cry, and after taking another piercing look at the tremendous gulf, ran away in desperate excitement, seeking some other crossing. By the time he got back, baffled of course, I had made a step or two. I dared not look back, but he made himself heard; and when he saw that I was certainly bent on crossing he cried aloud in despair. The danger was enough to daunt anybody, but it seems wonderful that he should have been able to weigh and appreciate it so justly. No mountaineer could have seen it more quickly or judged it more wisely, discriminating between real and apparent peril.

When I gained the other side, he screamed louder than ever, and after running back and forth in vain search for a way of escape, he would return to the brink of the crevasse above the bridge, moaning and wailing as if in the bitterness of death. Could this be the silent, philosophic Stickeen? I shouted encouragement, telling him the bridge was not so bad as it looked, that I had left it flat and safe for his feet, and he could walk it easily. But he was afraid to try. Strange so small an animal should be capable of such big, wise fears. I called again and again in a reassuring tone to come on and fear nothing; that he could come if he would only try. He would hush for a moment, look down again at the bridge, and shout his unshakable conviction that he could never, never come that way; then lie back in despair, as if howling, "O-o-oh! what a place! No-o-o, I can never go-o-o down there!" His natural composure and courage had vanished utterly in a tumultuous storm of fear. Had the danger been less, his distress would have seemed ridiculous. But in this dismal, merciless abyss lay the shadow of death, and his heartrending cries might well have called Heaven to his help. Perhaps they did. So hidden before, he was now transparent, and one could see the workings of his heart and mind like the movements of a clock out of its case. His voice and gestures, hopes and fears, were so perfectly human that none could mistake them; while he seemed to understand every word of mine. I was troubled at the thought of having to leave him out all night, and of the danger of not finding him in the morning. It seemed impossible to get him to venture. To compel him to try through fear of being abandoned, I started off as if leaving him to his fate, and disappeared back of a hummock; but this did no good; he only lay down and moaned in utter hopeless misery. So, after hiding a few minutes, I went back to the brink of the crevasse and in a severe tone of voice shouted across to him that now I must certainly leave him, I could wait no longer, and that, if he would not come, all I could promise was that I would return to seek him next day. I warned him that if he went back to the woods the wolves would kill him, and finished by urging him once more by words and gestures to come on, come on.

He knew very well what I meant, and at last, with the courage of despair, hushed and breathless, he crouched down on the brink in the hollow I had made for my knees, pressed his body against the ice as if trying to get the advantage of the friction of every hair, gazed into the first step, put his little feet together and slid them slowly, slowly over the edge and down into it, bunching all four in it and almost standing on his head. Then, without lifting his feet, as well as I could see through the snow, he slowly worked them over the edge of the step and down into the next and the next in succession in the same way, and gained the end of the bridge. Then, lifting his feet with the regularity and slowness of the vibrations of a seconds pendulum, as if counting and measuring *one-two-three,* holding himself steady against the gusty wind, and giving separate attention to each little step, he gained the foot of the cliff, while I was on my knees leaning over to give him a lift should he succeed in getting within reach of my arm. Here he halted in dead silence, and it was here I feared he might fail, for dogs are poor climbers. I had no cord. If I had had one, I would have dropped a noose over his head and hauled him up. But while I was thinking whether an available cord might be made out of clothing, he was looking keenly into the series of notched steps and finger-holds I had made, as if counting them, and fixing the position of each one of them in his mind. Then suddenly up he came in a springy rush, hooking his paws into the steps and notches so quickly that I could not see how it was done, and whizzed past my head, safe at last!

And now came a scene! "Well done, well done, little boy! Brave boy!" I cried, trying to catch and caress him; but he would not be caught. Never before or since have I seen anything like so passionate a revulsion from the depths of despair to exultant, triumphant, uncontrollable joy. He flashed and darted hither and thither as if fairly demented, screaming and shouting, swirling round and round in giddy loops and circles like a leaf in a whirlwind, lying down, and rolling over and over, sidewise and heels over head, and pouring forth a tumultuous flood of hysterical cries and sobs and gasping mutterings. When I ran up to him to shake him, fearing he might die of joy, he flashed off two or three hundred yards, his feet in a mist of motion; then, turning suddenly, came back in a wild rush end launched himself at my face, almost knocking me down, all the time screeching and screaming and shouting as if saying, "Saved! saved! saved!" Then away again, dropping suddenly at times with his feet in the air, trembling and fairly sobbing. Such passionate emotion was enough to kill him. Moses' stately song of triumph after escaping the Egyptians and the Red Sea was nothing to it. Who could have guessed the capacity of the dull, enduring little fellow for all that most stirs this mortal frame? Nobody could have helped crying with him!

But there is nothing like work for toning down excessive fear or joy. So I ran ahead, calling him in as gruff a voice as I could command to come on and stop his nonsense, for we had far to go and it would soon be dark. Neither of us feared another trial like this. Heaven would surely count one enough for a lifetime. The ice ahead was gashed by thousands of crevasses, but they were common ones. The joy of deliverance burned in us like fire, and we ran without fatigue, every muscle with immense rebound glorying in its strength. Stickeen flew across everything in his way, and not till dark did he settle into his normal fox-like trot. At last the cloudy mountains came in sight, and we soon felt the solid rock beneath our feet, and were safe. Then came weakness. Danger had vanished, and so had our strength. We tottered down the lateral moraine in the dark, over boulders and tree trunks, through the bushes and devil-club thickets of the grove where we had sheltered ourselves in the morning, and across the level mud-slope of the terminal moraine. We reached camp about ten o'clock, and found a big fire and a big supper. A party of Hoona Indians had visited Mr. Young, bringing a gift of porpoise meat and wild strawberries, and Hunter Joe had brought in a wild goat. But we lay down, too tired to eat much, and soon fell into a troubled sleep. The man who said, "The harder the toil, the sweeter the rest," never was profoundly tired. Stickeen kept springing up and muttering in his sleep, no doubt dreaming that he was still on the brink of the crevasse; and so did I, that night and many others long afterward, when I was overtired.

Thereafter Stickeen was a changed dog. During the rest of the trip, instead of holding aloof, he always lay by my side, tried to keep me constantly in sight, and would hardly accept a morsel of food, however tempting, from any hand but mine. At night, when all was quiet about the campfire, he would come to me and rest his head on my knee with a look of devotion as if I were his god. And often as he caught my eye he seemed to be trying to say, "Was n't that an awful time we had together on the glacier?"

■

Nothing in after years has dimmed that Alaska storm-day. As I write it all comes rushing and roaring to mind as if I were again in the heart of it. Again I see the gray flying clouds with their rain-floods and snow, the ice-cliffs towering above the shrinking forest, the majestic ice-cascade, the vast glacier outspread before its white mountain fountains, and in the heart of it the tremendous crevasse, —emblem of the valley of the shadow of death, —low clouds trailing over it, the snow falling into it; and on its brink I see little Stickeen, and I hear his cries for help and his shouts of joy. I have known many dogs, and many a story I could tell of their wisdom and devotion; but to none do I owe so much as to Stickeen. At first the least promising and least known of my dog-friends, he suddenly became the best known of them all. Our storm-battle for life brought him to light, and through him as through a window I have ever since been looking for deeper sympathy into all my fellow mortals.

None of Stickeen's friends knows what finally became of him. After my work for the season was done I departed for California, and I never saw the dear little fellow again. In reply to anxious inquiries his master wrote me that in the summer of 1883 he was stolen by a tourist at Fort Wrangel and taken away on a steamer. His fate is wrapped in mystery. Doubtless he has left this world— crossed the last crevasse—and gone to another. But he will not be forgotten. To me Stickeen is immortal.

14

Journey to the Sea

RACHEL L. CARSON

There is a pond that lies under a hill, where the threading roots of many trees—mountain ash, hickory, chestnut oak, and hemlock—hold the rains in a deep sponge of humus. The pond is fed by two streams that carry the runoff of higher ground to the west, coming down over rocky beds grooved in the hill. Cattails, bur reeds, spike rushes, and pickerel weeds stand rooted in the soft mud around its shores and, on the side under the hill, wade out halfway into its waters. Willows grow in the wet ground along the eastern shore of the pond, where the overflow seeps down a grass-lined spillway, seeking its passage to the sea.

The smooth surface of the pond is often ringed by spreading ripples made when shiners, dace, or other minnows push against the tough sheet between air and water, and the film is dimpled, too, by the hurrying feet of small water insects that live among the reeds and rushes. The pond is called Bittern Pond, because never a spring passes without a few of these shy herons nesting in its bordering reeds, and the strange, pumping cries of the birds that stand and sway in the cattails, hidden in the blend of lights and shadows, are thought by some who hear them to be the voice of an unseen spirit of the pond.

From Bittern Pond to the sea is two hundred miles as a fish swims. Thirty miles of the way is by narrow hill streams, seventy miles by a sluggish river crawling over the coastal plain, and a hundred miles through the brackish water

"Journey to the Sea" by Rachel L. Carson, from *Under the Sea-Wind* by Rachel L. Carson. Copyright 1941 by Rachel L. Carson. Copyright renewed © 1969 by Roger Christie. A Truman Talley Book. Used by permission of Dutton Signet, a division of Penguin Books USA Inc., and Frances Collin, Trustee.

of a shallow bay where the sea came in, millions of years ago, and drowned the estuary of a river.

Every spring a number of small creatures come up the grassy spillway and enter Bittern Pond, having made the two-hundred-mile journey from the sea. They are curiously formed, like pieces of slender glass rods shorter than a man's finger. They are young eels, or elvers, that were born in the deep sea. Some of the eels go higher into the hills, but a few remain in the pond, where they live on crayfish and water beetles and catch frogs and small fishes and grow to adulthood.

Now it was autumn and the end of the year. From the moon's quarter to its half, rains had fallen, and all the hill streams ran in flood. The water of the two feeder streams of the pond was deep and swift and jostled the rocks of the stream beds as it hurried to the sea. The pond was deeply stirred by the inrush of water, which swept through its weed forests and swirled through its crayfish holes and crept up six inches on the trunks of its bordering willows.

The wind had sprung up at dusk. At first it had been a gentle breeze, stroking the surface of the pond to velvet smoothness. At midnight it had grown to a half gale that set all the rushes to swaying wildly and rattled the dead seed heads of the weeds and plowed deep furrows in the surface waters of the pond. The wind roared down from the hills, over forests of oak and beech and hickory and pine. It blew toward the east, toward the sea two hundred miles away.

Anguilla, the eel, nosed into the swift water that raced toward the overflow from the pond. With her keen senses she savored the strange tastes and smells in the water. They were the bitter tastes and smells of dead and rain-soaked autumn leaves, the tastes of forest moss and lichen and root-held humus. Such was the water that hurried past the eel, on its way to the sea.

Anguilla had entered Bittern Pond as a finger-long elver ten years before. She had lived in the pond through its summers and autumns and winters and springs, hiding in its weed beds by day and prowling through its waters by night, for like all eels she was a lover of darkness. She knew every crayfish burrow that ran in honeycombing furrows through the mudbank under the hill. She knew her way among the swaying, rubbery stems of spatterdock, where frogs sat on the thick leaves; and she knew where to find the spring peepers clinging to grass blades, bubbling shrilly, where in spring the pond overflowed its grassy northern shore. She could find the banks where the water rats ran and squeaked in play or tusseled in anger, so that sometimes they fell with a splash into the water—easy prey for a lurking eel. She knew the soft mud beds deep in the bottom of the pond, where in winter she could lie buried, secure against the cold—for like all eels she was a lover of warmth.

Now it was autumn again, and the water was chilling to the cold rains shed off the hard backbones of the hills. A strange restiveness was growing in Anguilla the eel. For the first time in her adult life, the food hunger was forgotten. In its place was a strange, new hunger, formless and ill-defined. Its dimly perceived object was a place of warmth and darkness—darker than the blackest night over Bittern Pond. She had known such a place once—in the dim beginnings of life, before memory began. She could not know that the way to it lay beyond the pond outlet over which she had clambered ten years before. But many times that night, as the wind and the rain tore at the surface film of the pond, Anguilla was drawn irresistibly toward the outlet over which the water was spilling on its journey to the sea. When the cocks were crowing in the farmyard over the hill, saluting the third hour of the new day, Anguilla slipped into the channel spilling down to the stream below and followed the moving water.

Even in flood, the hill stream was shallow, and its voice was the noisy voice of a young stream, full of gurglings and tricklings and the sound of water striking stone and of stone rubbing against stone. Anguilla followed the stream, feeling her way by the changing pressure of the swift water currents. She was a creature of night and darkness, and so the black water path neither confused nor frightened her.

In five miles the stream dropped a hundred feet over a rough and boulder-strewn bed. At the end of the fifth mile it slipped between two hills, following along a deep gap made by another and larger stream years before. The hills were clothed with oak and beech and hickory, and the stream ran under their interlacing branches.

At daybreak Anguilla came to a bright, shallow riffle where the stream chattered sharply over gravel and small rubble. The water moved with a sudden acceleration, draining swiftly toward the brink of a ten-foot fall where it spilled over a sheer rock face into a basin below. The rush of water carried Anguilla with it, down the steep, thin slant of white water and into the pool. The basin was deep and still and cool, having been rounded out of the rock by centuries of falling water. Dark water mosses grew on its sides and stoneworts were rooted in its silt, thriving on the lime which they took from the stones and incorporated in their round, brittle stems. Anguilla hid among the stoneworts of the pool, seeking a shelter from light and sun, for now the bright shallows of the stream repelled her.

Before she had lain in the pool for an hour another eel came over the falls and sought the darkness of the deep leaf beds. The second eel had come from higher up in the hills, and her body was lacerated in many places from the rocks of the thin upland streams she had descended. The newcomer was a larger and more powerful eel than Anguilla, for she had spent two more years in fresh water before coming to maturity.

Anguilla, who had been the largest eel in Bittern Pond for more than a year, dived down through the stoneworts at sight of the strange eel. Her passage swayed the stiff, limy stems of the chara and disturbed three water boatmen that were clinging to the chara stems, each holding its position by the grip of a jointed leg, set with rows of bristles. The insects were browsing on the film of desmids and diatoms that coated the stems of the stoneworts. The boatmen were clothed in glistening blankets of air which they had carried down with them when they dived through the surface film, and when the passing of the eel dislodged them from their quiet anchorage they rose like air bubbles, for they were lighter than water.

An insect with a body like a fragment of twig supported by six jointed legs was walking over the floating leaves and skating on the surface of the water, on which it moved as on strong silk. Its feet depressed the film into six dimples, but did not break it, so light was its body. The insect's name meant "a marsh treader," for its kind often lived in the deep sphagnum moss of bogs. The marsh treader was foraging, watching for creatures like mosquito larvae or small crustaceans to move up to the surface from the pool below. When one of the water boatmen suddenly broke through the film at the feet of the marsh treader, the twiglike insect speared it with the sharp stilettos projecting beyond its mouth and sucked the little body dry.

When Anguilla felt the strange eel pushing into the thick mat of dead leaves on the floor of the pool, she moved back into the dark recess behind the waterfall. Above her the steep face of the rock was green with the soft fronds of mosses that grew where their leaves escaped the flow of water, yet were always wet with fine spray from the falls. In spring the midges came there to lay their eggs, spinning them in thin, white skeins on the wet rocks. Later when the eggs hatched and the gauzy-winged insects began to emerge from the falls in swarms, they were watched for by bright-eyed little birds who sat on overhanging branches and darted open-mouthed into the clouds of midges. Now the midges were gone, but other small animals lived in the green, water-soaked thickets of the moss. They were the larvae of beetles and soldier flies and crane flies. They were smooth-bodied creatures, lacking the grappling hooks and suckers and the flattened, stream-molded bodies that enabled their relatives to live in the swift currents draining to the brink of the falls overhead or a dozen feet away where the pool spilled its water into the stream bed. Although they lived only a few inches from the veil of water that dropped sheer to the pool, they knew nothing of swift water and its dangers; their peaceful world was of water seeping slow through green forests of moss.

The beginning of the great leaf fall had come with the rains of the past fortnight. Throughout the day, from the roof of the forest to its floor, there was a continuous downdrift of leaves. The leaves fell so silently that the rustle of their settling to the ground was no louder than the thin scratching of the feet of mice and moles moving through their passages in the leaf mold.

All day flights of broad-winged hawks passed down along the ridges of the hills, going south. They moved with scarcely a beat of their outspread wings, for they were riding on the updrafts of air made as the west wind struck the hills and leaped upward to pass over them. The hawks were fall migrants from

Canada that had followed down along the Appalachians for the sake of the air currents that made the flight easier.

At dusk, as the owls began to hoot in the woods, Anguilla left the pool and traveled downstream alone. Soon the stream flowed through rolling farm country. Twice during the night it dropped over small milldams that were white in the thin moonlight. In the stretch below the second dam, Anguilla lay for a time under an overhanging bank, where the swift currents were undercutting the heavy, grassy turf. The sharp hiss of the water over the slanting boards of the dam had frightened her. As she lay under the bank the eel that had rested with her in the pool of the waterfall came over the milldam and passed on downstream. Anguilla followed, letting the current take her bumping and jolting over the shallow riffles and gliding swiftly through the deeper stretches. Often she was aware of dark forms moving in the water near her. They were other eels, come from many of the upland feeder creeks of the main stream. Like Anguilla, the other long, slender fishes yielded to the hurrying water and let the currents speed their passage. All of the migrants were roe eels, for only the females ascend far into the fresh-water streams, beyond all reminders of the sea.

The eels were almost the only creatures that were moving in the stream that night. Once, in a copse of beech, the stream made a sharp bend and scoured out a deeper bed. As Anguilla swam into this rounded basin, several frogs dived down from the soft mud bank where they had been sitting half out of water and hid on the bottom close to the bole of a fallen tree. The frogs had been startled by the approach of a furred animal that left prints like those of human feet in the soft mud and whose small black mask and black-ringed tail showed in the faint moonlight. The raccoon lived in a hole high up in one of the beeches near by and often caught frogs and crayfish in the stream. He was not disconcerted by the series of splashes that greeted his approach, for he knew where the foolish frogs would hide. He walked out on the fallen tree and lay down flat on its trunk. He took a firm grip on its bark with the claws of his hind feet and left forepaw. The right paw he dipped into the water, reaching down as far as he could and exploring with busy, sensitive fingers the leaves and mud under the trunk. The frogs tried to burrow deeper into the litter of leaves and sticks and other stream debris. The patient fingers felt into every hole and crevice, pushed away leaves and probed the mud. Soon the coon felt a small, firm body beneath his fingers—felt the sudden movement as the frog tried to escape. The coon's grip tightened and he drew the frog quickly up onto the log. There he killed it, washed it carefully by dipping it into the stream, and ate it. As he was finishing his meal, three small black masks moved into a patch of moonlight at the edge of the stream. They belonged to the coon's mate and their two cubs, who had come down the tree to prowl for their night's food.

From force of habit, the eel thrust her snout inquisitively into the leaf litter under the log, adding to the terror of the frogs, but she did not molest them as she would have done in the pond, for hunger was forgotten in the stronger instinct that made her a part of the moving stream. When Anguilla slipped into the central current of water that swept past the end of the log, the two young coons and their mother had walked out onto the trunk and four black-masked faces were peering into the water, preparing to fish the pool for frogs.

By morning the stream had broadened and deepened. Now it fell silent and mirrored an open woods of sycamore, oak, and dogwood. Passing through the woods, it carried a freight of brightly colored leaves—bright-red, crackling leaves from the oaks, mottled green and yellow leaves from the sycamores, dull-red, leathery leaves from the dogwoods. In the great wind the dogwoods had lost their leaves, but they held their scarlet berries. Yesterday robins had gathered in flocks in the dogwoods, eating the berries; today the robins were gone south and in their place flurries of starlings swept from tree to tree, chattering and rattling and whistling to one another as they stripped the branches of berries. The starlings were in bright new fall plumage, with every breast feather spear-tipped with white.

Anguilla came to a shallow pool formed when an oak had been uprooted in a great autumn storm ten years before and had fallen across the stream. Oak dam and pool were new in the stream since Anguilla had ascended it as an elver in the spring of that year. Now a great mat of weeds, silt, sticks, dead branches, and other debris was packed around the massive trunk, plastering all the crevices, so that the water was backed up into a pool two feet deep. During the period of the full moon the eels lay in the oak-dam pool, fearing to travel in the moon-white water of the stream almost as much as they feared the sunlight.

In the mud of the pool were many burrowing, wormlike larvae—the young of lamprey eels. They were not true eels, but fishlike creatures whose skeleton was gristle instead of bone, with round, tooth-studded mouths that were always open because there were no jaws. Some of the young lampreys had hatched from eggs spawned in the pool as much as four years before and had spent most of their life buried in the mud flats of the shallow stream, blind and toothless. These older larvae, grown nearly twice the length of a man's finger, had this fall been transformed into the adult shape, and for the first time they had eyes to see the water world in which they lived. Now, like the true eels, they felt in the gentle flow of water to the sea something that urged them to follow, to descend to salt water for an interval of sea life. There they would prey semiparasitically on cod, haddock, mackerel, salmon, and many other fishes and in time would return to the river, like their parents, to spawn and die. A few of the young lampreys slipped away over the log dam every day, and on a cloudy night, when rain had fallen and white mist lay in the stream valley, the eels followed.

The next night the eels came to a place where the stream diverged around an island grown thickly with willows. The eels followed the south channel around the island, where there were broad mud flats. The island had been formed over centuries of time as the stream had dropped part of its silt load before it joined the main river. Grass seeds had taken root; seeds of trees had been brought by the water and by birds; willow shoots had sprung from broken twigs and branches carried down in flood waters; an island had been born.

The water of the main river was gray with approaching day when the eels entered it. The river channel was twelve feet deep and its water was turbid because of the inpouring of many tributary streams swollen with autumn rains. The eels did not fear the gloomy channel water by day as they had feared the bright shallows of the hill streams, and so this day they did not rest but pushed on downstream. There were many other eels in the river—migrants from other tributaries. With the increase in their numbers the excitement of the eels grew, and as the days passed they rested less often, pressing on downstream with fevered haste.

As the river widened and deepened, a strange taste came into the water. It was a slightly bitter taste, and at certain hours of the day and night it grew stronger in the water that the eels drew into their mouths and passed over their gills. With the bitter taste came unfamiliar movements of the water—a period of pressure against the downflow of the river currents followed by slow release and then swift acceleration of the current.

Now groups of slender posts stood at intervals in the river, marking out funnel shapes from which straight rows of posts ran slanting toward the shore. Blackened netting, coated with slimy algae, was run from post to post and showed several feet above the water. Gulls were often sitting on the pound nets, waiting for men to come and fish the nets so that they could pick up any fish that might be thrown away or lost. The posts were coated with barnacles and with small oysters, for now there was enough salt in the water for these shellfish to grow.

Sometimes the sandspits of the river were dotted with small shore birds standing at rest or probing at the water's edge for snails, small shrimps, worms, or other food. The shore birds were of the sea's edge, and their presence in numbers hinted of the nearness of the sea.

The strange, bitter taste grew in the water and the pulse of the tides beat stronger. On one of the ebb tides a group of small eels—none more than two feet long—came out of a brackish-water marsh and joined the migrants from the hill streams. They were males, who had never ascended the rivers but had remained within the zone of tides and brackish water.

In all of the migrants striking changes in appearance were taking place. Gradually the river garb of olive brown was changing to a glistening black, with underparts of silver. These were the colors worn only by mature eels about to undertake a far sea journey. Their bodies were firm and rounded with fat— stored energy that would be needed before the journey's end. Already in many of the migrants the snouts were becoming higher and more compressed, as though from some sharpening of the sense of smell. Their eyes were enlarged to twice their normal size, perhaps in preparation for a descent along darkening sea lanes.

Where the river broadened out to its estuary, it flowed past a high clay cliff on its southern bank. Buried in the cliff were thousands of teeth of ancient sharks, vertebrae of whales, and shells of mollusks that had been dead when the first eels had come in from the sea, eons ago. The teeth, bones, and shells were relics of the time when a warm sea had overlain all the coastal plain and the hard remains of its creatures had settled down into its bottom oozes. Buried millions of years in darkness, they were washed out of the clay by every storm to lie exposed, warmed by sunshine and bathed by rain.

The eels spent a week descending the bay, hurrying through water of increasing saltiness. The currents moved with a rhythm that was of neither river nor sea, being governed by eddies at the mouths of the many rivers that emptied into the bay and by holes in the muddy bottom thirty or forty feet beneath. The ebb tides ran stronger than the floods, because the strong outflow of the rivers resisted the press of water from the sea.

At last Anguilla neared the mouth of the bay. With her were thousands of eels, come down, like the water that brought them, from all the hills and uplands of thousands of square miles, from every stream and river that drained away to the sea by the bay. The eels followed a deep channel that hugged the eastern shore of the bay and came to where the land passed into a great salt marsh. Beyond the marsh, and between it and the sea, was a vast shallow arm of the bay, studded with islands of green marsh grass. The eels gathered in the marsh, waiting for the moment when they should pass to the sea.

The next night a strong southeast wind blew in from the sea, and when the tide began to rise the wind was behind the water, pushing it into the bay and out into the marshes. That night the bitterness of brine was tasted by fish, birds, crabs, shellfish, and all the other water creatures of the marsh. The eels lay deep under water, savoring the salt that grew stronger hour by hour as the wind-driven wall of sea water advanced into the bay. The salt was of the sea. The eels were ready for the sea—for the deep sea and all it held for them. Their years of river life were ended.

The wind was stronger than the forces of moon and sun, and, when the tide turned an hour after midnight, the salt water continued to pile up in the marsh, being blown upstream in a deep surface layer while the underlying water ebbed to the sea.

Soon after the tide turn, the seaward movement of the eels began. In the large and strange rhythms of a great water which each had known in the beginning of life, but each had long since forgotten, the eels at first moved hesitantly in the ebbing tide. The water carried them through an inlet between two islands. It took them under a fleet of oyster boats riding at anchor, waiting for daybreak. When morning came, the eels would be far away. It carried them past leaning spar buoys that marked the inlet channel and past several whistle and bell buoys anchored on shoals of sand or rock. The tide took them close under the lee shore of the larger island, from which a lighthouse flashed a long beam of light toward the sea.

From a sandy spit of the island came the cries of shore birds that were feeding in darkness on the ebb tide. Cry of shore bird and crash of surf were the sounds of the edge of the land—the edge of the sea.

The eels struggled through the line of breakers, where foam seething over black water caught the gleam of the lighthouse beacon and frothed whitely. Once beyond the wind-driven breakers they found the sea gentler, and as they followed out over the shelving sand they sank into deeper water, unrocked by violence of wind and wave.

As long as the tide ebbed, eels were leaving the marshes and running out to sea. Thousands passed the lighthouse that night, on the first lap of a far sea journey—all the silver eels, in fact, that the marsh contained. And as they passed through the surf and out to sea, so also they passed from human sight and almost from human knowledge.

Controversy

The line between fact and fiction in nature writing became a major issue in the first decade of the twentieth century. In 1903, John Burroughs attacked a number of nature writers, especially those writing wild animal stories, branding them "sham naturalists." He argued that the public was so eager to buy nature books that incompetent naturalists and charlatans were publishing bogus natural history books in an effort to take easy money from gullible readers. (We can see the influence of this controversy in Roberts', Seton's, and Long's prefaces, which acquired a somewhat defensive tone after 1903 as they emphasized the legitimacy of their stories.) The battle raged for four years, fought in newspapers, magazine articles, and book prefaces, until President Theodore Roosevelt joined the attack in 1907.

The Nature Fakers controversy involved three closely related questions. First, were nature writers reporting accurate natural history? In many cases they were not, and the controversy played an important role in establishing informal standards of accuracy in nature essays and animal stories. There was, though, a deeper question: what is the nature of "the" animal mind? Some people, including Burroughs, argued that animals are little more than instinct-driven machines. At the other extreme, some argued that there is little difference between animals and people. The truth is most likely somewhere in between these extremes, as Roosevelt proposed. Third, how should we balance scientific and emotional approaches to understanding nature and wildlife?

The following essays include some of the key documents in the Nature Fakers controversy, from Burroughs' initial attack, to William J. Long's spirited defense, to Roosevelt's killing blow. Of all the nature writers, Long mounted the most public and aggressive defense of himself and became the focus of the controversy. Ernest Thompson Seton's only public response was in the form of a humorous parable, "The Fate of Little Mucky." Jack London chose not to defend himself until the controversy had subsided. His response was one of the most articulate from the "Nature Fakers," athough it was marred by the racist notion (widespread then, as now) that non-European and non-European American races and cultures represent earlier stages in human evolution.

Some folks found the whole debate a bit funny and responded to it with political cartoons and humorous ditties. Some of the humor was unintentional, as when the director of the New York Zoological Park, William T. Hornaday, condemned those who humanize animals and then went on to describe parrots and cockatoos as "the most philosophic" of birds, cranes as "the most domineering," and gallinaceous birds as "having the least common-sense."[1] Many people, however, especially scientists, found little humor in the debate, and the participants often adopted unnecessarily extreme positions. Reflecting on the controversy from the distance of England, the English naturalist and author of *Green Mansions*, W. H. Hudson, found the controversy puzzling and overly strident. In any event, it was a lively debate.

The issues raised by the Nature Fakers controversy were often complex and not easily resolved. They are, nonetheless, important and some of them continue to be debated a century later. The controversy provides a valuable window through which to examine the images of animals presented in wild animal stories. It also sheds light on many of the debates about animals that are going on today. The concluding essay in this book, "Will the Real Wild Animal Please Stand Up!" examines the history of the controversy and some of its underlying issues.

Note

1. William T. Hornaday, *The American Natural History* (New York: Charles Scribner's Sons, 1904), xxii.

15

Real and Sham Natural History

JOHN BURROUGHS

I suppose it is the real demand for an article that leads to its counterfeit, otherwise the counterfeit would stand a poor show. The growing demand for nature-
books within the past few years has called forth a very large crop of these books,
good, bad, and indifferent, —books on our flowers, our birds, our animals, our
butterflies, our ferns, our trees; books of animal stories, animal romances, nature-study books, and what not. There is a long list of them. Some of these
books, a very small number, are valuable contributions to our natural history
literature. Some are written to meet a fancied popular demand. The current is
setting that way; these writers seem to say to themselves, Let us take advantage
of it, and float into public favor and into pecuniary profit with a nature-book.
The popular love for stories is also catered to, and the two loves, the love of
nature and the love of fiction, are sought to be blended in the animal story-
books, such as Mr. Charles G. D. Roberts's *Kindred of the Wild,* Mr. William
Davenport Hulbert's *Forest Neighbors,* Mr. Thompson Seton's *Wild Animals I
Have Known,* and the Rev. William J. Long's *School of the Woods.* Only the last
two writers seem to seek to profit by the popular love for the sensational and
the improbable, Mr. Long, in this respect, quite throwing Mr. Thompson
Seton in the shade. It is Mr. Long's book, more than any of the others, that
justifies the phrase "Sham Natural History," and it is to it and to Mr. Thompson Seton's *Wild Animals I ALONE Have Known,* if I may be allowed playfully
to amend his title to correspond with the facts, that I shall devote the major part
of this article.

But before I proceed with this discussion, let me briefly speak of the books

John Burroughs, "Real and Sham Natural History," *Atlantic Monthly* 91 (March 1903): 298–309.

that have lately appeared in this field that are real contributions to the literature of the subjects of which they treat. All of Mr. Bradford Torrey's bird studies merit this encomium. They have a rare delicacy, sweetness, and charm. They are the product of a shy, gentle, alert, birdlike nature, dwelling fondly, lovingly, searchingly, upon our songsters and the scenes amid which they live.

Mrs. Fannie Hardy Eckstorm's *Bird Book* and her work on the Woodpeckers are fresh, original, and stimulating productions. Mr. Leander S. Keyser's *Birds of the Rockies* tells me just what I want to know about the Western birds, — their place in the landscape and in the season, and how they agree with and differ from our Eastern species. Mr. Keyser belongs to the noble order of walkers and trampers, and is a true observer and bird-lover. Florence Merriam's (now Mrs. Bailey) books on Western bird life and Mr. Frank H. Chapman's various publications apart from their strict scientific value, afford a genuine pleasure to all nature-lovers. Mr. Ernest Ingersoll has been writing gracefully and entertainingly upon the lives of our birds and wild animals for more than twenty years, and his books foster a wholesome love for these things.

Another book that I have read with genuine pleasure is Mr. Dallas Lore Sharp's *Wild Life Near Home*, —a book full of charm and of real observation; the fruit of a deep and abiding love of Nature, and of power to paint her as she is. How delightful his sketch of the possum, and how true! Mr. Sharp is quite sure the possum does not faint when he "plays possum," as some naturalists have urged: "A creature that will deliberately walk into a trap, spring it, eat the bait, then calmly lie down and sleep until the trapper comes, has no nerves. I used to catch a possum, now and then, in the box-trap set for rabbits. It is a delicate task to take a rabbit from such a trap, for, give him a crack of chance and away he bolts to freedom. Open the lid carefully when there is a possum inside, and you will find the old fellow curled up, with a sweet smile of peace on his face, fast asleep. Shake the trap and he rouses yawningly, with a mildly injured air, offended at your rudeness, and wanting. to know why you should wake an innocent possum from so safe and comfortable a bed. He blinks at you inquiringly, and says, 'Please, sir, if you will be so kind as to shut the door and go away, I will finish my nap.' And while he is saying it, before your very eyes, off to sleep he goes."

Of all the nature-books of recent years, I look upon Mr. Sharp's as the best; but in reading it, one is keenly aware of the danger that is always lurking near the essay naturalist—lurking near me as well as Mr. Sharp, —the danger of making too much of what we see and describe, —of putting in too much senti- ment, too much literature, —in short, of valuing these things more for the literary effects we can get out of them than for themselves. This danger did not beset Gilbert White. He always forgets White, and remembers only nature. His eye is single. He tells the thing for what it is. He is entirely serious. He reports directly upon what he sees and knows without any other motive than telling the truth. There is never more than a twinkle of humor in his pages, and never one word of style for its own sake. Who in our day would be content to write with the same moderation and self-denial? Yet it is just these sane, sincere, moderate books that live.

In Mr. Charles G. D. Roberts's *Kindred of the Wild* one finds much to admire and commend, and but little to take exception to. The volume is in many ways the most brilliant collection of animal stories that has appeared. It reaches a high order of literary merit. Many of the descriptive passages in it of winter in the Canadian woods are of great beauty. The story called "A Treason of Nature," describing the betrayal and death of a bull moose by hunters who imitated the call of the cow moose, is most striking and effective. True it is that all the animals whose lives are portrayed—the bear, the panther, the lynx, the hare, the moose, and others—are simply human beings disguised as animals; they think, feel, plan, suffer, as we do; in fact, exhibit almost the entire human psychology. But in other respects they follow closely the facts of natural history, and the reader is not deceived; he knows where he stands. Of course it is mainly guesswork how far our psychology applies to the lower animals. That they experience many of our emotions there can be no doubt, but that they have intellectual and reasoning processes like our own, except in a very rudimentary form, admits of grave doubt. But I need not go into that vexed subject here. They are certainly in any broad generalization our kin, and Mr. Roberts's book is well named and well done.

Yet I question his right to make his porcupine roll himself into a ball when attacked, as he does in his story of the panther, and then on a nudge from the panther roll down a snowy incline into the water. I have tried all sorts of tricks with the porcupine and made all sorts of assaults upon him, at different times, and I have never yet seen him assume the globular form Mr. Roberts describes. It would not be the best form for him to assume, because it would partly expose his vulnerable under side. The one thing the porcupine seems bent upon doing at all times is to keep right side up with care. His attitude of defense is crouching close to the ground, head drawn in and pressed down, the circular shield of large quills upon his back opened and extended as far as possible, and the tail stretched back rigid and held close upon the ground. Now come on, he says, if you want to. The tail is his weapon of active defense; with it he strikes up like lightning, and drives the quills into whatever they touch. In his chapter called "In Panoply of Spears," Mr. Roberts paints the porcupine without taking any liberties with the creature's known habits. He paints one characteristic of the porcupine as felicitously as Mr. Sharp paints one of the possum: "As the porcupine made his resolute way through the woods, the manner of his going differed from that of all the other kindreds of the wild. He went not furtively. He had no particular objection to making a noise. He did not consider it necessary to stop every little while, stiffen himself to a monument of immobility, cast wary glances about the gloom, and sniff the air for the taint of enemies. He did not care who knew of his coming, and he did not greatly care who came. Behind his panoply of biting spears he felt himself secure, and in that security he moved as if he held in fee the whole green, shadowy, perilous, woodland world."

The father of the animal story as we have it to-day was doubtless Charles Dudley Warner, who, in his *A-Hunting of the Deer*, forever killed all taste for venison in many of his readers. The story of the hunt is given from the standpoint of the deer, and is, I think, the most beautiful and effective animal story yet written in this country. It is true in the real sense of the word. The line between fact and fiction is never crossed.

Neither does Mr. William Davenport Hulbert cross this line in his *Forest Neighbors*, wherein we have the life stories of the porcupine, the lynx, the beaver, the loon, the trout, made by a man who has known these creatures in the woods of northern Michigan from his boyhood. The sketches are sympathetically done, and the writer's invention is called into play without the reader's credulity ever being overtaxed. But in Mr. Thompson Seton's *Wild Animals I Have Known*, and in the recent work of his awkward imitator, the Rev. William J. Long, I am bound to say that the line between fact and fiction is repeatedly crossed, and that a deliberate attempt is made to induce the reader to cross, too, and to work such a spell upon him that he shall not know that he has crossed and is in the land of make-believe. Mr. Thompson Seton says in capital letters that his stories are true, and it is this emphatic assertion that makes the judicious grieve. True as romance, true in their artistic effects, true in their power to entertain the young reader, they certainly are but true as natural history they as certainly are not. Are we to believe that Mr. Thompson Seton, in his few years of roaming in the West, has penetrated farther into the secrets of animal life than all the observers who have gone before him? There are no stories of animal intelligence and cunning on record, that I am aware of, that match his. Gilbert White, Charles St. John, Waterton, Wallace, Darwin, Jefferies, and others in England—all expert students and observers; Bates in South America, Audubon roaming the whole country, Thoreau in New England, John Muir in the mountains of California and in the wilds of Alaska have nothing to report that comes within gunshot of what appear to be Mr. Thompson Seton's daily experiences. Such dogs, wolves, foxes, rabbits, mustangs, crows, as he has known, it is safe to say, no other person in the world has ever known. Fact and fiction are so deftly blended in his work that only a real woodsman can separate them. For instance, take his story of the fox. Every hunter knows that the fox, when pursued by the hound, will often resort to devices that look like cunning tricks to confuse and mislead the dog. How far these devices are the result of calculation we do not know, but hunters generally look upon them as such. Thus a fox hotly pursued will run through a flock of sheep. This dodge probably delays the hound a little, but it does not often enable the fox to shake him. Mr. Thompson Seton goes several better, and makes his fox jump upon the back of a sheep and ride several hundred yards. Of course no fox ever did that. Again, the fox will sometimes take to the railroad track, and walk upon the rail, doubtless with the vague notion of eluding his pursuers. Mr. Thompson Seton makes his fox so very foxy that he deliberately lures the hounds upon a long trestle where he knows they will be just in time to meet and be killed by a passing train, as they are. The presumption is that the fox had a watch and a time-table about his person. But such are the ways of romancers. The incident of the mother fox coming near the farmhouse at night to rescue her young, and, finding him held by a chain, digging a hole and burying the chain, thinking she had thus set him free, is very touching and pretty, and might well be true. It shows how limited the wit of the fox really is. But, finding herself unable to liberate her offspring, that she should then bring him poison is pushing the romantic to the absurd. In all the animal stories of Mr. Thompson Seton that I have read the same liberties are taken with facts. In his story of the rabbit, Raggylug, he says: "Those who do not know the animals well may think I have humanized them, but those who have lived so near them as to know something of their ways and their minds will not think so." This is the old trick of the romancer: he swears his tale is true, because he knows his reader wants this assurance; it makes the thing taste better. But those who know the animals are just the ones Mr. Thompson Seton cannot fool. Any country boy knows that the rabbit takes no account of barbed wire fences or of briers and brambles as a means of punishing the dog that is pursuing him. If these things were universal, it is possible that in the course of long generations rabbits might learn to interpose them between themselves and their enemies, —possible, but not probable.

Or take his story of the crow—Silver Spot; how truthful a picture is this? how much of the real natural history of the crow is here? According to my own observations of more than half a century, there is very little. In the first place, that these natural leaders among the fowls of the air ever appear I have no evidence. I have known crows almost as intimately as I have hens from my boyhood, and I have seen no evidence of it with them. For forty years I have seen crows in winter, in different parts of the country, passing to and fro between their rookeries and their feeding grounds, and I have never seen anything like leadership among them. They leave their roosting places at daybreak and disperse north and south or east and west to their feeding grounds, going in loose, straggling bands and silently, except in early spring and when they first leave their rookeries; and they return at night in the same way, flying low if it is stormy and windy, and high if it is calm, rising up or sheering off if they see a gunner or other suspicious object, but making no sound, uttering no signal notes. They all have eyes equally sharp and do not need to be warned. They are all on the alert. When feeding, they do post a sentry, and he caws when danger approaches, and takes to wing. They do not dart into a bush when pursued by a kingbird or a purple martin; they are not afraid of a hawk; they cannot count six, though such traditions exist (Silver Spot could count thirty!); they do not caw when you stand under them in winter to turn their course; they do not drill their young; they do not flock together in June; they cannot worry a fox into giving up half his dinner; they do not, so far as we know, have perpetual sentries; they have no calls that, we can be sure, answer to our words, "Mount," "Bunch," "Scatter," "Descend," "Form line," "Forage," —on these and other points my observations differ radically from Mr. Thompson Seton's.

Crows flock in September. Through the summer the different families keep pretty well together. You may see the old ones with their young foraging about the fields, the young often being fed by their parents. It may be permissible to say that the old are teaching the young how to forage; they are certainly setting them an example, as the mother hen or mother turkey is setting her brood an example when she leads them about the fields. The cat brings her kitten a mouse, but does she teach him how to deal with the mouse? Does he need to be taught?

From my boyhood I have seen that yearly meeting of the crows in September or October, on a high grassy hill or a wooded ridge. Apparently all the crows over a large area assemble at these times; you may see them coming, singly or in loose bands, from all directions to the rendezvous, till there are hundreds of them together. They make black an acre or two of ground. At intervals they all rise in the air, wheeling about, all cawing at once. Then to the ground again or to the treetops, as the case may be; then, wheeling in the air, they send forth the voice of the multitude. What does it all mean? Ask our romancer; they can tell you, I cannot. It is the meeting of the clan after the scattering of the breeding season, and they seem to celebrate the event. The crow is gregarious, he is social, he seems to have a strong community feeling; he will act as sentinel for the safety of his fellows. I have never seen crows quarrel over their food, or act greedy. Indeed, I am half persuaded that in hard times in winter they willingly share their food with one another. Birds of prey will rend one another over their food; even buzzards will make some show of mauling one another with their wings; but I have yet to see anything of the kind with that gentle freebooter, the crow.

What their various calls mean, who shall tell? That lusty *Caw-aw, caw-aw* that one hears in spring and summer, like the voice of authority or command, what does it mean? I never could find out. It is doubtless from the male. A crow will utter it while sitting alone on the fence in the pasture, as well as when flying through the air. The crow's cry of alarm is easily distinguished; all the other birds and wild creatures know it, and the hunter who is stalking his game is apt to swear when he hears it. I have heard two crows in the spring, seated on a limb close together, give utterance to very many curious, guttural, gurgling, ventriloquial sounds. What were they saying? It was probably some form of the language of love.

One very cold winter's morning after a fall of nearly two feet of snow, as I came out of my door, three crows were perched in an apple tree but a few rods away. One of them uttered a peculiar caw as they saw me, but they did not fly away. It was not the usual high-keyed note of alarm. It may have meant "Look out!" yet it seemed to me like the asking of alms: "Here we are, three hungry neighbors of yours; give us food." So I soon brought out the entrails and legs of a chicken, and placed them upon the snow. The crows very soon discovered what I had done, and with the usual suspicious lifting of the wings approached and devoured the food or carried it away. But there was not the least strife or dispute among them over the food. Indeed, each seemed ready to give precedence to the other. In fact, the crow is a courtly, fine-mannered bird. Yet suspicion is his dominant trait. Anything that looks like design puts him on his guard. He suspects a trap. A string stretched over and around a cornfield will often keep him away. His wit is not deep, but it is quick, and ever on the alert.

Since Mr. Thompson Seton took his reader into his confidence at all, why did he not warn him at the outset against asking any questions about the literal truth of his stories? Why did he not say that their groundwork was fact and their finish was fiction, and that if the reader find them entertaining, and that if they increase his love for, and his interest in, our wild neighbors, it were enough?

It is always an artist's privilege to heighten or deepen natural effects. He may paint us a more beautiful woman, or a more beautiful horse, or a more beautiful landscape, than we ever saw; we are not deceived even though he out-do nature. We know where we stand and where he stands; we know that this is the power of art. But when he paints portrait, or all actual scene, or event, we expect him to be true to the facts of the case. Again, he may add all the charm his style can impart to the subject, and we are not deceived; the picture is true, perhaps all the more true for the style. Mr. Thompson Seton's stories are artistic and pleasing, but he insists upon it that they are true to the fact, and that this is the best way to write natural history. "I believe," he says in his preface, "that natural history has lost much by the vague general treatment that is so common." Hence he will make it specific and individual. Very good; but do not put upon our human credulity a greater burden than it can bear. His story of the pacing mustang is very clever and spirited, but the endurance of the horse is simply past belief. What would not one give for the real facts of the case; how interesting they would be, no matter how much they fell short of this highly colored account! There should be nothing equivocal about sketches of this kind; even a child should know when the writer is giving him facts and when he is giving him fiction, as he does when Mr. Thompson Seton makes his animals talk; but in many of the narrations only a real woodsman can separate the true from the false. Mr. Thompson Seton constantly aims to convey the idea to his reader that the wild creatures drill and instruct their young, even punishing them at times for disobedience to orders. His imitator, the Rev. Mr. Long, quite outdoes him on this line, going so far as to call his last book the *School of the Woods*.

Mr. Long doubtless got the hint of his ridiculous book from Mr. Thompson Seton's story of the crow, wherein he speaks of a certain old pine woods as the crows' fortress and college: "Here they find security in numbers and in lofty yet sheltered perches, and here they begin their schooling and are taught all the secrets of success in crow life, and in crow life the least failure does not simply mean begin again. It means death." Now the idea was a false one before Mr. Long appropriated it, and it has been pushed to such length that it becomes ridiculous. There is not a shadow of truth in it. It is simply one of Mr. Thompson Seton's strokes of fancy. The crows do not train their young. They have no fortresses, or schools, or colleges, or examining boards, or diplomas, or medals of honor, or hospitals, or churches, or telephones, or postal deliveries, or anything of the sort. Indeed, the poorest backwoods hamlet has more of the appurtenances of civilization than the best organized crow or other wild animal community in the land!

Mr. Long deliberately states as possibly a new suggestion in the field of natural history "that animal education is like our own, and so depends chiefly upon teaching." And again: "After many years of watching animals in their native haunts [and especially after reading Thompson Seton] I am convinced that instinct plays a much smaller part than we have supposed; that an animal's success or failure in the ceaseless struggle for life depends, not upon instinct, but upon the kind of training which the animal receives from its mother." This is indeed a new suggestion in the field of natural history. What a wonder that Darwin did not find it out, or the observers before and since his time. But the honor of the discovery belongs to our own day and land!

Now let us see if this statement will bear examination. Take the bird with its nest, for instance. The whole art of the nest builder is concealment, —both by position and by the material used, —blending its nest with and making it a part of its surroundings. This is the way to safety. Does the mother bird teach her young this art? When does she do it, since the young do not build till they are a year old? Does she give them an object lesson on their own nest, and do they remember it till the next season? See, too, how all the ground birds and the females of nearly all the tree birds are protected by their neutral and imitative coloring. Is this, too, a matter of education? Or take any of our wild animals. Is the cunning of the fox a matter of education? or of inheritance? Is he taught in the school of the woods how to elude the hound, or how to carry a fat goose, or how to avoid a trap? Here is a neighborhood where a fox-trap has not been put out in fifty years. Go and bait your fox for a week in winter and then set your trap with your best art, and see if he comes and puts his foot or his nose in it. You may finally catch him, but not till you have allayed his suspicions and fairly outwitted him. He knows a trap from the jump, and it is not school knowledge, but inherited knowledge.

On what does the safety of the hare depend? On his speed, his sharp eyes and ears, and on his protective coloring; the deer likewise on its speed and on its acute senses; and so on through the list. Nature has instilled into them all the fear of their enemies and equipped them with different means in different degrees to escape them. Birds of prey have almost preternatural keenness of vision. Many of the four-footed creatures have equal sharpness of scent. A wild animal is a wild animal when it is born, and it fears man and its natural enemies as soon as its senses and its powers are developed. This fear, this wildness, can be largely eradicated from most of them, if we take them young enough, and it can be greatly increased by hunting them with guns and dogs. The gray squirrels in some of our city parks are as tame as cats. On the other hand, let a domestic cat rear its kittens in the woods, and they are at once wild animals. Wild geese are tame geese when hatched and reared by domestic geese, but when in the fall they hear the call of their migrating clan in the air above them, do they not know the language? do they have to be taught to spread their wings and follow after?

The question I am here arguing is too obvious and too well established to be considered in this serious manner, were it not that the popularity of Mr. Long's books, with their mock natural history, is misleading the minds of many readers. No pleasure to the reader, no moral inculcated, can justify the dissemination of false notions of nature, or of anything else, and the writer who seeks to palm off his own silly inventions as real observations is bound sooner or later to come to grief.

There is a school of the woods, as I have said, just as much as there is a church of the woods, or a parliament of the woods, or a society of united charities of the woods, and no more; there is nothing in the dealings of animals with their young that in the remotest way suggests human instruction and discipline. The young of all the wild creatures do instinctively what their parents do and did. They do not have to be taught; they are taught by nature from the start. The bird sings at the proper age, and builds its nest, and takes its appropriate food, without any hint at all from its parents. The young ducks take to the water when hatched by a hen as readily as when hatched by a duck, and dive, and stalk insects, and wash themselves just as their mothers did. Young chickens and young turkeys understand the various calls and signals of their mothers the first time they hear or see them. At the mother's alarm note they squat, at her call to food they come, on the first day as on the tenth. The habits of cleanliness of the nestlings are established from the first hour of their lives. When a bird comes to build its first nest and to rear its first brood, it knows how to proceed as well as it does years later, or as its parents did before it. The fox is afraid of a trap before he has had any experience with traps, and the hare thumps upon the ground at the sight of anything strange and unusual whether its mates be within hearing or not. It is true that the crows and the jays might be called the spies and informers of the woods, and that other creatures seem to understand the meaning of their cries, but who shall presume to say that they have been instructed in this vocation? Mr. Long would have us believe that the crows teach their young to fly. Does the rooster teach its young to crow, or the cock grouse teach the young males to drum? No bird teaches its young to fly. They fly instinctively when their wings are strong enough. I have often thought that the parent birds sometimes withheld food for the purpose of inducing their young to leave the nest, perching near by with it in their beaks and calling impatiently. The common dove will undoubtedly push its fully fledged young off the dovecot to make them use their wings. At a certain age young birds and young mice and squirrels and rabbits will leave their nests when disturbed, whether their parents are within hearing or not. Young hawks and young crows will launch out boldly into the air when they see or feel you shinning up the tree that holds their nest. Fear is instinctive in the young of all creatures, even of turtles. Yet Mr. Long would persuade us that young birds and animals are strangers to this feeling till their parents have taught them what to fear. Every farm boy knows that when old Brindle hides her calf in the woods, and he is sent to look it up when it is only a few hours old, that it is "as wild as a deer," as we say, and will charge him desperately with a loud agonized bleat. Had the old cow taught her young to be afraid of what she herself was not afraid? So with the human kind. Does the mother teach her baby to be afraid of strangers? When I was a small boy I remember being afraid of the first soaring hawk I had ever seen, and I ran and hid behind the fence.

What Mr. Long and Mr. Thompson Seton read as parental obedience is simply obedience to instinct, and of course in this direction alone safety lies, and there is no departure from it, as Mr. Long seeks to show in his story of "What the Fawns Must Know." The parents and the young are filled with the same impulse. Is it to be supposed that our white-footed mouse has taught her young to cling to her teats, when the plough throws out her nest, and thus be carried away by her? When did she drill them? Was it by word of command or by pinches and nudges? Are we to believe that the partridge teaches her just hatched brood to squat motionless upon the ground, or to stick their heads under leaves at a signal from her when a man or a dog appears? There they sit as if suddenly turned to stone while she blusters about and seeks to lead you away from the spot. Who taught her to try to play her confidence game upon you, to feign lameness, a broken wing, a broken leg, or utter paralysis? her parents before her? How interesting it would have been to have surprised them in their rehearsal! Nearly all the ground builders among our song birds try the same tactics when driven from their nests. When and how were they taught, and who was their teacher? The other day a lady told me she thought she had heard a robin in the summer teaching its young to sing. But, I said, the young do not sing till the following year, and then only the males. If they are taught, why don't the females sing? Is the singing school only for boys? It was not so when I was a youth.

Eternal vigilance is the price of life among the birds and the lower animals, and then they probably seldom die in their beds, as we say. They are like the people of a city in a state of siege, or like an army moving through, or encamped in, an enemy's country. They are surrounded by scalpers and sharpshooters;

yea, their camp is invaded by them. Guns, traps, snares, nets, snakes, weasels, cats, foxes, hawks, bloodsuckers, bone crushers, —foes in the air, in the bush, in the grass, in the water; foes by day, foes by night, foes that stalk, that glide, that swoop; foes that go by sight, that go by scent, that waylay, that spring from ambush, —how can they escape the fearful and the tragic, from the moose in his power to the hare in her timidity; from the fox with his speed and cunning to the mouse that he hunts in its meadow burrow? They cannot and they do not escape, and if Mr. Long had learned his lesson outside of his study, he might have found it out. Mr. Long often describes, with an extra show of exactness and particularity, incidents he has seen in the lives of the wood folk that no man ever saw or ever will see. He would make us believe that in the Northern woods (he does not name the spot) it is often difficult to frighten the moose out of your way; he says that they get in the way of your canoe in the water, or follow it threateningly, even though you fire your rifle to frighten them off; and that the bears are so tame that they stand in the path before you and dispute the right of way with you, but that if you look hard enough at them they may clamber up the rocks and look down upon you as you pass! We know that even the musk ox in the Arctic barren lands, that has never seen or known man, is wary and hard to approach. Mr. Long's book reads like that of a man who has really never been to the woods, but who sits in his study and cooks up these yarns from things he has read in *Forest and Stream,* or in other sporting journals. Of real observation there is hardly a vestige in his book; of deliberate trifling with natural history there is no end. He describes how on one occasion his attention was arrested by a curious sound among the bushes on the side of a hill. He could not make out what was coming But let me give the passage entire as a good sample of the tales of this Münchausen of our nature-writers: "It was not a bear shaking down the ripe beechnuts—not heavy enough for that, yet too heavy for the feet of any prowler of the woods to make on his stealthy hunting. *Pr-r-r-rush, swish! thump!* Something struck the stem of a bush heavily, and brought down a rustling shower of leaves; then out from under the low branches rolled something that I had never seen before, —a heavy grayish ball, as big as a half-bushel basket, so covered over with leaves that one could not tell what was inside. It was as if some one had covered a big kettle with glue and sent it rolling down the hill picking up dead leaves as it went. So the queer thing tumbled past my feet, purring, crackling, growing bigger and more ragged every moment as it gathered up more leaves, till it reached the bottom of a sharp pitch and lay still.

"I stole after it cautiously; suddenly it moved, unrolled itself. Then out of the ragged mass came a big porcupine. He shook himself, stretched, wabbled around a moment, as if his long roll had made him dizzy; then he meandered aimlessly along the foot of the ridge, his quills stuck full of dead leaves, looking big and strange enough to frighten anything that might meet him in the woods." And presently we are told he did frighten a hare almost out of its wits.

One would like to know what Mr. Long had for supper the night he dreamed this dream. He had probably just read or heard the old legend of the porcupine rolling over under an apple tree and walking off to his den with his quills stuck full of apples; this, with a late supper of Welsh "rabbit," had doubtless caused this fantastic vision to dance through his brain. But how did he come to believe it was a real experience? that is the mystery. One doubts his ever having met a porcupine in the woods, or he would know that these creatures do not cover their noses with their tails; the tail is always extended flat upon the ground and used as a weapon of defense. He ought to know, too, if he had had any such experience as he describes, that when a lynx, or any other wild animal, attacks a porcupine and gets its mouth full of quills, it does not lie down beside its murderer and die, as he represents. It lives for days, maybe weeks, wandering through the forest.

Or take Mr. Long's picture of the death—euthanasy—of an eagle, an occurrence which came under his own observation.

The eagle was circling in the air at a great altitude above the mountain top, and sending forth the loud, strident eagle scream, —advising Jove, no doubt, that his bird was ready to come. Presently the wheeling and the screaming ceased, the great bird set its wings and came sailing with great speed straight toward the earth, passing near the observer, who saw with wonder that the head with partly closed eyes "drooped forward as if it were heavy." "Only once did he veer slightly, to escape a tall stub that thrust its naked bulk above the woods athwart his path. Then with rigid wings he crossed the bay below the point! still slanting gently down to earth, and vanished silently into the drooping arms of the dark woods beyond" where Mr. Long soon found him, "his head lying across the moss-cushioned root of an old cedar, his wings outstretched among the cool green ferns—dead." Let us see how probable this event is: birds die as men do, suddenly, or from lingering disease and old age. We all know that when birds or poultry or caged eagles die of old age, or other causes, they sicken and droop for several days, refuse food, and refuse to use their wings, till some morning we find them dead under their perches. Sudden death with them is probably from apoplexy or something akin to it. I have heard of canaries suddenly falling dead from their perches, and of wild birds suddenly falling dead from great emotional excitement, when their nests were being robbed. It is possible that an old eagle might be smitten with apoplexy while high in air. In that case would he come sailing calmly to earth like a boy on a toboggan slide? Would he not rather collapse and come down in a heap as men and birds do?

It is not unusual for one to see hawks and eagles come to the earth from a great altitude with wings set in the manner that Mr. Long describes (all except the drooping head and the half-closed eyes); but who ever before fancied Death sitting astride their necks? The tale goes very well with the other of Mr. Long's, —of the playful porcupine rolling down the bank just for fun!

If it be urged that I discredit Mr. Long's stories simply because I myself have never seen or known the like, I say, no; that is not the reason. I can believe many things I have never seen or known. I discredit them because they are so widely at variance with all we know of the wild creatures and their ways. I discredit them as I do any other glaring counterfeit, or any poor imitation of an original, or as I would discredit a story of my friend that was not in keeping with what I knew of his character. There are many, very many, things in our own natural history that I do not know; I add a little to my knowledge of it every year, and hope to keep on doing so as long as I live; but I do know that Mr. Long draws the long bow when he says he has seen the great blue heron break up a frog and scatter the fragments upon the water and then wait to spear the little fish that might be thus attracted; or when he describes so circumstantially, in one of his late magazine articles, how he had a peep into the kingfisher's "kindergarten," and saw the old birds go fishing downstream and return with small minnows which they placed in a shallow pool near the main stream, and then went off and fetched their young to the spot and instructed them in diving for these shiners. If he had said that he saw the parent birds fishing with hook and line, or dragging a net of their own knitting, his statement would have been just as credible; or, his story of how he has seen the mother fishhawk train her young day after day to fish, even catching a fish for them and then dropping it back wounded into the water and then encouraging them to try for it! Our historian urges that if the young were not thus initiated into fishing they would relapse into the "old hawk habit of hunting in the woods, which is much easier." How does the Rev. Mr. Long know that they would go straight back to the "old hawk habit"? I once reared a marsh hawk, taken from the nest long before it was fledged. As it grew up it certainly needed no instruction as to how to use its talons. It would practice upon a dry leaf or a fragment of bark, striking it with unerring aim.

Equally fictitious is Mr. Long's account of what he calls the Roll Call of the Partridge—how, after the mother of the brood had been killed, he has seen a young male take her place and lead the flock, and, near nightfall, take up his stand upon a log and call till his mates came one by one and stood beside him to the number of nine. Still the leader called, —there should be two more, —the two that were in Mr. Long's game-bag; and who does not know that a smart young partridge, fresh from the school of the woods, can count eleven? Mr. Long saw him in the act of counting them. The family had at last become alarmed he asserts, and "huddled on the ground in a close group, all but the leader, who stood above them, counting them over and over, apparently, and anon sending his cry out into the darkening woods."

Why should any one palm off such stuff on an unsuspecting public as veritable natural history? When a man, writing or speaking of his own experience, says without qualification that he has seen a thing, we are expected to take him at his word. Mr. Long says his sketches were made in the woods with the subjects themselves living just outside his tent door; and that "they are all life studies, and include also some of the unusual life secrets of a score of animals and birds." We are not, therefore, to regard him as playing with natural history material for the amusement of his reader, or, like Mr. Thompson Seton, seeking to make up an artistic whole out of bits and fragments of the lives of the animals, gathered here and there, and heightened and intensified by a fertile fancy, but as an actual recorder of what he has seen and known. What the "life secrets" are that he claims to have discovered, any competent reader can see. They are all the inventions of Mr. Long. Of the real secrets of wild life, I do not find a trace in his volume. The only other book of Mr. Long's I have looked into is his *Beasts of the Field*, and here he is for the most part the same false prophet that he is in the *School of the Woods*. His statements are rarely convincing; rarely do they have the verisimilitude of real observations. His air is that of a witness who is trying to mislead the jury. What discoveries he has made! Among others, that the red squirrel has cheek pockets in which he can carry half a dozen chestnuts at a time! Has he really never seen a red squirrel, or does he not know him from a chipmunk? There is probably not a natural history museum in the land that would not pay a fine sum for a red squirrel with pouches in his cheeks.

What fun the fishermen and hunters and farmers must have with Mr. Long! Some fisherman along the coast told him that the fox catches crabs by trailing his brush over the water as a bait; the crab seizes it, whereupon the fox springs sway and jerks the crab to land. Mr. Long hopes to confirm the observation some time!

An old fox hunter found him still more gullible. He told him how one morning he made the discovery that a fox was in his hencoop killing his chickens. Approaching cautiously he closed the opening and had the fox a prisoner. On entering the coop a few moments later, what was his surprise to find one dead pullet and a dead fox beside it. He concluded the thief had tumbled down from the roost and broken his neck. He laid both the fox and his victim on a box outside the door. A minute later both fox and pullet were gone! The fox was only "playing possum," and when he left he took his chicken with him!

He knew of a black fox that played the same trick. A boy caught it in a trap, and found it in the morning apparently dead and frozen stiff. He carried it home in triumph over his shoulder. (Of course the fox had suppressed its animal heat also!) He removed the trap from the frozen leg, stroked and admired his beautiful prize, and then, as he turned his attention away for a moment, "he had a dazed vision of a flying black animal that seemed to perch an instant on the log fence and vanish among the spruces." Could credulity any further go?

It seems to me that Mr. Long's story of how an old fox captures chickens roosting beyond his reach in a tree does go a little further. The fox simply runs around the tree, going faster and faster, "jumping and clacking his teeth," and the chickens in trying to follow him with their eyes get dizzy and tumble off the roost! Mr. Long gives this as if it might have been his own observation, but doubtless some old farmer has "soaked" him with it. How the old humorist must have chuckled in his sleeve! I have read of an owl in South Africa which the natives believe can be made to twist its head off by a person walking round and round it. The curious bird follows you with his eyes, till, presto! his head is off. This story goes one or two better than that of our Natural History Münchausen!

16

The Modern School of Nature-Study and Its Critics

WILLIAM J. LONG

Two things should be borne in mind if one would understand the present interest in Nature-study, or classify the large number of books which minister to that interest:

First, the study of Nature is a vastly different thing from the study of Science; they are no more alike than Psychology and History. Above and beyond the world of facts and law, with which alone Science concerns itself, is an immense and almost unknown world of suggestion and freedom and inspiration, in which the individual, whether animal or man, must struggle against fact and law to develop or keep his own individuality. It is a world of *appreciation*, to express it in terms of the philosophy of Professor [Josiah] Royce, rather than a world of *description*. It is a world that must be interpreted rather than catalogued, for you cannot catalogue or classify the individuality for which all things are struggling. Here the "flower in the crannied wall" is analyzed, indeed, but not according to the principles of Gray's Manual; "the eagle that stirreth up her nest, fluttereth over her young, and beareth them on her wings," sweeps into our hearts without the might of a Latin name added; and the "poor, cowerin', timorous beastie" runs away and leaves us with a question that cannot be answered by telling us whether this mother mouse belongs to the long-tailed or jumping variety. This upper world of appreciation and suggestion, of individuality interpreted by individuality, is the world of Nature, the Nature of the

William J. Long, "The Modern School of Nature-Study and Its Critics," *North American Review* 176 (May 1903): 687–696.

poets and prophets and thinkers. Though less exact, it is not less but rather more true and real than Science, as emotions are more real than facts, and love is more true than economics—

> *"Und wenn Natur Dich unterweist*
> *Dann geht die Seelenkraft Dir auf,*
> *Wie spricht ein Geist zum andern Geist."*

That is the word which Goethe, himself a scientist and philosopher, put into the mouth of Faust, a man who knew all the sciences, but who cried out for the life of Nature. "I study facts and law; they are enough," says the scientist. "We know the tyranny of facts and law too well," answer the nature-students "Give us now the liberty and truth of the spirit."

Let me illustrate this difference clearly and simply by reference to two animals that I have followed, under difficulties, for many years. They are the beaver and the otter, both wonderful swimmers, more at home in the water than on the land. The beaver uses only his hind feet in swimming; the otter, except when playing on the surface, uses only his forefeet for the same purpose; when chasing a trout under water, the hind legs are trailed behind him with his tail. Why this difference in two powerful swimmers of the same waters? Again, both these animals are unusually peaceable at all seasons. Of all the wood-folk that mind their own business, the beaver is the most exemplary; and the otter, though a powerful fighter and belonging to the quarrelsome weasel family, is gentle and playful, lets the other animals severely alone, and makes the most docile of pets when you catch him. Yet these two peaceable animals fight like Kilkenny cats whenever they cross each other's path. Why?

Science has no answer here. It is not her field; and long ago she classified both animals and finished with them. The work of the nature-student, on the other hand, has hardly more than begun. Following these shy animals summer and winter, entering into their struggles, he has learned to interpret how, in their dim way, they think and feel, and how their interests are bound to clash. And he understands perfectly both their swimming and their animosities; for he sees the individuality which the scientist, with other interests, must always miss.

In a word, the difference between Nature and Science is the difference between a man who loves animals, and so understands them, and the man who studies Zoology; it is the difference between the woman who cherishes her old-fashioned flower-garden and the professor who lectures on Botany in a college class-room.

The second thing to remember is this: that the field of natural history has changed rapidly of late, and in the schools and nature clubs the demand is for less Science and more Nature. Formerly, the writer of natural history, working on the scientific plan, simply catalogued his facts and observations. Animals were assumed to be creatures of instinct and habit. They were described in classes, under the assumption that all animals of the same class are alike. Style and living interest were both alike out of place; for it was, and still is, asserted that a personal interest destroys the value of an observation.

The modern nature-student has learned a different lesson. He knows that animals of the same class are still individuals; that they are different every one, and have different habits; that they are not more alike than men and women of the same class, and that they change their habits rapidly—more so, perhaps, than do either governments or churches—when the need arises. When a student at the Theological Seminary, I watched a toad that lived under the stone door-step. Now, toads are not supposed to have much individuality; yet, though I have watched toads since I was a child, when I made pets of them, I recorded a dozen things of this one toad that I had never seen before, and that have never been observed, so far as I know, by any other naturalist.

The truth is, that he who watches any animal closely enough will see what no naturalist has ever seen. This is the simple secret of the wonderful cat story, or the incredible dog story, to be heard in almost every house. It means that, after you have catalogued dogs perfectly, you still have in every dog a new subject with some new habits. Every boy who keeps a pet has something to tell the best naturalist. Every audience to which I have ever lectured on animals has brought forward at least a dozen men and women, each with a true animal story that seems incredible. In the State of Maine alone I have talked with at least fifty different guides and trappers. They all follow the same classes of animals, yet every guide has a different record of the habits of those animals, and nearly every one of them has at least three or four animal stories that would not be believed if they were printed. That is not because they lie; for I have found them to be truthful and reliable men mostly; and, since their success as guides and hunters is at stake, they are keen to listen and learn about animals. The truth is, that they have discovered unconsciously the secret of animal individuality, which the old natural-history writers have missed; they see different habits, simply because they follow different animals in different localities.

For over twenty years, I have gone every season deep into the woods; have lived alone with the animals for months at a time; have followed them summer and winter with old Indians whose whole lives have been spent in hunting and trapping; have lain all night in my canoe or slept in the snow alone on their trail, that I might not lose the lesson of their awaking. Moreover, I have camped and tramped with a score of trappers, keen men whose eyes see everything and whose knowledge of animals is fatal in its accuracy. I have gone fifty miles out of my course to interview some famous old Indian or hunter, and ask for his verification or denial of my own observations. I have questioned these men about animals; have listened to them when, lying beside me on the same blanket after sharing my bread and fire, they spoke simply and spoke the truth as to what they had observed. And one result of all this watching and listening is this: that there is, for me at least, absolutely no limit to the variety and adaptiveness of Nature, even in a single species. If you cannot find two leaves alike on the same elm-tree, you certainly cannot write a list of habits that will cover even two animals perfectly, with their wild free life and their individuality struggling to express itself amidst a hundred dangers and unknown problems. When we consider the marvellous life of the bee and the ant and the water-spider, the wonder is, not that we have seen so much, but rather that we have seen so very little, of the more highly developed and individualized animals. There is another result also, namely this: that no animal story told me as a fact by an honest man will leave me incredulous; for in my note-books there are more incredible things written that I have seen myself, but that I have not dared to print until the observation shall have been confirmed. And this experience is true of many other naturalists who have written or spoken to me on the subject.

Sometimes the confirmation comes in unexpected ways. Years ago, when a small boy, I watched two orioles building their nest. The twig upon which they hung it forked too widely to suit them. They deliberated plainly upon the matter; then they brought up a twig from the ground, laid it across the forks, and tied it there with strings as a third support to the nest. Moreover, when they tied the strings, they took the ends in their beaks and hung their weight upon them so as to draw the knots tight. For twenty-five successive years I watched other orioles building, to see if this astonishing bit of calculation should be repeated. Then, last spring, two orioles built in a buttonwood tree, after having been driven away from their favorite elm by carpenters. They wanted a swinging nest, but the buttonwood's branches were too stiff and straight; so they fastened three sticks together on the ground in the form of a perfectly measured triangle. At each angle they fastened one end of a cord, and carried the other end over and made it fast to the middle of the opposite side. Then they gathered up the loops and fastened them by the middle, all together, to a stout bit of marline; and their staging was all ready. They carried up this staging and swung it two feet below the middle of a thick limb, so that some leaves above sheltered them from sun and rain; and upon this swinging stage they built their nest. The marline was tied once around the limb, and, to make it perfectly sure, the end was brought down and fastened to the supporting cord with a reversed double-hitch, the kind that a man uses in cinching his saddle. Moreover, the birds tied a single knot at the extreme end lest the marline should ravel in the wind. The nest hangs above my table now, the reward of a twenty-five years' search; but not one in ten of those who see it and wonder can believe that it is the work of birds, until in the mouths of two or three witnesses who saw the matter every word has been established.

There is one other thing that the modern nature-writer has learned, namely, that in this, as in every other field of literature, only a book which has style can live. And style is but the unconscious expression of personality. Not only may the personal element enter into the new nature-books; it must enter there if we are to interpret the facts truthfully. Every animal has an individuality, however small or dim; that is certain. (I know not how much farther one may safely go in the line of Leibnitz's philosophy and find the development of individuality below the animal.) And the nature-student must seek from his own individuality, which is the only thing that he knows absolutely (this is the centre of the philosophy of both Hume and Descartes) to interpret truthfully and sympathetically the individual before him. For this work he must have not only sight but vision; not simply eyes and ears and a note-book; but insight, imagination, and, above all, an intense human sympathy, by which alone the inner life of an animal becomes luminous, and without which the living creatures are little better than stuffed specimens, and their actions the meaningless dance of shadows across the mouth of Plato's cave.

With these general considerations in mind, it is a simple matter to estimate Mr. Burroughs's astounding criticism in a recent number of the *Atlantic Monthly*. Aside from the unwarranted personal attacks, which those who like him best will most deplore, the article has two evident faults that destroy the force of his criticism: (1) it overlooks entirely the individuality of animals and the adaptiveness of nature; (2) it weighs the universe with the scales of his own farm and barnyard. What the animals do there is the absolute measure and limit of what they will do in the Maine wilderness and the Canadian Rockies. From the mice and woodchucks of his pasture, where he is at home, he affirms what is true and false of the bear and caribou of the great forest where he has never been. One must deny at the outset the very grounds of his opposition.

These two faults are glaringly manifest in Mr. Burroughs's specific denials and assertions. He accuses Mr. Thompson-Seton of deliberate falsehood and misrepresentation, on the sole ground that he himself has not seen the things recorded and that, Therefore, they cannot be true. Frankly, I differ radically from Mr. Thompson-Seton in many of his theories and observations of animals. That is either because I have seen less, and less sympathetically, than he has, or because I have watched bears and wolves with different individual habits. But Mr. Thompson-Seton is a gentleman. When he tells me that he has seen a thing that is new and wonderful to me, though I know his animals well as a class, I shall simply open my own eyes wider, and question Indian hunters more closely, to know whether his observation is in error, or whether he saw some peculiar trait of some one animal, or whether the same thing has been seen by others in different places. For me to question his veracity, and deny what he has seen because I have not seen it, would be simply to show my own lack of courtesy, and arouse suspicion that I might be jealous of his hard-won and well-deserved success.

Mr. Burroughs denies, for instance, Mr. Thompson-Seton's record of a fox jumping on a sheep's back. He calls it pure invention, and assures us authoritatively that it never happened. Yet in my notes, among fifty other fox traits, is the record of a fox that did just that trick, in Boothbay, Maine, in 1887. This is the record: I was following a fox one day when I saw some sheep scatter suddenly; and, knowing that the fox was there, I ran down, calling-on the hound. There was soft snow on the ground, and every track in the field was plain as a footpath. A fox-trail came down to where the sheep were standing, and ended there; nor was there any further track that my own eyes or the hound's nose could discover. On the other side of the field I found the fox track again beside that of a frightened sheep. It began there, with no back track; and it was as certain as if seen and photographed that the fox had crossed on the sheep's back. No other way, except to fly or to jump a hundred yards, was possible.

Concerning Mr. Thompson-Seton's crow story, Mr. Burroughs is equally sure that it is largely falsehood; "for," says he, "crows do not flock in June. They flock only in September." Possibly this is true in Mr. Burroughs's own neighborhood. Elsewhere they are apt to flock at all seasons, and are always more or less gregarious. I have seen three or four hundred at once on the Chatham (N. B.) beaches in early July. On the island of Nantucket they even nest in flocks, contrary to their usual custom; and Mr. C. G. D. Roberts assures me this is also true in his home woods.

After denying Mr. Thompson-Seton's crow story, Mr. Burroughs tells one or two of his own. He tells us that crows in starvation times share their food with one another. He tells us of three crows that came, one winter day, to ask alms at his cabin; that he took them out food, and they came and ate it. This seems to me a much more incredible story than those he denies. Suppose we apply to it his own canons of criticism. We mete out to him the same measure of courtesy that he measures to his fellow naturalist; and we say: "This is deliberate falsehood. He made up that story and called it truth because he wanted to sell his books. We have seen starving animals from Maine to Florida, and they always fight for the biggest portions; we have seen crows in our orchard in winter, and they always fly away at our approach. It is a pretty story, but he should end it with the little sentence which is often found in parenthesis at the end of a long and elaborate Arabic manuscript: *'This is a lie!'*"

If we were so to criticize this story of his, and a score of others in his books, he himself would be the first to see how unjust, how inaccurate, and how arrogant was our criticism. Yet this is precisely the argument and the only argument he uses: "How could these upstart naturalists possibly see what Wallace and Darwin did not see?" he demands, authoritatively. And the answer is simple: Neither Darwin nor Wallace ever studied animals in this way. Their work was of a totally different kind. And these later naturalists follow different animals, with Indian hunters who know a thousand times more of the details of these animals' lives than Darwin or Wallace could possibly know. "How could Darwin see or dare to see what the great Cuvier had not seen?" we might ask with equal force. "How could Audubon see so many things that no one else had ever seen, and record twenty other things that we now know were mistakes?"

Simply because they dared to write what they saw, not what they were expected to see by the self-constituted authorities. And it is sad to remember that they also were vilified and insulted for their observations.

Mr. Burroughs treats my own books, and especially *School of the Woods*, with even scanter courtesy. He sweeps aside all the recorded facts of twenty years' patient observation. He has not seen these things on his farm, and therefore they must be false. The working theories, which alone seem to me to account for the facts, are denied *ex cathedra*. He denies absolutely that there is such a thing as a mother animal teaching her young. The answer to this is, not to accept any theory, but simply to open your eyes and see what goes on with wild mother-birds and animals as they lead their young out into the world. He gives the lie direct to the kingfisher that put minnows into a shallow pool for her young to catch, and to the fishhawk that wounded a fish in order that her young might learn how to strike it. Dr. Philip Cox, the best ichthyologist in Canada, found a new species of fish that the fishhawks had stored in a pool in just this way; and Mr. Mauran Furbish, who probably knows more of the New Brunswick wilderness than any other man, has told me since my book was written that he had seen the same thing. Moreover, the wild mother-sheldrakes to be seen on every wilderness lake often use this method to teach their little ones how to catch trout.

Mr. Burroughs declares absolutely—and here he is a type of the old school—that animals know no such thing as learning. "All animals do exactly and instinctively what their parents did," he affirms. How, then, are there any domestic animals? Why does the tame canary sing, while a wild canary or one brought up in solitude only chirps and twitters? How is a sheep-dog possible to-day, since his parents of yesterday ate the sheep?

He denies the absence of fear on the part of young fawns and moose. It is a little hard, but still only just, to point out here that his criticism is valueless, for he has no knowledge or experience of these creatures. He also forgets that early explorers in the Arctic found most of the animals, and especially the caribou, quite tame and fearless of men. Since then they have learned fear; but it is a denial of every theory of Weismann and Wallace to assert that the young can so soon inherit this fear. How, then, shall the young learn it except they be taught? The Hon. E. L. Scofield, Insurance Commissioner of Connecticut, had an experience with fawns in the Adirondacks precisely similar to that recorded in *School of the Woods;* and Mr. E. W. Deming, the artist, who knows the western animals as well as do the Indians whom he paints so splendidly, will tell him the same thing of elk and mountain sheep.

The critic denies my partridge story, a faithful record of what passed under my eyes one September day two years ago, on the curious ground that a partridge cannot count eleven. A very small grain of imagination here (imagination is good, even for a naturalist) might suggest that it may not be necessary to count in Arabic numerals. Among others of my congregation on a Sunday morning are some two or three hundred faces that I know well. A glance down is often enough to show me that one face is missing—and I never count the congregation. Over the way, my neighbor had a motherly old hen with a dozen or more chickens. I used often to watch her in the twilight clucking her brood under her wings. Just a glance as they come together, and she clucks again anxiously. She has missed one; and here he comes running from under the coop where he has been hiding. Possibly I could accept Mr. Burroughs's decree that no bird can count more than five, without asking how he knows; but, even so, I must believe my eyes, and give this old hen and the partridge credit for a bit of my own intuition. The point is, not that they counted eleven, but that they missed one whom they knew, and who was probably dear to them.

The critic, after denying what may be seen on a hundred wilderness lakes every summer, namely, a fishhawk teaching her young to strike fish, demands how I can know that the young left to themselves without the mother's teaching would probably go back to the old hawk habit of hunting. I answer: partly from a general knowledge of birds of prey; partly from specific experience. A boy whom I knew well had a young fishhawk that he took from a nest. Fish being scarce, he fed him mostly on scraps of meat and small animals. The moment he could use his wings the fishhawk swooped for a chicken. He never, so long as I watched him, tried to fish, but caught squirrels and chickens in true hawk fashion till he took a neighbor's setting hen from her eggs, one day, and was cudgelled to death as a nuisance.

On the subject of the red squirrel, Mr. Burroughs takes me to task for ignorance because I saw a red squirrel carrying some small chestnuts in his cheeks. "That is the word of a false witness," he says, "trying to mislead a jury." For red squirrels have no cheek-pouches like the chipmunks. Yet Mr. Burroughs must know well that red squirrels—and, indeed, all rodents from mice to musquash—will, in carrying grain or small objects, stuff their mouths and cheeks full, as if to remind Nature of the pouches she forgot to give them. It is possible, also, that at one time the red squirrel had pouches; but he no longer stores a winter's supply, and so his gifts have been taken away from him by long disuse, and only a shadowy memory of them remains.

Further analysis of the critic, and of those who, like him, regard animals only as creatures of instinct and fixed habit, would be superfluous. There are more things in heaven and earth, and in the heart of the wild things, evidently, than are seen on Mr. Burroughs's farm or dreamed of in his philosophy. Many will remember his cutting criticism of the poets [*Scribner's Monthly*, December, 1879] in which he ridicules Lowell for having buttercups and dandelions in the same field, and Bryant for giving fragrance to the yellow violet, and both poets for many other things which they had seen. Yet the poets were perfectly right; and Mr. Burroughs's quarrel was with the Almighty, not with the servants who did but interpret His works. Thomas Wentworth Higginson showed [*Atlantic Monthly*, March, 1880] how arrogant and inaccurate was this whole criticism;

but, though the article was modified in its book-form, it still takes the poets to task most unjustly for seeing many things as they are. The fault was, not that Mr. Burroughs did not know his buttercups, but that he overlooked the fact that his farm does not set bounds to the universe, and that the New England fields raised a crop of their own, of whose habits, even of whose species, he was unwittingly quite ignorant.

Indeed, whenever Mr. Burroughs leaves his own field for criticism, those of us who have been most delighted with what he has seen and recorded there will most regret his limitations. One recalls his harsh criticism of Maurice Thompson, a scholar and a gentleman, anent the classics. But how shall a man criticise the classics who does not read them? One remembers his criticism of Victor Hugo, in which, to borrow the great writer's own figure, "he confounds the constellations of profundity with the stars which a duck's feet leave in a puddle." One reads this arbitrary criticism of modern nature-writers, in which he hath put down the mighty from their seats and hath exalted them of low degree. No mention of Rowland Robinson, every one of whose pages is like a clear photograph; no allusion to Dr. Lockwood, the friend of Agassiz, who of all the nature-writers that America has produced was best fitted to write her natural history, and who, in his lectures and notes, has recorded more marvels of animal life than all the rest of us put together. He commends White, who is invariably dry as a stuffed owl, and has no word for Jefferies, who is fresh and inspiring as a morning in the English fields with the hawthorn all ablow. And as to those whom he foreordains and elects, one must take even more exceptions, and say frankly: this is not the voice of authority, as it was meant to be. For, in a word, criticism is not dogmatism. It is not bald assertion or denial: "this is so, sir, and that is false, upon my word and authority." Criticism is an art with a continuous historical development; and he who would criticise must first learn courtesy, and then he must understand the canons of criticism that prevail from Homer to Heine and from Bede to Balzac.

17

The Fate of Little Mucky

ERNEST THOMPSON SETON

Once there was a race with peculiar laws of growth. The people grew big in proportion to what they had done.

In a corner of their land was One who worked away very quietly for half his lifetime, thinking not about growth, but about doing certain things that were next his heart.

It so happened that many of his long tasks were finished about the same time, and so he seemed to grow very fast and become much bigger than the people near him.

Most of them rejoiced at his success, but there was one who had long schemed and aimed at "being big" without work, and so by the other natural law had kept on shriveling, while this one thought was in his small heart: "I cannot get anyone to notice me now, but if I throw a handful of mud at this Tall One that I hate, I shall at least have all eyes turned my way for a time." So he prepared a quantity of vileness, and by climbing a hill called Big Periodic, he reached high enough to throw the muck, and the tall Worker was plentifully bespattered. Every one turned in surprise, and saw the spindly Dwarf grinning with delight at his success, happy to be for a moment the center of observation.

At the first some of them laughed with the Dwarf, and every one wondered what the Worker would do. He would be quite justified in using his power. But he went on quietly with his work; the filth was easily brushed away, because it had no affinities there. The Dwarf grew smaller; people sniffed at him, after the first ripple of surprise and amusement. Furious now, he ran after the Worker to

Excerpted from Ernest Thompson Seton, "Fable & Woodmyth," *Century Magazine* 67 (February 1904): 500.

repeat his attack, since it seemed quite safe; but, not realizing that he had shrunk to a mere Pygmy, he fell into the hole where he had mixed the muck and was smothered.

Here endeth the tale of Little Mucky the Critic.

MORAL: *Notoriety is a poisonous substitute for fame.*

18

The Writings of William J. Long

W. F. GANONG

The last quarter of a century has seen a remarkable development of that form of literature which consists of charming popular writings about animals and their doings. A leader in this movement was John Burroughs, whose work combines literary grace with scientific truth to a degree not surpassed by that of any other modern nature writer, and there are several others in this country writing in the same spirit. Recently, however, there have arisen somewhat suddenly into prominence three writers on nature subjects whose works enjoy a popularity far surpassing that gained by any of their predecessors or contemporaries. These three are Mr. Thompson Seton (earlier known as Seton Thompson), Mr. W. J. Long and Mr. C. G. D. Roberts. Of the former I know little, but the two latter have written extensively of New Brunswick animals, and hence I have been much interested in their works, upon which I propose to make some comments from the point of view of New Brunswick natural history.

In examining the works of these two graceful writers, two queries naturally arise: First, as to the cause of their surpassing popularity, and second, as to their real scientific worth. The cause of their popularity is easily found. It does not lie in their literary charm primarily, for in this they do not so far surpass other nature books, but it consists in this, that they tell about animals, not as they are, but as people like to think they are. It is the humanization and idealization of animals, which, under the influence of the remarkable literary skill of these authors, has made their animal stories so popular. To accomplish this end, they have had to cut loose from the trammels of fact which hampered their

W. F. Ganong, "The Writings of William J. Long," *Science* 19 (April 15, 1904): 623–625. Originally read before the Natural History Society of New Brunswick, Canada, March 1, 1904.

predecessors, and have given their imaginations full play, thus producing fascinating works of fiction disguised as natural history. It is, however, this disguise which constitutes the chief ground of criticism against these works. We all agree that the use of animals as the heroes of romances is perfectly legitimate, but if such works pretend also to be accurate natural history, they unfairly deceive their readers and dishonestly claim a position to which they have no real title. It happens unfortunately that the works of both Mr. Long and Mr. Roberts are widely accepted as accurate in their natural history by the great majority of readers. Mr. Long positively claims that all he writes is accurate fact based on his personal observation, while Mr. Roberts allows an extensive personal knowledge of animals to be inferred, and takes no steps to correct this popular error.

Mr. Long has published five books on animals, containing many references to New Brunswick. The most characteristic feature of these books, especially of the later, is the marvelous character and remarkable number of the experiences the author claims to have had in his observations of animals. The aggregate of Mr. Long's reported observations, both as to quantity and character, is such that if all he reports is true, he has seen more widely and deeply into animal life than all other students of animal habits taken together. This I am not prepared to believe, especially in the light of the tone of his own writings, which seem to me to show that he possesses neither the temperament nor the training essential to a disinterested observer. I have no proof, with the single exception noted below, that any individual statement of Mr. Long's is untrue; but an experience in the New Brunswick wilderness at least as great as Mr. Long's has given me such a knowledge of the difficulties of observing wild animals in their native haunts that I can not believe that any man has had all of the remarkable experiences reported by Mr. Long. Furthermore, the one case in which I happen to know personally the evidence on which Mr. Long bases a statement does not allow me to entertain a high regard for his accuracy. In his book *School of the Woods* he claims to have seen fish hawks catch and wound fish which they then dropped back into the water in order to teach their young to dive for them. This statement is criticized by Mr. Burroughs in his article on 'Real and Sham Natural History' in the *Atlantic Monthly* for March, 1903, and in his reply to this article in the *North American Review* for May, Mr. Long reaffirms it, and adds: 'Mr. Mauran Furbish; who probably knows more of the New Brunswick wilderness than any other man, has told me since my book was written that he had seen the same thing.' Thinking I knew the incident on which this statement was based, I wrote Mr. Furbish, who has been my companion in two journeys into the wilderness of New Brunswick, asking what statement he had made to Mr. Long. He replied that he had simply told Mr. Long of our finding one day a wounded gaspereau[1] floating at the foot of a lake and that Mr. Long 'had furnished all the romance and the reason for their being there.' This incident, I believe, gives the clue to the character of much of Mr. Long's work. He does not deliberately invent, but some trifling basis of fact happening to fit in with some theory developed by his sympathies is accepted by him as confirming his surmises, which he thereupon considers and publishes as proven. Mr. Long's books undoubtedly contain a great deal of valuable fact, but this is so mixed with matter that can not possibly be accepted simply on Mr. Long's statement, that it makes his works practically valueless for any scientific purpose.

Mr. Roberts, I believe, nowhere makes any claim that the natural history basis for his animal writings rests on personal knowledge, but that is the impression left with the reader, and Mr. Roberts takes no steps to set him right. Those who know Mr. Roberts are aware that his literary work for several years past has not permitted him to make those journeys into wild New Brunswick essential to the study of its animal life, and that his few earlier trips had not this object in view and were not of a character to permit it. His knowledge of New Brunswick animals has been gained chiefly in the public libraries, museums and menageries of New York City; his material is hence mostly second hand, and it is unfair to his readers that they should be given the impression that these works are founded on a personal knowledge of the animals described. If Mr. Roberts would but state in the preface to his books that his studies are not based upon personal observation of their subjects, but are as accurate as he can make them from other sources of information, he would not only be dealing honestly with his readers but he would, in my opinion, greatly enhance the value of his really remarkable imaginative works.

So opposite are the standpoints from which the scientific and the literary man view animal life, and so entirely indifferent are they to one another's standards, that the two are not only nearly impossible to one person, but they are well nigh mutually exclusive. The charm of the study to the man of science is the triumph of demonstrating the truth. He makes this his sole standard as it is his sole reward. Slowly, patiently, laboriously, indifferent to popular opinion as to popular applause, he makes his resistless advances, testing and proving each step before a second is made. He naturally has little regard, therefore, for showy leaps from scanty fact to sensational generalization, and he has no respect at all for a presence of scientific knowledge not based upon an honest foundation. The literary man, especially the new nature writer, seems to view nature chiefly in the light of a fresh supply of literary material, and he values her phenomena in proportion to their adaptability for interesting and clever treatment. To him the truth is not of first importance, and imagination is allowed to improve upon nature whenever she can thereby be made more available for literary uses. All this may be legitimate in literature, but works thus inspired should not expect to be accepted also as science, nor should they pretend to an authority they do not possess.

---

1. *Editor's note: A fish, often called an Alewife.—RHL*

1 An advertising poster for Charles G. D. Roberts' *The Heart of the Ancient Wood* (1900). The contrast between the animals in this book and those in W. H. Hudson's *Green Mansions* (1904) illustrates the new approach of the realistic wild animal story. Editor's collection.

2 "Something made him turn his head quickly." By Charles Livingston Bull. From Charles G. D. Roberts, "The Rivals of Ringwaak," *The Watchers of the Trails* (Boston: L. C. Page, 1904).

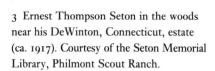

3 Ernest Thompson Seton in the woods near his DeWinton, Connecticut, estate (ca. 1917). Courtesy of the Seton Memorial Library, Philmont Scout Ranch.

4 "Lobo exposing the traps." By Ernest Thompson Seton. From his "Lobo: The King of the Currumpaw," *Wild Animals I Have Known* (New York: Charles Scribner's Sons, 1898).

5 Vix mourns her dead kits. By Ernest Thompson Seton. From his "The Springfield Fox," *Wild Animals I Have Known* (New York: Charles Scribner's Sons, 1898).

6 William J. Long. From *The Bookman* 25 (July 1907).

7 "Gripping his fish and *Pip-Pipping* his exaltation," the osprey learns how to fish. By Charles Copeland. From William J. Long, *School of the Woods* (Boston: Ginn, 1902).

8 The "woodcock genius" with the cast it applied to its broken leg. By Charles Copeland. From William J. Long, *A Little Brother to the Bear* (Boston: Ginn, 1903).

9 "A quick snap where the heart lay." Even the artist had a difficult time figuring out how a wolf could bite a caribou through the chest. By Charles Copeland. From William J. Long, *Northern Trails* (Boston: Ginn, 1905).

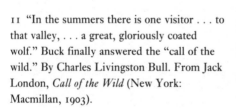

10 "Lying down when the moose
stood still," Buck rests from
harrying his quarry. By Charles
Livingston Bull. From Jack London,
Call of the Wild (New York:
Macmillan, 1903).

11 "In the summers there is one visitor . . . to
that valley, . . . a great, gloriously coated
wolf." Buck finally answered the "call of the
wild." By Charles Livingston Bull. From Jack
London, *Call of the Wild* (New York:
Macmillan, 1903).

12 The President and John Burroughs, at his right, just before entering Yellowstone Park in 1903. From John Burroughs, *Camping with President Roosevelt* (Boston: Houghton Mifflin, 1906).

13 Little Willie Long attacks an incontinent Teddy Roosevelt with his pen, as Johnnie Burroughs hides behind the Presidential chair. By Frank Wing. Courtesy of the Theodore Roosevelt Collection, Harvard College Library.

"Reason!"

Mr. London to his amanuensis: "Simple reflex action, compound reflex action, memory, habit, rudimentary reason, and abstract reason"

14 "Reason!" Jack London argues that animal can reason, although they may not be able to reason in the abstract. From *Collier's Weekly*, September 5, 1908.

"Instinct!"

The President and Mr. Burroughs observing carefully the antics of tom-tits and snipe. Theodore and John together: "Instinct, sheer instinct!"

15 "Instinct!" London did not realize that Roosevelt and Burroughs did not agree themselves over the extent to which animals are governed solely by instinct. From *Collier's Weekly*, September 5, 1908.

19

Truth Plain and Coloured

W. H. HUDSON

A good book is a gift to be grateful for, and here we have two, both very good;
yet it is enough to make even the weariest and saddest man smile to receive
these same two wrapped up together in one piece of brown paper and tied
round with one piece of string. It is as if your two dear friends, who hate each
other with a fierce hatred, should by an unhappy chance drop in upon you at
the same moment. Fortunately books are in a sense inanimate objects, else these
two on being released from the parcel would certainly rise up and fly at and
buffet one another, upsetting the ink and creating a tremendous confusion
among the papers on my writing-table. For it happens that these authors represent the two opposite and just now extremely antagonistic schools of nature
writing in North America. Both are now very well known in this country, and I
am inclined to think that readers at this distance, or on this side of the Atlantic,
are best able to appreciate their respective merits. The dust is washed off when
they reach us. John Burroughs is of the school we know best—the oldest man
among us has known it from his childhood; and when his first book, *Wake
Robin*, was issued in this country thirty or thirty-five years ago, it found a ready
public which he has never lost; on the contrary, it has grown with each succeed-
ing book, most of all perhaps with *Fresh Fields*, in which he describes his impressions of nature in England so delightfully. He would, and indeed does,
describe himself as a literary or "essay" naturalist, a student of nature in the
open air who aims at presenting his facts in a way to touch the emotions—to
produce in some degree the enjoyment we experience in the living reality. He is
scientific, too, since he is devoted to truth, only he sweetens his science with

W. H. Hudson, "Truth Plain and Coloured," *The Speaker* 13 (December 9, 1905): 248–249.

feeling and gives it literary form. His nature study, as he aptly says, is only science out of school, happy in the fields and woods, loving the flowers and animals which it observes, and finding in them something for the sentiments and emotions as well as for the understanding.

If Gilbert White had analysed his own feelings and aims with reference to his nature study and set it down, he would probably have anticipated much that the American naturalist says of himself in this book. And it is a fact, I think, that Burroughs, notwithstanding his modernity and American spirit, impatient of old ways, comes nearest in mind to the historian of Selborne of all living naturalists. In reading him I am often reminded of White's older followers—of Knapp, Jenyns, Moggridge, Jesse, and Knox of the *Ornithological Rambles,* rather than of any literary naturalist of the last fifty years. He is more emotional; he is also a very much better writer—there is no comparison; but he is undoubtedly of their tribe, his whole interest being in things as they are; his keener sympathy with all sentient life, and better gift of expression have never misled him into reading his own mind into that of the lower animals, nor tempted him to colour the simple truth as he finds it. "There is," he says, "but one interpretation of nature, and that is the scientific." And, again: "Jefferies tells how the flower, or the bird, or the cloud is related to his subjective life and experience. It means this or that to him; it may mean something entirely different from another, because he may be bound to it by a different tie of association. The poet fills the lap of earth with treasures not her own—the riches of his own spirit; science reveals the treasures that are her own, and arranges and appraises them."

To this point he returns again and again; the truth that to humanise animal life is to falsify, to caricature it, he ingeminates on page after page, dwelling on it with heat and eloquence. It is an almost angry protest against the new American-made romantic or sentimental school of nature study of which Thompson Seton, Long, and Charles Roberts are the leading exponents. Here in England one is surprised at the amount of feeling displayed in the book; but there is good cause; the trouble is that this new humanised natural history, which makes the beasts and birds a very much more intelligent nice-minded people than, say, the African pigmies or other low-down savages, is taken with tremendous seriousness on the other side of the water. They prefer it over there to the old sober sort of literary natural history, which dates back to the eighteenth century, and came from the village of Selborne. It is infinitely more interesting to the general reader—and it is truer! Again, it is distinctly flattering to the Transatlantic mind to know that this new method of finding out the truth is their own original invention, and that their soil and electrical atmosphere has produced not one but a whole crowd of writers who, in insight and knowledge of the animal mind, surpass all other naturalists who exist or have existed on the globe. We think a great deal of Professor Owen's feat in reconstructing the entire famework of the gigantic Dinornis, long extinct, from the fragment of a single bone. It is nothing compared to that of the new naturalists, who build you up the entire psychology, and whole life from the cradle to the grave, so to speak, of fox, and caribou, and bobcat, and chipmunk, and forty others from a few isolated facts concerning the habits of those animals.

Possibly the new writers were themselves astonished at the great reputation they had made, or which had been thrust on them; in any case, having got it, they are determined to keep it, and are not taking Mr. Burroughs's punishment lying down. There is not an incident in their animal biographies, they assert, however improbable or even incredible it may seem to those who do not know the mind that is in an animal, which has not been witnessed and put on record by some competent observer. Their critic, they say, has narrowed his point of view to the limits of his own personal experience; and they remind him loftily that they have been in the woods and lonely wildernesses, studying the creatures in their own homes, conversing, too, with Indians and trappers who have a life-long familiarity with the subject, and, finally, they tell him that he judges all animals from those he has seen on his own small farm. His retort is: "Your natural history knowledge of the East will avail you in the West. 'There is no country,' says Emerson, 'in which they do not wash the pans and spank the babies, and there is no country where a dog is not a dog or a fox a fox, or where a hare is ferocious or a wolf lamb-like.'"

That is how the matter stands; it is a pretty quarrel, amusing to the looker-on, but it does not concern us. We are a sober-minded people not at all likely to be carried away by anything this romantic school can send us, and this being so we can receive their books without apprehension and read and thoroughly enjoy them. For it can be said that they are delightful, and strike one as something new in literature. We have, it is true, something resembling it in our numerous animal biographies and auto-biographies, the best by far being Fortescue's *Life of a Wild Red Deer on Exmoor*. But these products are comparatively poor; in most cases the subjects are extravagantly over-humanised; they are by inferior writers or else by writers who do not possess all the qualities required to make such work really good.

Of the American writers who have made such a success in this line I should say that Charles Roberts is the foremost, and that *Red Fox*, his latest work, is a worthy successor of the *Kindred of the Wild* and *Watchers of the Trails*. All that the orthodox naturalists, and hunters, and trappers, know of the wild animals, he knows; and to his knowledge he adds a keen sympathy with Wild life, and, above all, he possesses imagination and invention. The result is a book which, purely as a story, is as delightful to read as the unforgettable adventures of Brer Rabbit and Brer Fox. At the same time, the author infuses his own into the animal mind with so nice a judgment and so much restraint that we do not regard his life of a fox, or of any other animal, as mere romance, but it does produce the right illusion, and knowing that it was founded on truth, that there is so much truth intermixed with it, we are pleased to take it as all true.

20

Nature as a Field for Fiction

MABEL OSGOOD WRIGHT

Some time ago when John Burroughs wrote his famous article for the *Atlantic Monthly* attacking the writings of Ernest Thompson Seton and William J. Long, he made one grave error, that of taking the point of view of the quasi scientific observer of nature's methods, instead of that of the naturalist facing a rather new literary phase where nature was seized as a field of fiction. Seton began with a virile originality, but worked his lode so greedily that he frequently sidetracked and bored through into sand. Long used as his stock in trade an incomprehensible mixture of enthusiasm, love of the beautiful, inverted observation, and folk-lore testimony of guides and halfbreeds, leavened by a weird credulity much broader than the wide but fixed limits of natural law, by which it must be judged, if his claims were to be regarded seriously.

Of course throughout all time natural history has been a setting for mythology, overdrawn conclusions, and errors of observation backed up by curious forms of ignorance such as made John Josselyn, gentleman of Kent, who, in writing his observations made in this country in 1638, state that "in the New World barley commonly degenerates into oats and Summer wheat often changeth into rye."

The difference between the creator of the hero of human fiction and the authentic record of the doings of a specific individual that constitute biography lies in this. The hero of fiction is in more or less degree a composite character, but all his attributes must be of course in accord with the known qualities of man, even though mixed in proportions to suit the author. This latter point

Excerpted from Mabel Osgood Wright, "Nature as a Field for Fiction," *New York Times Review of Books* (December 9, 1905), 872.

some of our creators of this new type of fiction forget, and insist not only upon the introduction of unprovable characteristics for their animal heroes, that do not add but rather detract from the strength of the situations, no matter in what light they are considered, but insist that the composite be considered as an individual pure and simple, whose comings and goings, and thoughts they have personally (or by proxy) watched and fathomed.

This position if foolish from any standpoint, for those who love a good, human story, both for its characterization and literary expression, do not care a penny-worth whether the hero is an actual man known to the author or a creature of his fancy, so long as a rational and convincing probability is maintained. It is when the authors in this new field insist that they are not only telling "the truth and nothing but the truth," which moreover, they have personally touched, tasted, swallowed, and digested, that a halt must be called.

Charles G. D. Roberts, the most consistent writer of this new school, as well as the one having the most artistic temperament, regarded from the literary standpoint, sounds the right note in the preface to his splendid story of *Red Fox* when he says:

> In the following story I have tried to trace the career of a fox of the backwoods district of Eastern Canada. The hero of the story, Red Fox, may be taken as fairly typical, both in his characteristics and in the experiences that befall him, in spite of the fact that he is stronger and cleverer than the average run of foxes. . . . This fact does not detract from his authenticity as a type of his kind. . . . As for any emotions which Red Fox may once in a great while seem to display, these may safely be accepted by the most cautious as fox emotions, not as human emotions. In so far as man is himself an animal, he is subject to and impelled by many emotions which he must share with not a few other members of the animal kindgom. Any full presentation of an individual animal of one of the more highly developed species must depict certain emotions not altogether unlike those which a human being experiences under like conditions. To do this is not by any means, as some hasty critics would have it, to ascribe human emotions to the lower animals.

William J. Long, however, in his latest volume, *Northern Trails*, persistently and foolishly, no matter what may be the standpoint, adheres to his old formula, which was made into kindling wood, burned, and the ashes scattered to the four winds by Burroughs's somewhat narrow criticism. This volume, with its spirited illustrations by Charles Copeland, is made up of eight stories. "Wayseeses the Strong One" (a wolf story, following many miles after "Lobo," Seton's first and best achievement); "In Quest of Weptonk the Wild," the pursuit of the wild goose in its breeding grounds"; Pequam the Fisher," the cunning robber of traps; "The Trail of the Cunning One"; "Out of the Deeps," dealing with whales, seals, sharks, and gulls; "Matwock of the Icebergs," a polar bear; "Where the Salmon Jump"; and "The Story of Kopseep," a salmon-colored romance.

Listen to the author's solemn guarantee of absolute veracity, and the completely identified individuality of each animal depicted, with one single exception in the case of Kopseep the Salmon, where, it being impossible to personally follow the fish under water from the sea to the river sources, the author was obliged "either to omit that part of his life or to picture it as best I could from imagination and the records of the salmon hatcheries and deep-sea travelers."

The reader who has not followed such trails before will ask at once, How many of these things are true? Every smallest incident recorded here is as true as careful and accurate observation can make it. In most of the following chapters, as in all previous volumes, will be found the direct results of my own experience among animals; and in the few cases where, as stated plainly in the text, I have used the experience of other and wiser men, I have taken the facts from first-hand and accurate observers, and have then sifted them carefully so as to retain only those that are in my own mind without a question as to their truth.

Ah, Mr. Long, here is another illustration of the glaring consistency of your methods. We, the reading public, must swallow whole any presentment you choose to make, but you reserve the right to question the statements born of the experience of "other and wiser men, first-hand and accurate observers," and retain only what appeals to you as being truth, thus confessing to a standard of veracity that, instead of being fixed, is to be wholly controlled by the personal equation of the author. Against this *a priori* the pen of criticism is powerless except to recommend a severe Winter course of pure logic as a possible cure. Aside from the controversial side as to whether these eight stories are to be classified as natural history or fiction, these tales of the northern trails are dull and lifeless. A certain entertaining quality that the author's earlier volumes, probable or improbable, possessed is missing. For some reason, we care very little about the animals portrayed; the stories are too much worked out; insistence upon truth and verbosity of detail and palpable word painting are not creative qualities, and nowhere is there a single breath of the genius such as makes the creatures of the jungle books as vitally probable to us as the little squirrel that gambols about the porch.

21

Roosevelt on the Nature Fakirs

EDWARD B. CLARK

Editor's Note—It is about time to call a halt upon misrepresentative nature studies. Utterly preposterous details of wild life are placed before school children in the guise of truth. Wholly false beliefs have been almost standardized. Only by an authoritative protest can the fraud be exposed. At this juncture it is fitting that the President should come forward. From every point of view he is the person in the United States best equipped for the task, and we are fortunate in being able to fire the first gun, so to speak, with a charge of Mr. Roosevelt's vigorous, clear-cut, earnest English.

"Theodore Roosevelt is the World's authority on the big game mammals of North America. His writings are fuller and his observations are more complete and accurate than those of any other man who has given the subject study."

This is the statement of Dr. C. Hart Merriam, Chief of the United States Biological Survey, a man whose knowledge of natural history and whose extensive field experience fit him to pass judgment on the comparative value of writings about the wild animals of this continent.

Dr. Merriam says that the truthfulness of none of the field notes of Theodore Roosevelt has ever been doubted. Mr. Roosevelt's field methods clearly account for the accuracy of his writings, for he makes his notes on the spot. Weights and measurements are taken at once, and these, with other observations, are set down forthwith, in order that nothing may be left to the possible fickleness of memory. Moreover, Mr. Roosevelt goes into the field knowing, to quote Dr. Merriam, "what is not known of animals." That is to say, if he falls in

Edward B. Clark, "Roosevelt on the Nature Fakirs," *Everybody's Magazine* 16 (June 1907), 770–774.

with the chance of observing wolves, cougars, bears, or other creatures of the wild, because of the breadth and accuracy of his knowledge he is able to eliminate at once from his study the habits or traits that have been already reported upon, and to watch only for what may be unknown to science.

These methods have, naturally enough, resulted not only in notes for which Dr. Merriam claims accuracy, but in specimens by means of which the scientists of the Biological Survey have been enabled materially to advance zoological knowledge. From bear specimens sent by Mr. Roosevelt from Mississippi, the scientists succeeded in reinstating a species of which they knew little. He gave to the Biological Survey the only cougar series extant in the museums of the country—a series of males, females, and immature specimens which has been of the greatest value for comparative purposes. Mr. Roosevelt has also given the Washington scientists specimens of the plains wolf, of the ordinary coyote, and of the Colorado bears, which have been extremely helpful in the work of securing final knowledge of these animals.

In the same spirit in which he observes land mammals, Mr. Roosevelt watches the small reminders of the wilderness that are not far from his window every day, winter and summer—for of course he is not entirely cut off from nature merely because he happens to live in the White House. He knows the birds as he does the big game animals of the West, and in his almost daily walks he watches for the cardinals, the juncos, the nuthatches, and the whitethroats with the same keen eye that watches elsewhere for the bear or the elk.

What Mr. Roosevelt Says

It is not surprising that a man who approaches nature with so sincere an interest and who himself observes so accurately should admire the writings of John Burroughs and other nature students who record truthfully what they see in the fields and the woods. Equally natural is it that, with hundreds of his fellow citizens who have smelled the smoke of the camp-fire and have taken the night sky for a blanket, Mr. Roosevelt should detest the misrepresentation of nature's ways.

The other night in the White House while sitting before a wood-fire suggestive of the camp, I asked him what he thought about the recent books of some of the nature "realists," and of certain nature "students" who declare in their prefaces that all they have set down is true.

Now, for a long time the men who have studied nature with a view to learning its truths have believed that the fiction that is put forth as fact by some of the most popular writers has injured the cause of nature study. These men have been stirred to alarm or indignation by the action of some of the school boards of the country in adopting as supplementary reading for the use of the children some of these fantastic animal stories which the writers claim are true to the minutest detail.

These things were in my mind when I asked Mr. Roosevelt what he thought about the subject, and he showed by his answer that they had been in his own mind for a long time.

"I don't believe for a minute," said Mr. Roosevelt, "that some of these men who are writing nature stories and putting the word 'truth' prominently in their prefaces know the heart of the wild things. Neither do I believe that certain men who, while they may say nothing specifically about truth, do claim attention as realists because of their animal stories, have succeeded in learning the real secrets of the life of the wilderness. They don't know, or if they do know, they indulge in the wildest exaggeration under the mistaken notion that they are strengthening their stories.

"As for the matter of giving these books to the children for the purpose of teaching them the facts of natural history—why, it's an outrage. If these stories were written as fables, published as fables, and put into the children's hands as fables, all should be well and good. As it is, they are read and believed because the writer not only says they are true but lays stress upon his pledge. There is no more reason why the children of the country should be taught a false natural history than why they should be taught a false physical geography.

"Dropping the matter of the school-books for a moment, take the stories of some of the nature writers who wish to be known as realists. Realism is truth. A writer like Stewart Edward White is true to nature; he knows the forest and the mountain and the desert; he puts down what he sees; and he sees the truth. But certain others either have not seen at all, or they have seen superficially. Nature writing with them is no labor of love. Their readers, in the main persons who have never lived apart from the paved street, take the wildest flights of the imagination of these 'realists' as an inspired word from the gospel of nature. It is false teaching."

Some Unnatural Nature Stories

"Take the chapter from Jack London's *White Fang* that tells the story of a fight between the great northern wolf, White Fang, and a bulldog. Reading this, I can't believe that Mr. London knows much about the wolves, and I am certain that he knows nothing about their fighting, or as a realist he would not tell this tale. Here is a great wolf of the northern breed; its strength is such that with one stroke it can hamstring a horse or gut a steer, and yet it is represented as ripping and slashing with 'long, tearing strokes' again and again and again a bull dog, not much more than a third its size, and the bulldog, which should be in ribbons, keeps on fighting without having suffered any appreciable injury. This thing is the very sublimity of absurdity. In such a fight the chance for the dog would be only one in a thousand, its victory being possible only through getting a throat grip the instant that the fight started. This kind of realism is a closet product.

"In the same book London describes a great dog-wolf being torn in pieces by a lucivee, a northern lynx. This is about as sensible as to describe a tom cat tearing in pieces a thirty-pound fighting bull terrier. Nobody who really knew anything about either a lynx or a wolf would write such nonsense. Now, I don't want to be misunderstood. If the stories of these writers were written in the spirit that inspired Mowgli and we were told tales like those of the animals at the Council Rock, of their deliberations and their something more than human conclusions, we should know that we were getting the very essence of fable and we should be content to read, enjoy, and accept them as fables. We don't in the least mind impossibilities in avowed fairy tales; and Bagheera and Baloo and Kaa are simply delightful variants of Prince Charming and Jack the Slayer of Giants. But when such fables are written by a make-believe realist, the matter assumes an entirely different complexion. Men who have visited the haunts of the wild beasts, who have seen them, and have learned at least something of their ways, resent such gross falsifying of nature's records."

How a Caribou Is Not Killed

"William J. Long is perhaps the worst of these nature-writing offenders. It is his stories, I am told, that have been put, in part, into many of the public schools of the country in order that from them the children may get the truths of wild animal life.

"Take Mr. Long's story of 'Wayeeses, the White Wolf.' Here is what the writer says in his preface to the story: 'Every incident in this wolf's life, from his grasshopper hunting to the cunning caribou chase, and from the den in the rocks to the meeting of wolf and children on the storm-swept barrens, is minutely true to fact, and is based squarely upon my own observation and that of my Indians.'

"As a matter of fact, the story of Wayeeses is filled with the wildest improbabilities and a few mathematical impossibilities. If Mr. Long wants us to believe his story of the killing of the caribou fawn by the wolf in the way that he says it was done, he must produce eye-witnesses and affidavits. I don't believe the thing occurred. Nothing except a shark or an alligator will attempt to kill by a bite behind the shoulder. There is no less vulnerable point of attack; an animal might be bitten there in a confused scuffle, of course, or seized in his jump so as to throw him; but no man who knows anything of the habits of wolves or even of fighting dogs would dream of describing this as the place to kill with one bite. I have seen scores of animals that have been killed by wolves; the killing or crippling bites were always in the throat, flank, or ham. Mr. George Shiras, who has seen not scores but hundreds of such carcasses, tells me that the death wounds or disabling wounds were invariably in the throat or the flank, except when the animal was first hamstrung.

"If Mr. Long's wolf killed the caribou fawn by a bite through the heart, as the writer asserts, the wolf either turned a somerset—or pretty near it—or else got his head upside down under the fore legs of the fawn, a sufficiently difficult performance. Wayeeses would have had to do this before he could get the whole breast of the animal in his mouth in order to crush it and bite through to the heart. It is very unlikely that any wolf outside of a book would be fool enough to attempt a thing like this even with a fawn caribou, when the killing could be done far more surely in so many easier ways.

"But the absurdity of this story is as nothing to the story of the killing of a bull caribou by the same wolf, using the same method. 'A terrific rush, a quick snap under the stag's chest just behind the fore legs, where the heart lay; then the big wolf leaped aside and sat down quietly again to watch.'"

Second-Hand Knowledge of Writers

"Mr. Long has Wayeeses, after tearing the caribou's heart, hold himself 'with tremendous will power from rushing in headlong and driving the game, which might run for miles if too hard pressed.'

"Now here Mr. Long is not thinking of anything he has ever seen, but has a confused memory of what he has heard or read of gut-wounded animals. A caribou with such a hurt may go on for a long distance before it drops, and it is wise not to follow it too closely, because if not followed it will often lie down, and in an hour or so will become too stiff to get up. But it would seem that even Mr. Long might know, what a child should know, that no caribou and no land mammal of any kind lives after the heart is pierced as he describes; whether followed or not, the caribou would fall in a few jumps. This, however, is the least of the absurdities of the story. That Wayeeses tore the heart of the bull caribou in the way that Mr. Long describes is a mathematical impossibility. The wolf's jaws would not gape right; the skin and the chest walls with all the protective bone and tissue could not possibly be crushed in; the teeth of the wolf could not pierce through them to the heart, for no wolf's teeth are long enough for the job, nor are the teeth of any other carnivorous land mammal. By no possibility could a wolf or any other flesh-eating land mammal perform such a feat. It would need the tusks of a walrus. Mr. Long actually cannot know the length of a wolf's fang; let him measure one, and then measure what the length would have to be to do the thing he describes; and then let him avow his story a pleasing fable. He will get a clear idea of just what the feat would be if he will hang a grapefruit in the middle of a keg of flour, and then see whether a big dog could bite through the keg into the grapefruit; it would be a parallel performance to the one he describes when he makes his picture-book wolf bite into the heart of a bull caribou.

"As a sort of a climax of absurdity to this 'true story of Wayeeses,' Mr. Long draws a picture of this wilderness wolf, savage from tip to tip, doing for some lost children the kindly service of leading them home through the forest. Now let me repeat that this would be all right if the story were avowedly a fairy tale, like Kipling's *Jungle Book*. But it is grotesque to claim literal truthfulness for such a tissue of absurdities."

The Lynx in Fiction and in Fact

"I wonder sometimes as I read the lynx stories of Mr. Long if this wilderness tramper ever saw a lynx to know it at all in any real sense. He has several stories of the lynx. They vary little in their grotesque inaccuracy. Take the story of 'Upweekis the Shadow,' which has place in a little book that I am now told is used as one of the supplementary readers from which American school children are expected to get accurate knowledge of wilderness ways. There are all kinds of absurdities in this lynx 'study.' In one place, for instance, Mr. Long describes a number of lynxes gathered around the nearly eaten carcass of a caribou, while a menagerie of smaller beasts, including a pine marten, circulates freely among them. Now, of course, a marten would circulate among a company of lynxes just about as long as a mouse would circulate among a company of cats. But the most comic feature of Mr. Long's lynx article is his account of various desperate encounters he had with the animal, which he evidently regards as a monster dangerous to man. We are told by the writer that a lone lynx made him exceedingly 'uncomfortable' for half an afternoon. The animal 'dogged' him hour after hour through the wilderness. He tells of making double time for four miles in order to reach camp before night should fall and give the lynx the advantage. Mr. Long declares that he had an encounter with the lynx before he succeeded in driving it from the trail. In reality, anyone is in just as much danger of being attacked by a domestic cat when walking through his own garden as Mr. Long was of being attacked by this lynx of the northern wilderness."

Writers Vouch for Misstatements

"Once more let me say that if the fairy-tale mark was put on the stories of these writers, criticism would pass. Apparently, however, they wish to be known as teachers, or possibly they have a feeling of pride that springs from the belief that their readers will think of them as of those who have tramped the wilds and met nature in its gentleness and in its fierceness face to face.

"Some of the writers who at times offend, at other times do excellent work. Mr. Thompson Seton has made interesting observations of fact, and much of his fiction has a real value. But he should make it clear that it *is* fiction, and not fact.

"Many of the nature stories of Charles G. D. Roberts are avowedly fairy tales, and no one is deceived by them. When such is the case, we all owe a debt to Mr. Roberts, for he is a charming writer and he loves the wilderness. But even Mr. Roberts fails to consult possibilities in some of his stories.

"The lynx seems to have an unholy fascination for these realists, and Mr. Roberts has succumbed to it. I wish he had learned a little of the real lynx, as distinguished from the Mr. Long lynx, before he wrote the story called 'On the Night Trail.'

"It's a big lynx that weighs over forty pounds. A fifty-pound lynx is a giant among the American species. An ordinary lucivee is about the size of a big Rocky Mountain bobcat. I have seen a light-weight dog, a cross between a bull terrier and a collie, take a full-grown, able-bodied lynx out of a hole, though this is a rather exceptional case. When the lynx is hard pressed and goes into a good place it will turn and fight just as a domestic cat will fight in the same circumstances, but it won't fight on its own initiative. In a hole it can usually stand off a good dog, but in the open any big fighting dog will kill it. I have known two ordinary foxhounds to kill a lucivee; several times I have seen a Rocky Mountain lynx, or bobcat, killed by a pack of half a dozen or more hounds and terriers, and in no case did the struggle last over a few seconds, the lynx being killed so quickly that it had no time to leave a serious mark on any one of its numerous foes.

"Now in this 'Night-Trail' story of Mr. Roberts a man catches a lynx in a trap, ties it up, puts it into a bag, and, swinging it over his shoulder, starts through the woods with his burden. On his way the man is attacked by eight wolves that form themselves in a crescent at his front. He is armed with an ax and as well as he can he fights off his wolf assailants. In the crisis, in order to give the lynx a chance for its life and perhaps a chance to create 'an effective diversion in his own favor,' the man slashes the sack open, cuts the lynx's bonds, and sets it free.

"The lynx, according to Mr. Roberts, goes into the fray with the wolves with a sort of savage exultation. Several of the wolves receive slashes which send them yelping out of the battle. Now the thing is so utterly ridiculous that any man who knows both the wolf and the lynx loses patience. Real wolves would have made shreds of a real lynx within a twinkling of the time they closed in to the attack. The animal of the story would have stood no more chance with the eight wolves than a house cat could stand in a fight with eight bull terriers.

"In one of the books that I understand is used as a supplementary reader is a story of 'the caribou school.' It is difficult to discus this story with patience. The writer, Mr. Long, vouches for the truth of everything in the book by saying that the sketches are the result 'of many years' personal observation in woods and fields.' He tells of finding half a dozen mother caribou and nearly twice as many little ones gathered together in a natural opening surrounded by dense underbrush—and this was their school-room. Then there follows a description of the mother caribou's method of teaching manners to the young, of giving them lessons in jumping and of impressing upon them the necessity of following the leader. Mr. Long allows little for instinct. He says: 'it was true kindergarten teaching, for under the guise of frolic the calves were being taught a needful lesson.' Such a tale, which the school children receive stamped with the word 'truth,' should need no comment; and it is rather startling to think of any school authorities accepting it.

"The preservation of the useful and beautiful animal and bird life of the country depends largely upon creating in the young an interest in the life of the woods and fields. If the child mind is fed with stories that are false to nature, the children will go to the haunts of the animal only to meet with disappointment. The result will be disbelief, and the death of interest. The men who misinterpret nature and replace fact with fiction, undo the work of those who in the love of nature interpret it aright."

22

"I Propose to Smoke Roosevelt Out"
—Dr. Long

"Mr. Roosevelt is a man who takes savage delight in whooping through the woods killing everything in sight. He goes with horses and dogs and guns. He doesn't know what a square deal means, either for wild animals or men.

"I am a gentle mollycoddle who can't bear the sight of suffering in beast or man. I go about with a pencil and a notebook instead of a rifle. But I have seen in the forest gentle-tempered animals whom it was not wise to rouse by unfair attack. I have been an inoffensive person going about my own business. The President has broken out against me, a private person, with an unprovoked and vicious attack upon my honor. I will not endure it. I will fight him on this issue until he is whipped. Mollycoddle that I am, no man shall give me the lie. He has stepped down from his high position to fire his shot, and having fired it he hurries back to the refuge of his office. But I propose to smoke Mr. Roosevelt out. He has given me the right to do it. He has made it incumbent on me to do it. And I expect to do it.

"Mr. Roosevelt says that he doesn't believe my account of the killing of the caribou fawn by the white wolf 'Wayeeses,' and remarks sneeringly that if I want him to believe it I must produce eyewitnesses and affidavits. I have already produced one affidavit, and I want to know whether Mr. Roosevelt is satisfied or whether he wants more (I can give him plenty more within a few days), or whether he proposes to refuse to receive the evidence which he asked for—whether he proposes to play the man and admit he was mistaken or to remain in hiding while he is shown to be a cowardly traducer of private citizens. For so surely as he refuses to do me justice, I shall do Mr. Roosevelt justice before the eyes of all men."

"'I Propose to Smoke Roosevelt Out'—Dr. Long," *New York Sunday Times,* Magazine Section, June 2, 1907, 2.

A Genuine Nature Lover

William J. Long, student of nature, is now forty years old. Since he was a tiny lad, when they would find him lying in the grass watching with a long afternoon's enchanted interest the rabbit or the ants, he has been a friend of the beasts. He grew up a scholar educated for the ministry. Before he took a pastorate he had taken a doctorate at Heidelberg and read in the Sorbonne and the Vatican library. He still shows a slight tendency to the stoop of the scholar, corrected, however, by much out-of-door life. He is six feet tall, and would weight about 175 pounds. He has an open and engaging, a rather boyish face; is nervous, and swift of foot and hand; looks you in the eye and talks with immense frankness and rapidity. He is full of his experiences with the animals, is apt to run off every few sentences into an anecdote, told with striking vividness of detail, and marked by certain simplicities of narration. It is impossible to talk five minutes with this man without concluding that what William J. Long says he saw he did see.

It is also impossible to doubt but that Mr. Long will keep after President Roosevelt until he gets some sort of satisfaction. The nature writer appears to have no animosity against the President, thought he abominates what he freely calls his "brutal" and "blood-thirsty" and "barbarous" methods in hunting the beasts. But Mr. Long is immensely in earnest in his conviction that where two gentlemen are concerned, a question of veracity cannot remain unsettled. He is modest and mild in countenance and manner, but he is a son of an Irishman, and he declines to go into the Ananias club without putting up an Irishman's fight.

He says:

"The idea of Mr. Roosevelt assuming the part of a naturalist is absurd. He is a hunter. He knows little or nothing concerning the beasts he hunts except how they try to escape death. He knows the outside of the animal; he collects their heads and hides and measures their exterior proportions. Who is he to write 'I don't believe for a minute that some of these nature writers know the heart of the wild things.' As to that, I find after carefully reading two of his big books that every time Mr. Roosevelt gets near the heart of a wild thing he invariably puts a bullet through it. From his own records I have reckoned a full thousand hearts which he has known thus intimately. In one chapter alone I find that he violently gained knowledge of eleven noble elk hearts in a few days and he tells us that this was 'a type of many such hunts'; in others he says he has been 'much more successful and often far excelled these figures' ('Elk Hunt at Two Ocean Pass'). Mr. Roosevelt certainly knows the hearts of the wild things. One nature writer whom he condemns has watched and followed animals for years, thinking that he could understand these wild hearts better if he left them beating warmly under their own soft skins; and he still perversely clings to this delusion.

"Mr. Roosevelt never gets near enough to animals of the forest to know anything about them. You stop 200 yards away to shoot a deer. I watch my friends from a point perhaps twenty or thirty yards away. I have been so close to wild animals that I could lie and watch their eyelids lift and fall. He has his horses and his dogs. What chance has he of getting near them in their native unconsciousness? I go alone into the woods and steal silently after the animals, never killing except in need of food, and then with a heartache. Thus I spend months of each year in the solitudes. I have had the good fortune to learn many things about the animals that had not been reported before. I couldn't help learning many things. I have discovered the individuality of animals and observed traits that had not been recognized before. I am only one of many men who will soon be doing the same thing—going out and getting acquainted with wild nature and learning how closely it is connected with human nature.

"The fact is, we are still barbarians in our attitude toward the animals. We are still living in the caves. Mr. Roosevelt is like a man of the stone age who sallied forth with his club to brain some beast and drag it home to display before his wives. But the stone age man needed meat for food; it wasn't entirely blood-lust with him. Which is the more pleasing picture, that of the hairy man with his club, slaughtering for food, or the gentleman who we see in Mr. Roosevelt's autobiography.

> He bore his antlers aloft; the snow lay thick on his mane; he snuffed the air as he walked. As I drew a bead his bearing of self-confidence changed to one of alarm. My bullet smote through his shoulder blades and he plunged wildly forward and fell full length on the blood-stained snow.
>
> I jumped off my horse, knelt and covered the fawn; as I pulled the trigger down went the deer, the bullet having gone into the back of its head. I felt much pleased with it.
>
> My nerves were thrilling and my heart beating with eager, fierce excitement. . . . Drawing a fine bead I pressed the trigger. He did not reel, but I knew he was mine, for the blood sprang from both his nostrils, and he fell dying on his side before he had gone thirty rods.
>
> My aim was true, and the huge beast crashed down hill, pulling himself on his forelegs for twenty rods, his hind quarters tailing. Racing forward, I broke his neck. Two moose birds followed the wounded bull as he dragged his great carcass down the hill, and pounced with ghoulish bloodthirstiness on the gouts of blood that sprinkled the green herbage.

Who Was Bloodthirsty?

"A nature writer would say here that the hungry birds were finding new food and eating it thankfully, like two children picking up red apples; and that the bloodthirstiness lay in the heart of the man who killed this elk when, according to his own record, he had already seven elk heads in camp, and the meat was of no possible use, being too strong for food at this season.

"I wonder if the cave-dweller was as poor a sportsman as the man we see in Mr. Roosevelt's autobiographical revelations! —the man who began his hunter's career by jacking deer in the Adirondacks and continued it by killing fawns and deer that came to his camp to drink. I have lain among the deer night after night and jacked them. I love to see their beautiful eyes, their fine nostrils and their lordly necks; no sportsman thus beguiles the creature and slaughters them while the light renders them helpless. Nor does any true sportsman butcher the deer that comes to his camp. It is an unwritten law of the camp that you may go after game when you need it, but must spare the animal that comes confidingly to your own door. But Mr. Roosevelt makes his own laws:

"Sitting on his veranda, a deer comes to drink at the river in front of him. The great huntsman records: 'Slipping stealthily into the house I picked up my rifle. . . . I held true, and as the smoke cleared away the deer lay struggling on the sands.'

"Too bad that deer did not know the heart of humanity as well as Mr. Roosevelt knows the heart of the wild things.

"He writes of two antelope: 'They stood side by side facing me, motionless, unheeding the cracks of the rifle.' He killed one, after four shots, and then took several vain shots at the mate as it ran away. 'This deer did not seem satisfied,' he says, 'but kept hanging around in the distance, looking at us.' A nature writer would say here that the deer was looking for his lost mate; but that, of course, would be a lie. He was merely ashamed of not letting himself be killed by so great a hunter.

"There was one last elk left in the country wherein Mr. Roosevelt had his ranch in the West. One day the lonely old fellow, the last of a noble race, wandered upon the ranch. He belongs to a gregarious tribe, and he probably felt that he might find a sort of companionship among the cattle. 'Of course,' writes Mr. Roosevelt, 'such a chance was not to be neglected.' He grabbed his rifle and rushed out:

> My bullet struck too far back, but made a deadly wound. The elk disappeared in a wild plunging gallop. We followed the bloody trail and found him dead in a thicket. . . . No sportsman can ever feel keener pleasure and self-satisfaction than when he walks up to a grand elk lying dead in the cool shade of the evergreen.

"You are mistaken Mr. Roosevelt, profoundly, absolutely, hopelessly mistaken. There was a better chance that you neglected when that lonely old elk, the last of his race, wandered to your ranch, seeing your cattle unmolested, and thinking, it may even be, in his dim, brute way, that here was a place where he might be safe from his enemies. And there is a keener pleasure than to walk up to a noble animal dead in the cool shade of the evergreen, his glad life gone, his symmetry distorted in the death struggle, his beautiful brown coat all clotted and bloodstained, and his soft eyes glazing rapidly as if to hide the reproach that is in them. There is a greater pleasure and wisdom than all this; but you will never know what they are. The bloody endings over which you gloat bring little 'self-satisfaction' to a thoughtful man who has seen the last look in the eyes of a stricken deer, and who remembers that even this small life has its mystery, like our own. You are not a sportsman, though you have slain your thousands; you are not a naturalist, though you have measured hides and horns; you do not and you cannot understand 'the hearts of the wild things,' though you have made a grievous quantity of them bleed. It needs no eyewitness nor any affidavit to support this statement. You have yourself furnished all the proof."

Does Tell Surprising Stories

"It is true that I tell some stories about wild animals that are surprising. I dare say there are thousands of still more surprising things I have not seen and do not tell. There are many incidents in my notebooks which I should not care to publish. I saw them. There is no mistake about them. But they would seem so extraordinary to the average reader that I prefer to wait until I have the corroborating testimony of another observer. It is constantly happening that these extraordinary stories are 'released,' so to speak, by the circumstance that a friend sees the same or a very similar incident.

"For instance, I had hesitated to publish that account of the woodcock who set his broken leg in a clay cast. When I was challenged on that I was able to produce the record of five similar cases in different parts of the country, with the affidavits of eight men and women witnesses. And since that publication I have received this additional confirmation of the possibility of the woodcock's feat."

Dr. Long took from a case the severed leg of a fowl, around which was bound a jacket of feathers glued together with some adhesive stuff. A shot wound could be seen in the bone of the leg underneath the jacket, which had worn loose.

"This," pointed out Dr. Long, "is the leg of a grouse which had bound up its wounded limb with a bandage of feathers plucked from its own body and cemented with some sticky substance the nature of which we have not been able to discover. It was sent me some months ago by friends in Scotland.

"One incident I narrated in a book was that of a race between two loons. Mr. Parkhurst of Boston, associated with my publishers, frankly expressed his disbelief in that incident. He told me that while he liked my books, that story he could not swallow. A year ago he said to me in the presence of a number of gentlemen: 'Dr. Long, I want to apologize to you for an injustice I did you. I did not believe in your loon race, and I am afraid I said so. I am now obliged to say that I have myself been witness to exactly such a race as you describe. Do you remember that bay of the Rangeley Lake where—' and he described a point I knew well, and proceeded to give an account of the scene he had witnessed. He was pushing along the bank close to an inlet when he heard a great clamoring of loons. He remembered my loon story, and, though without the slightest faith in it, it occurred to him to paddle softly and watch. When he reached the mouth of the inlet, he saw a flock of loons arrange themselves in orderly fashion in two lines, while two loons went to the top of the line, turned and came down the course at the top of their speed. 'What are they doing?' he whispered to his guide. 'By God, they're racing,' was the astonished answer. And so they were. The lines closed in back of the racers, all being eager to see the finish. When it was made, a great clattering went up.'"

Trout Do Jump

"I was myself incredulous about jumping trout. You know you often see fishing pictures in which the trout is represented as leaping out of the water. Now, I knew of no evidence that the trout had this habit. I had fished in half the trout streams from Labrador down to the south coast of Connecticut, and I had never seen a trout jump. Bass and salmon, yes; trout never. But one day I was canoeing through a Maine swamp and I observed that we were passing over the channel of a cold, clear stream. My guide laughed at me, but I began to whip the water. Sure enough trout began to rise. I took twenty within a very short while and of the twenty, eleven jumped.

"There are, I say, many incidents in my notebooks which I do not care to publish at present. But then every man who owns a pet dog has seen things which would lose him his reputation for veracity if he told them. The reason is that animals are individuals. There are dogs and dogs. There are deer and deer, and bears and bears. It has been a feature of my work that I have studied the individual. I have not tried to learn what are the habits of caribou or of coyotes. I have watched individual elks and individual wolves. And every incident related in any and all of my writings is there because I have myself seen or my guide has personally seen the thing happen. People may like or dislike my writings. They may think my fancy too active and my personifying disposition too strong. That does not matter. I may be wrong there. But as to facts, I am not wrong. I am absolutely certain of the fact always. Generally I can furnish corroborative testimony, and I am always glad to do this for any one who really desires to test honestly the value of my statements.

"My discovery has been the individuality of animals. Hasn't every owner of a dog seen him do things that he is sure no other dog ever did before? I once had a pet coon. I had to punish him when he was very young for killing a chicken. He appeared to be reformed, but after a while the chickens began to go again. There was no sign that he was guilty. But I observed him closely and suspected the worst. One day, looking with a strong glass from a window, I watched him at his meal. He left a little on his plate and lay down close by in the shadow of the little house he occupied. He appeared to be asleep with his nozzle between his paws, but through the glass I could see the glitter of his half-open eye.

Presently the chickens, looking for food, came up and began picking at the morsel on the coon's plate. Suddenly he sprang up—and had a chicken. He feasted to satisfaction, but before he lay down to a real sleep he buried the feathers and carcass.

"The next day I watched him undertake the same trick again, but this time I appeared on the scene before he had made way with his victim. As soon as the coon saw me coming he threw himself sprawling over the chicken, to hide it with his own body, and 'went to sleep.'

"Mr. Roosevelt denies certain details in two of my animals, the wolf of *Northern Trails* and the lynx of *Wilderness Ways,* which latter animal, he declares, has for me an 'unholy fascination.' He ridicules as 'grotesque absurdity' the fact that a big lynx once followed me in the big woods and made me feel 'uncomfortable.'

"Now, I have taken bear cubs from their mother and let them go again; have crawled into a cougar's den; have had hungry wolves too near me at night in midwinter, and I have still maintained that there is practically no danger to a quiet man from wild animals. It certainly was absurd for me to be disturbed by one lynx; but the fact remains that I was 'uncomfortable.' I was alone and unarmed with some fresh meat that the starving lynx wanted. Though I have met a few boasters in the woods, I have never yet met a real hunter who did not have a respect for the big Canada lynx, and who, if unarmed, would not go out of his way to avoid a band of lynxes in midwinter."

A Slight Difference

"Mr. Roosevelt never met the big lynx or wolf of Canada and Labrador, and is talking about smaller Western animals, and so far as I can discover from his books, he approaches a lynx after a pack of dogs has driven it into a tree. This, you see, makes a slight difference. If I were a lynx, and Mr. Roosevelt hunted me with a pack of savage dogs, so that I could not possibly get at his neck unawares, and behind the pack of dogs were horses, hunters and repeating rifles, I do not know what I would do. I might pitch savagely into the whole outfit; or I might collapse at the first nip of the first small dog. But when he declared dogmatically that any fighting dog will kill any of the big lynxes that I have tracked in the North, and that a lynx never begins a fight, I want some eyewitnesses and affidavits to support his statement. This is simply because only Mr. Roosevelt and God know all about lynxes, and God is modestly silent. Once I saw a big dog with a meddlesome disposition and a reputation as a fighter rush headlong upon a savage old mother lynx with kittens. In three minutes he looked like a beefsteak, and was heading for home howling. There are dogs and lynxes, and after some slight acquaintance with both I would hesitate to risk the remnants of my reputation upon any dogmatic utterances regarding either.

"Again, I was in camp once when a man came in pale and frightened, his clothes in ribbons, bleeding from a dozen ugly scratches. He said that while fishing in a trout stream through a rocky gorge a wild-cat, or small bay lynx had jumped on his back like a fury. Of course the man lied, since Mr. Roosevelt knows that a lynx never attacks; but what puzzles me is why that man should gash himself and spoil his clothes, and worry for a week over blood poisoning, just for the sake of making a story to fool one poor nature writer.

"As to the habit of wolves, which also Mr. Roosevelt knows all about, one who has ever studied them finds the subject one of immense fascination, and he cannot read their signs for a week, or talk an hour with an old wolf-hunter, without finding out how little he has discovered about this curious mixture of friendliness and savagery and unbelievable cunning."

The Wolf and the Fawn's Heart

"First, in the matter of the fawn's heart and the wolf's fangs. Mr. Roosevelt declares that it is a "mathematical impossibility" for a wolf to kill a deer in the manner described. 'By no possibility,' he said, 'could a wolf or any land mammal perform such a feat.' I think this is already sufficiently answered in the affidavit I have submitted; but it is still interesting as showing Mr. Roosevelt's methods and limitations. He advises me, if I would understand my own proposition, to 'hang a grapefruit in the middle of a keg of flour, and then see if a big dog could bite through the keg into the grapefruit.' If I would only examine a wolf's teeth, he declares, I would know better than to make such a statement.

"Well, long ago I did examine the skull and the teeth of the great northern wolf; for some of the nature writers take almost as much pains in preparing their statements as does Mr. Roosevelt, apparently, in promulgating laws and judgments on all possible subjects. I have also occasionally killed and dressed a deer, but I have never seen in his heart and chest any resemblance to a grapefruit hung in a keg of flour. What I did see and what any reader may see for himself is this: The lower part of a deer's chest is wedge-shaped and comparatively thin, and the point of the heart comes well down into the wedge. When the shoulder-blade slides far forward or back—as it does easily, not being attached to the skeleton—it leaves the edge of the deer's chest open for a wicked bite. Moreover, aside from spaces between the ribs, the bottom and front of the chest is not hard bone, as Mr. Roosevelt intimates, but a cartilage, which would offer slight resistance to the terrific snap of a big wolf's fangs. So much for the possibilities.

"As for the facts, I once found a small deer lying in the snow, still bleeding, with wounds on the lower chest as if made by long fangs. One of these had ripped into the chest and touched the heart. Beside the deer were tracks of a large wolf, which had probably slunk away as I approached. Again, my Indian, Matty Mitchell of Bonne Bay, was hunting in the interior of Newfoundland

and called a little caribou out to the edge of a thicket. As he raised his rifle he saw the deer suddenly rear; an enormous white wolf sprang up, reached for the chest and snapped. He tells me, from his own observation, that the big white wolf often kills caribou in this way. Sometimes they spring at the front chest; one snap tears into the cartilage, and a wrench lays the heart bare. If the first snap fails, others follow quicker than a man can open and shut his hand, and the heart is cut open before the caribou is fairly aware that he has been gripped. That this is an unusual method of killing goes without saying, but that a big wolf who had learned the trick could kill a deer in this way is both possible and probable. And there is hardly enough weight in Mr. Roosevelt's opinion or his keg of flour to make one doubt my own observation or the testimony of eyewitnesses.

"Chasing wolves with a pack of dogs and half a dozen yelling hunters, Mr. Roosevelt will never discover these two facts, for instance:

"The first is that the wolf is not always or often a savage, bloodthirsty creature, 'the arch type of ravin,' as Mr. Roosevelt describes him. On the whole, he is more like a big, shy, independent dog, than any other creature I know. The wolves were once numerous in our country, and are still abundant in the far north, but in the three hundred years of our history it is doubtful if ever a human being was killed by a wolf. In Newfoundland, where the huge white wolves were once numerous, I can discover no record of even a child being harmed or attacked by them. The fact that many people are killed each year by wolves in Europe does not change the record; it shows that wolves differ. Buffalo Jones, keeper of the animals in the National Park, once spent a Winter north of Athabasca catching musk-ox calves, and had Arctic wolves around him continually. At night they would crowd up to his skin tent, trying to get through for the calves; but when he came out they would draw back, though there were dozens of the big brutes and any one of them could have pulled down a man as easily as he would have killed a rabbit. They were hungry, too. Once he shot at the biggest of a score of wolves that threatened to carry off the calves from under his nose. The bullet shattered the animal's front leg, and at the smell of blood the wolf in its ravening hunger, tore off his own foot and swallowed it."

Wolves Like Companionship

"The other fact is that individual wolves occasionally display a strong interest in men and a timid desire for companionship, like a lost dog. Our dogs are all tamed wolves. A cub wolf taught by man often displays a loyalty to his master strongly suggesting a dog, and it is probable that the attraction which first drew wolf and man together and gave us our most loyal friends still exists in the wolf and is occasionally manifest.

"For instance, when a student in Paris, I read one morning that a pack of big

Siberian wolves had just arrived and were caged at the Jardin des Plantes. Within an hour I was there, neglecting lectures at the Sorbonne for the fascination of this epitome of the silent wilderness, so out of place in the most unnatural of cities. For days I haunted the spot, keeping as close as possible to the wolves, and finally bribed the keeper to allow me to go into the cage. The wolves had been caught in the late Spring, when they were ravenous with hunger, and had been shipped immediately to Paris. So far as I could learn from the authorities and from letters to Siberia, the wolves were absolutely wild and had never been approached by a human being. The keeper, who was new in the business, was horrified at the idea of my going among them, and assured me I would be torn to pieces. It took time and francs to overcome his objections, and when I went in he insisted on standing by the door with weapons and some big torpedoes. The wolves had eaten and were lying down when I entered and stood quietly near them. All sprang to their feet on the instant, but after a few minutes drew back to the furthest side of their cage; all but one, a young wolf, who advanced a step, keen, nervous, alert, and stood looking intently into my face. I spoke to him gently and presently he began to twist his head, as a pup does when you speak to him and he cannot understand. In a minute his tail wagged; soon, with immense caution, he thrust out his muzzle to sniff my open palm, and before I left the cage my fingers had rubbed him behind the ears.

"'It is a beautiful morning,' said the Englishman. 'It is a heavenly morning. Come, let us go out and kill something.' That is the idea of Mr. Roosevelt, and that is the idea the entertaining of which makes impossible the understanding of such work as I am trying to do. If it is charged that I do not understand nature as Mr. Roosevelt does, I stand up and plead guilty; yes, guilty in every page, every paragraph, every sentence. If my little books have done anything to undo the spirit of this man's work and make it regrettable, I am well content to have written them. Indeed, the fact that they have shown, by contrast, not by criticism, the crudeness of his primitive views, and have helped to bring a new spirit of gentleness and sympathy into our study of animal life, is perhaps the chief reason for his antagonism."

23

Charles G. D. Roberts Defends
His Nature Stories

While Charles George Douglas Roberts resents being put in President Roose-velt's list of "nature fakirs," he said last night on his arrival on the White Star liner *Adriatic* that he did not want to get into any controversy. He declared that he had much admiration for Mr. Roosevelt, but he thought the President was mistaken in criticizing some of his stories of animal habits and deeds in the article which appeared in the June *Everybody's*. The Author of *The Kindred of the Wild, The Return to the Trails,* and *Red Fox* said that he had read the article which brought out Mr. Long's challenge to the President while in Naples. He declared that he intended to write a defense.

"I am of the opinion," said Prof. Roberts, "that the whole question is not one of veracity but of judgment. The President undoubtedly when he referred to my story, 'On the Night Trail,' had in mind a different kind of lynx. In the story, I told of a fight in which a lynx was pitted against eight wolves. The lynx which the President has in mind is the *Felis rafa,* or the Rocky Mountain lynx, which is really the bobcat of the Rockies. The lynx of which I have written is a different kind. I wrote about the *Felis canadensis,* and he frequently weighs 50 or 60 pounds.

"In another respect the President probably labors under a mistake. I told of the wolves, and he in his criticism probably had in mind the big timber wolves of the West. I was not writing about them. The species I referred to was the Eastern wolf or the cloudy wolf of Canada, which is only about half the size of the Western wolf.

"The animals of which I wrote and those the President had in mind are entirely different, and I must assume that the President, whose experience in

"Defends Nature Stories," *New York Times,* June 14, 1907, 6.

the backwoods was limited to the Western part of the United States, is not familiar with the wild animals of other localities. A New Brunswick lumberman would laugh at the assertion of Mr. Roosevelt that the lynx could not take care of itself.

"I am going to send out a general and emphatic defense of the school of nature writers. I will go into the subject, but what I do will be entirely my affair, and I will assume no responsibility for the writings of Mr. Long, Ernest Seton Thompson and others."

Explaining further, he said:

"There are two classes of nature writers. One is headed practically by John Burroughs, who believes that the actions of animals are governed by instinct. The opposite school is concerned in animal psychology—and this is the view taken by backwoodsmen, trainers, and trappers. They have given the subject as much careful study as have the others. Mr. Hornaday is one of this last class. Animals are actuated in varying degrees by a process akin to reason. They do think and compare."

"What do you think of the President's opinions?" he was asked.

Prof. Roberts answered that he would in a friendly way try to correct some of Mr. Roosevelt's views, but that he wanted it understood that he had the greatest admiration for the President, and that he did not want to get into any altercation with him. He said:

"I have made slips that even John Burroughs and Mr. Roosevelt have not discovered. No, I am not going to say what they are, but I will correct them later."

24

Real Naturalists on Nature Faking

EDWARD B. CLARK

Editor's Note. —President Roosevelt's quoted comments on Nature Fakers in the June Everybody's, *provoked a heated controversy. In this the President did not intend to take any part, except to append a note on the subject to a forthcoming volume of his public papers. But, upon being informed that* Everybody's *meant to continue the discussion by presenting a symposium of the opinions of established naturalists on nature faking, he decided to publish the projected note in these columns, as a contribution to the controversy. The symposium which precedes President Roosevelt's article on "Nature Fakers," is made up of the opinions of men who are the most eminent working naturalists in America, and whose positions at the head of our leading scientific institutions, together with their practical work, give to their statements indubitable authority.*

In an interview given to me and published in *Everybody's Magazine* for June, President Roosevelt asserted that some of the stories of certain nature writers, although vouched for by them as the truth, were fiction rather than fact. The retort from one of the criticized was that the President was no naturalist and therefore had no right to sit in judgment. Mr. Roosevelt, however, is a naturalist, the best kind of a naturalist, for his studies have been followed in the field and not in the closet. Reiteration of this statement may be useless, for the men who deny probably will stick to their denials. There are men in the country, however, whose right to be called naturalists is of international record. Some of these naturalists have a word to say now about nature faking and nature fakers.

Edward B. Clark, "Real Naturalists on Nature Faking," *Everybody's Magazine* 17 (September 1907): 423–427.

What these scientists have set forth here is said voluntarily. Not long ago, in a New England paper, there appeared a statement from one of the writers who had felt the sting of Mr. Roosevelt's criticism, to the effect that the President was writing to some of the naturalists of the country to ask from them support for his published opposition to nature faking.

This assertion was absolutely untrue.

To go straight to the facts in the case, let me say that, early in June, I received a letter from Edward W. Nelson, who for nearly twenty years has been a field naturalist connected with the Biological Survey. The scientists of the country know Mr. Nelson well. In his letter to me he said this:

> In common with other American naturalists, I have been much displeased with the persistent misrepresentations of the fake natural history writers. The recent article in *Everybody's Magazine* expresses my sentiments and those of my naturalist friends. Heretofore the actual working naturalists whose lives have been spent mainly in the trained observation of animal life, have scarcely been heard from in this controversy. In view of the outrageous character of the claims set up by the fakers, it seems to me that a kind of symposium of the opinions of working naturalists on the subject of the Long style of natural history would be of some service in putting the matter on its proper basis. I have consulted various naturalist friends, and they coincide, and express a willingness to furnish material for such a set of statements.

As a direct result of Mr. Nelson's letter, the opinions of the men who know nature as it is have been collected and are herewith presented. Mr. Roosevelt knew nothing of the intention of these working field-students to say their word of rebuke to those who falsify nature's records, until he learned of it by accident some time after Mr. Nelson's letter to me was written.

The contributions from the naturalists are exhaustive, covering nearly every point in the matter that has been in controversy. I regret that it is impossible within the space at command to print these letters in full. Extracts only are given. The belief is that they will be found sufficient for their purpose.

William T. Hornaday, director of the New York Zoological Park, says:

> Contrary to the rule of indignant naturalists generally, I must say a good word for William J. Long. His books (of which I have five) have furnished me much amusement. His fiction tale of "Wayeeses, the White Wolf" is on its face nothing but a plain fairy story, and the blunders in it are of little consequence, one way or another; but in the other four—modest-looking little school books, selling at forty-eight cents each—he has left "Sinbad the Sailor" and "Baron Munchausen" far behind him.
>
> Whenever Mr. Long enters the woods, the most marvelous things begin to happen. There is a four-footed wonder-worker behind every bush and a miracle every hour. His animals are of superhuman intelligence, and the "stunts" they do for him surpass all that have been seen by all the real naturalists of the world added together. Furthermore, his tongue and pen are so plausible and entertaining that

thousands of persons now believe in him and swear that what he says "rings true."
Look at L. F. Brown of the Canadian Camp—who writes by the yard about
fishing and the woods—writing to the *Times* to indorse Long!

Apparently there is no imaginable intimacy with wild beasts and birds that this
gentleman has not struck up. To judge by *Wilderness Ways*, *Wood Folk at School*,
Ways of Wood Folk, and *A Little Brother to the Bear*, only God himself could know
the wild creatures as the Rev. William J. Long claims to know them, and only the
Omnipotent eye could see all the things that Mr. Long claims to have seen.

Mr. Hornaday, in his communication, takes up story after story in Mr.
Long's books and puts each where it belongs, in the realm of fiction. The bear
and her cubs; the caribou school; Cloud Wings, the Eagle; the woodcock that
set its broken leg; the kingfishers that taught their young to catch fish, and
others of the wilderness and waterside characters of Mr. Long's books, are
touched upon scientifically, if mercilessly. In closing, Mr. Hornaday says:

> In my opinion, any board of education which places W. J. Long's books in the
> schools under its control, or leaves them there after they have found their way in, is
> recreant to its duty and deserves severe censure. An unqualified approval of
> Long's books is, in my opinion, a sure index of profound ignorance regarding wild
> animals, their mental capacities and their ways.

Dr. J. A. Allen, curator of mammalogy and ornithology in the American
Museum of Natural History, New York City, entitles his contribution, "The
Real and the Sham in Natural History." In part Dr. Allen says:

> Omitting for the moment any reference to the many extraordinary things Long has
> said in his own defense, it has been evident to the naturalist that most of Mr.
> Long's defenders show by their own statements their thorough incompetence as
> judges in the case. They proclaim as facts of their own observation statements as
> impossible as those of Mr. Long. They attempt thus to defend him, but they really
> show that, while posing as experienced observers, they are not able properly to
> distinguish the very species of animals they suppose themselves to be writing
> about—as when in one case a writer attributes to a tree squirrel structural charac-
> teristics and habits that pertain only to the ground squirrel.

Touching Mr. Long's theory of the basis of the opposition of the naturalists
to his stories, Dr. Allen writes:

> From his point of view, it is due to his success (commercially) as a writer of nature
> books; his wares, he claims, are forcing theirs out of the market and they are
> consequently envious and revengeful, and call him bad names to injure him with
> the great public to which he so successfully appeals. Unfortunately for this expla-
> nation, the naturalists who have watched the incoming of Long with deepest regret
> and concern, do not write popular books on natural history and are thus in no way
> his commercial competitors. In their opinion, the Long style of nature books is
> pernicious; hence and solely, their opposition.

Edward W. Nelson, who spent four years in scientific explorations in Alaska, who was the Government's scientist accompanying the Corwin during her cruise on the Arctic search for the Jeannette, and who has studied the birds and beasts in nearly every North American and Central American field, calls the writers whom President Roosevelt condemned, "the animal novelists." He says:

> A number of the so-called nature writers have earned the hearty contempt of all naturalists and others who know and love the truth, by their persistence in claiming the exact truthfulness of every detail in their exaggerated animal novels. The animal heroes of these tales are often credited with sentiments which exist only among the more cultivated members of the human race. They are credited also with a marvelous degree of wisdom and prowess. Even granting the impossible and accepting the animals as described, there follows the necessity of believing in the equally amazing powers apparently possessed by these writers alone—that of getting at will into the closest and most intimate and prolonged companionship with even the shyest of the wood folk. No such birds and beasts as appear in these books have been met by any of my many naturalist and hunting friends nor by myself, in all our wanderings from Arctic to tropic America; and yet the least of these writers must be able, if taken at his word, to find them on almost any vacation morning.
>
> The claims made by the authors of these wonder tales of having actually witnessed such remarkable doings, may be accounted for in one of two ways either the animal novelists have the mystic power of creating about them a wonderland in which the ordinary birds and beasts become gifted beyond the gifts of men, or they are overworking their imaginative powers.
>
> The attractive style of some of the writers of false natural history gives their books a wide popularity This renders it the more imperative that all who know the truth and who care for honest nature study or for literary honesty should raise their voices against such writings.

Dr. C. Hart Merriam, who has been chief of the United States Biological Survey since the year 1885, writing on "The Rev. W. J. Long and His Nature Fables," says:

> After prolonged study, I have at length hit upon what I flatter myself is the real secret of the process by which W. J. Long endows animals with new cunning and new habits. The Rev. Dr. Long is possessed of that rare gift which Dr. Carroll D. Wright called the Creative Memory. Now, the Creative Memory is not taught in the schools. Its germ is inborn and susceptible of development.
>
> A nature writer blessed with the Creative Memory does not have to go about wasting valuable time waiting and watching for animals to appear and do something. For him it is quite sufficient to walk in the woods or fields until an animal is seen, or, if the animal is shy, until its track or other evidence of its presence is encountered. He may then hie homeward with the assurance that the Creative Memory will do the rest. For when he is ready to write, all he has to do is to press his finger on the proper cerebral button and set the Creative Memory going. This tells him promptly, and with the minutest attention to details, just what the animal

did, when, where, and under what circumstances, and what it was thinking about before and afterward.

Frederick A. Lucas, curator-in-chief of the Museums of Brooklyn Institute, uses the word "humanizer" instead of "faker" for the writers of certain kinds of nature books, and discusses the difference between the humanizer and the real naturalist. At the close of his article, the Brooklyn scientist writes this:

"Well," says the reader, "after all, if the writer of nature books does make statements of doubtful accuracy, what harm is done?" Now in spite of the depravity of the age, of which we read so much in the daily papers, there is a general impression that it is best to tell the truth, and the naturalist merely asks that "nature books" shall present facts, and not give any one's ideas or impressions as being facts. He regards this as an important matter, since these books are being widely introduced as reading books in public schools, and, knowing the importance of early impressions, he believes children should have the truth, and not fiction in the guise of truth. If good stories merely are wanted, we have Kipling, and no nature writer, *me judice*, has succeeded so well as Kipling in "'Er Majesty's Servants" in apparently looking at the world through the eyes of animals.

A man holding an important position in a Western school said that although the "humanizers" might be wrong in their statements, he would use their books in teaching natural history on account of their interest. It so happens that this same man is a teacher of history, and one cannot but wonder if he considers that the same rule applies to his own branch of study. Personally, "I'd rather not know so much than know so many things that ain't so."

Barton W. Evermann, who is the author of a number of standard works on the fishes of North America and who is in charge of the scientific inquiry department of the United States Bureau of Fisheries, takes strong exception to several of William J. Long's salmon stories. Of one of them he says:

In the National Bureau of Fisheries and in various State Fish Commissions are many fish-culturists and naturalists, men trained in the methods of science and skilled as observers, who have for years been studying the Atlantic salmon and the other species of the salmon family. They have studied the adult fish in the streams and on their spawning-beds and have hatched millions upon millions of salmon eggs in fish hatcheries They have also watched the eggs hatching in the streams and have followed the migrating fish from salt water to their spawning-beds far toward the head-waters of our northern streams. They have camped on these streams for weeks and months solely for the purpose of learning the habits of the salmon, which they watched day and night. . . . So regularly and carefully are these observations made and so frequently has each one of them been repeated and verified, that these fish-culturists and naturalists have come to believe that they know fairly well the facts in the life-history of the salmon.

But it has remained for Mr. Long, a man evidently wholly unfamiliar with the methods of science and equally untrained in the methods of accurate observation, to see many things in the life-history of the Atlantic salmon which no fish-culturist ever saw or believes to be true.

Salmon have hitherto not been regarded as possessed of any great amount of wisdom or common sense. Yet Mr. Long has evidently found them otherwise. Only a few of the astonishing things which his salmon do can be mentioned here. When ascending a stream and encountering a fall, before attempting to ascend it, they first jump out of the water a few times—simply "to get a good look at the falls" and pick out the best place to make the try, "to study the place and see where they must strike in order to succeed." Later, the salmon "springs out, flies in a great arc up to the rim of the falls, just touches the falling sheet, plunges over the brim, and disappears . . . into the swift water above." And the place selected was where the "water was thinnest, so that his tail could strike the rock beneath, and, like a bent spring, recoil from under him."

And if, perchance, he knocks off a few scales, and bacteria get into the wound, he at once turns tail and starts for salt water, knowing, wise being that he is, that a salt-water bath will kill the bacteria and heal the wound; and, further, "he feels within him the need of recuperation," that he may have strength to perform the long journey to the sea, so he begins eating everything in sight, a thing which, according to our author, he never does unless injured!

On the spawning-bed the female deposits her eggs and the male carefully covers them to "keep the current from washing them away." Fish-culturists have found that the covering of the eggs is a purely incidental result of other acts.

Then follows a marvelous account of the development of the little salmon in the egg. "Beginning his life with hunger, he had first eaten all that was left inside the egg besides himself, and was nibbling at the shell when it broke and let him out. . . . As the egg-shell wavered on his tail he whirled like a wink and swallowed it!"

Fish-culturists tell us that salmon come out of the egg tail first, not head first, and that they are totally unable to eat until many days after hatching.

The salmon that Mr. Long saw must, indeed, have been an exceptional and remarkable salmon. We are glad William J. Long saw it; for if we had seen it, we should not have believed it. But Dr. Long says that he saw it, and that "every smallest incident is as true as careful and accurate observation can make it."

The following letter is from George Shiras, 3d, who has hunted and photographed animals in Michigan and Central Canada for thirty-six years, and whose ingenuity in securing flashlight pictures of wild animals by night has been of great value to naturalists:

W. J. Long's latest book, *Northern Trails,* is largely devoted to the wonderful antics of the timber wolf, with Newfoundland for its stage.

In a long trip through the wild, northwestern portion of Newfoundland I saw no signs of wolves and understood from the guides and trappers that they likewise had been unable to find any trace of these animals in recent years. Considering this, the beginning of the doctor's recent tale of the Newfoundland wolf will prove amusing, if instructive. Here is what he says: "We came careening in through the tickle of Harbor Woe. There, in a disconsolate, rock-bound refuge of the Newfoundland coast, the Wild Duck swung to her anchor . . . while far away, like a vague shadow, a handful of gray houses hung like barnacles to the base of the great bare hill. . . . A long interval of profound silence had passed, and I could just make out the circle of dogs sitting on their tails, on the open shore, when suddenly faint and far away an unearthly howl came rolling down the mountain. . . . Suddenly Noel pointed upward and my eye caught something moving swiftly on the crest of the mountain. A shadow, with the slinking trot of a wolf, glided along the ridge between us and the moon, turned a pointed nose up to the sky, and the terrible howl of the great White Wolf tumbled down upon the husky dogs and set them howling as if possessed."

So here we have the keen-eyed doctor, pen in hand, sitting expectantly on the deck of a schooner and telling his readers just how a wolf looked and acted at night, half a mile or more away on the mountain top, behind the fishing village. An owl with a telescope over each eye could not have done better. Having looked this midnight wolf over carefully, the doctor then remarks: "This was my first glimpse of Wayeeses, the huge white wolf which I had come a thousand miles over land and sea to study." "All over the Long Range of the Northern Peninsula," he goes on, "I followed him, guided sometimes by rumor, a hunter's story or a postman's fright." Since the island of Newfoundland is considerably larger than Ireland, the idea of hunting a particular wolf by rumor or the aid of letter-carriers smacks of an originality that is most charming. As letter-carriers, wolves, and rumors were then unknown in the interior of Newfoundland—the doctor's triple alliance was a strong one.

He also tells how wolves round up great flocks of migratory plover; how the wild ducks, overcome with curiosity by the wolves' playful antics on the beach, swim close enough to be seized by these hungry gymnasts; how they catch the wary wild goose at night and "trot back to the woods, each with a burden on his shoulders"; how they chase alleged seals all over the low outlying reefs, in the broad glare of the sunlight, and how one "big seal tumbled into the tide, where the sharks following his bloody trail soon finished him." Next he writes of a big bull caribou viciously assaulting a band of wolves and tells how they considerately side-step each deadly lunge—because, as the doctor says, "the caribou's time had not come yet: besides he was too tough." From the fleet-winged plover to the tough venison, all this is frenzied fiction, as rare as it is raw.

Then he writes about the fearful raids made by the wolf upon certain fishing villages in Newfoundland and relates how "by night the wolf would come stealthily to prowl among the deserted lanes, and the fishermen sitting close by the stoves, behind barred doors, would know nothing of the huge, gaunt figures that flitted noiselessly past frosted windows. If a cat prowled about or an uneasy dog scratched to be let out, there would be a squall, a yelp—and the cat would not come back and the dog would never scratch the door again." This is really pathetic, and accounts for the "barred doors" of the stove-hugging inhabitants.

On the Newfoundland coast there reside about 250,000 brave, sturdy people, none of whom has ever seen a wolf or even a wolf track in the back yard, though they may have heard of these animals years ago from the lips of the midwinter trapper. The doctor, however, seeks to justify these wolf raids on the domestic pets by telling his readers that midwinter is the season of starvation for the wolf; although in fact, this is the very time when the myriad of caribou in Newfoundland would be utterly helpless, when, with the lakes and rivers frozen over, they could not escape the timber wolf if pursued. Ninety per cent of the deer killed by wolves meet their fate in midwinter for this very reason.

About five hundred American and English sportsmen hunt big game in the island of Newfoundland every year, and as none of these has killed a wolf, nor even seen one in recent years, they will unanimously vote that the doctor, having abandoned his degree of D.D., should have conferred upon him the new one of P.P. — Patron Prevaricator—of the Ancient Order of Ananias.

25

"Nature Fakers"

THEODORE ROOSEVELT

In the Middle Ages there was no hard-and-fast line drawn between fact and fiction even in ordinary history; and until much later there was not even an effort to draw it in natural history. There are quaint little books on beasts, in German and in English, as late as the sixteenth century, in which the unicorn and the basilisk appear as real creatures; while to more commonplace animals there are ascribed traits and habits of such exceeding marvelousness that they ought to make the souls of the "nature fakers" of these degenerate days swell with envious admiration.

As real outdoor naturalists, real observers of nature, grew up, men who went into the wilderness to find out the truth, they naturally felt a half-indignant and half-amused contempt both for the men who invented preposterous fiction about wild animals, and for the credulous stay-at-home people who accepted such fiction as fact. A century and a half ago old Samuel Hearne, the Hudson Bay explorer, a keen and trustworthy observer, while writing of the beaver, spoke as follows of the spiritual predecessors of certain modern writers:

> I cannot refrain from smiling when I read the accounts of different authors who have written on the economy of these animals, as there seems to be a contest between them who shall most exceed in fiction. But the compiler of the *Wonders of Nature and Art* seems, in my opinion, to have succeeded best in this respect; as he has not only collected all the fictions into which other writers on the subject have run, but has so greatly improved on them that little remains to be added to his account of the beaver besides a vocabulary of their language, a code of their laws,

Theodore Roosevelt, "'Nature Fakers,'" *Everybody's Magazine* 17 (September 1907): 427–430.

and a sketch of their religion, to make it the most complete natural history of that animal which can possibly be offered to the public.

There cannot be a greater imposition, or indeed a grosser insult on common understanding, than the wish to make us believe the stories [in question]. . . . A very moderate share of understanding is surely sufficient to guard [any one] against giving credit to such marvelous tales, however smoothly they may be told, or however boldly they may be asserted by the romancing traveler.

Hearne was himself a man who added greatly to the fund of knowledge about the beasts of the wilderness. We need such observers; much remains to be told about the wolf and the bear, the lynx and the fisher, the moose and the caribou. Undoubtedly wild creatures sometimes show very unexpected traits, and individuals among them sometimes perform fairly startling feats or exhibit totally unlooked-for sides of their characters in their relations with one another and with man. We much need a full study and observation of all these animals, undertaken by observers capable of seeing, understanding, and recording what goes on in the wilderness; and such study and observation cannot be made by men of dull mind and limited power of appreciation. The highest type of student of nature should be able to see keenly and write interestingly and should have an imagination that will enable him to interpret the facts. But he is not a student of nature at all who sees not keenly but falsely, who writes interestingly and untruthfully, and whose imagination is used not to interpret facts but to invent them.

True Nature Lovers

We owe a real debt to the men who truthfully portray for us, with pen or pencil, any one of the many sides of outdoor life; whether they work as artists or as writers, whether they care for big beasts or small birds, for the homely farmland or for the vast, lonely wilderness, whether they are scientists proper, or hunters of game, or lovers of all nature—which, indeed, scientists and hunters ought also to be. John Burroughs and John Muir, Stewart Edward White, and Frederic Remington, Olive Thorne Miller, Hart Merriam, William Hornaday, Frank Chapman, J. A. Allen, Ernest Ingersoll, Witmer Stone, William Cram, George Shiras—to all of these and to many like them whom I could name, we owe much, we who love the breath of the woods and the fields, and who care for the wild creatures, large or small. And the surest way to neutralize the work of these lovers of truth and nature, of truth in nature-study, is to encourage those whose work shows neither knowledge of nature nor love of truth.

The modern "nature faker" is of course an object of derision to every scientist worthy of the name, to every real lover of the wilderness, to every faunal naturalist, to every true hunter or nature lover. But it is evident that he completely deceives many good people who are wholly ignorant of wild life. Sometimes he draws on his own imagination for his fictions; sometimes he gets them secondhand from irresponsible guides or trappers or Indians.

Yellow Journalists of the Woods

In the wilderness, as elsewhere, there are some persons who do not regard the truth; and these are the very persons who most delight to fill credulous strangers with impossible stories of wild beasts. As for Indians, they live in a world of mysticism, and they often ascribe supernatural traits to the animals they know, just as the men of the Middle Ages, with almost the same childlike faith, credited the marvels told of the unicorn, the basilisk, the roc, and the cockatrice.

Of all these "nature fakers," the most reckless and least responsible is Mr. Long; but there are others who run him close in the "yellow journalism of the woods," as John Burroughs has aptly called it. It would take a volume merely to catalogue the comic absurdities with which the books of these writers are filled. There is no need of discussing their theories; the point is that their alleged "facts" are not facts at all, but fancies. Their most striking stories are not merely distortions of facts, but pure inventions; and not only are they inventions, but they are inventions by men who know so little of the subject concerning which they write, and who to ignorance add such utter recklessness, that they are not even able to distinguish between what is possible, however wildly improbable, and mechanical impossibilities. Be it remembered that I am not speaking of ordinary mistakes, of ordinary errors of observation, of differences of interpretation and opinion; I am dealing only with deliberate invention, deliberate perversion of fact.

"Uncle Remus" Wolves

Now all this would be, if not entirely proper, at least far less objectionable, if the writers in question were content to appear in their proper garb, as is the case with the men who write fantastic fiction about wild animals for the Sunday issues of various daily newspapers. Moreover, as a writer of spirited animal fables, avowed to be such, any man can gain a distinct place of some importance. But it is astonishing that such very self-evident fiction as that which I am now discussing should, when advertised as fact, impose upon any person of good sense, no matter how ignorant of natural history and of wild life. Most of us have enjoyed novels like *King Solomon's Mines*, for instance. But if Mr. Rider Haggard had insisted that his novels were not novels but records of actual fact, we should feel a mild wonder at the worthy persons who accepted them as serious contributions to the study of African geography and ethnology.

It is not probable that the writers in question have even so much as seen some of the animals which they minutely describe. They certainly do not know the first thing about their habits, nor even about their physical structure. Judging from the internal evidence of their books, I should gravely doubt if they had ever seen a wild wolf or a wild lynx. The wolves and lynxes and other animals which they describe are full brothers of the wild beasts that appear in "Uncle Remus" and "Reynard the Fox," and deserve the same serious consideration from the zoological standpoint. Certain of their wolves appear as gifted with all the philosophy, the self-restraint, and the keen intelligence of, say, Marcus Aurelius, together with the lofty philanthropy of a modern altruist; though unfortunately they are hampered by a wholly erroneous view of caribou anatomy.

Story-Book Beasts

Like the White Queen in "Through the Looking-Glass," these writers can easily believe three impossible things before breakfast; and they do not mind in the least if the impossibilities are mutually contradictory. Thus, one story relates how a wolf with one bite reaches the heart of a bull caribou, or a moose, or a horse—a feat which, of course, has been mechanically impossible of performance by any land carnivore since the death of the last saber-toothed tiger. But the next story will cheerfully describe a doubtful contest between the wolf and a lynx or a bulldog, in which the latter survives twenty slashing bites. Now of course a wolf that could bite into the heart of a horse would swallow a bulldog or a lynx like a pill.

In one story, a wolf is portrayed as guiding home some lost children, in a spirit of thoughtful kindness; let the overtrustful individual who has girded up his loins to believe this think of the way he would receive the statement of some small farmer's boy that when lost he was guided home by a coon, a possum, or a woodchuck. Again, one of these story-book wolves, when starving, catches a red squirrel, which he takes round as a present to propitiate a bigger wolf.[1] If any man seriously thinks a starving wolf would act in this manner, let him study hounds when feeding, even when they are not starving.

The animals are alternately portrayed as actuated by motives of exalted humanitarianism, and as possessed of demoniac prowess and insight into motive. In one story the fisher figures in the latter capacity. A fisher is a big marten, the size of a fox. This particular story-book fisher, when pursued by hunters on snow-shoes, kills a buck by a bite in the throat, and leaves the carcass as a bribe to the hunters, hoping thereby to distract attention from himself! Now, foxes are continually hunted; they are far more clever than fishers. What rational man would pay heed to a story that a fox when hunted killed a good-sized calf by a bite in the throat, and left it as a bribe to the hounds and hunters, to persuade them to leave him alone? One story is just as possible as the other.

In another story, the salmon is the hero. The writer begins by blunders about the young salmon which a ten minutes' visit to any government fish hatchery would have enabled him to avoid; and as a climax, describes how the salmon goes up a fall by flopping from ledge to ledge of a cliff, under circumstances which make the feat about as probable as that the fish would use a stepladder. As soon as these writers get into the wilderness, they develop preternatural powers of observation, and, as Mr. Shiras says, become themselves "invisible and odorless," so that the shyest wild creatures permit any closeness of intimacy on their part; in one recent story about a beaver colony, the alternative to the above proposition is that the beavers were both blind and without sense of smell.

Fact-Blindness

Yet these same writers, who see such marvelous things as soon as they go into the woods, are incapable of observing aright the most ordinary facts when at home. One of their stories relates how the eyes of frogs shine at night in the wilderness; the author apparently ignoring the fact that frog-ponds are common in less remote places, and are not inhabited by blazing-eyed frogs. Two of our most common and most readily observed small mammals are the red squirrel and the chipmunk. The chipmunk has cheek pouches, in which he stores berries, grain, and small nuts, whereas the red squirrel has no cheek pouches, and carries nuts between his teeth. Yet even this simple fact escapes the attention of one of the writers we are discussing, who endows a red squirrel with cheek pouches filled with nuts. Evidently excessive indulgence in invention tends to atrophy the power of accurate observation.

Fable Weavers and Believers

In one story a woodcock is described as making a kind of mud splint for its broken leg; it seems a pity not to have added that it also made itself a crutch to use while the splint was on. A Baltimore oriole is described as making a contrivance of twigs and strings whereby to attach its nest, under circumstances which would imply the mental ability and physical address of a sailor making a hammock; and the story is backed up by affidavits, as are others of these stories. This particular feat is precisely as possible as that a Rocky Mountain pack rat can throw the diamond hitch. The affidavits in support of these various stories are interesting only because of the curious light they throw on the personalities of those making and believing them.

If the writers who make such startling discoveries in the wilderness would really study even the denizens of a barnyard, they would be saved from at least some of their more salient mistakes. Their stories dwell much on the "teaching" of the young animals by their elders and betters. In one story, for instance, a wild duck is described as "teaching" her young how to swim and get their food. If this writer had strolled into the nearest barnyard containing a hen which had hatched out ducklings, a glance at the actions of those ducklings when the hen happened to lead them near a puddle would have enlightened him as to how much "teaching" they needed. But these writers exercise the same florid imagination when they deal with a robin or a rabbit as when they describe a bear, a moose, or a salmon.

It is half amusing and half exasperating to think that there should be excellent persons to whom it is necessary to explain that books stuffed with such stories, in which the stories are stated as facts, are preposterous in their worthlessness. These worthy persons vividly call to mind Professor Lounsbury's comment on "the infinite capacity of the human brain to withstand the introduction of knowledge." The books in question contain no statement which a serious and truth-loving student of nature can accept, save statements which have already long been known as established by trustworthy writers. The fables they contain bear the same relation to real natural history that Barnum's famous artificial mermaid bore to real fish and real mammals. No man who has really studied nature in a spirit of seeking the truth, whether he be big or little, can have any controversy with these writers; it would be as absurd as to expect some genuine student of anthropology or archeology to enter into a controversy with the clumsy fabricators of the Cardiff Giant. Their books carry their own refutation; and affidavits in support of the statements they contain are as worthless as the similar affidavits once solemnly issued to show that the Cardiff "giant" was a petrified pre-Adamite man. There is now no more excuse for being deceived by their stories than for being still in doubt about the silly Cardiff hoax.

The Guilty Ones

Men of this stamp will necessarily arise, from time to time, some in one walk of life, some in another. Our quarrel is not with these men, but with those who give them their chance. We who believe in the study of nature feel that a real knowledge and appreciation of wild things, of trees, flowers, birds, and of the grim and crafty creatures of the wilderness, give an added beauty and health to life. Therefore we abhor deliberate or reckless untruth in this study as much as in any other; and therefore we feel that a grave wrong is committed by all who, holding a position that entitles them to respect, yet condone and encourage such untruth.

Note

1. This particular incident was alleged to have taken place in Newfoundland, the wolf being the same as the hero of the caribou-heart-bite episode. Mr. George Shiras had informed me that there were no red squirrels in Newfoundland and that wolves were so scarce as to be practically non-existent, if they existed at all. He now writes me under date of July 19th as follows:

"I enclose a copy of a recent letter received from my guide—in Newfoundland—which shows that I did not err regarding the wolves and red squirrel.

"When Dr. Long alleges he was following, for weeks at a time, wolves in Newfoundland, this animal was extinct, or practically so. Squires is one of the best and most reliable trappers on this island, being one of the few who permanently reside in the interior, trapping in the most northerly and wildest portions of the country, where wolf sign would be instantly detected were the animals to be found on this island. Such audacity on the part of Dr. Long is simply astounding."

The letter from the guide, W. T. Squires, runs in part as follows:

"There are no squirrel of any kind here. Neither have I seen any sign of wolf in the last ten years."

26

The Other Animals

JACK LONDON

American journalism has its moments of fantastic hysteria, and when it is on the rampage the only thing for a rational man to do is to climb a tree and let the cataclysm go by. And so, some time ago, when the word *nature-faker* was coined, I, for one, climbed into my tree and stayed there. I happened to be in Hawaii at the time, and a Honolulu reporter elicited the sentiment from me that I thanked God that I was not an authority on anything. This sentiment was promptly cabled to America in an Associated Press despatch, whereupon the American press (possibly incensed because I had not climbed down out of my tree) charged me with paying for advertising by cable at a dollar per word—the very human way of the American press, which, when a man refuses to come down and be licked, makes faces at him.

But now that the dreadful storm is over, let us come and reason together. I have been guilty of writing two animal stories—two books about dogs. The writing of these two books, on my part, was in truth a protest against the "humanizing" of animals, of which it seemed to me several "animal writers" had been profoundly guilty. Time and again, and many times, in my narratives, I wrote, speaking of my dog heroes: "He did not think these things; he merely did them," etc. And I did this repeatedly, to the clogging of my narrative and in violation of my artistic canons; and I did it in order to hammer into the average human understanding that these dog-heroes of mine were not directed by abstract reasoning, but by instinct, sensation, and emotion, and by simple reasoning. Also, I endeavored to make my stories in line with the facts of evolution; I

Jack London, "The Other Animals," *Collier's* 41, (September 5, 1908): 10–11, 25–26.

hewed them to the mark set by scientific research, and awoke, one day, to find myself bundled neck and crop into the camp of the nature-fakers.

President Roosevelt was responsible for this, and he tried and condemned me on two counts. (1) I was guilty of having a big, fighting bulldog whip a wolf-dog. (2) I was guilty of allowing a lynx to kill a wolf-dog in a pitched battle. Regarding the second count, President Roosevelt was wrong in his field observations. He must have read my story hastily, for in my story I had the wolf-dog kill the lynx. Not only did I have my wolf-dog kill the lynx, but I made him eat the body of the lynx as well. Remains only the first count on which to convict me of nature-faking, and the first count does not charge me with diverging from ascertained facts. It is merely a statement of a difference of opinion. President Roosevelt does not think a bulldog can lick a wolf-dog. I think a bulldog can lick a wolf-dog. And there we are. Difference of opinion may make, and does make, horse-racing. I can understand that difference of opinion can make dog-fighting. But what gets me is how difference of opinion regarding the relative fighting merits of a bulldog and a wolf-dog makes me a nature-faker and President Roosevelt a vindicated and triumphant scientist.

Then entered John Burroughs to clinch President Roosevelt's judgments. In this unholy alliance there is no difference of opinion. That Roosevelt can do no wrong is Burroughs's opinion; and that Burroughs is always right is Roosevelt's opinion. Both are agreed that animals do not reason. They assert that all animals below man are automatons and perform actions only of two sorts—mechanical and reflex—and that in such actions no reasoning enters at all. They believe that man is the only animal capable of reasoning and that ever does reason. This is a view that makes the twentieth century scientist smile. It is not modern at all. It is distinctly medieval. President Roosevelt and John Burroughs, in advancing such a view, are homocentric in the same fashion that the scholastics of earlier and darker centuries were homocentric. Had not the world been discovered to be round until after the births of President Roosevelt and John Burroughs, they would have been geocentric as well in their theories of the Cosmos. They could not have believed otherwise. The stuff of their minds is so conditioned. They talk the argot of evolution, while they no more understand the essence and the import of evolution than does a South Sea Islander or Sir Oliver Lodge understand the noumena of radioactivity.

The President Short on Evolution

Now, President Roosevelt is an amateur. He may know something of statecraft and of big-game shooting; he may be able to kill a deer when he sees it and to measure it and weigh it after he has shot it; he may be able to observe carefully and accurately the actions and antics of tomtits and snipe, and, after he has observed it, to definitely and coherently convey the information of when the first chipmunk, in a certain year and a certain latitude and longitude, came out in the spring and chattered and gamboled—but that he should be able, as an individual observer, to analyze all animal life and to synthesize and develop and know all that is known of the method and significance of evolution, would require a vaster credulity for you or me to believe than is required for us to believe the biggest whopper ever told by an unmitigated nature-faker. No, President Roosevelt does not understand evolution, and he does not seem to have made much of an attempt to understand evolution.

Remains John Burroughs, who claims to be a thoroughgoing evolutionist. Now, it is rather hard for a young man to tackle an old man. It is the nature of young men to be more controlled in such matters, and it is the nature of old men, presuming upon the wisdom that is very often erroneously associated with age, to do the tackling. In this present question of nature-faking, the old men did the tackling, while I, as one young man, kept quiet a long time. But here goes at last. And first of all let Mr. Burroughs's position be stated, and stated in his words.

Reason Versus Instinct

"Why impute reason to an animal if its behavior can be explained on the theory of instinct?" Remember these words, for they will be referred to later. "A goodly number of persons seem to have persuaded themselves that animals do reason." "But instinct suffices for the animals . . . they get along very well without reason." "Darwin tried hard to convince himself that animals do at times reason in a rudimentary way; but Darwin was also a much greater naturalist than psychologist." The preceding quotation is tantamount on Mr. Burroughs's part, to a flat denial that animals reason even in a rudimentary way. And when Mr. Burroughs denies that animals reason even in a rudimentary way, it is equivalent to affirming, in accord with the first quotation in this paragraph, that instinct will explain every animal act that might be confounded with reason by the unskilled or careless observer.

Having bitten off this large mouthful, Mr. Burroughs proceeds with serene and beautiful satisfaction to masticate it in the following fashion. He cites a large number of instances of purely instinctive actions on the part of animals, and triumphantly demands if they are acts of reason. He tells of the robin that fought day after day its reflected image in a window-pane; of the birds in South America that were guilty of drilling clear through a mud wall, which they mistook for a solid clay-bank; of the beaver that cut down a tree four times because it was held at the top by the branches of other trees; of the cow that licked the skin of her stuffed calf so affectionately that it came apart, where upon she proceeded to eat the hay with which it was stuffed. He tells of the phoebe-bird that betrays her nest on the porch by tying to hid it with moss in similar fashion to the way all phoebe-birds hide their nests when they are built among rocks. He tells of the highhole that repeatedly drills through the clapboards of an empty house in a vain attempt to find a thickness of wood deep enough in which to build its nest.[1] He tells of the migrating lemmings of Norway that plunge into the sea and drown in vast numbers because of their instinct to swim lakes and rivers in the course of their migrations. And, having told a few more instances of like kidney, he triumphantly demands: Where now is your much-vaunted reasoning of the lower animals?

No schoolboy in a class debate could be guilty of unfairer argument. It is equivalent to replying to the assertion that $2 + 2 = 4$, by saying: "No; because $12 \div 4 = 3$. I have demonstrated my honorable opponent's error." When a man attacks your ability as a foot-racer, promptly prove to him that he was drunk the week before last, and the average man in the crowd of gaping listeners will believe that you have convincingly refuted the slander on your foot-racing ability. On my honor, it will work. Mr Burroughs has done it himself, and, I doubt not, pulled the sophistical wool over a great many pairs of eyes. No, no, Mr. Burroughs; you can't disprove that animals reason by proving that they possess instincts. But the worst of it is that you have at the same time pulled the wool over your own eyes. You have set up a straw man and knocked the stuffing out of him in the complacent belief that it was the reasoning of lower animals you were knocking out of the minds of those who disagree with you. When the highhole perforated the ice-house and let out the saw dust, you called him a lunatic.

But let us be charitable—and serious. What Mr. Burroughs instances as acts of instinct certainly are acts of instinct. By the same method of logic one could easily adduce a multitude of instinctive acts on the part of man and thereby prove that man is an unreasoning animal. But man performs actions of both sorts. Between man and the lower animals Mr. Burroughs finds a vast gulf. This gulf divides man from the rest of his kin by virtue of the power of reason that he alone possesses. Man is a voluntary agent. Animals are automatons. The robin fights its reflection in the window-pane because it is his instinct to fight and because he can not reason out the physical laws that make his reflection appear real. An animal is a mechanism that operates according to foreordained rules. Wrapped up in its heredity, and determined long before it was born, is a certain limited capacity and ganglionic response to external stimuli. These responses have been fixed in the species through adaptation to environment. Natural selection has compelled the animal automatically to respond in a fixed manner and a certain way to all the usual external stimuli it encounters in the course of a usual life. Thus, under usual circumstances, it does the usual thing. Under unusual circumstances it still does the usual thing, wherefore the highhole perforating the ice-house is guilty of lunacy and unreason, in short. To do the unusual thing under unusual circumstances, successfully to adjust to a strange environment for which his heredity has not automatically fitted an adjustment, Mr. Burroughs says is impossible. He says it is impossible because it would be a non-instinctive act, and, as is well known, animals act only through instinct. And right here we catch a glimpse of Mr. Burroughs's cart standing before his horse. He has a thesis, and though the heavens fall he will fit the facts to the thesis. Agassiz, in his opposition to evolution, had a similar thesis, though neither did he fit the facts to it nor did the heavens fall. Facts are very disagreeable at times.

Some Rollo Stories

But let us see. Let us test Mr. Burroughs's test of reason and instinct. When I was a small boy I had a dog named Rollo. According to Mr. Burroughs, Rollo was an automaton, responding to external stimuli mechanically as directed by his instincts. Now, as is well known, the development of instinct in animals is a dreadfully slow process. There is no known case of the development of a single instinct in domestic animals in all the history of their domestication. Whatever instincts they possess they brought with them from the wild thousands of years ago. Therefore, all Rollo's actions were ganglionic discharges mechanically determined by the instincts that had been developed and fixed in the species thousands of years ago. Very well. It is clear, therefore, that in all his play with me he would act in old-fashioned ways, adjusting himself to the physical and psychical factors in his environment according to the rules of adjustment which had obtained in the wild and which had become part of his heredity.

Rollo and I did a great deal of rough romping. He chased me and I chased him. He nipped my legs, arms, and hands, often so hard that I yelled, while I rolled him and tumbled him and dragged him about, often so strenuously as to make him yelp. In the course of the play many variations arose. I would make believe to sit down and cry. All repentance and anxiety, he would wag his tail and lick my face, whereupon I would give him the laugh. He hated to be laughed at, and promptly he would spring for me with good-natured, menacing jaws, and the wild romp would go on. I had scored a point. Then he hit upon a trick. Pursuing him into the woodshed, I would find him in a far corner, pretending to sulk. Now, he dearly loved the play, and never got enough of it. But at first he fooled me. I thought I had somehow hurt his feelings, and I came and knelt before him, petting him and speaking lovingly. Promptly, in a wild outburst, he was up and way, tumbling me over on the floor as he dashed out in a mad skurry around the yard. He had scored a point.

After a time it became largely a game of wits. I reasoned my acts, of course, while his were instinctive. One day, as he pretended to sulk in the corner, I glanced out of the woodshed doorway, simulated pleasure in face, voice and language, and greeted one of my schoolboy friends. Immediately Rollo forgot to sulk, rushed out to see the newcomer, and saw empty space. The laugh was on him, and he knew it, and I gave it to him, too. I fooled him in this way two or three times; then he became wise. One day I worked a variation. Suddenly looking out the door, making believe that my eyes had been attracted by a moving form, I said coldly, as a child educated in turning away bill collectors would say: "No, my father is not at home." Like a shot, Rollo was out the door, He even ran down the alley to the front of the house in a vain attempt to find the man I had addressed. He came back sheepishly to endure the laugh and resume the game.

And now we come to the test. I fooled Rollo, but how was the fooling made possible? What precisely went on in that brain of his? According to Mr. Burroughs, who denies even rudimentary reasoning to the lower animals, Rollo acted instinctively, mechanically responding to the external stimulus, furnished by me, that led him to believe that a man was outside the door. Since Rollo acted instinctively, and since all instincts are very ancient, tracing back to the predomestication period, we can conclude only that Rollo's wild ancestors, at the time this particular instinct was fixed into the heredity of the species, must have been in close, long-continued and vital contact with man, the voice of man, and the expressions on the face of man. But since the instinct must have been developed during the predomestication period, how under the sun could his wild undomesticated ancestors have experienced close, long-continued, and vital contact with man?

A Pinch of Brain-Stuff

Mr. Burroughs says that "instinct suffices for the animals," that "they get along very well without reason." But I say, what all the poor nature-fakers will say, that Rollo reasoned. He was born into the world, a bundle of instincts and a pinch of brain-stuff, all wrapped around in a framework of bone, meat, and hide. As he adjusted to his environment he gained experiences. He remembered these experiences. He learned that he mustn't chase the cat, kill chickens, nor bite little girl's dresses. He learned that little boys had little boy playmates. He learned that men came into back-yards. He learned that the animal man, on meeting with his own kind, was given to verbal and facial greetings. He learned that when a boy greeted a playmate he did it differently from the way he greeted a man. All these he learned and remembered. They were so many observations—so many propositions, if you please. Now what went on behind those brown eyes of his, inside what pinch of brain-stuff, when I turned suddenly to the door and greeted an imaginary person outside? Instantly, out of the thousands of observations stored in his brain, came to the front of his consciousness the particular observations connected with this particular situation. Next, he established a relation between these observations. This relation was his conclusion, achieved, as every psychologist will agree, by a definite cell-action of his gray matter. From the fact that his master turned suddenly toward the door, and from the fact that his master's voice, facial expression, and whole demeanor expressed surprise and delight, he concluded that a friend was outside. He established a relation between the various things, and the act of establishing relations between things is an act of reason—of rudimentary reason, granted, but none the less of reason.

Of course Rollo was fooled. But that is no call for us to throw chests about it. How often has every last one of us been fooled in precisely the same fashion by another who turned and suddenly addressed an imaginary intruder? Here is a case in point that occurred in the West. A robber had held up a railroad train. He stood in the aisle between the seats, his revolver presented at the head of the conductor who stood facing him. The conductor was at his mercy. But the conductor suddenly looked over the robber's shoulder, at the same time saying aloud to an imaginary person standing at the robber's back: "Don't shoot him." Like a flash the robber whirled about to confront this new danger, and like a flash the conductor shot him down. Show me, Mr. Burroughs, where the mental process in the robber's brain was a shade different from the mental process in Rollo's brain, and I'll quit nature-faking and join the Trappists. Surely, when a man's mental process and a dog's mental process are precisely similar, the much-vaunted gulf of Mr. Burroughs's fancy has been bridged.

I had a dog in Oakland. His name was Glen. His father was Brown, a Wolf-dog that had been brought down from Alaska, and his mother was a half-wild mountain shepherd dog. Neither father nor mother had had any experience with automobiles. Glen came from the country, a half-grown puppy, to live in Oakland. Immediately he became infatuated with an automobile. He reached the culmination of happiness when he was permitted to sit up in the front seat alongside the chauffeur. He would spend a whole day at a time on an automobile debauch, even going without food. Often the machine started directly from inside the barn, dashed out the driveway without stopping, and was gone. Glen got left behind several times. The custom was established that whoever was taking the machine out should toot the horn before starting. Glen learned the signal. No matter where he was nor what he was doing, when that horn tooted he was off for the barn and up into the front seat.

One morning, while Glen was on the back porch eating his breakfast of mush and milk, the chauffeur tooted. Glen rushed down the steps, into the barn, and took his front seat, the mush and milk dripping down his excited and happy chops. In passing, I may point out that in thus forsaking his breakfast for the automobile, he was displaying what is called the power of choice—a peculiarly lordly attribute that, according to Mr. Burroughs, belongs to man alone. Yet Glen made his choice between food and fun.

It was not that Glen wanted his breakfast less, but that he wanted his ride more. The toot was only a joke. The automobile did not start. Glen waited and watched. Evidently he saw no signs of an immediate start, for finally he jumped out of the seat and went back to his breakfast. He ate with indecent haste, like a man anxious to catch a train. Again the horn tooted, again he deserted his breakfast, and again he sat in the seat and waited vainly for the machine to go. They came close to spoiling Glen's breakfast for him, for he was kept on the jump between porch and barn. Then he grew wise. They tooted the horn loudly and insistently, but he stayed by his breakfast and finished it. Thus once more did he display power of choice, incidentally of control, for when that horn tooted it was all he could do to refrain from running for the barn.

The Dog and the Chauffeur's Joke

The nature-faker would analyze what went on in Glen's brain somewhat in the following fashion. He had had, in his short life, experiences that not one of all his ancestors had ever had. He had learned that automobiles went fast, that once in motion it was impossible for him to get on board, that the toot of the horn was a noise that was peculiar to automobiles. These were so many propositions. Now reasoning can be defined as the act or process of the brain by which, from propositions known or assumed, new propositions are reached. Out of the propositions which I have shown were Glen's, and which had become his through the medium of his own observation of the phenomena of life, he made the new proposition that when the horn tooted it was time for him to get on board.

But on the morning I have described, the chauffeur fooled Glen. Somehow, and much to his own disgust, his reasoning was erroneous. The machine did not start after all. But to reason incorrectly is very human. The great trouble in all acts of reasoning is to include all the propositions in the problem. Glen had included every proposition but one, namely, the human proposition, the joke in the brain of the chauffeur. For a number of times Glen was fooled. Then he performed another mental act. In his problem he included the human proposition (the joke in the brain of the chauffeur), and he reached the new conclusion that when the horn tooted the automobile was *not* going to start. Basing his action on this conclusion, he remained on the porch and finished his breakfast. You and I, and even Mr. Burroughs, perform acts of reasoning precisely similar to this every day in our lives. How Mr. Burroughs will explain Glen's action by the instinctive theory is beyond me. In wildest fantasy, even, my brain refuses to follow Mr. Burroughs into the primeval forest, where Glen's dim ancestors, to the tooting of automobile-horns, were fixing into the heredity of the breed the particular instinct that would enable Glen, a few thousand years later, capably to cope with automobiles.

Dr. C. J. Romanes tells of a female chimpanzee who was taught to count straws up to five. She held the straws in her hand, exposing the ends to the number requested. If she were asked for three, she held up three. If she were asked for four, she held up four. All this is a mere matter of training. But consider now, Mr. Burroughs, what follows. When she was asked for five straws and she had only four, she doubled one straw, exposing both its ends and thus making up the required number. She did not do this only once, and by accident. She did it whenever more straws were asked for than she possessed.

Did she perform a distinctly reasoning act? or was her action the result of blind, mechanical instinct? If Mr. Burroughs can not answer to his own satisfaction, he may call Dr. Romanes a nature-faker and dismiss the incident from his mind.

The Repartee of Mr. Burroughs

The foregoing is a trick of erroneous human reasoning that works very successfully in the United States these days. It is certainly a trick of Mr. Burroughs, which he is guilty of with distressing frequency. When a poor devil of a writer records what he has seen, and when what he has seen does not jibe with Mr. Burroughs's medieval theory, he calls said writer a nature-faker. When a man like Mr. Hornaday comes along, Mr. Burroughs works a variation of the trick on him. Mr. Hornaday has made a close study of the orang in captivity and of the orang in its native state. Also, he has studied closely many other of the higher animal types. Also, in the tropics, he has studied the lower races of man. Mr. Hornaday is a man of experience and reputation. When he was asked if animals reasoned, out of all his knowledge on the subject he replied that to ask him such a question was equivalent to asking him if fishes swim. Now Mr. Burroughs has not had much experience in studying the lower human types and the higher animal types. Living in a rural district of the State of New York, and studying principally birds in that limited habitat, he has been in contact neither with the higher animal types nor the lower human types. But Mr. Hornaday's reply is such a facer to him and his homocentric theory that he has to do something. And he does it. He retorts: "I suspect that Mr. Hornaday is a better naturalist than he is a comparative psychologist." Exit Mr. Hornaday. Who the devil is Mr. Hornaday anyway? The sage of Slabsides has spoken. When Darwin concluded that animals were capable of reasoning in a rudimentary way, Mr. Burroughs laid him out in the same fashion by saying: "But Darwin was also a much greater naturalist than psychologist"—and this despite Darwin's long life of laborious research that was not wholly confined to a rural district such as Mr. Burroughs inhabits in New York. Mr. Burroughs's method of argument is beautiful. It reminds one of the man whose pronunciation was vile, but who said: "Damn the dictionary; ain't I here?"

And now we come to the mental processes of Mr. Burroughs—to the psychology of the ego, if you please. Mr. Burroughs has troubles of his own with the dictionary. He violates language, from the standpoint both of logic and science. Language is a tool, and definitions embodied in language should agree with the facts and history of life. But Mr. Burroughs's definitions do not so agree. This, in turn, is not the fault of his education, but of his ego. To him, despite his well-exploited and patronizing devotion to them, the lower animals are disgustingly low. To him, affinity and kinship with the other animals is a repugnant thing. He will have none of it. He is too glorious a personality not to have between him and the other animals a vast and impassable gulf. The cause of Mr. Burroughs's medieval view of the other animals is to be found, not in his knowledge of those other animals, but in the suggestion of his self-exalted ego. In short, Mr. Burroughs's homocentric theory has been developed out of his own homocentric ego, and by the misuse of language he strives to make the facts of life jibe with his theory.

After the instances I have cited of actions of animals which are impossible of explanation as due to instinct, Mr. Burroughs may reply: "Your instances are easily explained by the simple law of association." To this I reply, first, then why did you deny rudimentary reason to animals? and why did you state flatly that "instinct suffices for the animals"? And, second, with great reluctance and with overwhelming humility because of my youth, I suggest that you do not know exactly what you do mean by that phrase "the simple law of association." Your trouble, I repeat, is with definitions. You have grasped that man performs what is called *abstract* reasoning, you have made a definition of abstract reason, and, betrayed by that great maker of theories, the ego, you have come to think that all reasoning is abstract and that what is not abstract reason is not reason at all. This is your attitude toward rudimentary reason. Such a process, in one of the other animals, must be either abstract or it is not a reasoning process. Your intelligence tells you that such a process is not abstract reasoning, and your homocentric thesis compels you to conclude that it can be only a mechanical, instinctive process.

The Climb of Reason from Mud to Man

Definitions must agree, not with egos, but with life. Mr. Burroughs goes on the basis that a definition is something hard and fast, absolute and eternal. He forgets that all the universe is in flux; that definitions are arbitrary and ephemeral; that they fix, for a fleeting instant of time, the things that in the past were not, that in the future will be not, that out of the past become, and that out of the present pass on to the future and become other things. Definitions can not rule life. Definitions can not be made to rule life. Life must rule definitions or else the definitions perish.

Mr. Burroughs forgets the evolution of reason. He makes a definition of reason without regard to its history, and that definition is of reason purely abstract. Human reason, as we know it to-day, is not a creation, but a growth. Its history goes back to the primordial slime that was quick with muddy life; its history goes back to the first vitalized inorganic. And here are the steps of its ascent from the mud to man: simple reflex action, compound reflex action, memory, habit, rudimentary reason, and abstract reason. In the course of the climb, thanks to natural selection, instinct was evolved. Habit is a development in the individual. Instinct is a race habit. Instinct is blind, unreasoning, mechanical. This was the dividing of the ways in the climb of aspiring life. The perfect culmination of instinct we find in the ant-heap and the bee-hive. Instinct proved a blind alley. But the other path, that of reason, led on and on even to Mr. Burroughs and you and me.

The Honey-Bee and the Dog

There are no impassable gulfs, unless one chooses, as Mr. Burroughs does, to ignore the lower human types and the higher animal types, and to compare human mind with bird mind. It was impossible for life to reason abstractly until speech was developed. Equipped with words, with tools of thought, in short, the slow development of the power to reason in the abstract went on. The lowest human types do little or no reasoning in the abstract. With every word, with every increase in the complexity of thought, with every ascertained fact so gained, went on action and reaction in the gray matter of the speech-discoverer, and slowly, step by step, through hundreds of thousands of years, developed the power of reason.

Place a honey-bee in a glass bottle. Turn the bottom of the bottle towards a lighted lamp so that the open mouth is away from the lamp. Vainly, ceaselessly, a thousand times, undeterred by the bafflement and the pain, the bee will hurl himself against the bottom of the bottle as he strives to win to the light. That is instinct. Place your dog in a back yard and go away. He is your dog. He loves you. He yearns toward you as the bean yearns toward the light. He listens to your departing footsteps. But the fence is too high. Then he turns his back upon the direction in which you are departing, and runs around the yard. He is frantic with affection and desire. But he is not blind. He is observant. He is looking for a hole under the fence, or through the fence, or for a place where the fence is not so high. He sees a dry-goods box standing against the fence. Presto! He leaps upon it, goes over the barrier, and tears down the street to overtake you. Is that instinct?

Talking Machine, Telephone and Mirror

Here, in the household where I am writing this, is a little Tahitian "feeding child." He believes firmly that a tiny dwarf resides in the box of my talking machine and that it is the tiny dwarf who does the singing and talking. Not even Mr. Burroughs will affirm that the child has reached this conclusion by an instinctive process. Of course the child reasons the existence of the dwarf in the box. How else could the box talk and sing? In that child's limited experience it has never encountered a single instance where speech and song were produced otherwise than by direct human agency. I doubt not that the dog is considerably surprised when he hears his master's voice out of the box.

The adult savage, on his first introduction to a telephone, rushes around to the adjoining room to find the man who is talking through the partition. Is this act instinctive? No. Out of his limited experience, out of his limited knowledge of physics, he reasons that the only explanation possible is that a man is in the other room talking through the partition.

But that savage can not be fooled by a hand-mirror. We must go lower down in the animal scale, to the monkey. The monkey swiftly learns that the monkey it sees is not in the glass, wherefore it reaches craftily behind the glass. Is this instinct? No. It is rudimentary reasoning. Lower than the monkey in the scale of brain is the robin, and the robin fights its reflection in the window-pane. Now climb with me for a space. From the robin to the monkey, where is the impassable gulf? and where is the impassable gulf between the monkey and the feeding child? between the feeding child and the savage who seeks the man behind the partition? ay, and between the savage and the astute financiers Mrs. Chadwick fooled and the thousands who were fooled by the Keeley Motor swindle?

Our Relatives, the Other Animals

Let us be very humble. We who are so very human are very animal. Kinship with the other animals is no more repugnant to Mr. Burroughs than was the heliocentric theory to the priests who compelled Galileo to recant. Not correct human reason, not the evidence of the ascertained fact, but the pride of ego, was responsible for the repugnance.

In his stiff-necked pride, Mr. Burroughs runs a hazard more humiliating to that pride than any amount of kinship with the other animals. When a dog exhibits choice, direction, control, and reason; when it is shown that certain mental processes in that dog's brain are precisely duplicated in the brain of man; and when Mr. Burroughs convincingly proves that every action of the dog is mechanical and automatic—then, by precisely the same argument, can it be proved that the similar actions of man are mechanical and automatic. No, Mr. Burroughs, though you stand on the top of the ladder of life you must not kick out the ladder from under your feet. You must not deny your relatives, the other animals. Their history is your history, and if you kick them to the bottom of the abyss, to the bottom of the abyss you go yourself. By them you stand or fall. What you repudiate in them you repudiate in yourself—pretty spectacle, truly, of an excited animal striving to disown the stuff of life out of which it was made, striving by use of the very reason that was developed by evolution to deny the processes of evolution that developed it. This may be good egotism, but it is not good science.

1. *Editor's Note: "Highhole" is a name once used for the Common Flicker, a species of woodpecker.—RHL*

27

Chipmunk Thoughts

JOHN BURROUGHS

One reaps his harvest, and it looks as if his acres would never yield another, but lo! as the seasons return, there springs a fresh crop of ideas and observations. It seems as if one never could get to the end of all the delightful things there are to know, and to observe, and to speculate about the world. Nature is always young, and there is no greater felicity than to share in her youth. I still find each day too short for all the thoughts I want to think, all the walks I want to take, all the books I want to read, and all the friends I want to see. But I will confide to my reader that there is one thing I am quite certain I have come to the end of, and that is the vexed question of the animal mind. Whether the dog, the cat, the cockroach reason or not, shall trouble me (and them) no more. While I write these lines in my outdoor study, a chipmunk whose den is near by, comes in and eagerly selects the hard, dry kernels of pop-corn from the soft unripe kernels of sweet corn which I have sprinkled upon the floor at my feet, stuffs his cheek pockets with them and hurries away to his den as if he knew that the dry corn would keep in his retreat, and that the green would not. After he has collected all the dry kernels, he falls to eating the green ones. I also sprinkle choke-cherries among the corn. These he finally proceeds to strip of their pulp and skins, and stuff his pockets with their pits, and rushes off to his den—thus putting no perishable food in his winter retreat. Does the pretty little rodent reason about all this? Ah! my reader, ask some one else! As for me, I will content myself with his companionship as he runs along my study table, pokes his nose under the arch made by my hand, under which the kernels lie, and

Excerpted from the Preface to John Burroughs, *The Summit of the Years* (Boston: Houghton Mifflin, 1913).

even climbs to the crown of my head. He sets me to thinking, and I, if I do not set him to thinking, at least aid him in adding to his winter supplies. We are both learning something; day unto day uttereth knowledge, and even a chipmunk shares a little of the wisdom that pervades the universe.

Interpretations

Scholars largely ignored wild animal stories for over half a century; but this began to change in the 1960s. The stories of Charles G. D. Roberts and Ernest Thompson Seton, in particular, were recognized as an important part of Canadian literature. In addition, they were seen to reflect distinctive qualities of the Canadian response to wilderness and as a literary response to Darwinism.

The opening essay in this book, "The Wild Animal Story: Animals and Ideas," reviewed some of this scholarship. The essays in this final part allow the scholars speak for themselves. At first glance, it may appear that scholars have as many different views of the genre as people have of animals. On reflection, though, these essays provide a richly textured perspective of an important branch of nature literature and its relationship with larger social issues.

Many of the issues over which the Nature Fakers controversy was fought remain with us generations later. They are issues that each generation must come to terms with in its own way. In what ways are wild animals like and unlike people? What does this mean in terms of our relationships with them? How is this best presented in print and non-print media? How have these understandings changed over time, and why? And in what ways do the wild animal stories of today reflect and inform us about the perceptions and concerns of our society and time?

28

Animal Victims

MARGARET ATWOOD

You'd think that the view of Nature as Monster so prevalent in Canadian literature would generate, as the typical Canadian animal story, a whole series of hair-raising tales about people being gnawed by bears, gored to death by evil-eyed moose, and riddled with quills by vengeful porcupines. In fact this is not the case; fangs and claws are sprouted by mountains and icebergs, it's true, but in stories about actual animals something much more peculiar happens, and it's this really odd pattern I'd like to pursue. In the course of the hunt I hope to demonstrate that the "realistic" animal story, as invented and developed by Ernest Thompson Seton and Sir Charles G. D. Roberts, is not, as Alec Lucas would have it in *A Literary History of Canada,* "a rather isolated and minor kind of literature," but a *genre* which provides a key to an important facet of the Canadian psyche. Those looking for something 'distinctively Canadian' in literature might well start right here.

The Canadian *genre* and its approach to its subject are in fact unique. It is true that stories ostensibly about animals appear in British literature; but as anyone who has read Kipling's Mowgli stories, Kenneth Grahame's *The Wind In The Willows,* or Beatrix Potter's tales can see, the animals in them are really, like the white rabbit in *Alice in Wonderland,* Englishmen in furry zippered suits, often with a layer of human clothing added on top. They speak fluent English and are assigned places in a hierarchical social order which is essentially British (or British-colonial, as in the Mowgli stories): Toad of Toad Hall is an upper-class twit, the stoats and ferrets which invade his mansion are working-class

From Margaret Atwood, *Survival: A Thematic Guide to Canadian Literature* (Toronto: Anansi, 1972). Used by permission of McClelland & Stewart, Inc., Toronto, *The Canadian Publishers.*

louts and scoundrels. The ease with which these books can be—and have been—translated into plays, ballets and cartoon movies, complete with song, dance, speech and costume, is an indication of the essentially human nature of the protagonists. Of note also are the invariably happy endings.

Animals appear in American literature minus clothes and the ability to speak English, but seldom are they the centre of the action. Rather they are its goal, as these "animal stories" are in fact hunting stories, with the interest centred squarely on the hunter. The white whale in *Moby Dick*, the bear in Faulkner's "The Bear," the lion in Hemingway's "The Short Happy Life of Francis Macomber," the grizzlies in Mailer's *Why Are We in Viet Nam?*, the deer glimpsed by the narrator in James Dickey's *Deliverance*—all these and a host of others are animals endowed with magic symbolic qualities. They are Nature, mystery, challenge, otherness, what lies beyond the Frontier: the hunter wishes to match himself against them, conquer them by killing them and assimilate their magic qualities, including their energy, violence and wildness, thus "winning" over Nature and enhancing his own stature. American animal stories are quest stories—with the Holy Grail being a death—usually successful from the hunter's point of view, though not from the animal's; as such they are a comment on the general imperialism of the American cast of mind. When Americans have produced stories which superficially resemble those of Seton and Roberts, they are likely to be animal success-stories, the success being measured in terms of the animal's adjustment to people—as in Jack London's *White Fang*, where the wolf-dog, mistreated in youth, begins by hating men but ends up loving them, saving them and living in California.

The animal stories of Seton and Roberts are far from being success stories. They are almost invariably failure stories, ending with the death of the animal; but this death, far from being the accomplishment of a quest, to be greeted with rejoicing, is seen as tragic or pathetic, *because the stories are told from the point of view of the animal.* That's the key: English animal stories are about "social relations," American ones are about people killing animals; Canadian ones are about animals *being* killed, as felt emotionally from inside the fur and feathers. As you can see, *Moby Dick* as told by the White Whale would be very different. ("Why is that strange man chasing me around with a harpoon?") For a Canadian version of whale-meets-whaler, see E. J. Pratt's *The Cachalot*, in which it's the whale's death—not the whaler's—that we mourn. (The whaler, incidentally, is from New England. . . .)

"The fact that these stories are true is the reason why all are tragic. The life of a wild animal *always has a tragic end*," says Seton in the Preface to *Wild Animals I Have Known*. He's defending his position as a realist, a purveyor of truth. However, "realism" in connection with animal stories must always be a somewhat false claim, for the simple reason that animals do not speak a human language; nor do they write stories. It's impossible to get the real inside story, from the horse's mouth so to speak. "Animal" stories must be stories written by people *about* animals, just as "Indian" stories have until very recently been stories written by white people *about* Indians. In the latter case the Indian tends to be made into a symbol; onto him the white man projects his own desire or fear. And so with the animal. "We and the beasts are kin," says Seton, all but acknowledging this connection.

The world of Nature presented by Seton and Roberts is one in which the animal is always a victim. No matter how brave, cunning and strong he is, he will be killed eventually, either by other animals (which these authors don't seem to mind too much; it's part of the game) or by men. Seton, especially, reverses the Nature-as-Monster pattern in stories such as "Lobo," "The Springfield Fox" and "Redruff." Here it is man who is the threat and the villain: the animals suffer much more through men, with their snares, traps, chains and poisons, than they would through other animals, who are at least quick. The amount of elegaic emotion expended over the furry corpses that litter the pages of Seton and Roberts suggest that "tragic" is the wrong word; "pathetic" would be a better one. Tragedy requires a flaw of some kind on the part of the hero, but pathos as a literary mode simply demands that an innocent victim suffer. Seton and Roberts rarely offer their victims even a potential way out. As James Polk says in his essay "Lives of the Hunted: The Canadian Animal Story and the National Identity,"

> These doleful endings and the number of stoic moose, tragic bears, grouse dying in the snow, woodchucks devoured, salmon failing to make it upstream, grief-stricken wolves and doomed balls of fur, feathers or quills squealing for dead mothers tend to instill a certain fatalism in the reader. . . .

If animals in literature are always symbols, and if Canadian animal stories present animals as victims, what trait in our national psyche do these animal victims symbolize? By now that should be an easily-guessed riddle, but before unravelling it more fully let's consider two later examples of the realistic animal story as *genre*.

Though Lucas claims that "Nature writing, particularly the animal story, had its hey-day in the late nineteenth and early twentieth centuries" and has "long passed," two widely-read books have appeared since then which refute him: Fred Bodsworth's *The Last of the Curlews* and Farley Mowat's *Never Cry Wolf.* In Bodsworth's novel the central characters are two birds, the last of their species. The book follows them through a season of their life; at its end the female curlew is shot by a man with a gun and the male curlew is left alone. Mowat's book is ostensibly a true-life account of the author's study of a pair of Arctic wolves. The wolves, seen at first as savage predators, emerge as highly commendable beings. But they too are doomed; in an epilogue the author tells us that soon after his visit a Predator Control Officer planted the wolves' den with cyanide, presumably finishing them off.

The difference between the earlier Seton and Roberts stories and the later

Bodsworth and Mowat ones is that in the former it is the individual only who dies; the species remains. But *The Last of the Curlews* is, as its name implies, the story of the death of a species, and Mowat indicates that not just the wolves but also the caribou and with them the whole Arctic ecological balance is threatened by the white man's short-sighted and destructive policies. Man is again the villain, but on a much larger scale.

The Canadian concern with doomed and slaughtered animals spreads far beyond the range of the "animal story," however. It is highly visible in poetry, and there's even a recent anthology of "animal poems." Both the title—*The Broken Ark*—and the jacket copy reveal editor Michael Ondaatje's stance, which is firmly in the tradition of Seton and Roberts:

> These are poems that look at animals from the inside out—not the other way round. We don't want to classify them or treat them as pets. We want you to imagine yourself pregnant and being chased and pounded to death by snowmobiles. We want you to feel the cage, and the skin and fur on your shoulders.

In fact, some of the poems in the book aren't this drastic; one is about walking the dog, one about bees, one about happy elephants. But the majority are in what we seem to have identified as the Canadian tradition: the animals in them are dead or dying, their deaths usually caused by man. In Alden Nowlan's "The Bull Moose," the moose is tortured before being killed; the imagery used of him makes him into a sacrificed-god figure, but his is a sacrifice that redeems no one. Irving Layton's "Cain" is a meditation on a frog he has himself killed with an air-rifle: presumably the title makes the frog his brother. Pat Lane's "Mountain Oysters" tells about the routine castration of rams; in Bill Bissett's "Killer Whale" the whales have been captured and will obviously die. In each case we are asked to sympathize with the animals, not with the men who are torturing or killing them.

There are many others that *The Broken Ark* misses. Prominent among them are Irving Layton's "The Bull Calf," in which the animal, like Nowlan's moose, is being sacrificed uselessly. Then there's Al Purdy's extraordinary poem "The Death of Animals," in which animal deaths and trivial human activities are juxtaposed, with the human activities seen as causal (though the poet claims, ironically, that there is "no connection"): the humans are taking over, replacing the animals:

> Fox in deep burrow suddenly imagined
> a naked woman inside his rubric fur,
> lacquered fingernails pushing, edging him out:
> and screamed, directly into the earth.

And castration again, in Alden Nowlan's "God Sour the Milk of the Knacking Wench."

Turning to recent prose fiction, we find the animal as victim making a significant appearance in the work of Dave Godfrey. *Death Goes Better with Coca*

Cola, Godfrey's first book, is essentially a collection of hunting stories. The point is made partly by the title, which links death with coca-cola, the great American beverage; partly by the initial quote, which is from biologist Konrad Lorenz's book *On Aggression* and which speaks of the destructive effect cultures regarded as "higher"—"as the culture of a conquering nation usually is"— have on those on "the subdued side"; and partly by the first story, "The Generation of Hunters," which is about a boy who is taught by his father how to shoot bears and who grows up to be a Marine. Americans, "the conquering nation," are the killers, Canadians are the killed, as the last story, "The Hard-Headed Collector," makes clear. The slaughter of moose and fish which occurs elsewhere in the stories, and which is performed in some cases by Canadians, is thus given an ironic framework: Canadians too can be hunters, but only by taking a stance towards Nature which is like the stance of America towards them. The only "authentic" hunters are those who must still kill to eat, the Indians and locals who "really live here." The rest are fakes, memento hunters, as the man who sets out to catch a flying fish in "The Flying Fish" learns when the fish he is allowed to hook turns out to be made of polyfoam. "It is something to mount on my wall," he says.

There's a fascinating poem by Alden Nowlan called "Hunters" which takes Americans-as-hunters a step further. The hunters, "Americans in scarlet breeches," have shot a bear which is roped to their car; one of them gets out to check the knots, looking "boyish," and Nowlan comments,

> . . . . One senses how this cowed
> and squalid beast enlivens him—its pain
> and cornered anger squelched in the dark wood
> that ornaments his world. It's like a child
> sprung from the violent act but tamed and good,
> decoratively. . . .

The Americans have been performing their ritual act of "taming" Nature by killing one of its animals, but somehow the thing is no longer real; the dark wood is now just ornamental, the dead animal a decoration, not something that can be seen as itself:

> . . . . He can't see it wild,
> alive in its own element. He might
> as well have bought it and perhaps he did:
> guides trap and sell them out by weight
> to hunters who don't want to hunt. The dead
> beast-thing secured, the car starts homeward. There
> bear skins are rugs, a den is not a lair.

Canada and America have interesting roles in this poem. America's hunter-energy is running down, though a dead animal can still produce an enlivening thrill. Canada is the place where Americans now come to hunt. The dead bear is

Canadian, a trophy to be taken from "here" to "there," and "there" is seen as civilized, safe, non-wild, a place of rituals that have lost their meaning and of fake surfaces, of living skins turned into rugs. The function of the Canadian "guides" is curious; they are the middlemen, converting their own live reality to dead trophies so they can sell it. The narrative stance hovers tantalizingly between sympathy for the bear and potential fear of it; at any rate, the bear is real for the narrator in a way that it is not for the Americans.

We've established that the animal as victim is a persistent image in Canadian literature; now here's a further clue to its possible meaning. Biologist Desmond Morris conducted a survey of people's reactions to animals, through which he made the not surprising discovery that the animals people choose to identify with depend on the size and age of the people. Small children like large 'parental' animals such as bears and elephants; slightly older children prefer white mice and squirrels and other things smaller than themselves which they can control; adolescents like companion or sexual-power figures such as dogs and horses; childless couples tend to favour substitute children such as cats, lapdogs and housebirds. Very rarely is an animal liked or disliked for itself alone; it is chosen for its symbolic anthropomorphic values.

Elderly people in England tended to identify with threatened or nearly-extinct species; obviously they themselves felt threatened or nearly-extinct. But in Canada it is the nation as a whole that joins in animal-salvation compaigns such as the protest over the slaughter of baby seals and the movement to protect the wolf. This could—mistakenly, I think—be seen as national guilt: Canada after all was founded on the fur trade, and an animal cannot painlessly be separated from its skin. From the animal point of view, Canadians are as bad as the slave trade or the Inquisition; which casts a new light on those beavers on the nickels and caribou on the quarters. But it is much more likely that Canadians themselves feel threatened and nearly extinct as a nation, and suffer also from life-denying experience as individuals—the culture threatens the "animal" within them—and that their identification with animals is the expression of a deep-seated cultural fear. The animals, as Seton says, are us. And for the Canadian animal, bare survival is the main aim in life, failure as an individual is inevitable, and extinction as a species is a distinct possibility.

A search for animal victims in Québec literature uncovers an interesting phenomenon: the "realistic" version of the animal victim is almost unknown. Animals, when they appear, are more likely to be Aesop-fable humanoids like the bull in Jacques Ferron's story "Mélie and the Bull." The explanation may lie in the persistence of the French fable tradition in Québec; or it may be that French Canadians have been more than willing to see themselves as victims, conquered and exploited, while English Canadians suppressed this knowledge of themselves—they won on the Plains of Abraham, didn't they? —and were able to project it only through their use of animal images.

However, there is one encounter with an animal in French Canadian literature which could be straight out of Ernest Thompson Seton: I'm thinking of the moment in Gabrielle Roy's *The Hidden Mountain* where Pierre, having hunted down a caribou, finally kills it and it turns upon him a gaze full of resignation and suffering. This gaze exchanged between a hunter and an animal either dying or threatened with death—and it's usually a deer, moose or caribou—is a recurring moment in Canadian literature; in it the hunter identifies with his prey *as suffering victim*. For an example from Seton, see *The Trail of the Sandhill Stag*, in which the narrator finally corners a stag after a long hunt but can't shoot because—during that meaningful gaze—he realizes that the stag is his brother.

In *The Bush Garden*, Northrop Frye notes "the prevalence in Canada of animal stories, in which animals are closely assimilated to human behaviour and emotions." I would add that the human behaviour and emotions in question are limited in range, being usually flight, fear and pain. Applying Morris' findings, we may infer that the English Canadian projects himself through his animal images as a threatened victim, confronted by a superior alien technology against which he feels powerless, unable to take any positive defensive action, and, survive each crisis as he may, ultimately doomed.

■

This is not to say that one shouldn't be humane towards animals or protect the wolf; one should, though in saying so I may simply be demonstrating my own Canadianism. But there comes a point at which seeing yourself as a victimized animal—naming your condition, as the crucial step from the ignorance of Position One through the knowledge of Position Two to the self-respect of Position Three—can become the *need* to see yourself as a victimized animal, and at that point you will be locked into Position Two, unable to go any further. This insight is explored with ruthless precision in Graeme Gibson's two novels, *Five Legs* and *Communion*. The central organizing images in both books are animal images, and the use Gibson makes of them pulls together everything I've said so far about animal victims in Canadian literature.

The title of the first novel, *Five Legs*, refers to a mutant water-buffalo which a nasty woman at a funeral in Southern Ontario has seen in a Mexican zoo. The animal has five legs instead of four, and because of its deformity people are laughing and throwing stones at it. The woman has vowed to become a collector of warped animals, and has already managed to locate a dog with three legs; she is currently looking for a deformed cat. She latches on to one of the novel's two protagonists, Felix Oswald, and her interest in him—he realizes with horror—is of the same kind: she sees him as a cripple, a victim and a freak. She's very perceptive, since this is in fact how he sees himself. The woman's pathological need to seek out victims is matched by Felix's pathological need to be one.

Later Felix changes the emphasis slightly: instead of a caged mutant, he has a fantasy of himself as a free wild animal, a moose. In the fantasy the moose is in flight from a group of pursuers, from which it is only barely managing to escape. (It's significant that Felix has acquired his moose image from the drunken monologue of a pitiful loser, who in the first section of the book is rambling on both about a moose he has allowed to get away and a deer he has shot and now feels remorseful about.)

The moose image is picked up in a later conversation, this time a discussion about hunting. There are two "sides" in the discussion: one taken by a group of conventional businessmen who emphasize the joys of the kill— "By George that's a, a satisfying feeling!" —and the other taken by Max, an eccentric old bohemian, who says he'd never shoot a moose or "any other of the round earth's living creatures" and goes on to tell, stealing his metaphors from the drunken driver in section one, how he once saw a moose "stumbling on the shore and rushing to the bush like a man in flames," and how when it looked at him it had "tears of blood in the eyes' dark corners." (There's that sacrificial victim imagery again, and the exchange of gazes between hunter and prey.) An American would have pulled the trigger, and in fact the men turn on Max, accuse him of being a subversive, claim that hunting is "the very BASIS of our social fabric," insist that they are successful; because "We know how to get things done," and extend their assumed usefulness even further: "we're hunters, that's right . . . The community needs people like us. The country . . . . whole free world!" These "practical" men are, it appears, not only capitalists but internationalists too; like the hunters in Godfrey's stories, they hunt for symbolic reasons, not because they need the dead animals for food.

Putting Gibson's patterns together, we find two sorts of people: those who are successful by "international" (or American) society's proclaimed standards, who are identified as hunters, soldiers, and aggressive moneymen; and those who are failures—the drunken driver, Max and Felix—who express sympathy with hunted animals and refuse to kill them. Felix, in fact, *is* an animal, a victim in flight; the "hunters," the forces of society, are in pursuit, and will capture and kill him if they can. No positive action, no defence, is possible for him; he can only run away—as he does, literally, at the end of the novel.

Even though he is running *away*, not towards anything, Felix does escape in *Five Legs*. But we know from Seton that animal stories—Canadian ones at least—always have a tragic end, and in *Communion* Gibson corrects any mistaken impression we might have had that Felix's escape could ever have been anything but temporary. Again, it is Felix's *need* to be a hunted animal that does it; his condition, though it is partly a reflection of his environment, seems as much willed as imposed. In *Communion* Gibson pushes the animal-victim identification as far as it can go: if you are determined to be a victim, that's exactly what you will be.

In *Communion* Felix is still in flight, but now he is escaping not only from society but from all human emotions and involvements, including sexual ones. He is in love with two stone statues in a cemetery, and he feels more for the diseased animals at the veterinarian's where he works than he does for anyone else. He singles out one particular animal, a sick husky dog, which is, like the crippled water buffalo in *Five Legs*, incurable. But whereas the buffalo can live with its deformity (however unpleasantly), the dog is mortally ill. Felix has fantasies of taking the dog out into the winter bush and freeing it, thereby freeing—perhaps—a part of himself, his own trapped and wounded life-energies. But when he acts out this fantasy, stealing the dog and driving it to a spot outside the city, it refuses to leave the car. Like Felix, it is choosing its own entrapment. When he finally manages to pry it loose, it runs along beside his moving car; he hits it by accident and it dies in agony. His attempted act of redemption has failed; but then, had he wanted success, he might have chosen a more redeemable subject.

His second attempted act of redemption fails also. In flight from everything by now, he gets a lift with a sadistic truck-driver and ends up in the United States. In the "Canadian" portion of *Communion*, the life-destroying forces are seen as mainly personal and internal: the paralyzing guilt, the inability to act, the incapacity to respond to authority by anything but flight, the sexual stasis, the sense of placelessness and exile, the lack of contact with any source of true feeling—all these are individual and private, rarely even verbalized. But once across the border the violence and destructiveness that is repressed and turned in upon itself in Canada is seen as external, *there* in the real world, rampantly at large. Ritson, the "American" character in *Communion*, is another hunted animal, but this time his condition is literal: he lives in a cellar, comes out at night to scrounge for food, and fights with other people who are also animals; the American city is the new locale, apparently, for Darwinian marginal survival. In America people-as-animals are not just victims, they are savage cornered beasts.

Felix dies trying to save his American *alter ego* from being burned up by a nightmarish group of children. In his attempt to stop the children he kills one of them and—as when he killed the dog by accident—he is so overcome with horror by the image of himself as predator rather than victim that he is paralyzed. Ritson escapes and Felix burns in his stead—ironically, since the life he has saved is scarcely human.

What Gibson has done in his two books is to take the naming of the condition a step further. Perhaps our condition is that of "exploited victim," but by now our *real* condition may be "those who *need* to be exploited victims." That's a tougher condition; the first could be changed by altering the external environment, but the second also involves the alteration of self, of the way we see ourselves. Felix's sexual, emotional and practical paralyses are all correlatives of never having accepted any role but that of victim.

■

I promised a ray of light at the end of each chapter, but for this one it isn't easy. However.

For other uses of animal images, you might try looking at some of Michael Ondaatje's animal poems. The aggressor-victim thing is still going on, but in Ondaatje the animal is more likely to incorporate a vitality and energy (which man finds threatening) than to be a suffering victim. Or you could look at Joe Rosenblatt's book *Bumblebee Dithyramb,* which has a number of animal poems in it. Rosenblatt also sees animals as centres of irrepressible vitality, though it sometimes seems as though he can approach this kind of vitality *only* through animals—it is somehow closed to man. Through his highly-charged use of language the animals can do and become things for him that human beings can't; they are surrogates for desire rather than for fear.

I'd like to end by looking at another Layton poem, "A Tall Man Executes A Jig." This is an astonishing poem, and it becomes even more astonishing when read in the light of everything I've said about animal victims. In it, the tall man proceeds through various meditations in a field full of purposeless gnats. He moves out of the field and stands waiting for a revelation, and what he gets is a revelation that is also a "temptation:" he sees "A violated grass snake that lugs / Its intestine like a small red valise." It's his reaction that's the astonishment:

And the man wept because pity was useless.
"Your jig's up; the flies come like kites," he said
And watched the grass snake crawl towards the hedge,
Convulsing and dragging into the dark
The satchel filled with curses for the earth,
For the odours of warm sedge, and the sun,
A blood-red organ in the dying sky.
Backwards it fell into a grassy ditch,
Exposing its underside, white as milk,
And mocked by wisps of hay between its jaws;
And then it stiffened to its final length.
But though it opened its thin mouth to scream
A last silent scream that shook the black sky,
Adamant and fierce, the tall man did not curse.

The temptation for the tall man would have been to see himself as the suffering and dying snake, "violated" and victimized, to see life as death, to see the only appropriate response as a hopeless cursing of all that is. What makes the tall man tall is that he resists temptation: he witnesses the suffering but he does not curse. Considering the almost overwhelming pressures of the great Canadian animal-victim tradition, this restraint is heroic.

29

The Revolt Against Instinct:
The Animal Stories of Seton and Roberts

ROBERT H. MACDONALD

In his introduction to *Kindred of the Wild*—a chapter that stands as a succinct apologia for the animal story—Sir Charles Roberts in 1902 explained the particular inspiration of the new genre practiced by Ernest Thompson Seton and himself. Animals and men, he said, were not so separate as had been supposed, for animals, far from being mere creatures of instinct, could and did reason, and what is more, frequently displayed to the discerning observer signs not only of their psychologies, but also of something which might appeal to man's spiritual self. "We have come face to face with personality, where we were blindly wont to predicate mere instinct and automatism." The animal story, Roberts concluded, was thus a "potent emancipator," freeing us from "shop-worn utilities" and restoring to us the "old kinship of earth," a spiritual and uplifting union with nature.[1]

These statements can be labelled "romantic," or "transcendental," and dismissed as a rather sentimental defence of the "inarticulate kindred" of the wild, who are distinguished from Black Beauty and Beautiful Joe only by the fact that they live in the woods. I propose, however, to take Roberts at his word, and to examine his and Seton's stories in the light of his crucial distinction between instinct and reason. The animal story, I shall show, is part of a popular revolt against Darwinian determinism, and is an affirmation of man's need for moral and spiritual values. The animal world provides models of virtue, and exem-

Robert H. MacDonald, "The Revolt Against Instinct: The Animal Stories of Seton and Roberts," *Canadian Literature*, no. 84 (Spring 1980), 18–29. Used by permission of the author.

plifies the order of nature. The works of Seton and Roberts are thus celebrations of rational, ethical animals, who, as they rise above instinct, reach towards the spiritual. This theme, inspired as it is by a vision of a better world, provides a mythic structure for what is at first sight, realistic fiction.

At the popular level, the chief implication of Darwin's theories of evolution and the principle of natural selection had been to diminish the distinction between man and the animals. We were descended from the apes, and if the apes were mere brutes, could we be very much different? All creatures, it seemed, owed their present form to certain inherited characteristics, which together with environmental influences, dictated their ability to survive. Nature was amoral; life was a power-struggle in which only the fittest survived. Instinct, to a large extent, seemed to govern animal behaviour; there was little place in nature for ethics or spirituality. Though man traditionally had been separated from the animals by his unique power of reason, could it not now be that man himself was little more than a brute beast?

By 1900 one of the most important controversies in the biological sciences was the question of animal behaviour: did animals act instinctively, or were they capable of learning? What was the nature of an animal's knowledge: was it inherited, or was it acquired? Were animals capable of reason? Did they learn from experience, did they teach each other? The weight of opinion, at least from the biologists, seemed to favour instinct and inheritance.[2] In their reaction to this controversy (and in a larger sense to the whole impetus of Darwinism), Seton, Roberts and their fellow nature writers rescued their public from the awful amorality of Darwinian nature. They reassured their readers, not so much that man was superior to animals, but that animals were superior in themselves, that they could reason, that they could and did educate their young, and that they possessed and obeyed laws of their own. Judging by the commercial success of their stories, this was a popular and much-needed antidote to Darwinian pessimism.

"The life of a wild animal," said Seton in *Wild Animals I Have Known* (1898), *"always has a tragic end."* By that he meant that all animals die, and since most of them prey upon each other, they frequently die violently. Both Seton and Roberts refused to evade this unpleasant fact: kill or be killed is the natural law. To this extent they were both Darwinians: nature was indeed red in tooth and claw, and only the best escaped for a time. Thus "Kneepads," the mountain ewe who took to kneeling as she grazed, was an easy prey for the mountain lion, and Red Fox's weaker and stupider siblings met an early death.[3] Survival does indeed go to the fittest.

In their biographies of animal heroes, both men repeatedly illustrate this central fact of the evolutionary theory. Their animals are not ordinary animals, but superior animals, distinguished by their size, skill, wisdom and moral sense. These animals have all learned to cope with a hostile environment; they endure. They are the leaders of their kind. Thus Wahb is the largest and most intelligent grizzly, Krag the noblest mountain sheep, Lobo a giant among wolves, Raggylugs a most sagacious rabbit, and so on. From the first Red Fox is the pick of his litter, larger, livelier, more intelligent, and, curiously, redder. Seton's comment on the old crow, Silverspot, will serve to characterize all these heroes: "once in awhile there arises an animal who is stronger or wiser than his fellow, who becomes a great leader, who is, as we would say, a genius, and if he is bigger, or has some mark by which men can know him, he soon becomes famous in his country, and shows us that the life of a wild animal may be far more interesting and exciting than that of many human beings."

Both Seton and Roberts took pains to establish that everything they wrote was within the bounds of truth. Their animal biographies were frequently "composite" biographies; that is, they included everything that had been done, or might have been done, by a crow, or a wolf, or a fox, but they contained nothing that was not possible. Thus Seton, in his preface to *Wild Animals I Have Known*, acknowledges having "pieced together some of the characters," but claims that there was, in at least three of the lives, "almost no deviation from the truth." Roberts, introducing Red Fox, makes the same point saying that in the life of his hero, "every one of these experiences has befallen some red fox in the past, and may befall other red foxes in the future." He has been, he assures his readers, "careful to keep well within the boundaries of fact." We may take these statements at face value: by and large, both men were astute and careful observers of nature, and in most of their writing give realistic, though fictionalized, descriptions of animal life.[4] Both also claim that though they have given their animals language and emotions, these are, within the demands of the genre, realistic, and not anthropomorphized.

However it is not realism that entirely inspires the art of Seton and Roberts, whatever strength that lends to their work, but certain ideas which frame and condition the realism, and which give to it symbolic form. The animal heroes may live and die in the wild, being only interesting specimens of their race, but their biographies, as literature, belong in the world of myth.[5] What matters is not that everything that is told *could* have happened to a fox, or a grizzly, but that it *did* happen, and that, for the author, the life of the animal was organized according to certain basic ideas, and that in its living it demonstrated certain fundamental truths. At the heart of the myth that gives structure to the work of both Seton and Roberts is their belief that animals are rational and ethical beings, and that they rise above instinct. This is demonstrated most clearly in the ways the animals train their young to survive, and the ways in which their young respond to the challenge.[6]

Seton's story of the cottontail rabbit, Raggylugs, will serve to illustrate. The young rabbit Raggylugs is "unusually quick and bright as well as strong," and he has in his mother Molly an extremely intelligent and valiant tutor, a "true heroine," a devoted mother who finally gives her life so that her son may survive. Here, as we might expect, are the superior animals, models of intelligence and mother love. Molly's first duty is to train her son, to educate him in the skills of life. His first duty, as a successful and superior animal, is to obey. "Molly was a good little mother and gave him a careful bringing up . . . he did as he was told." Rag learns the essential rabbit lessons, to "lay low," to "freeze," and to regard the briarbush as his best friend. "All the season she kept him busy learning the tricks of the trail, and what to eat and drink and what not to touch. Day by day she worked to train him; little by little she taught him." In some of his lessons he shows himself "a veritable genius," and he even goes on to take a "postgraduate course" in how to use water. On the one occasion he is disobedient—he sits up to watch his mother lose a dog—he is severely punished, being cuffed and knocked over by Molly.

Throughout this story Seton's emphasis is on the intelligence and skill of the successful animal, the "tricks" it uses to outwit its enemies, and the way in which it is able to educate its young. Molly shows her son how to run a dog into a barbed-wire fence, how to avoid snares, and how to use water as a last resource. Animals are not mere creatures of instinct, behaving according to a set of inherited responses, but capable, within their own terms, of intelligent reasoning, of teaching and learning, and of knowing right from wrong. Rabbits, for instance, have their own language: they "have no speech . . . but they have a way of conveying ideas by a system of sounds, signs, scents, whisker-touches, movements, and example that answers the purpose of speech. . . ."

■

It is worth pausing here to answer some questions: is Seton not right—do animals not have some very definite ability to communicate in a language of their own, and are they not capable of some kind of inductive reasoning? Do they not, in fact, educate their young, and is there not more to animal behaviour than a set of instinctive reactions?

The modern ethologist would almost certainly approach these problems with caution, for the whole question of animal behaviour has become one of immense complexity. In 1900 there seemed to be a straightforward contrast to be made between instinctive and learned behaviour; now the first point to be made is that rigid alternatives are simplistic.[7] Even the terms have changed. The "nature or nurture" controversy has been replaced by a discussion of innate or acquired characteristics, and behaviour is now classified as "environmentally stable" or "environmentally labile." The discovery of imprinting, the process by which certain animals when young respond as a species to certain stimuli, has been contrasted to "adaptive" learning. The mental processes of animals are not simple, but they are clearly not always automatic, or mechanical, or, in the old sense, simply instinctive. Apes have been taught to communicate with humans using American Sign Language: the higher mammals, it has been argued, have mental experiences and probably even a conscious awareness.[8]

In spite of the complexity of the problems, certain generalizations may be made. Many animals are able to learn from experience. Many animals do teach their young, chiefly by example.[9] Some animals are capable of inductive reasoning. Some other animals may be able to adapt their behaviour, by a process of trial and error, and though it might appear that they act rationally, they do not always seem to comprehend what they are doing. Considered in general terms, however, the observations and speculations of the nature writers are closer in many ways to current scientific thinking than those of their more sceptical, behaviourist contemporaries. Animals have complex means of communicating with one another: Seton's description of rabbit language, a "system of sounds, signs, scents, whisker-touches" and so on, is not fanciful, though modern naturalists might argue with the details. What matters is not the scientific accuracy of Seton's nature stories—although that itself is an interesting question—but the ideas which give his work symbolic form. By the lights of his day he played down instinct; his animals are rational creatures who educate their offspring to be obedient and successful. As such, they are intended to be models for human edification, and nature, though full of sudden and "tragic" death, is an ordered and in many ways superior world.

Seton, as a careful naturalist, frequently describes instinctive (or innate) behaviour in animals. In most cases, he regards it as an inherited substratum, a built-in defence against the early dangers of life. He speaks of an animal's "native instincts," which are supplemented by the twin teachers of life, experience and the example of fellow animals.[10] The little mountain lambs in *Lives of the Hunted*, surprised and chased by a hunter just after birth, are able to dodge and escape, for "nature had equipped them with a set of valuable instincts." Instinct, however, takes an animal only just so far. Its role in survival is subsidiary to reason. In the story of the Don Valley partridge, for instance, Seton tells us that the partridge chicks soon graduate from instinctive to rational behaviour: "their start in life was a good mother, good legs, a few reliable instincts, and a germ of reason. It was instinct, that is, inherited habit, which taught them to hide at the word from their mother; it was instinct that taught them to follow her, but it was reason which made them keep under the shadow of her tail when the sun was smiting down. . . . " And, Seton concludes, "From that day reason entered more and more into their expanding lives."[11]

Roberts treats instinct in much the same way, as a valuable though necessarily limited body of inherited knowledge. Thus Red Fox, as befits a superior animal, has an extra amount: "He seemed to inherit with special fulness and effectiveness that endowment of ancestral knowledge which goes by the name of instinct." At the same time, of course, we are told that he is more intelligent, that he can reason, and that he is "peculiarly apt in learning from his mother." Instinct is, too, a latent skill, which can surface when necessary: in the story of "Lone Wolf" (*Neighbours Unknown*), the tame circus wolf who escapes to the wilds, Roberts shows us its hero rediscovering "long buried memories" of how a wolf kills. "It was as if all his life Lone Wolf had been killing bulls, so unerring was that terrible chopping snap at the great beast's throat." These are perhaps unexceptionable ideas, yet elsewhere in Roberts' work there is the definite implication that instinct is a primitive force which must be controlled and subdued by reason. This is especially true when applied to man himself (though as the highest of the "kindred" what is true for man is also true for animals). In "The Moonlight Trails" (*Kindred of the Wild*), we are told of a boy who loves animals and is sensitive to their feelings, who accompanies the hired man on an expedition to the woods to snare rabbits. As they set the snares the boy is moved by the primitive lust of the hunter; he feels "stirrings of a wild, predatory instinct." When they return in the morning to see what they have caught the boy is still at first in the grip of the hunting passion, but when he sees the cruel tragedy of death his more civilized feelings come to the surface. "We won't snare any more rabbits, Andy," he tells the hired man.

The gap between man and the animals, Roberts insists, is very narrow. Animals "can and do reason."[12] *Red Fox* illustrates this thesis: the whole novel is a celebration of one animal's cunning and sagacity. We are repeatedly told of Red Fox's "nimble wits," his ingenious and deliberate schemes for evading his enemies, his prodigious memory, his ability to study a situation, to make plans, to reason. We hear how he outwits "the Boy," how he leads the hounds to their destruction, how he fools his enemy Jabe Smith. His qualities are quite obvious: "look at that cool and cunning eye," says one of his American captors. "He's got brains."

In his early education, Red Fox shows that instinct is subservient to reason. Red Fox must learn both from his mother and from experience. "It is possible (though some say otherwise!) to expect too much of instinct," Roberts tells us, and explains how a successful fox will learn his lessons, "partly by example and partly no doubt by a simple language whose subtleties evade human observation." Yet we notice that when instinct gets Red Fox into trouble, it is instinct that rescues him. His nose tells him to dig in a bees' nest for honey, and when they sting him, he runs blindly for a thicket, and automatically cools his smarting nose in the mud. These are inconsistencies: Roberts' dominant theme is the supremacy and efficacy of his hero's reason. The vixen's instructions to leave men alone have "their effect on [Red Fox's] sagacious brain," whereas his stupider brother thinks he knows better, and pays the price with his life. This incident, one should note, is at the same time an apt illustration of Darwinian theory, for it is the better animal that survives.

The intelligent young animal is also the obedient young animal. In the School of the Woods, obedience is a primary virtue. The child must obey the parent. "For a young animal," Seton said, "there is no better gift than obedience,"[13] and he demonstrated this again and again by showing us the fate of the disobedient, the young lambs who do not come when they are called, and are caught and killed, or the foolish partridge chicks who refuse to stay close to mother. The fate of Red Fox's siblings again makes the point: the weak and the foolish will not survive, but the disobedient bring trouble upon all.

The essential argument of this article should be clear by now: the fiction of both Seton and Roberts is inspired by their desire to present a moral and coherent order in the life of the wild, which is part of the greater order of the cosmos. That many of their observations of animal life are accurate is undeniable— animals do learn, they are intelligent in their way, and they are probably even capable of reason. Yet what is important in Seton and Roberts is the way the details are presented. Animals, we are told, are very much like ourselves. They obey certain laws, they demonstrate qualities we would do well to admire, they are our own kin. They inhabit what is often clearly a mythic world; they are symbols in our own ontological system. Nowhere is this more obvious than in the context of morality.

Each animal, first of all, must learn to obey the laws of its kind. Morality is not a human invention, but an integral part of all nature. "It is quite common," says Seton in *Lives of the Hunted*, "to hear conventionality and social rules derided as though they were silly man-made tyrannies. They are really important laws that, like gravitation, were here before human society began, and shaped it when it came. In all wild animals we see them grown with the mental growth of the species." The higher the animal, the more clearly developed the moral system. The better the animal—the more successful, or superior specimen—the more moral the animal. Thus superior animals fight fair, but the weak, the cowards, and the mean may well resort to dirty tricks. Krag the mountain sheep, whose strength, and size, and curling horns make him appear like a "demi-god" to his ewes, has to beat off two other rams to defend his rights to his harem. One ram fights fair and meets Krag horn to horn; the other fights foul, and attacks from the side. It is important that in this moral world the immoral ram "works his own destruction," running himself over a two hundred foot cliff to his death.

These animal laws would appear to be somewhat flexible, coloured as they are by the vision of the human observer, since occasionally even a "good" animal will break the rule of his kind to preserve himself or another. This is always done for a reason: the law may be broken in the name of the higher good. We are told, in "Raggylugs," that "all good rabbits forget their feuds when their common enemy appears." Rag's rival, the stranger, ignores this basic rule of rabbit society, trying to drive Rag into the reach of a goshawk. This is bad. Yet one sentence later we find Rag playing the same game to save himself and his mother, as he successfully lures old Thunder the hound into the nest of "the stranger." This, we infer, is good.

It is at moments like this that it is most evident that the animal story belongs not to the world of natural science, but to the world of literature. There are good animals and bad animals, and we, as readers, are always expected to be on

the side of morality. Seton, however, is usually careful not to denigrate a species: each animal, of whatever kind, has some quality that a man might admire.
Even the hated rat is courageous.[14] Roberts, on the other hand, lets his sympathies show: there are some species who exhibit only the worst. Such are lynx. In
"Grey Lynx's Last Hunting," we are shown a portrait of animal cruelty, self-
ishness and marital hatred, whose appropriate outcome is the sordid death of
the male, killed by his savage and mad mate. Both writers, in their desire to
make a moral point, cross from realism into romance. Seton has a story of
wolves who lynch an apparent cheat and liar,[15] and Roberts the fanciful tale of a
society of animals who voluntarily resolve not to kill "within eyeshot" of a
sensitive and disapproving child.[16]

Throughout Roberts' work there is an insistence on the meaning, the vitality,
the harmony and the morality of the struggle of life, and in Seton, of the
fairness and ultimate order of nature. Perhaps the most dramatic illustration of
their essentially similar moral philosophy is Seton's short *Natural History of the
Ten Commandments* (1907), in which he finds that the Mosaic laws are not
"arbitrary laws given to man, but are fundamental laws of all highly developed
animals." Animals, in their own way, observe the last six of the ten commandments, and in their occasional willingness to "throw themselves on the mercy of
some other power," manifest the beginnings of a spiritual life. Man, obeying
the first four commandments, acknowledges the Deity; the higher animals acknowledge man.

■

This is an idea which, in its implications of a natural cosmic order, testifies to
the true symbolic role of the animals. There is an obvious correspondence here
to the writing of Seton's contemporary, Kipling, and especially to the society of
the *Jungle Books* (1894, 1895). Roberts, in his Preface to *The Kindred of the
Wild*, praised the Mowgli stories, and although noting that the animals were
"frankly humanized," distinguished them as a different and a separate kind of
fiction from Seton's and his own. Yet the difference is one of degree, rather
than kind: Kipling's jungle animals are also rational creatures, who live in a
balanced and reasonably harmonious society, provided they obey the rules of
their kind. There are good and superior animals such as Bagheera the panther
and Baloo the bear, and evil animals such as Shere Khan the tiger and the whole
tribe of monkeys. The evil are punished and the good survive. The laws of the
jungle must be obeyed. Man, in the shape of Mowgli himself, is superior to all
the other animals.[17]

In their insistence on certain social principles—for instance the all-impor-
tant rule that the young must obey the old, and that obedience is both a necessity and a duty—Seton, Roberts and Kipling all use their animal stories to
exemplify clear and precise morality. The first law an animal learns, Seton tells
us, is obedience, and it is with the Fifth Commandment, "Against Disobe-

dience," that he begins his examination of the Mosaic code of nature. This is the law "which imposes unreasoning acceptance of the benefits derivable from the experience of those over us."[18] We remember from *Red Fox* "how sternly Nature exacts a rigid observance of her rules," and how Red Fox himself is always obedient to his mother, for "it was no small part of his intelligence that he knew how much better his mother knew than he." Obedience for Kipling is the first law of the jungle; every cub of the wolf pack must learn it:

> Now these are the Laws of the Jungle, and many and mighty are they;
> But the head and the hoof of the Law and the haunch and the hump is—Obey!

It could be argued that the evidence for the success of this moral philosophy, and the public acceptance of an anti-Darwinian optimism, can be found in the popularity of the nature writers. Both Seton's and Roberts' nature stories went through edition after edition at the beginning of the century, and one would suspect that Kipling's *Jungle Books* were read to generations of young listeners. All three writers supported the status quo; a child, if he paid attention to the moral lessons, would surely be improved. There is, however, one other means of estimating the popular encouragement given the nature writers, and that in a surprising though socially significant place—the Boy Scouts. The Scouts were also trained to be superior animals, to be brave, helpful, and especially, obedient. The third and most important part of the Scout Promise was obedience to the Scout Law. Curiously, their founder, General Robert Baden-Powell, used the work of the nature writers, and of Kipling, when he came to write the manual for his movement, *Scouting For Boys*.

"Any naturalist," Baden-Powell told his scouts, "will tell you that animals largely owe their cleverness to their mothers."[19] Older animals taught younger animals, and they taught them to obey. Instinct was not half as important as training. Seton was closely associated with the scouting movement from the first, having in fact organized a "woodcraft" group for the boys of America, and in *Scouting For Boys*, Baden-Powell used many of his ideas. Baden-Powell also recommended several of Seton's books to his readers, but when it came to the crucial questions of education, of training and obedience, and the naturalists' models of good conduct, he turned not to Seton or Roberts but to the American writer, William Long. Long's work has now sunk without trace; reading him one can see why he would appeal to a straightforward moralist like Baden-Powell. Much more sentimental and didactic than his contemporaries, and, one would guess, a less careful observer of animal life, Long made no pretense at Darwinism, but preferred to see in the school of the woods "no tragedies or footlight effects of woes and struggles, but rather a wholesome, cheerful life to make one glad and send him back to his own school with deeper wisdom and renewed courage."[20] He was quite clear on the unimportance of instinct, and he had no doubt at all about the necessity for obedience: "when one turns to animals, it is often with the wholesome, refreshing sense that here is a realm where the law of life is known and obeyed. To the wild creature obedience is everything. It is the deep, unconscious tribute of ignorance to wisdom, of weakness to power."

In *Scouting For Boys* Baden-Powell quoted Long at some length. "The Old Wolf" himself was a military man, and he believed in old-fashioned virtues; the scouting movement, though encouraging individual initiative, was authoritarian, its aim to turn out patriots and model citizens. It was important that boys be well trained, and if, in the stories of the nature writers, they had models of good behaviour, these were models that would naturally appeal to boys. Even the scout patrols were named after animals. When it came time to form the junior organization, Baden-Powell went to Kipling, and with his permission took his inspiration from *The Jungle Book*. Significantly, the first "law" of the Wolf Cubs was "the Cub gives in to the old Wolf."[21]

We have in this last detail the clue to the stories of animal heroes. Animals are not so much animals as emblems, symbols of a more perfect world. Baden-Powell called himself the "Old Wolf," and Seton used the wolf paw mark as his signature. To each, the wolf was a superior creature, a star in an ordered and moral universe. The animal stories thus are best considered mythopoeically: Old Silverspot, Seton's crow, drilling his troops and training his youngsters, could well be a model for General Baden-Powell. Red Fox, in his bravery and intelligence, might stand as a shining example to any young scout.

Seen in this light, the lives of the animals resemble, in their structure, the life of the mythic hero: they are born, go through early trials, win their kingdom and die. Some, like Seton's Krag, who returns after death to haunt his murderer, even have an apotheosis. Fate in the shape of a Darwinian catastrophe ensures in the evitable death of the hero a technical tragedy, though the prevailing note in both Seton and Roberts is one of life ever renewed. Man, especially in Seton's stories, may be part of a corrupt and decadent postlapsarian world. In Roberts, man's ignorance and callousness are crimes against nature, though innocence and goodness are often represented by a child or youth, the sensitive girl or boy who knows and loves the creatures of the woods. In Roberts also, the landscape is often magical or enchanted.

In all these details it is clear that the animal tales of both Seton and Roberts take their inspiration and structure as much from literature as from life. In their use of the conventions of the romance, in their echoing of a mythic pattern, and in their quite definite symbolic treatment of animal character, both men translate the indiscriminate facts of nature into the ordered patterns of art. At the centre of their fiction is their belief in moral and rational animals, which in its extensiveness and pervasive force, takes on the quality of an organizing myth. It is ironic that at a time when the forces of instinct, intuition and the unconscious were being rediscovered in man, the power of the Logos was found in the kingdoms of the brute beasts.

Notes

1. Charles G. D. Roberts, *The Kindred of the Wild: A Book of Animal Life* (1902; repr. Boston: L. C. Page, 1921), 15–29.

2. For a summary of the history of the concept of instinct, see W. H. Thorpe, *Animal Nature and Human Nature* (New York: Doubleday, 1974), 134 ff.

3. "Kneepads" appears in Seton's *Lives of the Hunted* (1901), "Red Fox" in Roberts' *Red Fox* (1905). Roberts wrote more than two hundred stories: I have chosen to refer only to those that are best known and written from the animal's point of view, or contain some statement on or illustration of the instinct problem.

4. Both Seton and Roberts were embroiled in a controversy over the realism of their stories, having, in 1903, come under attack from the naturalist, John Burroughs. W. J. Keith argues that the problem of realism is an important one: "the stories are convincing only in so far as they can be accepted as at least possible within the world of nature" (*Charles G. D. Roberts* [Toronto: Copp Clark, 1969], 93). This is a reasonable view, to which it is worth adding that it depends on the genre—if the author's intention is realism, and not romance. A difficult case is presented by, for example, Roberts' *The Heart of the Ancient Wood*, (New York: Silver Burdett, 1900), which, to use Northrop Frye's terms, falls into the mode of romance. In this tale a loving, intelligent, maternal bear named Kroof protects the child Miranda, and eventually rescues Miranda and her mother from a pair of wicked men. Did Roberts expect his readers to take this fairytale as "realistic" fiction?

5. See Joseph Gold, "The Precious Speck of Life," *Canadian Literature*, no. 26 (Autumn 1965): 22–32. In this important and provocative article, Gold argues for an archetypal and mythic interpretation of Roberts' animal stories. He sees the essential myth in Roberts as that of the vitality and persistence of life in its cycles. Roberts, he states, left a body of work "consistently arranged about a clear idea of the order of life itself."

6. These were the very points on which Seton and Roberts were challenged by John Burroughs, when he returned to the attack in 1905, in his book *Ways of Nature*. See Keith, *Roberts*, 91–92.

7. See Thorpe, *Animal Nature*, 151 ff. For more extensive discussion, see R. F. Ewer, *Ethology of Mammals* (London: Elek, 1973).

8. See Donald R. Griffin, *The Question of Animal Awareness* (New York: Rockefeller University Press, 1976).

9. See Ewer, *Ethology*, 277–278.

10. Ernest Thompson Seton, "Badlands Billy," in *Animal Heroes* (New York: Grosset and Dunlap, n.d.), 124–125.

11. Twenty-three years later Seton retreated from this position and declared that, "although an animal is much helped by its mother's teaching, it owes still more to the racial teaching, which is instinct. . . . " See his Foreword to *Bannertail: The Story of a Gray Squirrel* (London: Hodder and Stoughton, 1922).

12. Roberts, *Kindred*, 23.

13. Seton, *Lives of the Hunted*, 43.

14. See Ernest Thompson Seton, "The Rat and the Rattlers," *Mainly About Wolves* (London: Methuen, 1937), 171–179.

15. Seton, "The Wolf and the Primal Law," *Mainly About Wolves*, 121–121. Here, as so often in Seton, it is man himself who is the villain.

16. Roberts, *The Heart of the Ancient Wood*, 128.

17. For a discussion of the educational and moral didacticism of the *Jungle Books*, see Shamsul Islam, *Kipling's "Law"* (London: Macmillan, 1975), 122–131.

18. Ernest Thompson Seton, *The Natural History of the Ten Commandments* (New York: Scribner's, 1907), 7.

19. R. S. S. Baden-Powell, *Scouting For Boys* (London: Cox, 1908), 124.

20. William J. Long, *School of the Woods: Some Life Studies of Animal Instincts and Animal Training* (Boston: Ginn, 1902), 21.

21. R. S. S. Baden-Powell, *The Wolf-Cub's Handbook* (1916; repr. London: Pearson, 1923), 39.

30

The Realistic Animal Story:
Ernest Thompson Seton, Charles Roberts, and Darwinism

THOMAS R. DUNLAP

Darwinian evolution was the greatest intellectual problem facing Western civilization in the late nineteenth century. It challenged with the authority of science ideas that were fundamental parts of the culture. In tracing the social impact of Darwinism, historians have concentrated on issues of creation and humans' place in the world, but these were not the only problems the new theory caused. Since the late seventeenth century, science had been the basis of literary writings about nature; study had revealed the glories of God in creation and his guiding hand in the world around us. Darwinian evolution threatened this picture of order, harmony, and purpose. It stressed the struggle for existence, and nature now seemed chaotic, purposeless, and ruled by force. Nature writers could not easily make evolution serve their purposes. Because evolution was science, they could ignore or reject it only by abandoning their claims to the authority of science. If scientific theories dictated particular worldviews, and Darwin's ideas were as savage as they appeared, nature writers would have been forced to choose between science and sentiment. The choice, however, was not quite so stark. Scientific theories can generally be reconciled with many different views at least to the satisfaction of those making the effort. Those who

Thomas R. Dunlap, "The Realistic Animal Story: Ernest Thompson Seton, Charles Roberts, and Darwinism," *Forest & Conservation History* 36 (April 1992): 56–62. © 1992 Forest History Society. Used by permission of the Forest History Society and the author.

believe in a literal seven day creation, for example, reject evolution, but many less fundamentalist Christians accept it. It is therefore not surprising to find that nature writers attempted to interpret evolution in ways that would emphasize law and purpose in nature.

The most successful were two Canadian nature writers, Ernest Thompson Seton and Charles G. D. Roberts. Born in 1860, they came of age in the heat of the debate over Darwinism. They began writing in the late 1880s and, as public debate and interest declined, by 1910 drifted away from the animal story. Seton turned to life histories of mammals and Roberts to other literary forms (although he continued to grind out animal stories for another twenty years). They presented their vision of an ordered, but Darwinian, nature in a new form, the "realistic" animal story. In these tales animals were the central characters, observed from within, and given the mental characteristics attributed to them by animal psychology (itself a science stimulated by Darwinian ideas). Presenting animals as thinking and feeling beings allowed Seton and Roberts to dramatize from within the struggle and death so prominent in Darwinian evolution. These stories were presented not as fiction or fable but as the fruits of nature study backed by science. The authors used these episodes to show that struggle and death were not chaotic, but purposeful. The stories allowed people to accept evolution and struggle without losing the vision of nature as an ordered realm. Seton and Roberts made an apparently hostile theory the vehicle for emotional identification with nature.

The stories were immensely popular. Roberts had some difficulty selling his first efforts in the early 1890s (editors did not know quite what to make of them), but in 1894 the public and scientists alike praised Seton's "The King of Currumpaw: A Wolf Story." His first collection, *Wild Animals I Have Known* (1898), went through nine printings in eighteen months. The stories appeared in the best magazines: *Century* took "Biography of a Grizzly," the *Ladies' Home Journal* printed "Billy, the Big Wolf."[1] Roberts never enjoyed quite the same popularity, but his first collection, *Kindred of the Wild* (1902), went through ten printings in five years, and he sold about a hundred stories in the next fifteen years.[2]

That the stories were more than entertainment is evident in the "Nature Faker" controversy touched off by nature writer John Burroughs' blast in 1903. His article condemning the false natural history he found in popular animal stories attracted national attention. The ensuing debate was covered in the most important magazines, including *Science,* the journal of the American Association for the Advancement of Science. It went on for five years, involved the President of the United States, and was popular enough to be satirized by the prominent humorist Finley Peter Dunne.[3]

Part of this popularity and interest was attributable to the rising interest in nature.[4] Industrialization, urbanization, and immigration were producing a generation little acquainted with rural life. The culturally dominant "old stock"

Americans, fearing that their way of life would soon be swamped, reacted by including nature in education. Elementary schools around the country added nature studies to the curriculum, and nature stories filled popular magazines.[5] Social conditions, however, do not explain the popularity of these particular stories or the intense concern of authors and critics with their scientific accuracy. Seton and Roberts were popular because they met people's needs. Backed by science and their own experience, they showed that the struggle in nature was not only compatible with order, but part of that order. The tales were a major component of a new American nature myth, and their authors were interpreters of nature for a generation of North Americans. The visions Seton and Roberts presented and the differences between their views provide a window on popular acceptance of Darwinian ideas.

What made the animal story possible was the new science of animal psychology. From the seventeenth century the idea that animals had feelings and emotions had been growing, but it was still a long leap to seeing them as thinking beings. Darwin made that leap. There was "no fundamental difference between man and the higher mammals in their mental faculties . . . [even] the lower animals . . . feel pleasure and pain, happiness and misery . . . [and] possess some power of reason."[6] With this, animal psychology became possible, and by the 1880s a school of animal psychologists was forming a new picture of animals for the public.[7] These psychologists found considerable evidence (due in part to their own ideas and research methods) of mental activity in animals. They began with observation. Watching an animal, or hearing a report of what it did, the psychologist decided what he would think in the circumstances and from that inferred the animal's mental state. This technique was treacherous at best (and the experimental psychologists who began work in the 1890s felt impelled to tear down the entire structure and start over), but it formed the basis for theories that held the field for a generation.[8] The psychologists also recognized only two mental states. There was instinct, conceived of as a stereotyped reaction to a stimulus, and reason. When people began observing animals closely, instinct became untenable. Even simple creatures did things that were far too complicated to be built-in mechanical reactions. Once instinct fell, the conclusion was inevitable: animals could think.

W. Lauder Lindsay's *Mind in the Lower Animals* (1880) said precisely that. Even the lowest organisms possessed many "advanced" mental faculties. Protozoa showed a "whole series of mental phenomena . . . will, purpose, choice, ingenuity, observation, feeling. . . . " Fish were capable of "conjugal and parental love . . . [f]idelity, [s]elf sacrifice . . . [and] . . . feelings of indignation or disgust." Birds had articulate speech and language, including gestures intelligible to man; could perpetrate practical jokes; and appreciated domestic comfort. At least some dogs had a religious and moral sense, understood language and the use of money, and had ideas of time, tune, number, and order.[9] George Romanes, a friend of Darwin and a careful and critical observer, believed that the higher animals shared almost all of man's characteristics. The more advanced crustaceans had reached the level of reason and had progressed in the emotional scale to the point of affection. Among the carnivores, rodents, and ruminants he found grief, cruelty, benevolence, and an understanding of mechanisms. Apes and dogs could feel shame and remorse, and were capable of an "indefinite morality," a state equivalent to that of a fifteen-month-old child.[10]

Seton and Roberts built their fiction on this portrait of animals' mental life. Roberts described "the modern animal story" as a "psychological romance constructed on a framework of natural history." We have attempted, he said, to explain animal behavior by instinct and coincidence. We have stretched these to their limits, but they have failed. "We now believe that animals can and do reason."[11] He made the point in his stories. Sometimes he was tentative: a bear, if he was "capable of reflection—a point on which the doctors differ with some acrimony—he perhaps reflected that. . . ." "Boy," an autobiographical figure, surveys a beaver dam and smiles, thinking "how inadequate what men call instinct would be to such a piece of work as this."[12] More often he took a bolder stand. An Arctic fox, a "Master of Supply," caches his food in frozen ground, using knowledge "which he could only have arrived at by the strictly rational process of putting two and two together—he understood the efficacy of cold storage."[13] "The Ringwaak Buck" had instinct as his "first, and most important, source" of knowledge. Beyond that was

> experience, which teaches varying lore, according to variation in circumstances and surroundings. . . . But after instinct and experience have accounted for everything that can reasonably be credited to them, there remains a considerable and well authenticated residuum of instances where wild creatures have displayed a knowledge which neither instinct nor experience could well furnish them with. In such cases observation and inference seem to agree in ascribing the knowledge to parental teaching.[14]

Seton's stories showed wild animals learning from their parents and their own experience, supplementing instinct with instruction. One, "Tito: The Story of the Coyote That Learned How," is virtually a lecture on animal learning. We watch the captive coyote cub being introduced to all the tricks and traps of humans—dogs, rifles, steel traps, and poison. We then see him teaching his fellows after he has gotten free. Animals, Seton said, have three sources of wisdom. The first, instinct, had been "hammered into the race by ages of selection and tribulation." The "experience of his parents and comrades, learned chiefly by example," was a second. Finally, the "personal experience of the animal itself came into play."[15]

Both authors saw science as a means to the appreciation of nature. "The field of animal psychology so admirably opened [by the modern nature story]," said Roberts, "is an inexhaustible world of wonder."[16] The animal story helps us "to return to nature, without requiring that we at the same time return to barbarism.

It leads us back to the old kinship of earth, without asking us to relinquish by way of toll any part of the wisdom of the ages, any fine essential of the 'large result of time.'" Our life in nature, "far behind though it lies in the long upward march of being," is nevertheless a touchstone, a life to which we can and must return for refreshment and wisdom. The animal story will be our guide.[17] In "The Kangaroo Rat," Seton made science the key to Romantic appreciation of nature. Finding the tracery trails of the little rodents, he had been tempted to take them for the marks of fairies. "Would it not be delightful? . . . But for me, alas! it was impossible, for long ago, when my soul came to the fork in the trail marked on the left 'To Arcadie,' on the right 'To Scientia,' I took the flinty, upland right-hand path." Studying the kangaroo rats, however, he finds in them "the Little Folk, and nearer, better, and more human Little Folk than in any of the nursery books. My chosen flinty track had led me to Upper Arcadie at last."[18]

Both authors preached sympathy with animals. Seton declared that he wished people to find in his stories "a moral as old as Scripture—we and the beasts are kin."[19] Since "animals are creatures with wants and feelings differing in degree only from our own, they surely have their rights." His stories, each showing the "real personality of the individual, and his view of life" made the point. When they did not, he made it himself. Over the body of Redruff the partridge, caught in a snare, he orated: "Have the wild things no moral or legal rights? What right has man to inflict such long and fearful agony on a fellow-creature, simply because that creature does not speak his language?"[20] Roberts made the same points more subtly, through the structure of his stories. "The Kill" inverted the usual hunting tale, telling it from the point of view of the hunted, wounded, and ultimately slain moose.[21] Another story described a bull moose being lured to his death by a hunter imitating the call of a cow moose. The title was "A Treason of Nature."[22] "The Aigrette" switched back and forth between a woman dressing for a fashionable occasion and the scene of slaughter at the egret rookery that yielded the feathers for her hat.[23]

Seton and Roberts agreed that nature was ordered and full of meaning for humans, and man was kin to the beasts, but they differed on what that order was and how humans fit into it. In those differences and the public's clear preference for Seton, we can see the kind of nature turn-of-the-century Americans wanted. That Seton was the more popular was never in doubt. Roberts sold his stories; Seton became an icon. Roberts' reputation is embalmed in studies of Canadian literature; Seton's books are still for sale. Seton's talents for self-promotion and art (he provided profuse and excellent illustrations for his tales) help explain the difference in popularity, but that is hardly enough, and literary quality will not help. As a writer, Roberts was much superior to Seton, whose prose was, at best, serviceable. People may have rejected William J. Long, Burroughs' chief target in the nature-faking controversy, for telling incredible tales, but few knew or cared that Seton based his on long hours of field and museum work, while Roberts drew on books and childhood memories.[24]

Seton was the more popular because he was more comfortable. He softened harsh nature and cruel fate to a much greater extent than Roberts. His was a "realistic" nature, but one that mirrored human moral values.

The moral links between the worlds of animals and people were central to Seton's fiction. "I have tried to emphasize our kinship with the animals," he said, "by showing that in them we can find the virtues most admired in Man. Lobo stands for Dignity and Love-constancy; Silverspot, for Sagacity. . . ."[25] In animals' lives virtues were rewarded, vice punished. Courage, strength, quickness of mind and body, and obedience (particularly of the young to their mothers) brought life. Sloth, improvidence, and foolishness killed. The stakes were higher than those risked or sought by the aspiring boys in the Horatio Alger stories, but the moral was the same. Seton went even further, arguing in *The Ten Commandments in the Animal World* that those species that most closely followed the biblical commands—which were, for instance, monogamous rather than polygamous—stood higher in the scale of development and were more successful.[26]

Seton provided not only virtues and order but *Animal Heroes*. His characters were creatures above their fellows in strength, cunning, and character. Lobo was the "King of the Currumpaw," Redruff a "wonder to all who [knew] him." "Krag, the Kootenay Ram" had the most magnificent horns in the mountains, and his death is such a tragedy that "the Ram's own Mother White Wind, from the Western Sea," takes revenge on the hunter who shot him.[27] Roberts, in contrast, rarely named his animals or gave them individual character, and did not present them as heroes or moral symbols.

Roberts wrote about a less human and less moral nature. Virtue was not rewarded and indeed hardly appeared. Strength ruled, although only at the moment, for at the center of his stories was an iron law. Each lived because another died; death was the price of life.[28] That was clear in his first story, "Do Seek Their Meat from God" (1892). It seems to be, at first glance, a standard melodrama. Two "panthers" (Eastern mountain lions) leave their cubs in the den and set out on a night's hunting. Hearing a child crying, they move toward the sound. It is a farmer's son. He has gone to see his playmate, the squatter's child, but the squatter has that very day moved on. The boy, afraid to pass through the now dark woods to his home, sits crying in the abandoned shanty. His father, returning from town, almost passes by, thinking it is only the "squatter's brat." Moved by pity, he turns aside. Man and panthers meet in the clearing, just as the animals are nosing at the broken door. The father kills them, one in hand-to-hand combat. Only then does he discover that it is his own child he has saved.

What sets this story apart is the point of view. As man and animals converge on the cabin, Roberts pauses to disabuse the reader of his prejudices and to drive home the implicit moral of the title (a quotation from Psalm 104 extolling the order of the world established by the Creator).[29] "Theirs was no hideous or unnatural rage, as it is the custom to describe it. They were but seeking with the strength, the cunning, the deadly swiftness given them to that end, the food convenient for them." Nor does the story end with the father's discovery that it is his own child he has saved. It ends "not many weeks afterward," when the farmer, following a bear that has killed one of his sheep, finds a wild animal's den and in the back "the dead bodies, now rapidly decaying, of two small panther cubs."[30] This nature has an order certainly, but not Seton's comfortable and familiar one.

In "When Twilight Falls on the Stump Lots," a hungry mother bear, seeking food in the early spring, attacks a cow and her calf. Driven off and gored, she dies on the way back to the den. Her cubs are "spared . . . some days of starving anguish" when two foxes find them. The story ends with the calf, whose "fortune was ordinary. Its mother, for all her wounds, was able to nurse and cherish it through the night; and with morning came a searcher from the farm and took it, with the bleeding mother, safely back to the settlement. There it was tended and fattened, and within a few weeks found its way to the cool marble slabs of a city market."[31] This tale shares with others an irony and a moral nihilism Seton never approached.

■

Death, too, has a different significance. In Roberts' fiction death is the usual end of the story. Many of his tales are strings of deaths, the victor of one combat falling in turn to another. "The Little Wolf of the Pool" describes a dragonfly larva hunting in the pond. He kills a tadpole, then a minnow. The story ends with the insect's metamorphosis to the adult phase. The hideous monster becomes "a gem-like, opalescent shining thing." "The Little Wolf of the Air" continues the tale. A dragonfly, fleeing a shrike, lights on a man's shirt. It leaves, returning with its latest prey, a grasshopper. It goes off again to lay its eggs. A frog catches and eats it, thus avenging "(though about that he cared as little as he knew) the lives of a thousand tadpoles."[32] The same scenes occur with larger animals. Life is short, death is certain.

In theory Seton did not blink at the suffering and death in nature. "The fact that these stories are true," he said in an introduction to *Wild Animals I Have Known*, "is the reason why all are tragic. The life of a wild animal *always has a tragic end*."[33] In practice, Seton did blink. In that collection "Raggylug" survives, as does "The Springfield Fox." Lobo dies of a broken heart after being trapped through his devotion to his mate, and his faithfulness moves Seton and transforms his view of the wolf. "The Pacing Mustang" hurls himself over a cliff rather than accept captivity. "Bingo," Seton's dog, dies of poison set out for the wolves. "Wully," the "Yeller Dog," is ruined by bad handling, becomes a sheep-killing sheepdog, and is slain for his treachery. "Redruff" dies in a snare. Only "Silverspot" the crow dies the normal, "tragic" end of the wild animal, and he dies offstage.

Seton and Roberts also saw humans and their relationship to nature in different ways. In Seton's stories people are almost always dangerous intruders into the natural world. Men kill Wahb's family in "The Biography of a Grizzly" and Tito's in "Tito: The Story of the Coyote That Learned How." They hunt down the Pacing Mustang and the great ram Krag. Cuddy, the "shiftless loafer" snares the Don Valley partridges in "Redruff." Speaking of Cuddy, Seton said he had changed the name, "as it is the species, rather than the individual, that I wish to expose."[34] About sport hunting he wrote:

> There was once a wretch who, despairing of other claims to notice, thought to achieve a name by destroying the most beautiful building on earth. This is the mind of the head-hunting sportsman. The nobler the thing that he destroys, the greater the deed, the greater his pleasure, and the greater he considers his claim to fame.[35]

On the other side, almost alone, stand the autobiographical Yan from *The Trail of the Sandhill Stag* and the child who befriends the Winnipeg Wolf. Only innocence is permitted love, but the reader implicitly is in that company.[36] Roberts is more ambiguous. Some of his humans are good, some bad, and while he condemns the slaughter of animals he accepts hunting in most of his characters, the backwoodsmen of his native New Brunswick, as part of the natural order. In "Savoury Meats," for instance, a young farmer kills a doe for his old, sick father. The two "made a joyous meal. The old man ate as he had not eaten for months and the generous warmth of the fresh meat put new life into his withered veins." There is, of course, the inevitable ending—the doe's fawn falls prey to a wildcat that night—but the man, like the panthers in "Do Seek Their Meat from God," was seeking what he needed with the strength given him.[37]

Seton and Roberts are part of a chain going back to the seventeenth century, a continuing effort to incorporate science, the culture's authoritative source of knowledge, into the nature myths of the society. They are distinguished for the difficulty of their task and the ingenuity of their solution. Darwin has apparently destroyed the partnership between science and religion, observation and awe. To make evolution a servant of the sublime seemed as impractical as turning Frankenstein's monster into a man about town. Nevertheless, they succeeded. Millions read their stories and bought those stories for their children. They were an important part of a current that made predation and death acceptable even in stories for young children.[38] Seton's continuing popularity and the recent revival of Roberts scholarship suggest that they may have done better than they knew. Although they were speaking to their generation, they attracted a later audience as well, one informed by popular ideas of ecology but still struggling with the problems of humans' place in the natural world.

That we are still struggling may be seen in the shifting emphasis of nature literature. In the 1920s, nature literature returned to personal essays, people's reactions to individual occurrences and events. In 1944, when Edwin Way Teale compiled a list of great nature books for the Audubon Society, it was heavily weighted toward Romantic and Transcendental nature writers. In the 1950s, animal stories returned, but with a different focus. Farley Mowat, Fred Bodsworth, and Roger Caras, popular writers of the period, took for granted animals' thinking and the round of life and death. They did not emphasize struggle and death, but saw predators as an essential part of the natural order. Their great theme, matching the rising concern with environmental problems, was human destruction of the natural world.[39]

More recently, the decline in strict behaviorism and laboratory science and increasing interest in field studies have begun a process that may result in a new kind of animal story. Darwin threw down the barriers separating humans from animals, but only in the last generation have we begun to take seriously animal behavior as social behavior. Studies of chimps and gorillas have shown human (sometimes distressingly human) behavior in our nearest relatives, and continuing studies of wolves, wild dogs, and other animals are revealing layers of social behavior even Seton and Roberts never suspected. Farley Mowat's *Never Cry Wolf* was a pioneer effort in using field observation as the basis for animal stories, and others may follow. If they do, they will find a well-beaten path.

Notes

Acknowledgment: The author acknowledges financial support from the Virginia Tech Center for Programs in the Humanities.

1. Ernest Thompson Seton, *Wild Animals I Have Known* (New York: Charles Scribner's Sons, 1898); Seton, "Biography of a Grizzly," *Century* (November–December 1899, and January 1900); Seton, *Animal Heroes* (New York: Charles Scribner's Sons, 1905); Seton, *Lives of the Hunted* (New York: Charles Scribner's Sons, 1901). On Seton, see H. Allen Anderson, *The Chief: Ernest Thompson Seton and the Changing West* (College Station: Texas A&M University Press, 1986), and John Henry Wadland, *Ernest Thompson Seton: Man in Nature and the Progressive Era, 1880–1915* (New York: Arno, 1978).

2. Printings can be gauged in a rough way from the National Union Catalog and library copies. On Seton, see Wadland, *Seton*, and Anderson, *The Chief.* On Roberts, the nature story, and its audience, see Joseph Gold, "The Ambivalent Beast," in *The Proceedings of the Sir Charles C. D. Roberts Symposium*, ed. Carrie MacMillan (Sackville, New Brunswick: Centre for Canadian Studies, Mount Allison University, 1984), 77–86; W. J. Keith, "A Choice of Worlds: God, Man and Nature in Charles G. D. Roberts," in *Colony and Confederation: Early Canadian Poets and Their Background*, ed. George Woodcock (Vancouver: University of British Columbia Press, 1974), 87–102.

3. William Morton Wheeler, "Woodcock Surgery," *Science* 19 (February 1904): 347–350; John Burroughs, "Real and Sham Natural History," *Atlantic Monthly* 91 (March 1903): 298–309. There is a basic bibliography on nature-faking in Loren Owings, *Environmental Values, 1860–1972* (Detroit, Mich.: Gale Research Co., 1976), 212–215. The most recent and thorough examination of this episode is Ralph H. Lutts,

The Nature Fakers: Wildlife, Science & Sentiment (Golden, Color.: Fulcrum, 1990). Dunne's column is in the *New York Times*, June 2, 1907.

4. On the boom, see Peter J. Schmitt, *Back to Nature: The Arcadian Myth in Urban America* (New York: Oxford University Press, 1969); Roderick Nash, *Wilderness and the American Mind*, 3d ed. (New Haven: Yale University Press, 1982). Paul Brooks, *Speaking for Nature* (San Francisco: Sierra Club Books, 1980), presents a nonhistorical survey of this literature in America. Owings' *Environmental Values* provides an excellent bibliography of nature writing. See also Phillip Marshall Hicks, "The Development of the Natural History Essay in American Literature," Ph.D. diss., University of Pennsylvania, 1924.

5. Botany was the most popular science for teaching students about nature; see Ronald Tobey, *Saving the Prairies* (Berkeley: University of California Press, 1981), chap. 2.

6. Charles Darwin, *The Descent of Man*, 2d ed. (New York: H. M. Caldwell, 1874), 81, 84, 90.

7. James C. Turner, *Reckoning with the Beast* (Baltimore: Johns Hopkins University Press, 1980); Keith Thomas, *Man and the Natural World* (New York: Pantheon, 1983). Important contemporaneous books include George J. Romanes, *Mental Evolution in Man* (New York: D. Appleton, 1889; repr. Washington, D.C.: University Publications of America, 1975); Romanes, *Animal Intelligence* (New York: D. Appleton, 1883; repr. Washington, D.C.: University Publications of America, 1977); W. Lauder Lindsay, *Mind in the Lower Animals:* vol. 1, *Mind in Health*, vol. 2, *Mind in Disease* (New York: D. Appleton, 1880).

8. On the next generation, see Edward L. Thorndike, *Animal Intelligence: Experimental Studies* (1911; repr. New York: Hafner, 1965); Thorndike, "Do Animals Reason?" *Popular Science Monthly* 55 (August 1899): 480–490; C. Lloyd Morgan, *Animal Behavior* (London: Edward Arnold, 1900); Morgan, "Limits of Animal Intelligence" (1893; repr. in *Significant Contributions to the History of Psychology, 1750–1920*, series D, vol. 2 [Washington, D.C.: University Publications of America, 1977]).

9. Lindsay, *Mind in the Lower Animals*, vol. 1, 52, 70, 75. The lower races of man, in contrast, were sadly lacking. In Lindsay's scheme, as one modern critic noted, the cultured English gentleman was closer to his bulldog than to the Eskimos. Peter H. Klopfer, *An Introduction to Animal Behavior: Ethology's First Century* (Englewood Cliffs, N.J.: Prentice-Hall, 1974), 20.

10. Romanes, *Animal Intelligence*, and *Mental Evolution in Man*.

11. Charles G. D. Roberts, *The Kindred of the Wild: A Book of Animal Life* (Boston: L. C. Page, 1902), 24, 28.

12. Charles G. D. Roberts, "In the Year of No Rabbits," in *The Feet of the Furtive* (New York: Macmillan, 1913; repr. Toronto: Ryerson, 1947), 52–70; Charles G. D. Roberts, *The House in the Water* (Boston: L. C. Page, 1908), 27.

13. Charles G. D. Roberts, *Hoof and Claw* (New York: Macmillan, 1914), 56–57.

14. Charles G. D. Roberts, *The Haunters of the Silences* (Boston: L. C. Page, 1907), 175; Wadland, *Ernest Thompson Seton*, 217–218.

15. Seton, "Tito," in *Lives of the Hunted*, 284–285.

16. Roberts, "The Animal Story," *Kindred*, 29.

17. Roberts, "the Animal Story," *Kindred*, 24.

18. Seton, *Lives of the Hunted*, 228, 231, 251.

19. Seton, *Wild Animals I Have Known*, 11.

20. Seton, *Wild Animals I Have Known*, 357

21. Charles G. D. Roberts, *The Watchers of the Trails* (Boston: L. C. Page, 1904), 197–208.

22. Roberts, "A Treason of Nature," *Kindred*, 180–196.

23. Charles G. D. Roberts, *The Secret Trails* (New York: Macmillan, 1916), 77–89.

24. Ernest Thompson Seton, *Trail of an Artist-Naturalist* (Salem, N.H.: Ayer Co. Publishers, 1940), 367–371; Wadland, *Ernest Thompson Seton*, 180–191.

25. Seton, *Lives of the Hunted*, 11.

26. Ernest Thompson Seton, *The Ten Commandments in the Animal World* (1907; repr. New York: Doubleday, 1925). Seton's *Lives of Game Animals* contained many of the same arguments. See, for instance, vol. 1, pt. 1 (1909–1925; repr. Boston: Charles T. Branford, 1953), for comments on the wolf.

27. Seton, *Animal Heroes;* Seton, *Lives of the Hunted*, 103.

28. Joseph Gold, "The Precious Speck of Life," *Canadian Literature* 26 (Autumn 1965): 22–32. See also Gold's Introduction to a collection of Roberts' work, *King of Beasts* (Toronto: Ryerson, 1967); James Polk, "Lives of the Hunted," *Canadian Literature* 53 (Summer 1972): 51–59.

29. Psalms 104: 21. Roberts used a similar passage from Job 38:41 or Psalms 147:9 for another early story, "The Young Ravens That Call on Him," *Earth's Enigmas* (1895; repr. Boston: L. C. Page, 1903). That, too, extols the order of the world and the oversight of the Creator. Keith, "A Choice of Worlds," discusses the titles as ironic comments, for the meat the panthers seek is man and the young ravens (eagles in the story) feed on a lamb whose cries have gone unheard.

30. Roberts, "Do Seek Their Meat from God," *Harper's* 86 (December 1892): 122.

31. Roberts, *Kindred*, 283–284.

32. Roberts, *Watchers of the Trails*, 65–70, 73–80.

33. Seton, *Wild Animals I Have Known*, 11, emphasis in original.

34. Seton, *Wild Animals I Have Known*, 11, 267–269; Seton, "Biography of a Grizzly"; Seton, *Lives of the Hunted*.

35. Seton, *Lives of the Hunted*, 84.

36. Ernest Thompson Seton, *The Trail of the Sandhill Stag* (New York: Charles Scribner's Sons, 1899); Wadland, *Ernest Thompson Seton*, 119, on the Winnipeg Wolf.

37. Roberts, *Kindred*, 152. Much the same theme occurs in "Wild Motherhood," *Kindred*, 93–113. Roberts does not, however, believe that people can fully become part of nature. On this theme, see the analysis of Roberts' *The Heart of the Ancient Wood* (New York: Lippincott, 1900) in Thomas R. Dunlap, " 'The Old Kinship of Earth': Science, Man and Nature in the Animal Stories of Charles G. D. Roberts," *Journal of Canadian Studies* 22 (Spring 1987): 104–120.

38. See the works of Thornton W. Burgess, produced from about 1906 to 1930, on this (Burgess' works are now being reprinted by Aeonian Press and Little, Brown).

39. Edwin Way Teale, "The Great Companions of Nature Literature," *Audubon* 46 (November–December 1944): 363–366. See Farley Mowat, *Never Cry Wolf* (Boston: Little, Brown, 1963); Fred Bodsworth, *The Last of the Curlews* (New York: Dodd, Mead, 1955); Roger Caras, *The Custer Wolf* (Boston: Little, Brown, 1966).

Stickeen and the Moral Education of John Muir

RONALD H. LIMBAUGH

More than a century has passed since John Muir and a mongrel dog named Stickeen crossed a treacherous Alaskan glacier on a stormy day in the summer of 1880. The story of that singular day, perfected by numerous retellings and published seventeen years later in a popular national magazine, became one of Muir's best-known nature adventures.

The story unfolded during Muir's second trip to Alaska, following close on the heels of his first exploration of Glacier Bay in the fall of 1879. With him were three native Alaskans and a missionary friend, S. Hall Young. They remained in camp while Muir and the dog trekked across the glacier. Although details of the story changed over a fifteen-year period, the dog remained central to the tale both in its oral and written form. In the most familiar version, as Muir left camp the dog tagged along despite Muir's warning words and the foul weather. Crossing the glacier diagonally by following flow lines and jumping crevasses, they reached the opposite shore, traced the path for several miles, then headed back near dusk on a different route. As darkness loomed they entered a heavily crevassed area. Some gaps could be jumped, others had to be crossed by straddling or gingerly stepping on icy connecting bridges, which Muir smoothed with his ice axe for Stickeen's benefit, while still requiring long looping detours. Soggy from the rain, without food since the breakfast bread,

Ronald H. Limbaugh, "Stickeen and the Moral Education of John Muir," *Environmental History Review* 15 (Spring 1991): 25–45. Used by permission of the American Society for Environmental History and the author.

nearly exhausted from the long walk and handicapped by the dimming twilight, Muir and the dog soon found themselves stranded on an island with the only escape a badly deteriorated spiny bridge. How they made it across is the thrilling climax.

The manuscript Muir ultimately prepared for publication was not a true-life adventure but an allegory on the worth of animals and their importance to mankind. That fiction grew from fact is clear by comparing Muir's original narrative in his 1880 journal with the final draft he submitted to *Century* in 1897. The most striking difference is the total lack of any reference to a dog in the 1880 journal, directly or indirectly. Did Stickeen really exist or was he a product of the author's fertile imagination? That was the question I first asked after deciphering the badly smudged and nearly illegible original journal, accessible to scholars only since the 1970s and now available on microfilm.[1] But surely the dog was real; his presence was confirmed by the testimony of Muir's missionary companion, S. Hall Young, whose own book on Muir is filled with Stickeen references from the 1880 trip and who cooperated with Muir in writing a reminiscence about the dog.

Then why did Muir leave the dog out of his original written account? The most plausible answer is that he never recognized the dog's importance until the early 1890s. In the intervening years he had become a gentleman farmer with a handsome income and an indulgent wife. As the son-in-law and business partner of Dr. John Strentzel, physician and pioneer horticulturist in the Alhambra Valley just south of Martinez, California, Muir had new responsibilities but also new opportunities. Muir scholars tend to exaggerate the frustrations Muir experienced in the 1880s. Exchanging the wild Yosemite days for a prosperous life in Alhambra Valley was a willful act that brought with it security and fortune, things he had never known before. Now down from the mountains, he traded the book of nature for the literal book, the aggregate knowledge of mankind bound in cloth and hard leather. His expanding book collection was indicative of his intellectual growth, both made possible by time and affluence, two precious gifts he received from his generous new partners, the Strentzels. They gave him the instruments of a new education, and he richly repaid them by mastering the practical science of horticulture even as he submersed himself in the literature of the Western world. The fortune he earned as a fruit farmer paled in comparison to the wealth of knowledge he gleaned from his books. They broadened and deepened his perspective on nature and life. The man who wrote the dog story in the 1890s was more reflective and philosophical than the effervescent explorer of earlier years.

John Muir told his friends *Stickeen* was the hardest story he had ever composed. Reading it nearly eighty years later I could not understand why at first. After all, from a writer's perspective the story line is uncomplicated. Drafting a first-person descriptive narrative of an exciting single event was one of my first assignments as a college freshman. After nearly twenty years of working with the Muir Papers, reading all the preliminary manuscripts and relevant correspondence, tracing the origins of key words, ideas and phrases, and following the convoluted literary spoor left behind in the marginalia and endnotes of over one hundred books from his personal library, I have begun to understand what Muir meant.[2]

The Stickeen story evolved over a fifteen-year period after the adventure of 1880. For thirteen of those years Muir told the story repeatedly to family and friends, yet apparently thought little more about it until Robert Underwood Johnson, *Century*'s associate editor, cajoled him into writing "the dog and glacier story in your livliest [sic] style."[3] Muir eventually promised he would, but for two years was distracted by other obligations, including the completion of his first book, *The Mountains of California*. By the spring of 1895 he was ready to start in earnest on what he called the "Canis project."

For more than two years he worked, intermittently but intensely, on what he considered the hardest writing job of his career. Scholars can follow his tortuous literary labors through both the books he used for inspiration and the manuscripts and notes he prepared as preliminary steps to drafting a manuscript. They can also trace his struggle through two separate notebooks and numerous draft fragments he left behind.[4] What is most significant is not the mechanical details but the intellectual growth revealed in the process. All of Muir's creative energies went into the writing of *Stickeen*. What began as a simple adventure story—the kind R. U. Johnson had in mind for *Century*— ended in a profoundly moving narrative, a classic commentary on the rights of animals and their place in nature.

Why this shift? The answer lies in Muir's psychic struggles after he began working in earnest on the dog narrative. What was the real meaning of the 1880 adventure? As he labored that question drove him deeper into philosophical and psychological and ethical dimensions. Johnson wanted a simple descriptive narrative, just the way he remembered Muir telling it. But Muir realized that was no longer enough. As a freelance writer for a popular magazine he was bound by the prescriptive guidelines of its editor, but he wanted to educate as well as entertain. His reading and reflection since 1880 had sharpened his thinking about animals and their role in nature.

Evolution Controversy: The Context for *Stickeen*

Stickeen was now more than just a dog; he was a messenger, a harbinger of good news about the natural world. It was a timely message. The story of Stickeen emerged out of the intellectual foment of the 1890s, a disruptive decade of panic and depression, industrial exploitation and labor violence, class consciousness and racism, imperialism and war. Accompanying these unsettling economic and social forces were profoundly disturbing scientific and intellectual challenges. After a generation of controversy, Darwinism still headed the list.[5] American society at the turn of the century generally accepted the evidence of evolution but was deeply divided over its implications. Humans and animals were closely related, but was that good or bad?

Pessimists portrayed a dim future. To them Darwinism meant a literal descent of man to the level of animals, a Hobbesian confirmation that underneath the ethical facade were baser instincts that controlled human behavior. They lamented the loss of divinity, the moral as well as physiological diminution of the human species. Man now had little to look forward to but the bleak "struggle for existence" like his cousin the brute. Novelists explored the dark side of human nature in fantasies such as *Dr. Jekyll and Mr. Hyde* and in realistic novels such as *McTeague* and *Maggie: Girl of the Streets*. Henry Adams summed up the somber implications: "In plain words, Chaos was the law of nature; Order was the dream of man."[6]

Optimists, in contrast, found ways to cushion society from such negative forebodings. One way was to tone down the materialist implications of Darwinism. Even Darwin himself was unwilling to openly reject theism.[7] Perhaps the human spirit, if not the human body, still contained the divine spark, the promise of dignity and nobility and progress. A whole new era of post-Darwinian Christian activism, led by Protestant liberals and modernists, developed from this premise.[8]

John Muir, a lifelong student and admirer of Darwin, saw only the bright side. To him the ennobling qualities of life in humans and the higher animals confirmed the divine spark. Beauty and harmony in the physical world were patent evidence of a benevolent and loving creator. Instead of demonstrating might makes right, evolution was purposive, ongoing and progressive, all part of the divine plan.

Another Darwinian riposte was to elevate the moral status of animals. Using animals to teach moral truths was nothing new in literature. Nature writing in the 1890s expanded upon a premise explored a half-century earlier by Romantic primitivists: nature was a source of moral truth, free from the corrupting influences of ignoble humanity. To Americans in the Victorian era raw nature was less appealing than pastoral nature, tamed and modified by human hands but still embodying primal virtues.[9] Even the family pet might have admirable mental and moral qualities. The result was a new literary genre, the noble animal story.[10]

Stickeen thus emerged reborn on paper, a dog with deeper and more enduring elements of character than had been observed in life or described by word of mouth. The new Stickeen required some remodeling and a certain amount of poetic license. But Muir was convinced the dog story could be shaped into a powerful didactic instrument, a tool to help Americans understand and appreciate their fellow creatures.

Muir and the Great Chain of Being

Stickeen's moral worth rested not on the logic of Darwinian materialism but on Muir's belief that all living things are linked by a chain of creation. Adapted from Greek epistemology by Christian theologians to explain the origin and organization of life in the universe, the "Great Chain of Being" theory influenced Western thought from the eighth to the eighteenth century.[11] Extolled by medieval and Enlightenment scientists, philosophers and poets alike, it postulated a coherent and preordained sequence of creatures beginning with the lowest and ascending in orderly steps to the ultimate creator-god. Chain theory slowly disintegrated after 1800 as empirical science exposed the fallacy of a priori assumptions about the natural world, but not before it was "temporalized" and energized by the Romantic emphasis on individuality. Instead of a static and finite creation, Romantics conceived of a boundless and dynamic process of creativity that found underlying unity in diversity—thus opening the door to evolutionary thinking without utterly destroying the religious premise on which chain theory was based. Emerson led the way, asserting in "Correspondences" that:

> the universe is represented in every one of its particles. Everything in nature contains all the powers of nature. Everything is made of one hidden stuff; as the naturalist sees one type under every metamorphosis, and regards a horse as a running man, a fish as a swimming man, a bird as a flying man, a tree as a rooted man. Each new form repeats not only the main character of the type, but part for part all the details, all the aims, furtherances, hindrances, energies, and whole system of every other.[12]

Post-Darwinian creation-scientists such as Asa Gray, Alfred Russel Wallace and John Muir had little trouble reconciling empirical biology with belief in a purposive and harmonious universe.[13] They took their cue from Darwin himself, who initially found no contradiction between physiological evolution and the idea of a divine Master Plan. Muir noted with approval a passage from Darwin's "Beagle" journal, speculating that a systematic study of ovenbirds in Bahia Blanca "ultimately may assist in revealing the grand scheme, common to the present and past ages, on which organized beings have been created."[14] All life was still linked and unified by a cosmic chain, but the chain had become more organic than linear.

Through the books of his personal library Muir absorbed the ideas of numerous defenders of the Chain, including Addison, Pope, Goldsmith, Kant, Herder, Schiller, Swedenborg, Emerson, Thoreau and Carlyle. Holographic notes and marginalia show how important chain theory was to the development of Muir's own thinking. From Emerson's words quoted above, Muir formulated his own general theory of oneness, insisting, like Emerson, that "all of Nature is found in man. Squeeze all the universe into the size & shape of a perfect human soul & that is a whole man."[15] In the back of a volume of Asa

Gray's scientific papers, Muir noted the Harvard botanist's affirmation of the "Infinite Variety in Unity which characterizes the Creator's works."[16] In Carlyle's *Life of John Sterling*, Muir underscored Sterling's reference to the "sense of a oneness of life and power in all existence," but rephrased it to the "sense of a oneness of life & destiny in all existence."[17] An original aphorism Muir penciled in Wallace's metaphysical treatise, *The World of Life*, expresses even more directly the influence of chain theory on the California Scot: "Every cell, every particle of matter in O [the world] requires a Captain to steer it into its place JM."[18] Finally, in the midst of a lengthy series of Stickeen notes written on the endpages of Hawthorne's *The Scarlet Letter*, Muir tried to draft a more explicit statement on oneness:

> Like a voice from the upper heights came the message you & I are one/ Through so humble a medium came the apostolic message dog & man all animals/ & man are one/ Looking into the eyes/ watching the attitudes of snakes bedbugs etc., I felt dimly that no line of demarcation separated us.[19]

Here Muir's creator imagery blurred the distinctions between species and asserted a biocentric view of life in the cosmos. Peel back superficial differences and life forms become indistinguishable, either by the nature of their essences or by their moral worth. This was the central message Muir found in reassessing the meaning of Stickeen. The logic of the Great Chain of Being led him to a reaffirmation of the moral equality of dogs and men and all other elements in the endless span of creation. In an advanced draft of the dog manuscript he reinforced the point in a mystical acknowledgment of Stickeen's role as heavenly messenger:

> The vast mysterious chain of being—about as little known as are the inhabitants of other stars. That they should in such lively demonstrative multitudes be with us & remain so strangely apart from us is most wonderful.[20]

Pre-Darwinian Views of the Moral Worth of Animals

Stickeen was thus a special dog, an individual personality with inherent worth. Muir's nature writing, flowing from what has been called the humanitarian branch of the conservation movement, asserted the individuality of animals both as a way to uplift their moral value in the eyes of the reading public and as a ploy against utilitarian conservationists who sought scientific studies of animal populations and who tended to treat animals as objects to be "managed" like forests and grasslands.[21] The humanitarians deplored the depersonalization of species and emphasized individual personality characteristics. "It is the denial of 'personality' to animals that is at the root of the evil," wrote Henry Salt, one of the more outspoken humanitarians.[22] By appealing to reader sympathies, humanitarians helped expand popular interest in the cause of animal rights. Yet by describing individual animal characteristics in anthropomorphic terms, many popular writers enveloped nature with a Romantic gloss.[23]

In his study of nature Muir stood somewhere between the scientific method and unadulterated anthropomorphism. By describing the dog's personality traits Muir sought to make his nature and actions more understandable to the ordinary reader of popular magazines. His friend John Burroughs also recognized the need to observe and describe animals in human terms, but warned against trying to make more out of animal behavior than the facts warranted. He scornfully rejected the anthropomorphic characterizations of most Romantic nature writers, but praised Muir's story for elucidating animal character without stretching credulity. "It is true that Muir makes his dog act like a human being under the press of great danger," he wrote,

> but the action is not the kind that involves reason; it only implies sense perception, and the instinct of self-preservation. Stickeen does as his master bids him, and he is human only in the human emotions of fear, despair, joy that he shows.[24]

But Burroughs did not know the original Stickeen, the dog Muir described in the first written version which his editor, Robert Underwood Johnson, gutted. That version implied the dog had more than mere "sense perception."

Burroughs, Muir, Wesley Mills and other contemporary naturalists drew conclusions based on field observations of individual specimens, but they leaned toward evidence that was anecdotal rather than empirically testable. Sustained field observation, rather than laboratory testing, was the approved method of nature study in late nineteenth century.[25] Studies of animal behavior moved from the field to the laboratory only with the development of modern comparative and experimental psychology after 1900.[26] Yet the old ways died hard, as John Burroughs demonstrated in criticizing lab tests. They "prove what the animal does not know and cannot do under artificial conditions, but do they show what it does know and can do under natural conditions?"[27] Muir would have thought it a fair question. He was no specialist on dogs, but after nearly a month of togetherness in the field he believed he knew Stickeen thoroughly.

Muir's moral egalitarianism drew him closer to activists in the cause of animal rights. Like so many other modernist trends near the turn of the century, the late Victorian movement for animal rights grew out of the foment over the intellectual and moral implications of natural selection. Before Darwin, the Christian world had been dominated by the dogmas built upon classical Greek philosophy that posited the moral superiority of humans over animals. Plato's distinction between mind and body not only exalted humans as the only creatures with souls but also gave them a loftier material status. They were, in effect, gods in an animal body. While disputing Plato's taxonomy, Aristotle also elevated humans by defining them as the highest order in the animal kingdom. He endowed both humans and animals with souls, but distinguished between the immortal soul of the human species and the material soul of animals which died with the body. For much of western history, animals had no place in the hereafter and thus no moral worth.[28]

Moral and biological superiority, however, did not justify mistreatment. Medieval Christian stewardship doctrine, exemplified by the teachings of St. Francis—to some eco-philosophers the patron saint of the modern environmental movement[29] —sanctified the protection of animals from wanton cruelty.[30] Regardless of whether they had souls, the higher animals, at least, felt pain, and it was an egregious sin to consciously expose any creature to needless suffering. Sympathy for animals surrendered during the eighteenth-century Enlightenment to the mechanistic rationalism of René Descartes. He reduced all but human life to the status of "dumb" animals or plants. Even though both animals and man were machines, he wrote, only humans had souls and only souls were sentient.[31]

By asserting the primacy of human over all other life forms, Cartesian dualism reinforced the idea of human progress at the expense of less worthy objects. From Descartes to Darwin, the Industrial Revolution swept across the Western world, sanctified by an anthropocentric and masculine philosophy and armed with new technology that accelerated nature's conquest and domination. In this two-hundred-year era, Romanticism was the only popular intellectual movement to challenge the logic of exploitation, but much of its psychic energy was siphoned off in sentimental appeals on behalf of life's downtrodden, including slaves, orphans, aborigines, imbeciles, women and "dumb" animals.

In the meantime, Cartesian dualism came under increasing pressure from moral philosophers and materialists. John Locke, David Hartley and Étienne de Condillac, forerunners of modern animal psychology, did not reject dualism but recognized "continuous degrees of intelligence at various levels of the scale of beings." De La Mettrie's sensational *L'Homme machine* (1748), proposed a wholly mechanistic view of the Chain of Being, with all mental functions having a physiological origin and "with no break in the continuum from crude matter through plants and animals to man."[32] Up to the mid-nineteenth century, the emerging disciplines of psychology and biology struggled to reconcile the idea of a continuous chain with older portions that separated mind from matter.

Then came Darwin and the revolutionary implications of natural selection. By the 1890s Darwinism had nearly demolished both Cartesian and Romantic views of the animal-man relationship. In trumpeting the common biology of animals and humans, radical Darwinians, as distinguished from post-Darwinian creationists, replaced Transcendental metaphysics with materialism. Even if Darwin himself was reluctant to abandon creationism publicly, his German apostle Ernst Haeckel was much bolder. He antagonized both Neo-Platonists and orthodox Christians by insisting that all higher brain functions, like all motor functions, evolved from lower organisms.[33]

The Darwinian Impact on *Stickeen*

Despite resistance from theists like Muir, the implications of Haeckel's uncompromising materialism extended the debate over the causes of animal behavior as well as the moral status of animals. The holographic marks and margin notes in books Muir read during this era demonstrate how closely he followed these debates. They also show his effort to expand the dog story into a larger study of animal behavior and its lessons for humanity.

Darwinians raised four troubling issues of special interest to Muir: the ethical relationship between humans and animals, the nature and extent of animal intelligence, the status of the soul in higher animals, and the rights of animals. By insisting that sentience was a product of natural selection common to all higher animals along with ganglia and the central cortex, strident evolutionists cast a shadow over traditional ethics that ignored or discounted nonhuman species. If making others suffer is unethical, any being that can experience pain deserves respect and consideration. Jeremy Bentham had first postulated this principle in the late eighteenth century, and it was taken up in earnest in the renewed debates of the 1890s.[34]

The debate over the question of sentience led to a renewed dispute over the question of animal intelligence. Muir's belief in the cognition of animals found common ground with Haeckel and other Darwinians who rejected Cartesian logic along with Romantic sentiment. Both had assumed animal behavior was motivated solely by instinct. But if humans and animals have similar nervous systems and brain functions, why should reasoning ability be exclusively human? Darwin and his "bulldog," Thomas Huxley, found it difficult to reject that logic.[35] They were reinforced by other post-Darwinians, including George Romanes, a pioneer in the field of comparative psychology, who wrote in 1883 that "common sense" suggests animals and humans may develop similar "mental states." In a passage Muir read and underscored, Romanes extrapolated from that premise to explain animal intelligence by a modernized version of chain theory:

> Just as the theologians tell us and logically enough—that if there is a Divine Mind, the best, and indeed only, conception we can form of it is that which is formed on the analogy, however imperfect, supplied by the human mind; so with 'inverted anthropomorphism' we must apply a similar consideration with a similar conclusion to the animal mind.[36]

Filled with anecdotes describing animal behavior analogous to that of humans in species ranging from insects to primates, Romanes' study made a deep impression on Muir.[37] He was particularly interested in the chapters on bees and dogs—both species he had personally investigated. Although cautioning himself in an endnote on a back page of Romanes' book that "analogies in nature studies [are] apt to be misleading,"[38] he nevertheless found in the Romanes tract reinforcement for his conviction that Stickeen's action on the glacier was more than mere instinct. "The reasoning displayed by dogs may not always be of a high order," wrote Romanes in a passage Muir found of special interest, "but little incidents, from being of constant occurrence among all dogs, are the more important as showing the reasoning facility to be general to these animals."[39] Applying this conclusion to Stickeen, Muir wrote on the back pages of Romanes' book:

> Can we conceive any human being reasoning more correctly under the desperate circumstances than Stick[een]/ Not from a mere love of anecdote do I write this but to throw light on the vast animal world/ The fear of thoughts & feelings that I saw (under a stern death & life press) in this lit[tle] d[og] cannot I think fail to interest every human thinker/ Never as far as I know had a d[og] ever before been confronted by so stern & fateful a problem . . . all his movements & gestures became fairly luminous with reason & intelligence.[40]

Muir and the Movement for Animal Rights

If animals could think like humans, did they also have fundamental rights? The moral implications of Darwinism were not lost on a new coalition of animal rights activists who emerged as the nineteenth century closed. One of the most vocal—and widely read—was an English liberal, Henry S. Salt, whose 1892 treatise summed up the new case for animal rights. By setting humans apart from animals, by denying animal immortality or sentience, said Salt, Christian dogma and Cartesian epistemology share the blame for centuries of indifference and cruelty to animals. Now science has demonstrated that animals and humans share a similar biological heritage. Extrapolating from that premise, Salt concluded that animals have "individuality, character, reason; and to have those qualities is to have the right to exercise them, insofar as surrounding circumstances permit."[41]

Salt's impassioned plea called public attention to issues that had been debated for years among intellectuals both in Europe and the United States. Before Darwin, sympathy for "dumb" animals was the common denominator by which animal advocates appealed for better treatment. Darwinism added a new twist by strengthening the argument of activists who asserted animals were intelligent as well as morally equivalent to humans.

A revolutionary affirmation, indeed, but conditioned by the pragmatic realities of "surrounding circumstances." Like other moral reformers, animal rights activists had to overcome the inertia and indifference of established traditions and institutions. The church, the political system, the schools, mass opinion— all resisted change. "Animal rights" sounded ominous to the working man, especially if he depended on animal exploitation for a livelihood. Even Darwinism itself could be used to work against social intervention for any reason. By drawing dubious analogies between natural selection among species and "survival of the fittest" in human society, English sociologist Herbert Spencer transformed Social Darwinism into a justification for economic and social laissez-faire. Thus public indifference, even public hostility, greeted early advocates of animal rights. Before corrective action could be taken, the movement would have to gather allies, to build a broad base of sympathy and support.

Muir's extant library does not contain Salt's 1892 treatise, but the book may have been one of the 500 lost after 1914. That Muir and Salt knew the work of each other, however, is more than just surmise: the Muir papers contain correspondence from Salt after 1900, and one of Salt's later books, personally inscribed by the author and annotated by Muir in endnotes, resides in the Holt-Atherton Library. Muir shared Salt's view on the deleterious effects of Christian dogma, the damage done by Cartesian dualism and the need to recognize and respect animal rights. But he went beyond Salt and most humanitarians in defending predators.[42] Twenty years before Salt's publication, Muir had proclaimed rights for all living things:

> Ours is an age [of] liberal principles yet we find but little charity that is broad enough to include bears. A Burns may step outside the selfish circle of his species with sympathy for a suffering daisy or to claim the mousie as fellow mortal but in the smug highwalled realms of the civilized such souls are rare indeed & it is boasted as a grand consumation [sic] of "universal charity" that now all the human race black brown & yellow are recognized as in some sence [sic] brethren capable of Christianity & even admissible to the Anglo Saxon heaven, but bears are allowed no part nor loft in our celestial regions & are begrudged the air & light . . . all long toothed poisonous uneatable uncivilizable animals & plants which carry prickles are vaguely considered diabolical or . . . in some way referrable to man's first disobedience. . . . Man forms but a small portion of the great unit of creation & bears & snakes have rights as well as he.[43]

Despite growing interest in protecting animals, the Victorian world was not ready for such revolutionary ethics. Most of Muir's statements defending predators remained in the closet during his lifetime, and even his literary executors were reluctant to reveal the real Muir.[44] Salt, however, had no such qualms. His 1892 publication, even though it stopped short of calling for predator rights, established his reputation as a leader of the animal rights movement.

By that time Muir was also famous but much less controversial. His popularity rested on carefully crafted published descriptions of the beautiful Western wilds where he had wandered and preached the gospel of preservation. Thousands had read his eloquent prose in *Scribner's* and *Harper's* and *Century* magazines; they knew him not as a revolutionary but as the spokesman for America's rich natural heritage. And they were willing listeners if not ready converts, for the 1890s was an era of reflection, a time for soul-searching and reassessment. If the nation owed its greatness to the frontier, as Frederick Jackson Turner asserted, what would the future offer now that the frontier was but a memory? Muir's charming portraits of redwood giants and sublime vistas and animal personalities tamed the Wild West with evocative word pictures. He was a popularizer, a spokesman for the picturesque, a naturalist with a national following. Both he and his editors recognized the power of his persuasive but gentle rhetoric. But there were also penalties for popularity. Writing for the masses placed boundaries on literary discretion. Johnson's editorial hand kept Muir confined to words and themes and values the American people were ready to read.

But Salt's work and the animal rights movement stirred Muir's conscience and rekindled the revolutionary fires that smoldered within. The momentum for change seemed to be leaning his way: witness the string of recent conservation victories—the new park bills for Yosemite and Sequoia and the founding of the Sierra Club. If he could popularize conservation, perhaps he could do the same for animal rights. The trick was to challenge traditional attitudes in an inoffensive way; to reach the public's heart with a sentimental story that unobtrusively introduced radical concepts.

That was a formidable task that infinitely complicated the writing of *Stickeen*. Even demonstrating the dog's intelligence was made more difficult by Johnson's insistence upon following literary conventions. To retain the element of surprise, the *Century* editor wanted Muir to introduce Stickeen as a "dull" dog with little hint of intellect until confronted by the great crevasse. For months the author struggled to find just the right phrase. On the back pages of books, on tablets and scraps of paper he tried out various combinations: "Serenity seemed only dullness";[45] "a dull sleepy sagacity";[46] "dull glum feeble dignity";[47] "the little dull dumbness of a dog";[48] "a dull silly semi-imbecile look";[49] and the more alliterative "small black dumpling of dullness."[50] After at least 60 different expressions, he finally settled on 6 separate characterizations of the dog's evident dim-witted behavior in the 1897 final draft. Johnson cut those down to three in the published version.

Thus the little dog on the wrong side of the abyss was an unknown entity, a canine "of the dull solemn kind,"[51] ponderous and stoical, an unlikely object of human interest or concern. Why was he so insipid? The primitivist in Muir initially claimed the dog was "dulled by civilization,"[52] but on second thought, nineteenth-century Alaska was hardly the place to stake that claim. By the final draft he vaguely attributed it to the heritage of "generations of downtrodden ancestors" worn out by hard work and hunting.[53]

The Soul and Animal Immortality

A dog with hidden intellectual powers, that was the message. To cross the crevasse, courage had to conquer fear, inspiration to triumph over instinct. But courage and inspiration were more than just discrete intellectual gifts. They were attributes of the soul, the central "organizing principle" that gave meaning to much of mankind in the late Victorian era.[54] Darwinian materialism had undermined the metaphysical pedestal on which the soul rested, yet the defenders of tradition fought back in popular journals such as *Nineteenth Century* and *Atlantic Monthly*. The result was a resurgent debate over the nature, existence and immortality of the soul, a dialogue that reached its peak during the writing of *Stickeen*.

Defenders of tradition had to respond to two types of criticism. One came from materialists, like Huxley and Haeckel, who either insisted that all psychic processes follow the "law of substance," or who took refuge in Voltairian agnosticism. To "cultivate your own garden" meant avoiding irrelevant metaphysical questions.[55] The other type was less materialistic but equally disturbing, for it granted the existence of souls but heretically broadened the concept to include the higher nonhuman species. All things were related by a common substance, but did that include mind as well as matter, and did each level of life contain all the attributes of the soul? Emerson had opened a metaphysical Pandora's Box by finding a common denominator in the "hidden stuff" with which all things are created.

Other creationists also saw the logic of continuity, especially as Darwinism continued to chip away at theoretical distinctions between humans and other animals. If there were no differences in material substance, why should there be differences in spirit? Huxley in the 1870s had preferred an organic distinction: evolution explains consciousness, but higher brain functions, that is, the soul, may develop only at the higher stages of evolution. But lest religionists take comfort in believing animals "do not possess immortal souls," he admitted that his theory would not "prevent any one from entertaining the amiable convictions ascribed by Pope to his untutored savage, that, when he passed to the realms of the blessed, his faithful dog should bear him company."[56]

Muir had probably read and enjoyed Pope's anecdote as much as Huxley. On the immortality of dog souls he stood four-square with the savages. While conventional America was not prepared to go that far, Muir found a sympathetic ear among old friends in the nearby Berkeley Hills. One was Sarah J. McChesney, an Oakland feminist and director of the Oakland Society for the Prevention of Cruelty to Animals. Twenty years after Muir had boarded in the McChesney household while drafting his Sierra glaciation theories, Mrs. McChesney boldly spoke out on the implications of Darwinism. To an enquiring reporter she said evolution had reversed Cartesian logic. If souls were necessary for sentience, then "most assuredly" animals had souls. The remark of course had religious implications, for orthodox Christianity denied that animals were immortal. On that question both McChesney and her colleague, Charles B. Holbrook of the San Francisco SPCA, boldly asserted that dogs and other sentient animals had a rightful place in heaven.[57]

That same logic could also be used against antifeminists who denied that women had souls. This was simply a religious extension of Cartesian theory, based on the pre-Darwinian premise that souls were necessary for sentience and that women were less sentient than men. Mrs. McChesney's reported remarks stopped short of challenging the conventional Western religious view of women, but another Muir friend was more outspoken. Mary McHenry Keith, a San Francisco attorney and wife of Muir's closest friend William Keith, played a prominent regional role in the cause of women's rights.[58] She was also an animal rights activist, asserting, with Sarah McChesney, that animal sentience no longer could be disputed. In response to a reporter's inquiry she boldly linked the cause of women and animals. Both were sentient beings with immortal souls. Mrs. Keith even suggested western Christianity could learn something from Hindu teachings on the "transmigration of souls" after death.[59]

Muir closely followed the debates on Darwin and religion in the press and kept an extensive clipping file. While ambivalent on the question of women's rights, the arguments of McChesney and Keith augmented his own thoughts on animal sentience, and he tried to incorporate them into the Stickeen story. He was intrigued by metempsychosis, the belief that animal and human souls "transmigrate" after death into another life form. It was an old idea, traced back at least as far as Pythagoras in the Western world and ancient Hindu philosophy in the East.[60] The concept fostered belief in the immortality of souls and also laid the cornerstone for a broader ethic that respected all living things. In the West, faith in incarnate immortality, if not reincarnation, remained a fundamental tenet of Christianity long after the transmigration theory declined. But the notion resurfaced and gained considerable attention by the 1890s as part of the backwash of Darwinism.

Could the soul of Stickeen be human in origin? That was one of the questions Muir now asked himself as he worked on the manuscript. That the dog had a soul was to him beyond doubt, but would elevating it to human status make the idea more palatable to his readers? As the plot of the story began to take form, he conceived the ice bridge as a metaphor for baring the soul.

The moment of truth came in Stickeen's decision to cross the bridge. Here was the crisis that "like white light laid the mind and soul bare."[61] "Now his whole soul & body to the end of every hair was revealed."[62] What Muir perceived was a confirmation of oneness, a symbolic union of human and animal. For in beholding the soul of the little dog, Muir saw himself. Stickeen was a boy growing up, a child suddenly transformed by crisis. The glacier journey was a metaphor for life, with Muir and the dog at the height of danger reduced to a single entity, a merging of mind and spirit, a coalescence of the primal elements of creation. "Soul of our soul," wrote Muir in an 1896 passage.[63] In the back of George Eliot's *Wit and Wisdom,* he expressed it differently: "Under the stress of this supreme trial Stickine became a living human soul."[64]

If the bridge was the connecting link between the species, the abyss symbolized the dark unknown, the void of superstition and fear that separates human from other life forms. Bridging the gap represented not only oneness and immortality—a uniting of souls in a spiritual victory over death—it also signified a "triumphant joy of deliverance"[65] over the nether world of ignorance that prevented mankind from recognizing its physical and spiritual kinship with the rest of creation. Leaving the void behind was symbolic affirmation of the human-animal bond.

With dog and man as one, Muir came back to the transmigration theory and tested it out on paper, first in the back of Hawthorne's *Our Old Home,* then in his 1896 draft notes. "No wonder the belief is so wide of the transmigration of souls & everybody obsessed with psychological speculations as to whether they have souls," he wrote in Hawthorne.[66] By 1896 he had worked that cumbersome passage down into a terse: "No wonder so many believe the souls of men enter animals."[67] In an advanced draft of 1897, he took a more precautionary tack: "No wonder so many believe or half believe the Pathagorian notion (doctrine) of transmigration of souls."[68] He even worked in a Hindu reference. The "Little black horizontal philosopher" of earlier years was rewritten by 1897. Now Muir speculated that the dog "might be some old Hindoo [*sic*] philosopher" in disguise.[69] Johnson deleted the transmigration paragraph before publishing the story in 1897.

The question of animal souls led to the question of animal immortality. Here Muir stood solidly with Sarah McChesney and other animal rights activists. A lifelong critic of sectarian dogmas, he rejected all arguments that smacked of speciesism. Long a student of American Indian culture, like Pope, he saw the irony in contrasting "primitive" and "civilized" religions. "Even in religion animals are mostly ignored," he wrote:

> We throw our heaven open to every vertical mammal but close it against all the horizontal ones. Indians are more charitable. They allow their dogs to follow them into their happy hunting grounds.[70]

Johnson also threw out this passage, presumably on the ground that it would offend too many *Century* readers.

From its initial telling in the 1880s to the final version submitted in 1897, Muir's dog story, like Darwin's ovenbirds, changed over time. What began as an exotic adventure evolved into a lesson in moral equality and oneness. Incorporating concepts gleaned from nearly two decades of reading and reflection, the final narrative contained unconventional ideas, some his editor in the waning Victorian years found too sensitive to publish in a popular magazine.[71] But he left intact the author's bedrock lessons, the culminating wisdom of his moral education. Outspoken defender of wilderness values, John Muir was also an eloquent spokesman for animals. Convinced that dogs and other higher animals were endowed with the creator's gifts of intellect, sentience and immortality, as proof he offered firsthand evidence gathered on a glacier in 1880 with a "little hank of hair" named Stickeen.

Notes

1. John Muir, From Wrangel Up Cost Sum Dum Takou, etc. (AMS Journal, August 16–31, 1880), in *The John Muir Papers,* Microform edition (Alexandria, Va.: Chadwyck-Healey, 1986), Reel 26 at 02114, hereafter cited as JMP Microfilm.

2. It is impossible in this abbreviated format to describe the Muir book collection or its contents in detail More than 1,000 of the 1,600 volumes described in Muir's probate records of 1915 have been located. The bulk are now part of the John Muir Papers at the Holt-Atherton Library; another 250 are in the Huntington Library. A few scattered volumes are still in family hands. As a working library rather than a drawing-room collection, these volumes contain much of the best of late eighteenth- and nineteenth-century British and American literature, poetry, science, philosophy and history. Over 50 percent of the extant volumes contain Muir holograph endnotes and marginalia—a wealth of information that scholars have yet to systematically investigate. What they will find remains to be seen, although my work in deciphering Muir's Stickeen notes leaves me convinced that much of Muir's literary style and substance as both writer and nature philosopher can be traced through the books he read.

3. R.U. Johnson to John Muir, May 17,1894, JMP Microfilm 8/04536.

4. Although the books have yet to be duplicated and made widely available, facsimiles of the manuscript drafts and notebooks have been published as part of *The John Muir Papers, 1858–1957* (Microform edition). It is not my purpose here to analyze the content of this voluminous literary record, or to discuss the process by which Muir went about composing his dog story. That has been done in my book, *John Muir's "Stickeen" and the Lessons of Nature* (College: University of Alaska Press, 1996).

5. Roderick Nash, *Wilderness and the American Mind,* 3rd ed. (New Haven: Yale University Press, 1982), 143–145.

6. Lisa Mighetto, "Science, Sentiment and Anxiety: American Nature Writing at the Turn of the Century," *Pacific Historical Review* 54 (February 1985): 33–34; James Turner, *Reckoning with the Beast: Animals, Pain, and Humanity in the Victorian Mind* (Baltimore: Johns Hopkins University Press, 1980), 62, 67; Henry Adams, *The Education of Henry Adams* (1918; repr. Boston: Houghton Mifflin, 1961), 451.

7. Before publication of *Origin of the Species,* Darwin defended the idea of a creator-god as the First Cause or ultimate source of life but not directly responsible for new species. After the 1850s he rejected theism, at least in private; see Maurice Mandelbaum, *History, Man & Reason. A Study in Nineteenth-Century Thought* (Baltimore: Johns Hopkins University Press, 1971), 85–87. After his death his literary heirs apparently suppressed correspondence that sounded too atheistic while agreeing to publish letters expressing agnosticism; see Gertrude Himmelfarb, *Darwin and the Darwinian Revolution* (Garden City, N.Y.: Doubleday Anchor, 1962), 384.

8. The emergence of a "Christian Darwinism" illustrates Gertrude Himmelfarb's observation "The basic religious quarrel provoked by the Origin was not between the theists who rejected it and the atheists who favored it, as has been thought, but rather between the reconcilers and the irreconcilables, those who believed the Origin to be compatible with Christianity and those who thought that it was not" (*Darwin and the Darwinian Revolution,* 397).

9. Muir was disappointed to learn that even Emerson, the progenitor of Muir's own

nature philosophy, distinguished between wilderness advocacy and total submission. Declining Muir's invitation to spend a week together in the Yosemite wilds, the aging Bostonian offered a pragmatic aphorism: "solitude . . . a sublime mistress but an intolerable wife." Emerson to Muir, February 5, 1872, *The Life and Letters of John Muir*, vol. 1 (Boston: Houghton Mifflin, 1923), 259–260.

10. Mighetto, "Science, Sentiment and Anxiety," 33–37; Turner, *Reckoning with the Beast*, 60–77. Leo Marx explored the pastoral idea and its cultural implications in his classic study, *The Machine in the Garden: Technology and the Pastoral Ideal in America* (New York: Oxford University Press, 1967).

11. Arthur O. Lovejoy, *The Great Chain of Being: A Study of the History of an Idea* (1936; repr. New York: Harper Torchbooks, 1960), esp. 24–66, 183–207, 242–314. Stephen Jay Gould has summarized the biological fallacies of chain theory in *The Flamingo's Smile: Reflections in Natural History* (New York: Norton, 1985), 281–290.

12. Ralph W. Emerson, *Prose Works*, vol. 1 (Boston: Fields, Osgood, 1870), 269, in Beinecke Library, Yale University. This was Muir's copy, and the passage quoted is marked in Muir's hand.

13. Gray even called for the development of an "evolutionary teleology"; see Himmelfarb, *Darwin and the Darwinian Revolution*, 390.

14. Charles Darwin, *Journal of Researches into the Natural History and Geology of the Countries Visited During the Voyage of the H.M.S. Beagle Round the World* (London: T. Nelson & Sons, 1891), 121, in John Muir's Library Collection, University of the Pacific, Western American collection (Stockton, Calif.), hereafter cited as JML, UOPWA.

15. See the paraphrase of Emerson in Muir's 1872 journal, as quoted in R. H. Limbaugh, "The Nature of Muir's Religion," *Pacific Historian* 29 (Summer–Fall 1985): 25.

16. *Scientific Papers of Asa Gray*, vol. 1 (Boston & New York: Houghton, Mifflin, 1889), JML, UOPWA.

17. Thomas Carlyle, *The Life of John Sterling* (London: Chapman & Hall, 1870), JML, UOPWA.

18. Muir holograph endnote in Alfred Russel Wallace, *The World of Life. A Manifestation of Creative Power, Direction Mind and Ultimate Purpose* (New York: Moffat, Yard & Co., 1911), JML, UOPWA.

19. Muir holographic endnote in Nathanial Hawthorne, *The Scarlet Letter* (Boston: Houghton Mifflin, 1884), JML, UOPWA.

20. John Muir, advanced holograph draft fragments of Stickeen manuscript, JMP Microfilm 42/09018, 66.

21. Mighetto, "Science, Sentiment, and Anxiety," 37–42; Mighetto, "Wildlife Protection and the New Humanitarianism," *Environmental Review* 12 (Spring 1988): 37–41.

22. Henry S. Salt, "The Rights of Animals," *International Journal of Ethics* 10 (January 1900): 206.

23. Muir went further than most of his humanitarian contemporaries by praising unpopular predators as well as more desirable creatures. But few of his thoughts on predation reached the reading public during his lifetime; his editors deleted passages that might prove offensive. Lisa Mighetto, "John Muir and the Rights of Animals," *Pacific Historian* 29 (Summer–Fall 1985): 107–109. Although he showed ecological insight in describing the importance of predators for balancing certain habitats, modern ecology owes more to George Perkins Marsh than to Muir.

24. John Burroughs' *My Dog Friends*, ed. Clara Barrus (Boston & New York:

Houghton Mifflin, 1928), 76–77; "On Humanizing the Animals," *Century* 67 (March 1904): 780.

25. For example, see Wesley Mills, *The Nature & Development of Animal Intelligence* (New York: Macmillan, 1898), 6–7. Some time after 1897 Muir clipped two book notices from the papers and filed them in an envelope labeled "books to buy." The books were the volume by Mills and *Our Friend the Dog* by Maurice Maeterlinck. The Muir Library at UOP contains neither of these.

26. Robert M. Young, "Animal Soul," *The Encyclopedia of Philosophy*, editor-in-chief Paul Edwards (New York: Macmillan–Free Press, 1967), vol. 1:122–127; David McFarland, *The Oxford Companion to Animal Behavior* (Oxford & New York: Oxford University Press, 1982), 310–311.

27. John Burroughs, *The Summit of the Years* (Boston & New York: Houghton Mifflin, 1913), 167.

28. For a discussion of pre-Darwinian ethics, see *Ethics and Animals*, ed. Harlan B. Miller and William H. Williams (Clifton, N.J.: Humana Press, 1983), esp. 2–4.

29. See, for example, Lynn White, Jr., "The Historical Roots of Our Ecologic Crisis," *Science* 155 (March 10,1967): 1207; Joseph Wood Krutch, as cited in Lawrence Buell, "The Thoreauvian Pilgrimage: The Structure of an American Cult," *American Literature* 61 (May 1989): 193.

30. Limbaugh, "Nature of John Muir's Religion," 25–27; Bernard E. Rollin, *Animal Rights and Human Morality* (Amherst, N.Y.: Prometheus Books, 1981), 6–9.

31. Rollin, *Animal Rights and Human Morality*, 10–11; Miller and Williams, *Ethics and Animals*, 3, 6.

32. Young, "Animal Soul."

33. *Encyclopedia of Philosophy*, vol. 3:399–402. Professor William D. Gunning, a Unitarian minister and Haeckel protégé, toured the West Coast in 1878, but he shocked audiences with outrageous evolution stories, asserting, for instance, that Adam and Eve were black and covered with hair. His mockery of orthodox religion won few sympathizers. Asked his opinion of Gunning, Muir said not to waste time with such "poor game": they will "destroy themselves" with lies (Letter, Muir to Annie K. Bidwell, February 13, 1878, JMP Microfilm 3/01703).

34. Modern philosophers are still debating the ethical and moral ramifications. See Peter Singer, *Animal Liberation: A New Ethics for Our Treatment of Animals* (New York: New York Review, 1975), 2–9. Singer's controversial book attempted to strike a middle ground in the modern debate over animal rights, but his utilitarian argument has been challenged by some ethicists. See David Lamb, "Animal Rights and Liberation Movements," *Environmental Ethics* 4 (Fall 1982): 215–233.

35. Huxley, in a passage marked by Muir, quoted with approval a post-Darwinian essay discussing the biological linkage of primates and then carried the argument further: "I may add the expression of my belief that the attempt to draw a psychical distinction is equally futile, and that even the highest faculties of feeling and of intellect begin to germinate in lower forms of life"; see Thomas H. Huxley, *Man's Place in Nature and Other Anthropological Essays* (New York: Appleton, 1894), 152, JML, UOPWA.

36. George J. Romanes, *Animal Intelligence* (New York: D. Appleton, 1883), 10, JML, UOPWA.

37. In 1896 Muir gave the book to his eldest daughter on her fifteenth birthday. His

inscription is revealing: "To Wanda, nurse & friend & lover of all her feeble fellow mortals . . . " Romanes, *Animal Intelligence*, JML, UOPWA.

38. Holograph endnote in Romanes, *Animal Intelligence*, JML, UOPWA.

39. Romanes, *Animal Intelligence*, 460.

40. Holograph endnote in Romanes, *Animal Intelligence*.

41. Henry S. Salt, *Animals' Rights Considered in Relation to Social Progress* (New York: Macmillan, 1894), 1–22. In 1908 Salt corresponded with Muir and sent him a copy of his most recent book, *On Cambrian and Cumbrian Hills*. It now resides with the Muir Library Collection at UOP. For Salt's importance on the humanitarian faction of the animal rights movement, see Mighetto, "Wildlife Protection and the New Humanitarianism," 37–49.

42. Lisa Mighetto, *Muir Among the Animals* (San Francisco: Sierra Club Books, 1986), xxxxii.

43. "Bears," holograph ms., ca. 1872, JMP Microfilm 34/02018.

44. For example, see Linnie Marsh Wolfe's heavily emended version of Muir's statement on bears in *John of the Mountains: The Unpublished Journals of John Muir* (1938; rpt. Madison: University of Wisconsin Press, 1979), 82–83.

45. Muir holograph note in Walter Bagehot, *Literary Studies (Miscellaneous Essays)*, vol. 3 (1895), JML, UOPWA.

46. Holograph note in Bagehot, *Literary Studies*, vol. 3, JML, UOPWA.

47. Holograph note in Brown, *Horae Subsecivae*, vol. 2 (1889), JML UOPWA.

48. Holograph note in *The Wit and Wisdom of George Eliot* (Boston: Robert Bros., 1885), JML, UOPWA.

49. Holography note in Hawthorne, *Scarlet Letter* (1884), JML, UOPWA.

50. Holograph note in Brown, *Horae Subsecivae*, vol. 1 (1889), JML, UOPWA.

51. JM holograph note in the endpages of Thomas Carlyle, *Wilhelm Meister's Apprenticeship and Travels* (London: Chapman & Hall n.d.), vol. 1, JML, UOPWA.

52. Muir holograph note in Hawthorne, *Septimius Felton, with an Appendix Containing The Ancestral Footstep* (Boston: Houghton Mifflin, 1884), JML, UOPWA.

53. Muir holograph notes in [Stickeen] draft notebook 06474, 33/011344. Muir used the words "dull" or "dullness" at least 35 different times in a variety of draft passages trying to describe the dog's character prior to crossing the ice bridge. See especially the endnotes in books by Hawthorne, John Ruskin and Hippolyte-Adolphe Taine in the Muir Collection at the Holt-Atherton Library, and in Muir's 1896 draft notebook, 06474, 33/01338–01384.

54. James F. Clarke, "Have Animals Souls?" *Atlantic Monthly* 34 (October 1874): 422.

55. Vernon L. Kellogg, "Ernst Haeckel: Darwinist, Monist," *Popular Science Monthly* 76 (February 1910): 136–142; Thomas H. Huxley, "Are Animals Automatons?" *Popular Science Monthly* 5 (October 1874): 732–733.

56. Huxley, "Are Animals Automatons?" 730–732.

57. "Have Animals Souls," San Francisco *Chronicle*, Sunday Supplement, May 26, 1901, 31, in the unfilmed John Muir Papers, Series VI, JMP, UOPWA.

58. *San Francisco Call*, May 6, 1896, 10–11; May 21, 1896, 13, cols. 3–4; Ida Husted Harper, ed., *The History of Woman Suffrage* (New York: National American Woman Suffrage Association, 1922), vol. 4: 480, 483.

59. "Have Animals Souls," JMP, UOPWA. Another controversial woman leader in both feminist and animal causes was the wife of Charles Holbrook, the San Francisco

SPCA secretary. In 1903 anonymous accusations were brought against both Holbrooks, he for "neglecting his duty in order to visit theaters and music halls," she for conducting herself "in an unladylike manner in the society's offices," "being generally disagreeable," and, on her absentee husband's behalf, having "administered the affairs of the charity during his absence." A majority of trustees, however, recognizing her outstanding efforts to educate schoolchildren on the proper treatment of animals, supported both and dismissed the charges. *San Francisco Call,* February 22, 1903, 27, cols. 2.

60. J. Donald Hughes, "The Environmental Ethics of the Pythagoreans," *Environmental Ethics* 2 (Fall 1980): 195–213.

61. Muir holograph note in Brown, *Horae Subsecivae,* vol. 1, JML, UOPWA.

62. Muir holograph note in Carlyle, *History of Friedrich II,* vol. 2, JML, UOPWA.

63. Muir draft passage in [Stickeen] manuscript, JMP Microfilm 06474, 13/01357.

64. Muir holograph note in Eliot, *Wit and Wisdom,* JML, UOPWA. "Stickine" is the accepted spelling for the river and the Indian people in southeast Alaska, and was in common use both before and after the 1880s. Muir most often used the variant spelling for the dog, probably because of its phonetic advantages. But he was inconsistent, especially in 1897 while he gathered data on the Stickine River and the Indians. Young's reminiscence of 1897 spells the dog's name "Stickine," and occasionally Muir did the same. His story-title of "Stickeen" however, fixed the accepted spelling, even though in the same draft he used the variant at times—which the *Century* editors caught before publishing.

65. This is Muir's phrase as expressed in his notes at the back of Taine's *History of English Literature.* He tried various other versions. See endnotes in Carlyle's *The French Revolution,* vol. 1, and Oliver Cromwell's *Letters and Speeches,* vol. 1, as well as those in Eliot, *Wit and Wisdom* and in the 1896 Stickeen draft. All are in JML, UOPWA and JMP Microfilm, manuscript 06474, 33/01367.

66. Muir holograph note in Hawthorne, *Our Old Home, and English Note-Books* (Boston: Houghton Mifflin, 1884), vol. 1, JML, UOPWA.

67. Muir holograph note in [Stickeen] manuscript, JMP Microfilm 06474, 33/01376.

68. Muir note in advanced draft of "An Adventure with a Dog and a Glacier," JMP Microfilm 07876, 43/09449.

69. Muir holograph notes in Eliot, *Wit and Wisdom,* JML, UOPWA, and in advanced draft of "An Adventure with a Dog and a Glacier," JMP Microfilm 07874, 43/09449.

70. Muir holograph passage in "An Adventure with a Dog and a Glacier," advanced draft fragments, JMP Microfilm 42/09018.

71. It should be noted that Muir later restored many of R. U. Johnson's textual emendations in a revised version published by Houghton Mifflin in 1909 under Muir's original title, *Stickeen.*

Will the Real Wild Animal Please Stand Up! The Nature Fakers

RALPH H. LUTTS

The beginning of the twentieth century witnessed an explosion of public interest in nature that has been equaled only in the years following Earth Day 1970. This interest had its roots in the Romantic and Transcendental movements and a number of trends that developed and merged throughout the nineteenth century, reaching a peak in the first years of the twentieth. The increased ease of river and rail transportation, along with an increase in affluence, led many people to travel the American landscape and visit its wilds—a practice that steamboat and railroad companies promoted heavily. Recreational travel, camping, hiking, and sightseeing increased, bringing more people in contact with nature as they vacationed at resorts, camps, and lodges, and journeyed into the wilderness. Outdoor clubs such as the Appalachian Mountain Club and the Sierra Club (founded in 1876 and 1892, respectively) further promoted recreation in the wilderness.

Public interest in nature topics was fed by a burgeoning number of magazine articles and books. In the latter part of the nineteenth century, the development of the nature study movement as an approach to both outdoor recreation and educational reform led still more children and adults out of doors and into the fields and woods in search of birds, wildflowers, and ferns. Some people heard

This essay is a revised and enlarged version of Ralph H. Lutts, "The Nature Fakers: Conflicting Perspectives of Nature," *Ecological Consciousness: Essays from the Earthman X Colloquium, University of Denver, April 21–24, 1980* (Washington, D.C.: University Press of America, 1981). Used by permission of University Press of America.

the call of the back-to-the-land movement and left their town houses to take up farming and live the simple life. The federal government also turned its attention to the environment with the creation of forest, range, and water management programs, the establishment of national parks, the development of the conservation movement, and the creation of the National Conservation Commission in 1908. By that time, public interest in nature was so great that social critics, concerned by what they feared was a retreat from society, began to decry the pervasive presence of "nature lovers" and the "nature cult."[1]

John Burroughs and the Sham Naturalists

John Burroughs (1837–1921) was a prominent figure in the development of popular interest in nature. Between the publication of his first nature piece in 1861 and his death in 1921, he produced a wealth of nature books and articles that found few equals. The warmth and deceptive simplicity of his essays had a wide appeal. In a review of his second book, Henry James, Jr., referred to him as "a sort of reduced, but also more humorous, more available, and more social Thoreau."[2] Reading one of Burroughs' essays is much like going on a walk with the author, noting the plants and animals (especially the birds) and taking pleasure in them. He was a keen observer and helped his readers sharpen their own powers of observation. His landscape was farm, garden, and woodlot. What he saw and reported was a part of the environment of many of his readers and fed the nostalgia of others who were only a generation away from farm life. His style, avoiding overblown emotions and rhetoric, led his readers to believe that they, too, could step outside and see what he saw. He became one of the best known and loved authors in America. In later years, his life as a farmer in New York's Hudson River Valley was continually interrupted by a procession of admirers: writers, scientists, publicists, industrialists, teachers, students and a president all beat a path to his door.

In 1887 Burroughs' publishers issued a special school edition of his essays. This was the first of a number of readers based on his work. Teachers found that their students were interested in nature and used this motivation, along with Burroughs' books, to develop their students' reading skills. Between 1889 and 1906 more than three hundred thousand copies of his school readers were sold, introducing a generation of children to nature.[3]

Burroughs was a central figure in the development of nature writing as literature in the United States and he played an important role in defining the role of the literary naturalist. In his view, the literary naturalist combined qualities of both scientist and poet. He used the metaphor of a honeybee to make his point. Just as the nectar of a flower does not become honey until it has passed through the chemistry of the bee's body, nature does not become literature until it has passed through the naturalist-writer's mind:

The literary naturalist does not take liberties with facts; facts are the flora upon which he lives. The more and the fresher the facts the better. I can do nothing without them, but I must give them my own flavor. I must impart to them a quality which heightens and intensifies them. . . .

If I name every bird I see in my walk, describe its color and ways, etc., give a lot of facts or details about the bird, it is doubtful if my reader is interested. But if I relate the birds in some way to human life, to my own life, —show what it is to me and what it is in the landscape and season, —then do I give my reader a live bird and not a labeled specimen.[4]

The requirement that the author adhere both to facts and the poetic spirit, the objective and the subjective approaches to nature, means that he or she is obligated to combine elements of both scientist and artist. The tension between these elements lay, as we will see, at the heart of the Nature Fakers controversy.[5]

The public developed a great appetite for books and articles about nature. By the turn of the century, most popular magazines carried nature pieces and nature books appeared on lists of books recommended for summer reading and Christmas gifts. With the mushrooming demand came a great increase in the number of authors trying to satisfy it. In the first years of the twentieth century, many established nature writers became concerned that the general quality of the literature was deteriorating as less-qualified writers were attracted to the market. John Burroughs voiced this concern in his 1903 article, "Real and Sham Natural History," published in the *Atlantic Monthly*.

Burroughs was a quiet man who shied away from controversy. But he had reached the limit of his patience, and in a rare public display of temper he accused some authors of writing nature books primarily for profit. The brunt of his attack was directed at two of the most popular nature writers, Ernest Thompson Seton and William J. Long. "Only the last two writers," he wrote, "seem to seek to profit by the popular love for the sensational and the improbable, Mr. Long, in this respect, quite throwing Mr. Seton in the shade." Burroughs argued that "the line between fact and fiction is repeatedly crossed, and that a deliberate attempt is made to induce the reader to cross, too, and to work such a spell upon him that he shall not know that he has crossed and is in the land of make believe." He called this practice "sham natural history."[6]

Both Seton and Long claimed that what they wrote was true. Seton began his *Wild Animals I Have Known* (which Burroughs felt should have been entitled *Wild Animals I ALONE Have Known*) by stating, "These stories are true. Although I have left the strict line of historical truth in many places, the animals in this book are all real characters. They lived the lives I have depicted, and showed the stamp of heroism and personality more strongly by far than it has been in the power of my pen to tell." Long's Preface to *School of the Woods* asserted, "Most of the following sketches were made in the woods, with the subjects themselves living just outside my tent door. They are all life studies, and include also some of the unusual life secrets of a score of animals and birds."[7] Although both books were entertaining and enjoyable, the authors also wanted to build a sympathetic appreciation of nature in their readers. They tried to accomplish this by writing about the daily lives of selected animals and the authors' encounters with them.

Seton was a co-creator, along with Charles G. D. Roberts, of the realistic wild animal story, a branch of nature writing that tried to present nature from the animals' perspectives. Wild animal stories found an eager audience, beginning in the late 1890s. This new literary genre challenged the popularity of the more traditional nature essayists such as Burroughs. Perhaps Burroughs' complaints were in part motivated by sour grapes, but there was more to it. In trying to understand an animal's own experiences of nature, wild animal story writers were always in danger of projecting themselves on the animals and writing overly anthropomorphized tales.

Burroughs felt that Long, Seton, Roberts, and other writers went too far in constructing their stories. He pointed to Seton's tales of foxes: riding across a field on the back of a sheep in order to escape the hounds, luring dogs into the path of an oncoming railroad train, and bringing poison to its captured and chained kit when it was unable to set it free, favoring death to captivity. Burroughs was particularly upset by Long's stories about animals consciously schooling their young in the same way as humans do. Long wrote, for example, that kingfishers and osprey catch and injure (but do not kill) fish and drop them into practice pools where their fledglings are taught to fish. In another of Long's stories, a playful porcupine curled into a sphere and rolled downhill, gathering leaves speared upon its quills. Burroughs' complaint was not that they wrote tall tales, but that they had the audacity to represent them as truthful.

Burroughs had sent a draft of his article to Dallas Lore Sharp for comment. Sharp, a literature professor and fellow literary naturalist, responded with praise and wrote that he expected the piece to "clear the air and settle things."[8] Actually, "Real and Sham Natural History" neither cleared the air nor settled anything. Rather, the smoke of debate rose. There were a number of writers who, although they supported Burroughs' basic position, felt that he had dealt too harshly with the offenders, who had made important contributions to the public understanding of nature: Burroughs himself to the appreciation of natural history and Seton and Long to the development of a love of nature.

Ernest Thompson Seton (1860–1946) remained silent. He had reason to feel secure in his qualifications as a naturalist. Although his formal training was as an artist, he had a great deal of experience in the field and had been named Naturalist to the Government of Manitoba, Canada. His earliest volume, *Studies in the Art Anatomy of Animals* (1896), the first book of animal anatomy specifically written for artists, capitalized upon both of these interests. His artwork and his field journals provide proof of his skills as an observer and his attention to detail. His approach to identifying birds by field marks would later be adopted by Roger Tory Peterson in his famous *A Field Guide to the Birds.*[9]

A few weeks after Burroughs' article was published the two writers met at a dinner given by Andrew Carnegie for fifty prominent authors. According to Seton's account of their meeting, he arranged to be seated beside the elder naturalist and during the meal put him on the spot, interrogated Burroughs about his experience with wolves and learned that he had no experience with the animals. When Seton then asked how he could feel competent to make the attack that he had made in the *Atlantic*, Burroughs became flustered and said, "Well there are fundamental principles of interpretation and observation that apply to all animals alike." Seton then toyed with Burroughs, saying of Long (whom he did not know), "He is telling the truth sincerely as he sees it. Now he is crushed and broken, sitting desolate on the edge of his grave. Mr. Burroughs, if you hear of a terrible tragedy in that boy's home in the near future, you can lay it to only one cause—the blame will be wholly yours." At this, he claimed, the old man burst into tears.[10]

Seton published this account of their meeting forty years later and his memory may not have been entirely accurate. Others who were present that evening do not recall the event quite that way. Seton did not record the confrontation in his journal, and Burroughs wrote home to his son that night that he had met Seton. "He behaved finely and asked to sit next to me at dinner," Burroughs wrote, "he quite won my heart."[11] In any event, Burroughs accepted Seton's invitation to visit his home in Connecticut, where he saw Seton's museum of bird and mammal skins, library and photographic collections, and field journals. Convinced of Seton's qualifications, he still felt the stories were too fanciful. A year later he wrote, "Mr. Thompson Seton, as an artist and *raconteur*, ranks by far the highest in this field, and to those who can separate the fact from the fiction in his animal stories, he is truly delightful."[12]

Seton never entered the public debate directly. He did, however, publish a fable about a critic called Little Mucky who climbed to the top of a hill named Big Periodic and threw mud at a newcomer who was drawing attention away from him. As a result, Little Mucky got smaller and smaller. "MORAL: *Notoriety is a poisonous substitute for fame*." In 1907 Seton acknowledged in a letter to Burroughs that some authors had abused the wild animal story and that he was going to do something better.[13] Seton set to work on a study of North American mammals that led to the publication of his two-volume *Life Histories of Northern Animals* in 1909 and his four-volume *Lives of Game Animals* nearly twenty years later. Both received critical acclaim and demonstrated his competence as a naturalist. The latter work, ironically, earned him the honor, in 1927, of being the second person to receive the Burroughs Medal awarded by the John Burroughs Memorial Society.

Seton thus escaped the brunt of the debate about sham naturalists. William J. Long (1866–1952), however, became its focus. In part, this was because critics saw him as a far greater offender than Seton. In addition, he mounted a strong public defense, which made him a lightning rod for criticism. Long, who held a

Ph.D. in philosophy from the University of Heidelberg, was a Congregational minister in Stamford, Connecticut. Despite what his detractors said, he was an active outdoorsman who spent months each year in the woods of Canada and northern Maine—a practice that continued until 1952, the year of his death at the age of eighty-six.[14]

In his response to Burroughs, Long pointed out that it is important to realize two things:

> First, the study of Nature is a vastly different thing from the study of Science; they are no more alike than Psychology and History. Above and beyond the world of facts and law, with which alone Science concerns itself, is an immense and almost unknown world of suggestion and freedom and inspiration, in which the individual, whether animal or man, must struggle against fact and law to develop or keep his own individuality. . . . Though less exact, it is not less but rather more true and real than Science, as emotions are more real than facts, and love is more true than Economics.[15]

The second point was "that the field of natural history has changed rapidly of late, and in the schools and nature clubs the demand is for less Science and more Nature." The scientific view of animals, Long claimed, placed them in categories of like individuals, eliminating their individuality. The modern school of nature-study, however, is interested in the uniquely individual animal and such a study will, he argued, reveal things that the scientific attempt to describe general patterns fails to recognize. "Every boy who keeps a pet," he wrote, "has something to tell the best naturalist."[16]

There is strength in Long's points. Statements about the behavior of a broad category of animals are generalities based on many observations. The scientific goal is to understand animal behavior in terms that are general, rather than anecdotal. But the process of generalizing can gloss over individual variations. The literary naturalist and writers of wild animal stories are, as Burroughs himself pointed out, interested in nature as personally experienced. Long wanted to write about animals as he experienced them, not about animals and their behavior as categorical abstractions. In addition, he wanted to stimulate in his readers an appreciation of, and fellow feeling toward these animals. That he accomplished this was repeatedly proven in the admiring testimony of his defenders.

Long pointed out that there can be a great deal of variation in behavior. How, though, are we to distinguish between an honest, careful observation and a fanciful one? If questioned, each reporter can fall back upon the defense that the observation was of a unique phenomenon. Are there no criteria that can be used to separate truth from fancy? Long wrote "that no animal story told me as a fact by an honest man will leave me incredulous" and went on to say he had heard fifty different guides and trappers each tell different accounts of the behavior of the same animal. He accounted for this by arguing that each had seen different individuals in different locations.[17]

His criterion of truthfulness, then was the trustworthiness of the reporter, rather than a general understanding of the behavioral parameters of the animal or efforts to verify the report by careful observations. For example, Long wrote of Seton:

> Frankly, I differ radically from Mr. Thompson-Seton in many of his theories and observations of animals. That is either because I have seen less, and less sympathetically, than he has, or because I have watched bears and wolves with different individual habits. But Mr. Thompson-Seton is a gentleman. When he tells me that he has seen a thing that is new and wonderful to me, though I know his animals well as a class, I shall simply open my own eyes wider, and question Indian hunters more closely, to know whether his observation is in error, or whether he saw some peculiar trait of some one animal, or whether the same thing has been seen by others in different places. For me to question his veracity, and deny what he has seen because I have not seen it, would be simply to show my own lack of courtesy, and arouse suspicion that I might be jealous of his hard-won and well-deserved success.[18]

Long has transformed the problem of verifying observations into an issue of courtesy. Long appears to have been a gentleman in an Old World sense, who placed great value upon honor, respect, and gentlemanly conduct.[19] A gentleman assumes the best of another gentleman. This is quite at odds with the scientist's view that everything must be open to question and subject to verification. How does one verify ephemeral and unique phenomena? We may open our eyes wider, but we can open them only so wide and the point must come at which we are forced to judge the reliability of our informants. Long's approach opens the door to legitimate unique observations that might not be scientifically verifiable. However, can a gentleman not sometimes be wrong?

Burroughs' view was that there were certain universal principles of animal behavior that one can apply to verify, or at least to test, the plausibility of a reported observation. He viewed Long as an imposter who only pretended to be a careful observer. Long, in turn, believed that Burroughs ignored the individuality of animals and expected all of nature to conform to the limited world of his own farm.[20]

There was more at the root of the controversy. The two men differed fundamentally in their views of the nature of the animal mind. Animals were governed solely by instinct in Burroughs' view. He considered them to be "almost as much under the dominion of absolute nature, or what we call instinct, innate tendency, habit of growth, as are the plants." Long felt that animals shared in the creation and are reflections of the mind of God. As a result, animal minds, including those of humans, differ only in degree, not in kind. A person who notices human characteristics in animals, Long wrote, "is simply finding, as all do find who watch animals closely, many things which awaken a sympathetic response in his own heart, and which he understands more or less clearly, in precisely the same way that he understands himself and his own children."[21] Burroughs' interpretation of animal behavior was grounded in mechanistic instinctive reflexes. Long's interpretation was based on empathy. This led to a great difference in the ways in which each was predisposed to interpret behavior. The polarization of their views is not surprising, since the psychology of their day offered only instinct and reason as options for interpreting animal behavior.

In one of his stories Long recalled watching a woodcock apply a mud cast to its broken leg. This became the object of a series of letters in *Science* initiated by William Morton Wheeler. After commending Burroughs' "Real and Sham Natural History" (which he felt was "too temperate"), Wheeler cut into Long's woodcock story, pointing out that, "Mr. Long virtually claims that a woodcock not only has an understanding of the theory of casts as adapted to fractured limbs, but is able to apply this knowledge in practice. . . . The bird is familiar with the theories of bone formation and regeneration—in a word, with osteogenesis, which, by the way, is never clearly grasped by some of our university juniors."[22]

Most respondents supported Wheeler's view of Long, but one writer came to Long's defense. She argued that "Long tells us in simple language what he has seen, offering neither inferences nor generalizations. It is his critic, Mr. Wheeler, who 'virtually' affirms that a woodcock could not apply mud to a broken leg without knowledge of surgery; and it is much as if he should say that a man who blows on his fingers to warm them or on his tea to cool it has the knowledge of the laws of thermodynamics and is ready to discuss entropy and an indicator diagram." Long's lengthy letter in his defense included notarized affidavits by people who claimed to have seen similar things.[23]

A year later William Brewster, a leading ornithologist, and Harold Bowditch were corresponding about a sandpiper that had been found with what appeared to be a cast on its leg. They thought it might shed light on the debate over Long's woodcock. After studying the specimen and consulting with colleagues, they determined that the leg was broken and that the "cast" was created when the bird's feathers adhered to fluids seeping from the injury. In 1988 the specimen, which was stored in Harvard's Museum of Comparative Zoology, was X-rayed and the leg was found to be out of joint. There had been considerable bleeding at the site of the injury, which had clotted and eventually calcified, creating a practical but natural cast.[24] Long's description of his woodcock and the casts described by his informants seem very similar to the "cast" on this sandpiper. It is very likely that they found birds with similar injuries. The stories about birds setting their own broken legs and applying casts to them were a product of Long's vivid imagination. His assumption that birds are capable of such things made it that much easier for him to leap to this conclusion.

Theodore Roosevelt and the Nature Fakers

One of the most pleasing letters that Burroughs received in response to his "Real and Sham Natural History" article came from Theodore Roosevelt. The President praised the article and invited Burroughs to travel with him to Yellowstone Park. Thus began a long friendship and correspondence, in which they continued to discuss sham natural history, focusing their criticism on Long. In addition, Roosevelt often wrote privately to Long's publishers and to those who wrote articles in his support urging them not to provide a forum for Long's views.[25]

The President was an accomplished naturalist and he encouraged Burroughs' work and read drafts of some of his articles. Roosevelt's views of animal behavior were not so mechanistic as were Burroughs'. He felt, for example, that the relative roles of learning and instinct varied in different groups of animals; that learning played a greater role in the lives of monkeys than salamanders. He often urged Burroughs to moderate the tone of his articles. Both lamented the fact that Long continued to publish his stories. Burroughs urged his friend to speak out publicly against Long. Roosevelt was eager to attack, but found it difficult to do so as President. Finally, however, in 1907 he felt he needed a diversion and granted an interview with a reporter in which he spoke his mind about Long, Jack London, and other offending writers.[26] The reporter was Edward B. Clark, a friend of the President's, who asked Roosevelt to revise and approve the written interview.[27] The article, "Roosevelt on the Nature Fakirs," reignited the controversy and with the President involved, the flames burned even hotter than before. The term "nature fakirs" quickly altered to "nature fakers," which became the name of the entire controversy.

In Clark's interview the President repeated Burroughs' original complaints, criticized an assortment of authors, and again turned to William J. Long. He poked holes in a number of his stories, giving special attention to Long's tale of a wolf killing a caribou with a single bite to the heart. "I have seen scores of animals that have been killed by wolves;" he said, "the killing or crippling bites were always in the throat, flank, or ham." A naturalist who has seen hundreds of wolf kills verified his opinion. A bite in the chest area must be extremely rare and, even if it were inflicted, could not pierce the heart, Roosevelt argued, because of the limited size of the wolf's teeth and gape of its jaws, the breadth and toughness of the caribou's rib cage, and the unusual position the wolf would have to assume in order to make the bite. He required that Long "produce eye-witnesses and affidavits."[28]

The President was upset over Long's books being used in schools. If they were presented as fairy tales, there would be no problem. He had no complaint, for example, with Kipling's *Jungle Book* tales. But Long's were being presented to innocent students as the truth.

The preservation of the useful and beautiful animal and bird life of the country depends largely upon creating in the young an interest in the life of the woods and fields. If the child mind is fed with stories that are false to nature, the children will go to the haunts of the animal only to meet with disappointment. The result will be disbelief, and the death of interest. The men who misinterpret nature and replace fact with fiction, undo the work of those who in the love of nature interpret it aright.[29]

It was impossible for Long to take this quietly. In a letter to Roosevelt he proclaimed, "There are two noticeable things about your article: its bad taste and its denials and assertions which are too easily disproved; it is not worthy of a gentleman's consideration. Unfortunately your high position gives weight even to your foolish words; and for the sake of the truth, and of the thousands who read and love my books, I am obliged to answer you publicly." A week later he sent Roosevelt a notarized affidavit by a Sioux Indian who reported having seen wolves kill cattle and horses by biting in the chest region. The President did not answer, nor did he answer a letter received a few days later from a man who reported seeing a deer killed in Michigan by wolf bites in back of its forelegs.[30]

Long's public reply to the President was given an entire page in the *New York Times Sunday Magazine*. In it he both asserted the truthfulness of his own stories and attacked Roosevelt as a bloodthirsty killer.

The idea of Mr. Roosevelt assuming the part of a naturalist is absurd. He is a hunter. He knows little or nothing concerning the beasts he hunts except how they try to escape death. He knows the outside of the animal; he collects their heads and hides and treasures their exterior proportions. Who is he to write "I don't believe for a minute that some of these nature writers know the heart of the wild things." As to that, I find after carefully reading two of his big books that every time Mr. Roosevelt gets near the heart of a wild thing he invariably puts a bullet through it. From his own records I have reckoned a full thousand hearts which he has known thus intimately.[31]

The public response to the controversy was much more vocal now that the President was at its center. Political cartoonists took full advantage. One cartoon depicted Long and other nature writers being welcomed into Roosevelt's "Ananias Club for Liars"—Long walking forward, pig under his arm, saying, "Pigs make their nests in Chicago." Another had the President hunting, rifle in hand, confronted by a rabbit carrying the sign, "Immune, a friend of John Burroughs," and a mountain lion with, "Immune, testified against the fakirs." Yet another cartoon represented the principals as children, with Willie Long attacking Teddy with a pen, while Johnnie Burroughs hides behind the presidential chair.[32]

In an effort to deliver a final, fatal blow to the Nature Fakers, Clark, with the assistance of Edward W. Nelson, future chief of the U. S. Biological Survey, put together an article summarizing the opinions of a number of professional naturalists. "Real Naturalists on Nature Faking" included comments by such outstanding scientists of the day as William T. Hornaday, director of the New York Zoological Park; J. A. Allen, curator of mammalogy and ornithology of the American Museum of Natural History; and C. Hart Merriam, chief of the Biological Survey. They all testified to Roosevelt's qualifications as a naturalist and strongly supported the President's position. An accompanying article by Roosevelt, "Nature Fakers," restated his views and echoed his private letters to Long's editorial supporters. "Men of this stamp will necessarily arise from time to time, some in one walk of life, some in another. Our quarrel is not with these men, but with those who given them their chance."[33]

The heat of the controversy cooled, although its embers glowed for many years. One author of children's animal stories reminisced that the controversy made him realize "that if I ever made a bad break in regard to my natural history statements that I was doomed." He was just one of many writers who began to exercise greater care in his stories. Publishers, too, became more careful in their selection of manuscripts. Long, although he did continue to write some nature stories, turned his attention to English and American literature and wrote a number of very successful textbooks. He did not publish another nature book until 1919, the year of Roosevelt's death.[34]

But this did not bring an end to Long's books that Burroughs and Roosevelt had criticized. Ginn & Co. kept some of his school readers in print for years; one of them remained in print until 1940. Part of the reason for this may have been that his publisher, Edwin Ginn, shared some of Long's views. Ginn was a Unitarian and Long had been criticized for his Unitarian leanings while he was a Congregational minister. Ginn was also an idealist, founding the World Peace Foundation and envisioning a time when animals would not be killed for food. Nevertheless, Ginn & Co. kept the books in print long after Ginn's death in 1914. The simple truth is that there was a demand for Long's books. They were good reading and presented an appealing vision of nature.[35]

The Underlying Issues

The Nature Fakers controversy was fought over the responsibility of nature writers, whether writers of nature essays or wild animal stories, to report honest and accurate natural history. An important underlying issue was that of the nature of animal mentality. Burroughs considered animals to be bundles of instincts that are activated by their environment. Roosevelt was much more flexible in his views, allowing the "higher" animals some ability to learn from experience and to use some degree of reasoning. Long, on the other hand, believed that animals think much like humans. Neither Burroughs nor Roosevelt agreed with Long's view and they accused him of anthropomorphic fantasies. "Nature Faker," then, can be used in two often overlapping ways. It can refer to a person who fakes facts and to one who interprets animal behavior with excessive anthropomorphism. Both are sins against scientific objectivity, but does this account for the heat, duration, and popularity of the debate?

An important element in the life of the controversy was the prominence of the accusers, John Burroughs and Theodore Roosevelt. It was simply impossible to ignore their charges. They were both sincere, articulate, and forceful in expressing their views, and there was a receptive public already interested in nature and prepared for the debate. The issue of truthfulness was an important one, but it was not sufficient to account for the magnitude of the controversy. The question of the nature of animal psychology ran deeper, reaching to basic assumptions about natural history and the interpretation of animal behavior. Psychology at that time offered only the options of instinct and reason, with little in between. Darwin, however, had shown that evolution had produced a wide range of possibilities. Wild animal stories were a response to this realization and they provided visions of the natural world that responded to the Darwinian perspective and resonated in their readers.[36] They emphasized the kinship between humans and other animals. They also reflected growing public interest in animal welfare, as well as nascent ideas about animal rights. Long's stories reflected similar views, although they originated from his religious views, rather than Darwinism. His efforts, though, were severely compromised by his carelessness in the ways he observed animals in the field and interpreted their behavior.

As it turned out, many of the Nature Fakers' views that animals (at least some of them) could reason made a positive contribution, countering the erroneous assumption that even the most evolutionarily "advanced" animals are governed only by instinct. Jack London, for example, argued that animals can display types of reasoning that are not necessarily the "abstract reasoning" that characterizes humans. Animal psychology is much more complex than most scientists of the time were willing to acknowledge—a prejudice that inhibited progress in their field. Donald Griffin, for example, has argued, "It seems possible that the variety of communications conveyed by the dances of bees might have been discovered by Frisch in the 1920s, if anything like complex communication among insects had not been so utterly unthinkable." He also argued, "It seems more likely than not that mental experiences, like many other characters, are widespread, at least among multicellular animals, but differ greatly in nature and complexity."[37] Ethologists such as Jane Goodall, Dian Fossey, and Biruté Galdikas have demonstrated that primates have capabilities remarkably similar to humans. Where many Nature Fakers erred, however, was in interpreting the mental states of wild animals primarily in human terms.

There was a third issue underlying the Nature Fakers debate. In 1910 there appeared a short story, "The Nature Faker," that satirized the nature lovers of the day. It opened with a description of a wealthy gentleman who, having been rejected in love, decided to become a lover of nature. There are, after all, no

disappointments or heartaches in that kind of love. The description of his estate, created from an abandoned farm in Connecticut, is a delightful spoof of
nature lovers (and, probably, of Ernest Thompson Seton's own Connecticut
estate):

> The game preserve was his own special care and pleasure. It consisted of two
> hundred acres of dense forest and hills and ridges and rocks. It was filled with
> mysterious caves, deep chasms, tiny gurgling streams, nestling springs, and wild
> laurel. . . . Around the preserve was a high fence stout enough to keep poachers on
> the outside and to persuade the wild animals that inhabited it to linger inside. . . .
> Every day, in sunshine or in rain, entering through a private gate, Herrick would
> explore this holy of holies. . . . In time he grew to think he knew and understood
> the inhabitants of this wild place of which he was the overlord. He looked upon
> them not as his tenants, but as his guests. And when they fled from him in terror to
> caves and hollow tree-trunks, he wished he might call them back and explain he
> was their friend, that it was due to him they lived in peace. He was glad they were
> happy. He was glad it was through him that, undisturbed, they could live the
> simple life.[38]

This mockery did not directly address the issues of animal intelligence or
accurate observations that were at the core of the original debate. It had lost
touch with the earlier meanings of the term and turned the Nature Faker into a
nature sentimentalizer: one who is interested more in his or her feelings about
nature than in the intrusive reality of nature itself. "What the nature-lover
really desires is not to be a part of nature, but to be a part of himself," wrote a
critic of the nature cult. "He could cast away 'worldly cares' and city life with
its difficulties, as well as farm life with *its* difficulties, so that he might be, like
the inhabitants of the Garden of Eden, 'free to roam and to reminisce under the
pines.'"[39]

The sentimental view of nature was also a focus of a debate over goals within
the nature study movement. This educational movement contributed to important pedagogical reforms and the development of progressive education. Some
educators saw the goals of nature study as improving the sensory, discrimina-
tory, and other mental faculties of their students. Others believed it to be teaching the methodological approaches of the sciences. Still others felt that the goal
should be to teach useful skills. Finally, there was a strong contingent of educators who believed that education should build upon the child's enjoyment of
nature and emphasize its aesthetic and inspirational value. The conflict over
these four rationales was a significant factor that eventually led to the disin-
tegration of the movement. The Nature Fakers controversy was a literary expression of the conflict between the fourth goal, since called the natural harmony rationale, and the scientific methodology approach.[40]

Liberty Hyde Bailey was a strong proponent of the natural harmony rationale. He pointed out, "Nature-study is not science. It is not knowledge. It is not
facts. It is spirit. It is concerned with the child's outlook on the world." It is, he

believed, an attempt to bring students into a personal relationship and sympathy with nature. An opponent within the movement argued, "The idea that nature-study is not science leads to serious results, the responsibility for accuracy seems to disappear, and much of the nonsense and weak sentimentalism that has brought discredit on the subject is due to this fundamental error."[41] The leaders of the natural harmony approach (and certainly Bailey, a distinguished scientist) never intended that accuracy be sacrificed, even though they felt that the scientific approach to nature was not sufficient in itself.

Burroughs would have been the last to argue that scientific knowledge alone is sufficient for the nature writer. He wrote that he must have facts, "but I must give them my own flavor." This human element is what makes nature writing literature. William J. Long appears to have been an honorable and sincere man, but he seems to have sometimes made the error of confusing his sentiments with what he was observing. His readers, though, found their own sentiments reflected in his books, and thus the attacks upon Long were also attacks upon them. It is not surprising then, that the controversy was so lively. Long was right in arguing that the sympathetic appreciation of nature must go beyond scientific knowledge. (Unfortunately, his was an antiscience and anti-Darwinian stance.) Scientific knowledge gains personal significance only when it ceases to be an alienated abstraction and becomes psychologically meaningful. The same is true of all experiences of nature. This personal significance, in addition to scientific accuracy, is necessary if we are to have a populace motivated, as both the Nature Fakers and their critics intended to preserve wildlife and our environment.

Media Manifestations

The realistic wild animal story went into a decline in the decades following the Nature Fakers controversy. It was revived and revitalized in the 1940s with the publication of Rachel Carson's *Under the Sea-Wind* and Sally Carrighar's *One Day on Beetle Rock.* Twenty years later, Farley Mowat's very popular *Never Cry Wolf* hit the bookstores. In those twenty years, the animal story leaped to the new media, film and television. Popular interest in nature and what came to be called the environment began to grow as the twentieth century entered its final decades until it reached a level equaled only by that at the beginning of the century. This, again, created a booming market for nature books, films, and television programs. It is not surprising that some of those who created products for that market were accused again of presenting distorted accounts of nature and wildlife.[42]

Farley Mowat and *Never Cry Wolf* received early criticism after the book first appeared in 1963. His autobiographical account of studying wolves in Northern Canada at the behest of the Canadian Wildlife Service presented the public with a new view of wolves and reported a number of amazing exploits, from experimenting with a diet of mice to crawling into an occupied wolf den. But was what he reported factual? A. W. F. Banfield, who had supervised Mowat's field work (whom Mowat lampooned as the "Chief"), was not pleased with the book. He characterized it as "semi-fictional." Mowat's "career with the Federal Government lasted only about six months," he reported. "As the reader is well able to confirm, Farley wasn't cut out to be a civil servant." (*Never Cry Wolf* certainly confirms this point.) Banfield was obviously displeased with Mowat's characterization of the Wildlife Service, including its supposedly bungled job of supplying his field expedition. As to this, Banfield offered that Mowat had provided the list of supplies that he wanted and all had been provided him. Furthermore, he was not alone in the wilderness, but part of a team of three biologists and was never alone with the wolves. More to the point, Banfield complained that Mowat "borrowed" some of the conclusions in Banfield's own report of the survey's results. In addition, during his training Mowat had read a number of books on wolves, including Adolph Murie's *The Wolves of Mount McKinley.* "Any resemblance between *Never Cry Wolf* and that book is *not* coincidental," he argued. "Much is familiar, including first names for the wolves and the crawl into the burrow. 'Squib' disproved no scientific concepts about wolves—only his own misconceptions." If Banfield is correct, Mowat had fictionalized his account and used it as a vehicle to popularize not only his own discoveries, but those of others. Mowat was not pleased with Banfield's review. However, his humorous response, written in the voice of the wolf Uncle Albert, did not refute these points.[43]

Another zoologist came to a similar conclusion after reading Mowat's published accounts of his study and the report he submitted to the Wildlife Service. "[*Never Cry Wolf*] is based on a grain of fact," he reported, "he did work for the Wildlife Service, and he did observe wolves (although in much less detail than is indicated in [the book]). However, that is close to being the full extent of the fact behind the book. The remainder is a blend of fancy, fantasy, and the published data of other workers, to whom no reference is made in the book." This view was supported by John Goddard, who interviewed Mowat and studied documents at the National Archives of Canada and Mowat's personal papers at McMaster University. He reported that Mowat spent less than four weeks, only ninety hours, observing wolves. Mowat did not lack companionship; he was assisting his friend Andy Lowrie in the study, and Mowat's wife joined him for a couple of months. Goddard, who found numerous discrepancies between the facts and what Mowat reported in his early books, quoted Mowat as saying, "I never let the facts get in the way of the truth!"[44]

Although Mowat played loose with the facts regarding the circumstances of his study and the sources of his information, it appears that the information about wolves in *Never Cry Wolf* was correct. Although fictionalized, the book cannot be faulted as nature-faking on its natural history. Whether he should be faulted for misrepresenting his account as nonfiction is another matter. Ernest Thompson Seton fictionalized his wild animal stories, but at least he made it clear to readers that his animal heroes were composites based on observations and tales of many animals. And Thoreau told his readers that he spent two years at Walden Pond, although his book described his experiences in the cycle of one.

Must the nature writer be completely honest, so long as the natural history is accurate? In doing the magic of creating literature, must the writer reveal the tricks? Where is the boundary between fiction and nonfiction, especially in the field of creative nonfiction, to which much of nature literature belongs? Loren Eiseley did not tell his readers that many of his "autobiographical" essays were fictionalized. Nor did Annie Dillard tell readers of *Pilgrim at Tinker Creek* that the incident of the cat leaving bloody paw prints on her chest had really happened to someone else, or that she never saw a Giant Water Bug suck the life out of a frog; these omissions had upset many scholars.[45] Eiseley, Dillard, and other nature writers present literary personas and incidents designed to achieve specific literary goals. The line between fact and fiction is often a continuum, rather than a sharp boundary. Authors should be allowed a good deal of literary flexibility, but there comes a point at which representing fiction as autobiography has entered the realm of deception and Mowat appeared to have reached that point.

The translation of *Never Cry Wolf* from print to film only increased the gap between autobiographical fact and what the audience was given. Filmmakers are notorious for changing novels as they adapt them to a different medium and also add their own creative flair. In this case, not only did they rewrite Mowat's tale, they also had to cross the bridge from nature writing to nature cinematography. It is relatively easy for an author to put thoughts onto paper. It is more difficult to make nature perform on cue for the camera. Filmmakers often cannot wait and must stage "natural" events. Nearly a third of the expense of filming Disney's version of *Never Cry Wolf* (1983) was invested in shooting the six minutes of scenes in which the Mowat character ran naked amid a herd of caribou as he observed wolf kill behavior. The director, Carroll Ballard, used horsemen and helicopters repeatedly to locate and drive a herd of domesticated caribou into camera range. The animals did not cooperate and, after weeks of effort, the filming of these scenes had to wait until the next year. In addition, the trained wolves used in the film had to be taught how to hunt.[46]

It is not unreasonable for filmmakers to use this sort of manipulation to make a nature film, so long as the resulting depiction of nature is not unduly distorted. Filmmakers working on Walt Disney's True-Life Adventure series sometimes fenced their subject into compounds of up to 50 acres in size. "It was a short cut," one of his writers pointed out. "We're not faking nature." In a sense, these devices are akin to a writer's selection from, and manipulation of,

284 ■ RALPH H. LUTTS

experience in order to craft a story or essay. The extraordinary film version of James Oliver Curwood's *The Grizzly King* (1916) went to even greater extremes. In addition to using trained bears, the film, titled *The Bear* (Columbia, 1989), included animation and Jim Henson puppetry to supplement the live "actors." The greatest criticism of this extraordinarily beautiful and emotionally effective film, however, was directed at the way it anthropomorphized bears. Pauline Kael called it "a nature fake" and went on to write, "It's saying that we shouldn't kill bears, because they're so much like us—after it fakes the evidence that they are."[47] In addition, the basic premise of both book and film, that an adult male bear will adopt an orphaned cub, stretches credulity. Book and film do, however, make it clear that the adult bear initially wanted nothing to do with the cub, although he relented when the cub provided comfort by licking his gunshot wound.

Anthropomorphism has been a frequent problem in nature films. Movies in Walt Disney's True-Life Adventure series were severely criticized for just this. This film series, which began with *Seal Island* (1948), established a new cinematic standard for nature films that has had a lasting influence on nature films and videos and introduced millions of people to the wonders of the natural world. Disney, nevertheless, approached these films as entertainment. "Any time we saw an animal doing something with style or personality—say a bear scratching its back," said one of his writers, "—we were quick to capitalize on it." As a result, they ended up selecting footage that emphasized the humanlike quality of wild animals. In addition, Disney went out of his way to present some animals as heroes and others as villains. When a wasp did battle with a tarantula in *The Living Desert* (1953), the wasp was cast as the hero. Disney further anthropomorphized the animals in his True-Life tales by using cinematic tricks to make them appear to dance to music or by selecting music that fit the pattern of their movements. In the same film, a pair of scorpions mated to the tune of a square dance, complete with a caller. The series' director was asked "how we possibly [can] get animals to move in time to music." Disney was stunned by the criticism, but he cut much of the cutesy stuff out of subsequent films.[48]

The countless wildlife films and television programs that were inspired and influenced by Disney's True-Life Adventure series had to come to terms with similar issues. Many avoided anthropomorphism by emphasizing the animals' life cycles and the Darwinian struggle in their story lines. And there is a continuing emphasis on the threats that humans pose for wildlife (which tended to place the animals on higher moral ground than people). In their efforts to create human interest, however, others fell, to varying degrees, into traps similar to those into which Disney had stumbled. It is difficult to avoid overly humanizing animals, even unwittingly. One reviewer found that the narrative structure of programs on the Discovery Channel's "Wild Discoveries" show was similar to that of television situation comedies.

I saw one of these recently in which a jackal family had a teen-aged daughter who finds a suitor but when he comes to visit the father threatens him—though the suitor "exhibits himself in his most submissive posture." The daughter leaves home with the suitor. I channel surfed to the Family Channel and saw the same show with this exception: the daughter was wearing a dress and they left in the boyfriend's car.[49]

The sheer volume of nature films that flood the market, particularly via television, have led inadvertently to another problem. Viewers would be bored to tears by a film that faithfully recorded the average walk in the woods; they would see very little happening. Thus, filmmakers must select sequences in which there is something happening; where there is action. As a result, nature films unwittingly raise expectations and, thus, disappointment when their viewers head out to see the real thing. Oftentimes, they feel that nature is just not "real" enough. While on a safari in East Africa, Colin Turnbull met a couple who planned to visit Disneyland. They told him that "they expected to find Disneyland both more 'real' and more 'natural.'"[50]

Richard Schickel argued that children try to interpret the world in terms of themselves. They invest the objects around them with their own personality. However, as a child matures:

> he learns that there are other forces in the world beyond his own personality, and education rightly conceived is the process by which he learns to value those forces, mastering and turning to his own uses those that he can, respecting those he cannot. Disney never could seem to learn this simple distinction, and confronted with things that were inexplicable to him, he either turned away in disgust or willfully falsified them by reshaping them in terms that he understood and approved.[51]

Disney was not alone in this misapprehension. Interpreting wild animals in terms of our own personality is a common phenomenon that inhibits our ability to come to terms with wild animals, organic evolution, and the natural world.

The popular "save the whale" and other "save the critter" films of the 1990s displayed this relationship with wild animals. Perhaps this is inevitable, given that they were produced as "Family" films, which means they appealed to children. *Free Willy* (Warner, 1993), *Free Willy II* (Warner, 1995), *The Amazing Panda Adventure* (Warner, 1995), and *Fly Away Home* (Columbia, 1996)[52] each featured a youthful protagonist who bonded with one or more animals. The bond between child and animal was one of the friendship between child and pet. In the process, the wild animals were anthropomorphized—outrageously so in the Willy films. Still, in each, the child heroes saved their animal friends from the evil deeds of humans, most often by releasing them to the wild. On one level, this symbolizes the child's growing to recognize that the Orca or Canada Geese are autonomous creatures with beings independent of his or her own personality. The audience is left, nevertheless, with a humanized image of wild animals. There is an advantage to this in that viewers recognize their kinship with wild animals. On another level, they are denied the opportunity to recognize and understand their "otherness," which we must learn to respect if we really want to save them.

We *do* share many qualities in common with other animals, in varying degrees depending on the species. It is important to recognize these commonalities and this kinship. It is equally important, however, to recognize their differences from humans. We cannot respect other species unless we also respect their "otherness." Turning wild animals into furry and feathery people may satisfy our sentimental fancies, but it does violence to the animals' nature by making them something they are not.

We live in a world of our own psychological creation, as well as in one that has an existence apart from our own minds. The inner world is of enormous importance, but it should not be in too great conflict with the outer one. As the conflict is reduced, nature-faking fades. Nature Fakers are still with us and we must take care to avoid their seductions. We must take equal care, though, that in rooting out the fakers we do not also rob ourselves of our ability to address our whole environment as whole human beings.

Notes

Acknowledgments: I thank Hampshire College, which provided a research grant, and Elizabeth Burroughs Kelley and Frances Long Woodbridge for their valuable assistance. I also thank Kenneth Hoffman, Vicky Hovde, Douglas Riggs, David Smith, and Arthur Westing for their comments on this essay.

1. This sketch is intended only to suggest the scope of what we now call environmental interests at the beginning of the twentieth century. For detailed examinations, see Samuel P. Hays, *Conservation and the Gospel of Efficiency* (Cambridge: Harvard University Press, 1959); Hans Huth, *Nature and the American* (Berkeley: University of California Press, 1957); Peter J. Schmidt, *Back to Nature: The Arcadian Myth in Urban America* (1969, repr. Baltimore: Johns Hopkins University Press, 1990); Roderick Nash, *Wilderness and the American Mind*, 3rd ed. (New Haven: Yale University Press, 1982); and David E. Shi, *The Simple Life: Plain Living and High Thinking in American Culture* (New York: Oxford University Press, 1985).

2. Henry James, Jr., *The Nation* (January 27, 1876), 66.

3. Clara Barrus, ed., *The Life and Letters of John Burroughs*, 2 vols. (Boston: Houghton Mifflin, 1925), vol. 1:285; Mary E. Burtt, "Introduction," in John Burroughs, *Birds and Bees* (Boston: Houghton Mifflin, 1887), 3–6; sales figures clipped to a letter from Burroughs to Houghton Mifflin, August 20, 1907, Houghton Mifflin Papers, Houghton Library, Harvard University.

4. John Burroughs, *Wake Robin*, Riverside Ed. (Boston: Houghton Mifflin, 1895), xvi.

5. For a detailed discussion of this controversy, see Ralph H. Lutts, *The Nature Fakers: Wildlife, Science & Sentiment* (Golden, Colo.: Fulcrum Publishing, 1990).

6. John Burroughs, "Real and Sham Natural History," *Atlantic Monthly* 91 (March 1903): 298, 300.

7. Ernest Thompson Seton, *Wild Animals I Have Known* (New York: Charles Scribner's Sons, 1898), 9; William J. Long, *School of the Woods* (Boston: Ginn, 1902), vii.

8. Dallas Lore Sharp to Burroughs, December 20, 1902, Sharp Papers, Boston University Library.

9. Roberts also avoided a public debate with Burroughs. On Seton's life and work, see Ernest Thompson Seton, *Trail of an Artist-Naturalist* (New York: Charles Scribner's Sons, 1940); John Henry Wadland, *Ernest Thompson Seton: Man in Nature and the Progressive Era, 1880–1915* (New York: Arno Press, 1978); and H. Allen Anderson, *The Chief: Ernest Thompson Seton and the Changing West* (College Station: Texas A&M University Press, 1986). On Seton's influence on Peterson, see Ernest Thompson Seton, *Two Little Savages* (New York: Doubleday, Page, 1903), 385–393; and Roger Tory Peterson, *A Field Guide to the Birds*, rev. ed. (Boston: Houghton Mifflin, 1939), v.

10. Seton, *Trail of an Artist-Naturalist*, 367–371.

11. Elizabeth Burroughs Kelley, *John Burroughs: Naturalist* (New York: Exposition Press, 1959), 175. See also, Lutts, *Nature Fakers*, 45–49.

12. John Burroughs, "The Literary Treatment of Nature," *Atlantic Monthly* 94 (July 1904): 42. In his autobiography, *Trail of an Artist-Naturalist*, Seton misquoted this passage to his advantage: "Mr. Thompson Seton, as an artist and raconteur, ranks by far the highest in his field; he is truly delightful" (371). When Burroughs reprinted this essay in one of his books, the sentence was altered to read, "Mr. Thompson Seton, as an artist and *raconteur*, ranks by far the highest in his field, but in reading his works as natural history, one has to be constantly on guard against his romantic tendencies" (*Ways of Nature* [Boston: Houghton Mifflin, 1905], 203).

13. Ernest Thompson Seton, "Fable & Woodmyth: The Fate of Little Mucky," *Century* 67 (February 1904): 500. Seton to Burroughs, November 18, 1907, collection of Burroughs' granddaughter, Elizabeth Burroughs Kelley.

14. Dorothy G. Wayman, "Pastor Irked T. R. on Hunting Ethics," *Boston Sunday Globe*, August 17, 1952, 1, 38; "Retired Cleric, 86, A Noted Writer on Outdoor Life," *Stamford* (Conn.) *Advocate*, November 10, 1952, 1, 16; interview with Long's daughter, Frances Long Woodbridge, August 11–13, 1979. The only extended examination of Long's life and work appears in Lutts, *Nature Fakers*.

15. William J. Long, "The Modern School of Nature-Study and its Critics," *North American Review* 176 (May 1903): 687.

16. Long, "Modern School," 689–690.

17. Long, "Modern School," 690–691.

18. Long, "Modern School," 693.

19. This interpretation is based on my reading of the literature and was confirmed in an interview with Frances Long Woodbridge, August 11–13, 1979.

20. Long, "Modern School," 693. Less than two years after the beginning of this controversy, which called into question Long's powers as an observer, Long went blind. An item on the first page of the December 10, 1904 *New York Times* noted, "For years one of his eyes was weak, and chiefly on that account he retired from the ministry in 1903. Last week he lost the sight of both eyes. He is confined in a dark room and bears his affliction with cheerfulness." He later recovered his sight and his blindness may have been stress-related. See Lutts, *Nature Fakers*, 86–87, 222–223 n. 36.

21. John Burroughs, "Current Misconceptions in Natural History," *Century* 67 (February 1904): 515. See also Burroughs' essays in *Ways of Nature* (Boston: Houghton Mifflin, 1905) and *Leaf and Tendril* (Boston: Houghton Mifflin, 1908). William J. Long, *Northern Trails* (Boston: Ginn, 1905), xvi.

22. William J. Long, *A Little Brother to the Bear* (Boston: Ginn, 1903), 101–116; William Morton Wheeler, "Woodcock Surgery," *Science* 19 (February 26, 1904): 349.

23. Ellen Hayes, *Science* 19 (April 22, 1904): 625; William J. Long, "Science, Nature and Criticism," *Science* 19 (May 13, 1904): 760–767. For other parts of the correspondence, see *Science* 19 (March 4, 1904): 387–389; (April 1, 1904): 550–551; (April 22, 1904): 667–675; and (May 13, 1904): 623–625.

24. Lutts, *Nature Fakers*, 81–82, 221–222 n. 24.

25. Elting Morison et al., *The Letters of Theodore Roosevelt*, 8 vols. (Cambridge: Harvard University Press, 1951–1954), vol. 3:441–443, 467–470; vol. 5:39–41, 700–704.

26. Roosevelt to Burroughs, August 1, 1903; Roosevelt to Burroughs, May 29, 1905; Roosevelt to Burroughs, November 28, 1903; Burroughs to Roosevelt, December 3, 1903; and Roosevelt to Burroughs, October 16, 1905; all in Theodore Roosevelt Papers, Library of Congress, Washington, D.C. See also, Morison et. al., *Letters*, vol. 5:617.

27. Edward B. Clark to Roosevelt, February 6, 1907, Theodore Roosevelt Papers, Library of Congress; Clark to Hermann Hagedorn, December 30, 1921, Theodore Roosevelt Collection, Houghton Library, Harvard University.

28. Edward B. Clark, "Roosevelt on the Nature Fakirs," *Everybody's Magazine* 16 (June 1907): 770–774.

29. Clark, "Roosevelt on the Nature Fakirs," 774.

30. William J. Long to Roosevelt, May 22, 1907; Long to Roosevelt, May 29, 1907; affidavit dated May 24, 1907; George R. Smith to Roosevelt, June 2, 1907; all in Theodore Roosevelt Papers, Library of Congress.

31. William J. Long, "'I Propose to Smoke Roosevelt Out'—Dr. Long," *New York Times Sunday Magazine*, June 2, 1907, pt. 5, 2. Long submitted this letter to a number of newspapers throughout the United States, several of which published portions of it.

32. *New York Evening Journal*, May 24, 1907, 22; Albert Shaw, *A Cartoon History of Roosevelt's Career* (New York: Review of Reviews, 1910), 159; cartoon by Frank Wing, Theodore Roosevelt Collection, Houghton Library, Harvard University.

33. Edward B. Clark, "Real Naturalists on Nature Faking," *Everybody's Magazine* 17 (September 1907): 423–427; Theodore Roosevelt, "'Nature Fakers,'" *Everybody's Magazine* 17 (September 1907): 430.

34. Clarence Hawkes, *The Light That Did Not Fail* (Boston: Chapman & Grimes, 1935), 118. Long's English literature text, first published in 1909, was in print for sixty-three years; the enlarged edition did not go out of print until 1972. He published three nature books, statements of his understanding of animal life, in the four years following Roosevelt's death and then returned to writing American and English literature textbooks: William J. Long, *English Literature* (Boston: Ginn, 1909); *How Animals Talk, and Other Pleasant Studies of Birds and Beasts* (New York: Harper & Bros., 1919); *Wood-Folk Comedies: The Play of Wild-Animal Life on a Natural Stage* (New York: Harper & Bros., 1920); *Mother Nature: A Study of Animal Life and Death* (New York: Harper & Bros., 1923).

35. The dates at which Long's books went out of print, when available, are shown in the Long bibliography in Lutts, *Nature Fakers*, 205–207. Also see, Ralph H. Lutts,

"John Burroughs and the Honey Bee: Bridging Science and Emotion in Environmental Writing," in *Sharp Eyes: Proceedings of a Conference on John Burroughs and Environmental Writing at the State University of New York College at Oneonta, July* 1994, ed. Charlotte Zoe Walker, Kay D. Benjamin, and George Dunham (New York: SUNY Oneonta, 1995), 54–55.

36. Robert H. MacDonald, "The Revolt Against Instinct: The Animal Stories of Seton and Roberts," *Canadian Literature,* no. 84 (Spring 1980), 18–29; Thomas R. Dunlap, "'The Old Kinship of Earth': Science, Man and Nature in the Animal Stories of Charles G. D. Roberts," *Journal of Canadian Studies* 22 (Spring 1987): 104–120; Dunlap, "The Realistic Animal Story: Ernest Thompson Seton, Charles Roberts, and Darwinism," *Forest & Conservation History* 36 (April 1992): 56–62.

37. Jack London, "The Other Animals," *Collier's* 41 (September 5, 1908): 10–11, 25–26; Donald R. Griffin, *The Question of Animal Awareness: Evolutionary Continuity and Mental Experience,* rev. and enlarged (New York: Rockefeller University Press, 1981), 134, 170. See also, Griffin, *Animal Thinking* (Cambridge: Harvard University Press, 1984).

38. Richard Harding Davis, "The Nature Faker," *Collier's* 46 (December 10, 1910): 17. This is probably a parody of Charles G. D. Roberts' description of Seton's two-hundred-acre Connecticut estate in "Home of a Naturalist," *Country Life in America* 5 (December 1903): 152–156.

39. Norman Foerster, "The Nature Cult Today," *The Nation* 94 (April 11, 1912): 358.

40. Tyree G. Minton, "The History of the Nature-Study Movement and Its Role in the Development of Environmental Education," Ed.D. diss., University of Massachusetts, Amherst, 1980; Richard Raymond Olmsted, "The Nature-Study Movement in American Education," Ed.D. diss., Indiana University, 1967, 64–157. The Nature Fakers controversy and the conflict between the natural harmony and scientific methodology rationales for nature study are also expressions (although clouded and distorted by a variety of issues) of the tensions between what Donald Worster has called arcadian and imperial ecology. Arcadian ecology, typified by Gilbert White, author of *The Natural History and Antiquities of Selborne* and a progenitor of literary natural history, emphasizes a holistic fellow feeling with nature. Imperial ecology, with its detached analysis and desire for managerial control, is an extension of Baconian science. Donald Worster, *Nature's Economy: A History of Ecological Ideas* (1977; repr. Cambridge: Cambridge University Press, 1985).

41. L. H. Bailey, *The Nature-Study Idea* (New York: Doubleday, Page, 1903), 5; W. E. Praeger, *The Nature-Study Review* 4 (February 1908): 43.

42. Rachel L. Carson, *Under the Sea-Wind: A Naturalist's Picture of Ocean Life* (New York: Simon & Schuster, 1941); Sally Carrighar, *One Day on Beetle Rock* (New York: Alfred A. Knopf, 1944); Farley Mowat, *Never Cry Wolf* (Boston: Little, Brown, 1963).

43. A. W. F. Banfield, Review, "Never Cry Wolf," *Canadian Field-Naturalist* 78 (January–March 1964): 52–54; F. M. [Farley Mowat], Letter to the Editor, *Canadian Field-Naturalist* 78 (July–September 1964): 206.

44. Douglas H. Pimlott, Review, "Never Cry Wolf," *Journal of Wildlife Management* 30 (January 1966): 236. For a more generous review of the book, see A. M. Stebler, "Never Cry Wolf," *Journal of Wildlife Management* 29 (October 1965):906–907. John Goddard, "A Real Whopper" [http://www.enews.com/magazines/sn/archive/

960501–002.html], seen July 10, 1997 (this is the text of an article that appeared in *Saturday Night*, May 1, 1996).

45. Gale E. Christianson, *Fox at the Wood's Edge: A Biography of Loren Eiseley* (New York: Henry Holt, 1990), 110, 279–280, 392–394, 412–414; Annie Dillard, *Pilgrim at Tinker Creek* (New York: Harper's Magazine Press, 1974), 1–2, 5–6. Dillard is reported to have acknowledged at the 1996 Key West Seminar on Nature Writing that she did not experience all the incidents she described in her book. For a discussion of this, see the exchange of messages on the Association for the Study of Literature and the Environment (ASLE) Discussion List at its web site archive, "Dillard's Bug" [http:// wsrv.clas.virginia.edu/~djp2n/discussion/home.html], mostly in February 1997. See also "Fiction/Nonfiction" at the same site, mostly in June 1996.

46. Robert DeRoos, "The Magic Worlds of Walt Disney," in *Disney Discourse: Producing the Magic Kingdom*, ed. Eric Smoodin (New York: Routledge, 1994), 58; Tim Cahill, "Call of the Wolf," *Rolling Stone*, no. 408 (November 10, 1983), 68–79; Bruce Brown, "Filming 'Never Cry Wolf,'" *New York Times Magazine*, October 16, 1983, 84– 91. See the video *Never Cry Wolf* (Burbank, Calif.: Walt Disney Home Video, n.d.).

47. James Oliver Curwood, *The Grizzly King* (Garden City, N.Y.: Doubleday, Page, 1916); Pauline Kael, "Current Cinema," *New Yorker*, November 13, 1989, 121–23. For a more laudatory review, see "The Bear," in *The Motion Picture Guide, 1990 Annual* (Evanston, Ill.: CineBooks, 1990), 16–17.

48. DeRoos, "Magic Worlds of Walt Disney," 56 (quotation), 58–59; Leonard Maltin, *The Disney Films* (New York: Bonanza Books, 1973), 18–20, 113–15 (quotation on 115); Richard Schickel, *The Disney Version: The Life, Times, Art and Commerce of Walt Disney*, rev. & updated (New York: Simon & Schuster, 1985), 284–293.

49. John Gilgun, "Re: Deconstructing Wild Discoveries," forwarded to the ASLE Discussion List by Scott Olsen, archived at [http://wsrv.clas.virginia.edu/~djp2n/discussion/home.html], February 15, 1996.

50. Colin Turnbull, "East African Safari," *Natural History* 90 (May 1981): 26. On television nature films, see Peter Steinhart, "Electronic Intimacies," *Audubon* 90 (November 1988): 10–13; Charles Siebert, "The Artifice of the Natural," *Harper's Magazine* 286 (February 1993): 43–51; and the letters in response to Siebert's article, "When Nature Is Televised," *Harper's Magazine* 286 (May 1993): 2–3, 77.

51. Schickel, *Disney Version*, 290–291.

52. See the videos *Free Willy* (Burbank, Calif.: Warner Home Video, 1993), *Free Willy II: The Adventure Home* (Burbank, Calif.: Warner Home Video, 1995); *The Amazing Panda Adventure* (Burbank, Calif.: Warner Home Video, 1996); and *Fly Away Home* (Culver City, Calif.: Columbia TriStar Home Video, 1996).

About the Writers

MARGARET ATWOOD is an award-winning Canadian poet, novelist, and nonfiction writer. Her works include *The Circle Game, The Edible Woman, The Handmaid's Tale,* and her study of Canadian literature, *Survival.*

JOHN BURROUGHS (1837–1921), naturalist, bank examiner, and farmer, was the foremost nature essayist of the late nineteenth- and early twentieth-century United States. Beginning with *Wake Robin,* his lively and accessible descriptions of birds and rural natural history were very popular in an increasingly urbanized nation. He helped to elevate nature writing to a new literary standard.

RACHEL CARSON (1907–1964) is best known as author of *Silent Spring,* one of the most influential books of the twentieth century, which has been credited with beginning the contemporary environmental movement. She was also an eloquent interpreter of the ocean and of marine life through her earlier books, *Under the Sea-Wind, The Sea Around Us,* and *The Edge of the Sea.*

EDWARD B. CLARK (1859–1941) was a journalist, soldier, and amateur ornithologist. He reported from the field during the Sioux war (1890–91), the Garza uprising in Texas in 1892, and World War I in France. He was decorated by France as Chevalier of the Legion of Honor. He was also an organizer and vice president of the Illinois Audubon Society.

THOMAS R. DUNLAP is professor of history at Texas A & M University. He is the author of *DDT: Scientists, Citizens and Public Policy* and *Saving America's Wildlife* and is currently working on an analysis of attitudes toward nature in Australia, Canada, New Zealand, and the United States.

W. F. GANONG (1864–1941), botanist and historian, was born in New Brunswick and taught for nearly forty years at Smith College in Massachusetts. He wrote several botany textbooks including *A Text Book of Botany for Colleges.* He was a corresponding member of the Royal Society of Canada and served as president of the Botanical Society of America.

W. H. HUDSON (1841–1922), born in Argentina, became one of England's great nature writers. His books include *The Purple Land* and his autobiography, *Far Away and Long Ago*. Hudson is best known for his novel *Green Mansions*.

RONALD H. LIMBAUGH is Rockwell Hunt Professor of California History and Director of the John Muir Center for Regional Studies at University of the Pacific. He is author of *John Muir's "Stickeen" and the Lessons of Nature*.

JACK LONDON (1876–1916) was a United States writer and adventurer. His *Call of the Wild* became one of the most successful of dog stories. His many other books include *White Fang* and *The Sea-Wolf*. At one point, he was the best known and highest paid American author.

WILLIAM J. LONG (1866–1952), a Massachusetts-born author and Congregational minister, received a Ph.D. from the University of Heidelberg. His early nature books, including *School of the Woods* and *Northern Trails*, were very popular but were nevertheless attacked as fraudulent natural history. He went on to write a series of very successful textbooks in English and American literature.

RALPH H. LUTTS is a member of the faculty of Goddard College. He is author of *The Nature Fakers: Wildlife, Science & Sentiment*, past president of the American Nature Study Society and a recipient of the Forest History Society's Ralph W. Hidy Award. His work in environmental history bridges natural history and ecology, literature and popular culture.

ROBERT H. MACDONALD is an adjunct professor of English at Carleton University, Ottawa. He is interested in the ideology of imperialism and, in particular, in the construction of masculinity through social myths. His latest book is *The Language of Empire: Myths and Metaphors of Popular Imperialism, 1880–1918*.

JOHN MUIR (1838–1914), was a founder of the wilderness preservation movement in America, first president of the Sierra Club, and a leading figure in the history of American environmentalism. After early years as a mechanic and wilderness explorer, he became a California fruit grower. Muir later turned to writing such books as *The Mountains of California* and *Our National Parks* to promote wilderness preservation.

CHARLES G. D. ROBERTS (1860–1943), co-creator of the realistic wild animal story, was a Canadian novelist and poet. His nature books include *The Heart of the Ancient Wood* and *The Kindred of the Wild*. He has been called the father of Canadian literature, and his contributions were recognized with a knighthood in 1935.

THEODORE ROOSEVELT (1858–1919), politician, naturalist, and sportsman, was the twenty-sixth president of the United States. He authored books on American history, western life, hunting, and exploration, including *The Winning of the West, Hunting Trips of a Ranchman*, and *African Game Trails.* The United States' first recipient of the Nobel Prize, he received the 1906 Prize for Peace.

ERNEST THOMPSON SETON (1860–1946), co-creator of the realistic wild animal story, was a Canadian naturalist, artist, and author. His best known book, *Wild Animals I Have Known,* has remained in print throughout the twentieth century. He was co-founder of the Boy Scouts of America and received the Burroughs Medal for his four-volume *Lives of Game Animals.*

MABEL OSGOOD WRIGHT (1859–1934) was an important figure in the early bird protection movement. She was founder and first president of the Connecticut Audubon Society, and served on the board of directors of the National Audubon Society. Wright wrote one of the first modern bird guides, *Birdcraft,* and was associate editor of the magazine *Bird-Lore.* Her other books included *Citizen Bird, Four-Footed Americans and their Kin,* and a number of novels.

Index

Illustrations (following page 157) are indicated herein by their illustration numbers, which appear in *italics*.

Blanca (wolf), 3, 49, 50, 55
Bodsworth, Fred, 11, 217–18, 245
Bowditch, Harold, 275
Brewster, William, 275
Brier-Patch Philosophy (Long), 9
Broken Ark (Ondaatje), *The*, 218
Buck (dog), 6, 91–102; joins wolves, 94–95, 100–102, *10, 11*
Buddhism, 9, 46
"Bull Calf" (Layton), 218
"Bull Moose" (Nowlan), 218
Bumblebee Dithyramb (Rosenblatt), 224
Burroughs, John, 269–70, *12, 13, 15*; on animal psychology, 211–12, 254, 274–75; on chipmunk, 211–12; compared with Long, 274–75; critical of poets, 151–52; on death, 140; *Fresh Fields*, 158; Hudson on, 158, 160; London on, 201–4, 206–9, 210; Long on, 148–52; on Long, 135–43; meets Long, 272; on nature writing, 269–70, 281; "Real and Sham Natural History," 129–43, 156, 161, 238, 270–71, 275, 276; on reason vs. instinct, 211–12; Roberts responds to, 30; on Roberts, 131–32; and Roosevelt, 276; Roosevelt on, 193; on Seton, 129, 142, 232–35, 272, 287 n.12; on sham naturalists, 8; on Sharp, 130; on *Stickeen*, 254; *Summit of Years, The*, 211–12; *Wake Robin*, 158; on White, 130–31; Wright on, 161; on writer's responsibility, 135, 141–42
Bush Garden (Frye), *The*, 221

"Cachalot" (Pratt), 216
Call of the Wild (London), ix, 6, 91–102, *10, 11*; *Call of the Wild* (films), 12
Canadian literature, 4, 5, 215–24, 225–36
Canadians as victims, 221–23
Caras, Roger, 245
Cardiff Giant, 197
Caribou, 6, 85, 167–69, 195, 283, *9*
Carnegie, Andrew, 272
Carrighar, Sally, 10–11, 281
Carson, Rachel, 10, 11; "Journey to the Sea," 117–25; *Under the Sea-Wind*, 10, 117–25, 281
Chapman, Frank H., 130, 193
Christian Darwinism, 263 n.8
Christianity, 26, 254, 255, 257, 258
Clark, Edward B., 164–71, 184–91, 276, 277–78

Communion (Gibson), 221–23
Condillac, Étienne de, 255
Cox, Philip, 150
Cram, William, 193
Curwood, James Oliver, 6, 13, 284

Darwin, Charles, 201, 207, 263 n.7, 279
Darwinian Revolution, 7
Darwinism, 7–8, 12, 16, 201–3, 225–36, 237–47, 250–51, 259, 260, 263 n.8, 279
"Death Goes Better with Coca Cola" (Godfrey), 218–19
"Death of Animals" (Purdy), 218
DeBakey, Michael, ix
deer, 2–3
"Deliverance" (Dickey), 216
Deming, E. W., 150
Descartes, René, 3, 255
Desmond Morris survey, 220, 221
Dickey, James, 216
Dillard, Annie, 283, 290 n.45
Disney, Walt, 12, 13–14, 283–84, 285
Disneyland, 285
"Do Seek Their Meat from God" (Roberts), 3, 4, 31–35, 242–43, 244
Dr. Jekyll and Mr. Hyde (Stevenson), 251
"Drummer on Snowshoes" (Seton), 3
Dunlap, Thomas, 8, 237–47
Dunn, Finley Peter, 238

Earth Day, 168
Earth's Enigmas (Roberts), 3
Eckstorm, Fannie Hardy, 130
eel, 118–25
Eiseley, Loren, 283
Emerson, Ralph Waldo, 252, 260, 263–64 n.9
English literature, 159–60, 215–16
English Literature (Long), 288 n.34
Evermann, Barton W., 188–89
evolution. *See* Darwinism

fact vs. fiction, 23–24, 135, 161–63, 194, 227, 283
"Fate of Little Mucky" (Seton), "The," 127, 153–54, 272
Faulkner, William, 5, 216
Felis canadensis, 182
Felis rafa, 182
Ferron, Jacques, 220